The Two-Story House
A Level Above In Gracious Living

Design V23325

First Floor: 1,595 square feet
Second Floor: 1,112 square feet
Total: 2,707 square feet

Horizontal clapboard siding, varying roof planes and finely detailed window treatments set the tone for this delightful family farmhouse. The central foyer unfolds excellent traffic patterns. The living and dining rooms are free of unnecessary cross-room traffic and function very well together. Note the four, double-hung windows in the living room that provide an abundance of natural light to this area. For informal occasions, a spacious family room and breakfast room extend a wealth of livability. In the family room, a raised-hearth fireplace acts as the focal point. Large glass doors provide an extra measure of natural illumination and direct access to the rear terrace. The U-shaped kitchen, with a tile floor, utilizes a work island supplemented by plenty of cabinet, cupboard and counter space. The sleeping accommodations of this plan include a master bedroom suite with a walk-in closet in addition to a long wardrobe closet. The master bath has a tub plus a stall shower and twin lavatories. The main bath also features twin lavatories. The rear bedroom will make a fine study, guest room or fourth bedroom.

For generations, Americans have "gone upstairs to bed." This comfortable living pattern, which emanated from the early Colonial period, continues today in beautiful and thoroughly livable designs. The omnipresent two-story represents not only the best return per construction dollar spent, but also a budget-smart residence option in the long-run.

The "stacked livability" features of the two-story house rival other designs in allowing efficiency of construction and operating costs. The full two-story creates a doubling of livable square footage without incurring the additional roof or foundation costs required for a similar size one-story.

Another construction advantage is the ease with which plumbing and heating/cooling systems can be installed. Having two stories means shorter wiring and ductwork runs. Also, single-stack plumbing for toilet facilities is possible when upstairs bathrooms are located above those on the first floor.

Before the days of central heating, the two-story chimney often served two or more fireplaces. The rooms on each floor relied upon the fireplace for warmth and comfort. While today the fireplace is no longer a heating necessity, it is a popular amenity. A common and cost-saving practice continues to be the utilization of a single chimney for the first- and second-floor fireplaces.

Two-story houses also make the most effectual use of building sites. This is a significant economic factor when deciding between a one- or two-story house. The exterior dimensions of a two-story can be much smaller than those of a one-story house with the same square footage. Because of this, a smaller and consequently less expensive site can be purchased. Narrow, or modest-sized sites are used to full advantage when two-story units are built upon them. With today's inflated land prices, utilizing a smaller, less expensive lot allows the direction of more money to actual construction, thereby allowing for a larger and more amenity-filled home. Hence, the popularity of the two-story house as attested by the numerous subdivisions throughout the United States.

Two-story houses can be L-shaped, U-shaped, in-line or even angular. Two-stories can also be part one-story. Sometimes it is even sensible to add a one-story wing for a family room or living room to a two-story home. Winged two-story houses, such as Design V22683 on page 149, provide a spacious, appealing alternative.

While the rectangular, two-story configuration is the most economical to build for the amount of livable square footage it delivers, there are other popular shapes that can be wisely used. Consider, for example, the L-shaped two-story with a front-projecting garage. This plan fits on a smaller site than if the garage were appended to the side of the main house.

Two-story houses become even more practical when attic space is completed. This can also be the case when the basement is developed into bonus recreational, hobby and storage areas.

Elegant features which can complement the two-story design include grand full-height foyers and sweeping staircases. And for those who like a more open feeling, amenities such as second-story bridges, interior balconies and lounges are good choices.

With a sloping site, the basement can often be exposed and windows and door-walls installed to allow for the creation of light, airy living spaces. This can turn a two-story house into a three-story or hillside home in a most cost-effective manner. See Design V22511 on page 340. If two-story design is your choice, our collection is sure to please.

CREATIVE HOMEOWNER PRESS®

MOST POPULAR

TWO-STORY HOMES

Design V23309

478 Designs
To Suit a Range of Styles and Budgets

Contents

Note: Many of the homes features in this book have a matching or corresponding Landscape or Deck Plan available. Some have both. These plans have an **L** or a **D** following their design number and square-footage notations. For information on how to order plans for landscapes and decks, see pages 402-411.

Copyright © 1994 Home Planners, Inc.

Printed in the United States of America.

Published by Creative Homeowner Press®
A Division of Federal Marketing Corp.
24 Park Way
Upper Saddle River, NJ 07458

Current Printing (last digit)
10 9 8 7 6 5 4 3 2 1

Library of Congress Number: 93-74014

ISBN: 1-880029-34-0

On The Cover: Making a grand Victorian statement, our plan V23309 graces the cover. For more information about this home, see page 235.
Photo by Andrew D. Lautman.

Design V23310

First Floor: 1,668 square feet
Second Floor: 905 square feet
Total: 2,573 square feet

The angular design of this home allows not only facade interest, but creates an interesting floor plan. The master suite on the first floor is split from family bedrooms. Note the balconies on these second-floor sleeping areas.

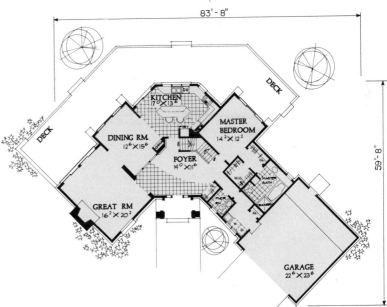

Design V23558

First Floor: 2,328 square feet
Second Floor: 603 square feet
Total: 2,931 square feet

One-story livability is possible in a two-story home. Notice how the living areas and master suite occupy the main living area and secondary bedrooms are upstairs. A lovely open staircase brightens the foyer and gallery.

The Cost of a Mortgage

Monthly principal and interest per $1,000 of mortgage

Mortgage rate	15-year loan	20-year loan	25-year loan	30-year loan
5.000%	7.91	6.60	5.85	5.37
5.125%	7.97	6.67	5.92	5.44
5.250%	8.04	6.74	5.99	5.52
5.375%	8.10	6.81	6.07	5.60
5.500%	8.17	6.88	6.14	5.68
5.625%	8.24	6.95	6.22	5.76
5.750%	8.30	7.02	6.29	5.84
5.875%	8.37	7.09	6.37	5.92
6.000%	8.44	7.16	6.44	6.00
6.125%	8.51	7.24	6.52	6.08
6.250%	8.57	7.31	6.60	6.16
6.375%	8.64	7.38	6.67	6.24
6.500%	8.71	7.46	6.75	6.32
6.625%	8.78	7.53	6.83	6.40
6.750%	8.85	7.60	6.91	6.49
6.875%	8.92	7.68	6.99	6.57
7.000%	8.99	7.76	7.07	6.66
7.125%	9.06	7.83	7.15	6.74
7.250%	9.13	7.91	7.23	6.83
7.375%	9.20	7.98	7.31	6.91
7.500%	9.28	8.06	7.39	7.00
7.625%	9.35	8.14	7.48	7.08
7.750%	9.42	8.21	7.56	7.17
7.875%	9.49	8.29	7.64	7.26
8.000%	9.56	8.37	7.72	7.34
8.125%	9.63	8.45	7.81	7.43
8.250%	9.71	8.53	7.89	7.52
8.375%	9.78	8.60	7.97	7.61
8.500%	9.85	8.68	8.06	7.69
8.625%	9.93	8.76	8.14	7.78
8.750%	10.00	8.84	8.23	7.87
8.875%	10.07	8.92	8.31	7.96
9.000%	10.15	9.00	8.40	8.05
9.125%	10.22	9.08	8.48	8.14
9.250%	10.30	9.16	8.57	8.23
9.375%	10.37	9.24	8.66	8.32
9.500%	10.45	9.33	8.74	8.41
9.625%	10.52	9.41	8.83	8.50
9.750%	10.60	9.49	8.92	8.60
9.875%	10.67	9.57	9.00	8.69
10.000%	10.75	9.66	9.09	8.78
10.125%	10.83	9.74	9.18	8.87
10.250%	10.90	9.82	9.27	8.97
10.375%	10.98	9.90	9.36	9.06
10.500%	11.06	9.99	9.45	9.15
10.625%	11.14	10.07	9.54	9.25
10.750%	11.21	10.16	9.63	9.34
10.875%	11.29	10.24	9.72	9.43
11.000%	11.37	10.33	9.81	9.53
11.125%	11.45	10.41	9.90	9.62
11.250%	11.53	10.50	9.99	9.72
11.375%	11.61	10.58	10.08	9.81
11.500%	11.69	10.67	10.17	9.91
11.625%	11.77	10.76	10.26	10.00
11.750%	11.85	10.84	10.35	10.10
11.875%	11.93	10.93	10.44	10.20
12.000%	12.01	11.02	10.54	10.29
12.125%	12.09	11.10	10.63	10.39
12.250%	12.17	11.19	10.72	10.48
12.375%	12.25	11.28	10.82	10.58
12.500%	12.33	11.37	10.91	10.68
12.625%	12.41	11.45	11.00	10.77
12.750%	12.49	11.54	11.10	10.87
12.875%	12.58	11.63	11.19	10.97
13.000%	12.66	11.72	11.28	11.07

Note: Multiply the cost per $1,000 by the size of the mortgage (in thousands). The result is the monthly payment, including principal and interest. For example, for an $80,000 mortgage for 30 years at 10 percent, multiply 80 x 8.78 = $702.40.

A Checklist For Plan Selection

Developing an architectural plan from the various wants and needs of an individual or family that fits into lifestyle demands and design elegance is the most efficient way to assure a livable plan. It is not only possible but highly desirable to design a plan around such requirements as separate bedrooms for each member of the family, guest suites, a quiet study area, an oversized entertainment area, a two-car garage, a completely private master suite, and a living room fireplace. Incorporated into this can be such wants as Tudor styling, 1½-stories, a large entry hall, decks and balconies, and a basement.

While it is obviously best to begin with wants and needs and then design a home to fit these criteria, this is not always practical or even possible. A very effective way around this problem is to select a professionally prepared home plan which meets all needs and incorporates as many wants as possible. With careful selection, it will be possible to modify sizes and make other design adjustments to make the home as close to custom as can be. It is important to remember that some wants may have to be compromised in the interest of meeting budgetary limitations. The trick is to build the best possible home for the available money while satisfying all absolute needs.

Following are some cost-controlling ideas that can make a big difference in the overall price of a home:

1. Square or rectangular homes are less expensive to build than irregularly shaped homes.
2. It is less expensive to build on a flat lot than on a sloping or hillside lot.
3. The use of locally manufactured or produced materials cuts costs greatly.
4. Using stock materials and stock sizes of components takes advantage of mass production cost reductions.
5. The use of materials that can be quickly installed cuts labor costs. Prefabricating large sections or panels eliminates much time on the site.
6. The use of prefinished materials saves significantly on labor costs.
7. Investigating existing building codes before beginning construction eliminates unnecessary changes as construction proceeds.
8. Refraining from changing the design or any aspect of the plan after construction begins will help to hold down cost escalation.
9. Minimizing special jobs or custom-built items keeps costs from increasing.
10. Designing the house for short plumbing lines saves on piping and other materials.
11. Proper insulation saves heating and cooling costs.
12. Utilizing passive solar features, such as correct orientation, reduces future maintenance costs.

To help you consider all the important factors in evaluating a plan, the following checklist should be reviewed carefully. By comparing its various points to any plan and a wants-and-needs list, it will be possible to easily recognize the deficiencies of a plan or determine its appropriateness. Be sure to include family members in the decision-making process. Their ideas and desires will help in finding exactly the right plan.

CHECKLIST

The Neighborhood

1. _____ Reasonable weather conditions
2. No excess
   _____ a. wind
   _____ b. smog or fog
   _____ c. odors
   _____ d. soot or dust
3. _____ The area is residential
4. There are no
   _____ a. factories
   _____ b. dumps
   _____ c. highways
   _____ d. railroads
   _____ e. airports
   _____ f. apartments
   _____ g. commercial buildings
5. _____ City-maintained streets
6. No hazards in the area
   _____ a. quarries
   _____ b. storage tanks
   _____ c. power stations
   _____ d. unprotected swimming pools

7. Reasonably close to
   _____ a. work
   _____ b. schools
   _____ c. churches
   _____ d. hospital
   _____ e. shopping
   _____ f. recreation
   _____ g. public transportation
   _____ h. library
   _____ i. police protection
   _____ j. fire protection
   _____ k. parks
   _____ l. cultural activities
8. _____ Streets are curved
9. _____ Traffic is slow
10. _____ Intersections are at right angles
11. _____ Street lighting
12. _____ Light traffic
13. _____ Visitor parking
14. _____ Good design in street
15. _____ Paved streets and curbs
16. _____ Area is not deteriorating
17. _____ Desirable expansion
18. _____ Has some open spaces

19. _____ Numerous and healthy trees
20. _____ Pleasant-looking homes
21. _____ Space between homes
22. _____ Water drains off
23. _____ Near sewerage line
24. _____ Storm sewers nearby
25. _____ Mail delivery
26. _____ Garbage pickup
27. _____ Trash pickup
28. _____ No city assessments

The Lot

1. _____ Title is clear
2. _____ No judgments against the seller
3. _____ No restrictions as to the use of the land or the deed
4. _____ No unpaid taxes or assessments
5. _____ Minimum of 70 feet of frontage
6. _____ House does not crowd the lot
7. _____ Possible to build on
8. _____ Few future assessments (sewers, lights, and so forth)
9. _____ Good top soil and soil percolation
10. _____ Good view
11. _____ No low spots to hold water
12. _____ Water drains off land away from the house
13. _____ No fill
14. _____ No water runoff from high ground
15. _____ If cut or graded there is substantial retaining wall
16. _____ Permanent boundary markers
17. _____ Utilities available at property line
18. _____ Utility hookup is reasonable
19. _____ Utility rates are reasonable
20. _____ Taxes are reasonable
21. _____ Water supply is adequate
22. _____ Regular, simply shaped lot
23. _____ Trees
24. _____ Do not have to cut trees
25. _____ Privacy for outside activities
26. _____ Attractive front yard
27. _____ Front and rear yards are adequate
28. _____ Front yard is not divided up by walks and driveway
29. _____ Outdoor walks have stairs grouped

The Floor Plan

1. _____ Designed by licensed architect
2. _____ Purchased from a reputable stock plan company
3. _____ Supervised by skilled contractor
4. Orientation
   _____ *a.* sun
   _____ *b.* view
   _____ *c.* noise
   _____ *d.* breeze
   _____ *e.* contour of land
5. _____ Entry
6. _____ Planned for exterior expansion
7. Planned for interior expansion
   _____ *a.* attic
   _____ *b.* garage
   _____ *c.* basement
8. _____ Simple but functional plan
9. _____ Indoor recreation area
10. _____ Wall space for furniture in each room
11. Well-designed hall
   _____ *a.* leads to all areas
   _____ *b.* no congestions

_____ *c.* no wasted space
_____ *d.* 3' minimum widths
12. _____ Easy to clean
13. _____ Easy to keep orderly
14. _____ Plan meets family's needs
15. _____ All rooms have direct emergency escape
16. Doorways functional
   _____ *a.* no unnecessary doors
   _____ *b.* wide enough for moving furniture through
   _____ *c.* can see visitors through locked front door
   _____ *d.* do not swing out into halls
   _____ *e.* swing open against a blank wall
   _____ *f.* do not bump other subjects
   _____ *g.* exterior doors are solid
17. Windows are functional
   _____ *a.* not too small
   _____ *b.* enough but not too many
   _____ *c.* glare-free
   _____ *d.* roof overhang protection where needed
   _____ *e.* large ones have the best view
   _____ *f.* easy to clean
   _____ *g.* no interference with furniture placement
   _____ *h.* over kitchen sink
   _____ *i.* open easily
18. _____ No fancy gadgets
19. _____ Room sizes are adequate
20. _____ Well-designed stairs
   _____ *a.* treads are 9" minimum
   _____ *b.* risers are 8" maximum
   _____ *c.* 36" minimum width
   _____ *d.* 3' minimum landings
   _____ *e.* attractive
   _____ *f.* easily reached
21. _____ Overall plan "fits" family requirements
22. _____ Good traffic patterns
23. _____ Noisy areas separated from quiet areas
24. _____ Rooms have adequate wall space for furniture
25. _____ Halls are 3'6" minimum

The Living Area

1. _____ Minimum space 12' x 16'
2. _____ Front door traffic does not enter
3. _____ Not in a traffic pattern
4. _____ Windows on two sides
5. _____ Has a view
6. _____ Storage for books and music materials
7. _____ Decorative lighting
8. _____ Whole family plus guests can be seated
9. _____ Desk area
10. _____ Fireplace
11. _____ Wood storage
12. _____ No street noises
13. _____ Privacy from street
14. _____ Acoustical ceiling
15. _____ Cannot see or hear bathroom
16. _____ Powder room
17. _____ Comfortable for conversation
18. Dining room
   _____ *a.* used enough to justify
   _____ *b.* minimum of 3' clearance around table
   _____ *c.* can be opened or closed to kitchen and patio
   _____ *d.* can be opened or closed to living room
   _____ *e.* electrical outlets for table appliances

19. Family room
　　_____ *a.* minimum space 10' x 12'
　　_____ *b.* room for family activities
　　_____ *c.* room for noisy activities
　　_____ *d.* room for messy activities
　　_____ *e.* activities will not disturb sleeping area
　　_____ *f.* finish materials are easy to clean and durable
　　_____ *g.* room for expansion
　　_____ *h.* separate from living room
　　_____ *i.* near kitchen
　　_____ *j.* fireplace
　　_____ *k.* adequate storage
20. _____ Dead-end circulation
21. _____ Adequate furniture arrangements

The Entry

1. _____ The entry is a focal point
2. _____ The outside is inviting
3. _____ The landing has a minimum depth of 5'
4. _____ Protected from the weather
5. _____ Has an approach walk
6. _____ Well planted
7. _____ Coat closet
8. _____ Leads to living, sleeping, and service areas
9. _____ Floor material attractive and easy to clean
10. _____ Decorative lighting
11. _____ Space for table
12. _____ Space to hang mirror
13. _____ Does not have direct view into any room

The Bedrooms

1. _____ Adequate number of bedrooms
2. _____ Adequate size—10' x 12' minimum
3. _____ Open into a hall
4. _____ Living space
5. _____ Children's bedroom has study and play area
6. _____ Oriented to north side
7. In quiet area
　　_____ *a.* soundproofing
　　_____ *b.* acoustical ceiling
　　_____ *c.* insulation in walls
　　_____ *d.* thermal glass
　　_____ *e.* double doors
　　_____ *f.* closet walls
8. _____ Privacy
9. _____ 4' minimum wardrobe rod space per person
10. Master bedroom
　　_____ *a.* bath
　　_____ *b.* dressing area
　　_____ *c.* full-length mirror
　　_____ *d.* 12' x 12' minimum
11. Adequate windows
　　_____ *a.* natural light
　　_____ *b.* cross-ventilation
　　_____ *c.* windows on two walls
12. _____ Room for overnight guests
13. _____ Bathroom nearby
14. _____ Wall space for bed, nightstands, and dresser
15. _____ Quiet reading area

The Bathroom

1. _____ Well designed
2. _____ Plumbing lines are grouped
3. _____ Fixtures have space around them for proper use
4. _____ Doors do not interfere with fixtures
5. _____ Noises are insulated from other rooms

6. _____ Convenient to bedrooms
7. _____ Convenient to guests
8. _____ Ventilation
9. _____ Heating
10. _____ Attractive fixtures
11. _____ No windows over tub or shower
12. _____ Wall area around tub and shower
13. _____ Light fixtures are water tight
14. _____ Large medicine cabinet
15. _____ Children cannot open medicine cabinet
16. _____ No bathroom tie-ups
17. _____ Good lighting
18. _____ Accessible electrical outlets
19. _____ No electric appliance or switch near water supply
20. _____ Towel and linen storage
21. _____ Dirty clothes hamper
22. _____ Steamproof mirrors
23. _____ Wall and floor materials are waterproof
24. _____ All finishes are easy to maintain
25. _____ Curtain and towel rods securely fastened
26. _____ Grab bar by tub
27. _____ Mixing faucets
28. _____ Bath in service area
29. _____ No public view into open bathroom door
30. _____ Clean-up area for outdoor jobs and children's play

The Kitchen

1. _____ Centrally located
2. _____ The family can eat informally in the kitchen
3. _____ At least 20' of cabinet space
　　_____ *a.* counter space on each side of major appliances
　　_____ *b.* minimum of 8' counter work area
　　_____ *c.* round storage in corners
　　_____ *d.* no shelf is higher than 72"
　　_____ *e.* floor cabinets 24" deep and 36" high
　　_____ *f.* wall cabinets 15" deep
　　_____ *g.* 15" clearance between wall and floor cabinets
4. _____ Work triangle is formed between appliances
　　_____ *a.* between 12' and 20'
　　_____ *b.* no traffic through the work triangle
　　_____ *c.* refrigerator opens into the work triangle
　　_____ *d.* at least six electric outlets in work triangle
　　_____ *e.* no door between appliances
5. _____ No space between appliances and counters
6. _____ Window over sink
7. _____ No wasted space in kitchen
8. _____ Can close off kitchen from dining area
9. _____ Snack bar in kitchen
10. _____ Kitchen drawers are divided
11. _____ Built-in chopping block
12. _____ Writing and telephone desk
13. _____ Indoor play area visible from kitchen
14. _____ Outdoor play area visible from kitchen
15. _____ Exhaust fan
16. _____ Natural light
17. _____ Good lighting for each work area
18. _____ Convenient access to service area and garage
19. _____ Durable surfaces
20. _____ Dishwasher
21. _____ Disposal
22. _____ Built-in appliances
23. _____ Bathroom nearby

24. _____ Room for freezer
25. _____ Pantry storage

The Utility Room

1. _____ Adequate laundry area
2. _____ Well-lighted work areas
3. _____ 240-volt outlet
4. _____ Gas outlet
5. _____ Sorting area
6. _____ Ironing area
7. _____ Drip-drying area
8. _____ Sewing and mending area
9. _____ On least desirable side of lot
10. _____ Exit to outdoor service area
11. _____ Exit near garage
12. _____ Sufficient cabinet space
13. _____ Bathroom in area
14. _____ Accessible from kitchen
15. _____ Adequate space for washer and dryer
16. _____ Laundry tray
17. _____ Outdoor exit is protected from the weather
18. _____ Window

Working Areas

1. _____ Home repair area
2. _____ Work area for hobbies
3. _____ Storage for paints and tools
4. _____ Garage storage
5. _____ Incinerator area
6. _____ Refuse area
7. _____ Delivery area
8. _____ Near parking
9. _____ 240-volt outlet for power tools

Storage

1. _____ General storage space for each person
2. _____ 4' of rod space for each person
3. _____ Closet doors are sealed to keep out dust
4. _____ Minimum wardrobe closet size is 40" x 22"
5. _____ Cedar closet storage for seasonal clothing
6. _____ Bulk storage area for seasonal paraphernalia
7. _____ Closets are lighted
8. _____ Walk-in closets have adequate turnaround area
9. Storage for:
_____ a. linen and towels
_____ b. cleaning materials
_____ c. foods
_____ d. bedding
_____ e. outdoor furniture
_____ f. sports equipment
_____ g. toys—indoor
_____ h. toys—outdoor
_____ i. bicycles
_____ j. luggage
_____ k. out-of-season clothes
_____ l. storm windows and doors
_____ m. garden tools
_____ n. tools and paints
_____ o. hats
_____ p. shoes
_____ q. belts
_____ r. ties
_____ s. bridge tables and chairs
_____ t. camping equipment
_____ u. china
_____ v. silver
_____ w. minor appliances
_____ x. books

10. _____ Closets are ventilated
11. _____ Closets do not project into room
12. _____ Toothbrush holders in bathrooms
13. _____ Soap holders in bathrooms
14. _____ Adequate built-in storage
15. _____ Drawers cannot pull out of cabinet
16. _____ Drawers slide easily
17. _____ Drawers have divided partitions
18. _____ Adult storage areas easy to reach
19. _____ Children storage areas easy to reach
20. _____ Guest storage near entry
21. _____ Heavy storage areas have reinforced floors
22. _____ Sides of closets easy to reach
23. _____ Tops of closets easy to reach
24. _____ No wasted spaces around stored articles
25. _____ Sloping roof or stairs do not render closet useless
26. _____ Entry closet

The Exterior

1. _____ The design looks "right" for the lot
2. _____ Design varies from other homes nearby
3. _____ Design fits with unity on its site
4. _____ Definite style architecture—not mixed
5. _____ Simple, honest design
6. _____ Garage design goes with the house
7. _____ Attractive on all four sides
8. _____ Colors in good taste
9. _____ Finish materials in good taste
10. _____ Has charm and warmth
11. _____ Materials are consistent on all sides
12. _____ No false building effects
13. _____ Well-designed roof lines—not chopped up
14. _____ Window tops line up
15. _____ Bathroom windows are not obvious
16. _____ Does not look like a box
17. _____ Easy maintenance of finish materials
18. _____ Windows are protected from pedestrian view
19. _____ Attractive roof covering
20. _____ Gutters on roof
21. _____ Downspouts that drain into storm sewer
22. _____ Glass area protected with overhang or trees
23. _____ Dry around the house
24. _____ Several waterproof electric outlets
25. _____ Hose bib on each side
26. _____ Style will look good in the future

Outdoor Service Area

1. _____ Clothes hanging area
2. _____ Garbage storage
3. _____ Can storage
4. _____ On least desirable side of site
5. _____ Next to indoor service area
6. _____ Near garage
7. _____ Delivery area for trucks
8. _____ Fenced off from rest of site

Outdoor Living Area

1. _____ Area for dining
2. _____ Area for games
3. _____ Area for lounging
4. _____ Area for gardening
5. _____ Fenced for privacy
6. _____ Partly shaded
7. _____ Concrete deck at convenient places
8. _____ Garden walks

9. _____ Easy access to house
10. _____ Paved area for bikes and wagons
11. _____ Easy maintenance

Landscaping

1. _____ Planting at foundation ties
2. _____ Garden area
3. _____ Well-located trees
4. _____ Healthy trees
5. _____ Plants of slow-growing variety
6. _____ Landscaping professionally advised
7. _____ Garden walks
8. _____ Easy maintenance
9. _____ Extras as trellis or gazebo

Construction

1. _____ Sound construction
2. _____ All work complies to code
3. _____ Efficient contractor and supervision
4. _____ Honest builders
5. _____ Skilled builders
6. _____ Constructed to plans
7. Floors are well constructed
    _____ a. resilient
    _____ b. subfloor diagonal to joints
    _____ c. flat and even
    _____ d. slab is not cold
    _____ e. floor joists rest on 2" of sill—minimum
    _____ f. girder lengths are joined under points of support
8. Foundation is well constructed
    _____ a. level
    _____ b. sill protected from termites
    _____ c. vapor barrier
    _____ d. no cracks
    _____ e. no water seepage
    _____ f. no dryrot in sills
    _____ g. garage slab drains
    _____ h. waterproofed
    _____ i. walls are 8" thick
    _____ j. basement height 7'6" minimum
    _____ k. sills bolted to foundation
    _____ l. adequate vents
9. Walls are well constructed
    _____ a. plumb
    _____ b. no waves
    _____ c. insulation
    _____ d. flashing at all exterior joints
    _____ e. solid sheathing
    _____ f. siding is neat and tight
    _____ g. drywall joints are invisible
10. Windows are properly installed
    _____ a. move freely
    _____ b. weatherstripped
    _____ c. caulked and sealed
    _____ d. good-quality glass
11. Doors properly hung
    _____ a. move freely
    _____ b. exterior doors weatherstripped
    _____ c. exterior doors are solid-core
    _____ d. interior doors are hollow-core
12. Roof is well constructed
    _____ a. rafters are straight
    _____ b. all corners are flashed
    _____ c. adequate vents in attic
    _____ d. no leaks
    _____ e. building paper under shingles
13. _____ Tile work is tight

14. _____ Hot water lines are insulated
15. _____ Mortar joints are neat
16. _____ Mortar joints do not form shelf to hold water
17. _____ Ceiling is 8'0" minimum
18. _____ No exposed pipes
19. _____ No exposed wires
20. _____ Tight joints at cabinets and appliances
21. _____ Stairs have railings
22. _____ Neat trim application
23. _____ Builder responsible for new home flaws

The Fireplace

1. _____ There is a fireplace
2. _____ Wood storage near the fireplace
3. _____ Draws smoke
4. _____ Hearth in front (minimum 10" on sides; 20" in front)
5. _____ Does not project out into the room
6. _____ Has a clean-out
7. _____ Chimney top 2' higher than roof ridge
8. _____ No leaks around chimney in roof
9. _____ No wood touches the chimney
10. _____ 2" minimum air space between framing members and masonry
11. _____ No loose mortar
12. _____ Has a damper
13. _____ Space for furniture opposite fireplace
14. _____ Doors minimum of 6' from fireplace
15. _____ Windows minimum of 3' from fireplace
16. _____ On a long wall
17. _____ Install "heatilator"
18. _____ Install glass doors to minimize heat loss

Equipment

1. _____ All equipment listed in specifications and plans
2. _____ All new equipment has warranty
3. _____ All equipment is up to code standards
4. _____ All equipment is functional and not a fad
5. _____ Owner's choice of equipment meets builder's allowance
6. _____ Public system for utilities
7. _____ Private well is deep; adequate and healthy water
8. Electrical equipment is adequate
    _____ a. inspected and guaranteed
    _____ b. 240 voltage
    _____ c. 120 voltage
    _____ d. sufficient electric outlets
    _____ e. sufficient electric circuits—minimum of six
    _____ f. circuit breakers
    _____ g. television aerial outlet
    _____ h. telephone outlets
    _____ i. outlets in convenient places
9. Adequate lighting
    _____ a. all rooms have general lighting
    _____ b. all rooms have specific lighting for specific tasks
    _____ c. silent switches
    _____ d. some decorative lighting
    _____ e. light at front door
    _____ f. outdoor lighting
10. _____ Plumbing equipment is adequate
    _____ a. inspected and guaranteed
    _____ b. adequate water pressure
    _____ c. hot water heater—50-gallon minimum
    _____ d. shut-off valves at fixtures

_____ e. satisfactory city sewer or septic tank
_____ f. septic tank disposal field is adequate
_____ g. septic tank is large enough for house (1000 gallons for three-bedroom house, plus 250 gallons for each additional bedroom)
_____ h. water softener for hard water
_____ i. siphon vertex or siphon reverse-trap water closet
_____ j. clean-out plugs at all corners of waste lines
_____ k. water lines will not rust
_____ l. water pipes do not hammer
_____ m. waste lines drain freely
_____ n. cast iron with vitreous enamel bathtub
11. _____ Good ventilation through house and attic
12. Heating and cooling systems are adequate
_____ a. insulation in roof, ceiling, walls
_____ b. air conditioning system
_____ c. heating and cooling outlets under windows
_____ d. air purifier
_____ e. thermostatic control
_____ f. walls are clean over heat outlets
_____ g. comfortable in hot or cold weather
_____ h. automatic humidifier
_____ i. furnace blower is belt-driven
_____ j. quiet-heating plant
_____ k. ducts are tight
13. _____ Windows are of good quality
_____ a. storm windows
_____ b. secure locks
_____ c. screened
_____ d. double glazed in extreme weather (thermal)
_____ e. glass is ripple-free
_____ f. safety or safe thickness of glass
_____ g. moisture-free
_____ h. frost-free
14. Doors are of good quality
_____ a. secure locks on exterior doors
_____ b. attractive hardware
_____ c. hardware is solid brass or bronze
15. All meters easily accessible to meter readers
16. _____ Fire extinguisher in house and garage
17. _____ Acoustical ceiling
18. _____ Facilities to lock mail box
19. _____ Facilities to receive large packages
20. _____ Gas or electric incinerator
21. Adequate small hardware
_____ a. soap dishes
_____ b. toilet-paper holders
_____ c. toothbrush holders
_____ d. towel holders
_____ e. bathtub grab bars
_____ f. door and drawer pulls

The Garage

1. _____ Same style as the house
2. _____ Fits with house
3. _____ Single garage 12' x 22' minimum
4. _____ Double garage 22' x 22' minimum
5. _____ Larger than minimum size if used for storage or workshop
6. _____ Protected passage to house
7. _____ Doors are safe
8. _____ Access to overhead storage

Financial Checklist

1. _____ Do you understand conveyancing fees (closing costs)?
2. _____ Is the house a good investment?
3. _____ Is the total cost approximately three times your annual income?
4. _____ Have you shopped for the best loan?
5. _____ Do you have a constant payment plan (sliding principal and interest)?
6. _____ Is there a prepayment penalty?
7. _____ Will a week's salary cover the total housing expense for one month?
8. _____ Are all the costs itemized in the contract?
9. Do you understand the following closing costs?
_____ a. title search
_____ b. lawyer
_____ c. plot survey
_____ d. insurance, fire, and public liability
_____ e. mortgage tax
_____ f. recording mortgage
_____ g. recording deed
_____ h. bank's commitment fee
_____ i. state and county taxes
_____ j. state and government revenue stamps
_____ k. title insurance (protects lender)
_____ l. homeowner's policy (protects owner)
_____ m. transferring ownership
_____ n. mortgage service charge
_____ o. appraisal
_____ p. notarizing documents
_____ q. attendant fee (paying off previous mortgage)
_____ r. personal credit check
10. _____ Do you have extra cash to cover unforeseen expenses?
11. Can you afford to pay the following?
_____ a. closing costs
_____ b. old assessments or bonds
_____ c. new assessments or bonds
_____ d. downpayment
_____ e. immediate repairs
_____ f. immediate purchases (furniture, appliances, landscape, tools, fences, carpets, drapes, patio)
_____ g. adequate insurance
_____ h. mortgage payments
_____ i. general maintenance
_____ j. utilities (water, heat, electricity, phone, gas, trash pickup)
_____ k. special design features wanted
_____ l. extras not covered in plans and contract
_____ m. prepayment of interest and taxes for first month of transition
_____ n. moving
_____ o. gardener
_____ p. travel to work
_____ q. interest on construction loan
_____ r. advances to contractors
12. _____ Who will pay for the following?
_____ a. supervision costs of architect or contractor
_____ b. inspection fees
_____ c. increased costs during building
_____ d. building permits
_____ e. difficulties in excavation
_____ f. dry wells
_____ g. extra features the building inspector insists upon

The above Checklist is used with permission. It is taken from Home Planners' Guide to Residential Design _by Charles Talcott, Don Hepler, and Paul Wallach; 1986; McGraw-Hill, Inc._

EARLY COLONIAL DESIGNS . . .

as found in this section feature a wide variety of sizes and shapes with a myriad of charming exterior design details which recall our architectural heritage. The saltbox and gambrel roofed structure has been an enduring and highly identifiable form. These houses, together with full two-story, are depicted here with a wide range of living potential for varying budgets and family sizes. Worthy of note are the fine traffic patterns that emanate from the numerous center entry houses shown here. With the excellent sleeping, living and work area potential these are truly homes for family living.

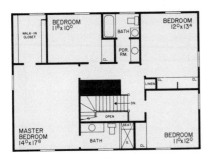

Design V22666

First Floor: 988 square feet
Second Floor: 1,147 square feet
Total: 2,135 square feet

● Charming Colonial detailing in multi-paned windows and twin coach lamps grace the exterior of this two-story. A spacious country kitchen highlights the interior. Its features include an island workcenter, fireplace, beamed ceiling, and sliding glass doors leading to the rear terrace. A washroom and a side door are only steps away. A second fireplace is in the large living room which also has sliding glass doors to the rear.

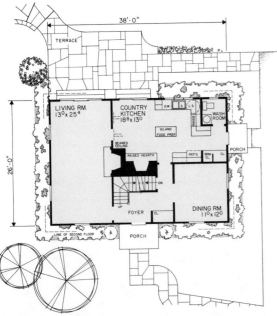

Design V22998

First Floor: 2,243 square feet
Second Floor: 1,532 square feet
Total: 3,775 square feet

● Symmetrical and simply lovely, this gambrel-roofed two-story is a fine example of historical homes. Its details will enchant the most particular enthusiast of early architecture. The floor plan is a classic as well. Note the formal dining and living rooms flanking the entry hall. The living room has a fireplace and the dining room a bay window. A media room/study also sports a fireplace and has access to a rear terrace. The family room connects to the kitchen via a through snack bar. There's also another fireplace here. On the second floor are three bedrooms and two full baths. The third floor contains unfinished space which acts as superb storage and can be developed later into more bedrooms if needed.

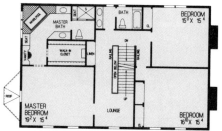

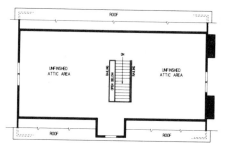

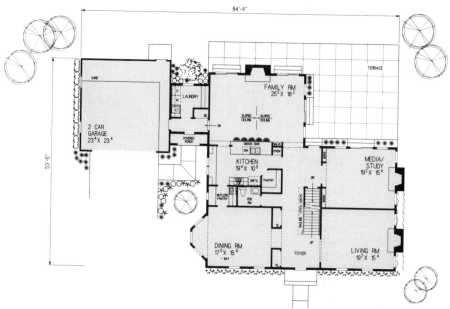

Design V22990

First Floor: 2,615 square feet
Second Floor: 1,726 square feet
Guest Bedroom: 437 square feet
Total: 4,878 square feet

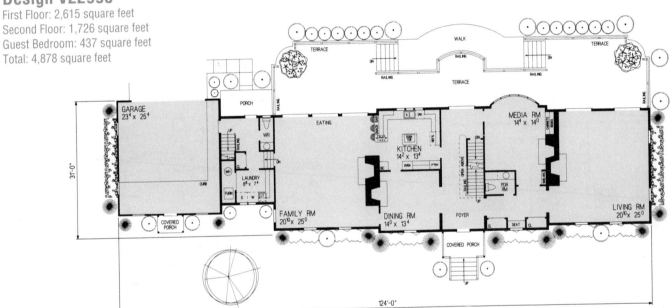

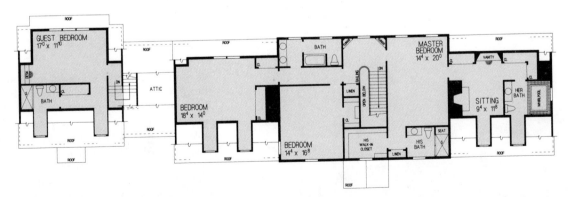

● Designed to resemble the St. George Tucker house in Williamsburg, this stately home offers a floor plan for today's family. First-floor rooms include a family room with informal dining space at one end of the plan and a formal living room at the other end. In between are the media room, guest powder room, dining room and kitchen. Three second-floor bedrooms include a luxurious master suite with sitting room. There is also a guest room with private bath over the garage.

15

Design V22994

First Floor: 1,736 square feet

Second Floor: 1,472 square feet

Total: 3,208 square feet

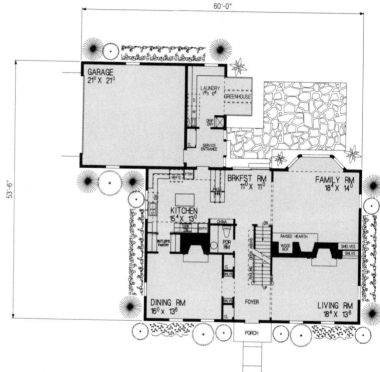

● Modeled after the homes of successful merchants in Amherst, New Hampshire, this lovely two-story plan presents an historical facade. Two chimney stacks, fluted pilasters and a bracketed pediment add their distinctive details. The floor plan is equally as classic with center hall separating living and dining rooms and leading back to the family room. All three living spaces have fireplaces. The second floor holds three bedrooms including a gracious master suite with two walk-in closets and whirlpool tub. Secondary bedrooms share a full bath with dual lavatories.

Design V22989

First Floor: 1,972 square feet
Second Floor: 1,533 square feet
Total: 3,505 square feet

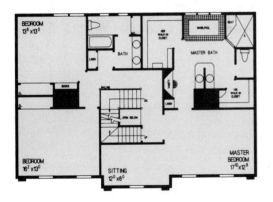

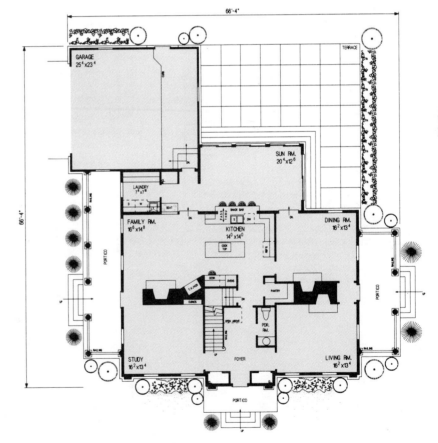

● This dramatic residence, patterned after one built in 1759 by Major John Vassall in Cambridge, offers a floor plan that is intriguing in its wealth of amenities. On the first floor are the formal living and dining rooms, each with fireplace. A front study connects to the family room with built-ins and another fireplace. Opening to the rear terrace is a most-welcome sun room with pass-through snack bar to the kitchen. Upstairs are three bedrooms. The master has a sitting room, double vanity, whirlpool tub, His and Hers closets, and built-in vanity. Two family bedrooms share a full bath.

Design V22687
First Floor: 1,819 square feet
Second Floor: 1,472 square feet; Total: 3,291 square feet

L D

● Exterior styling of this home is reminiscent of the past but its floor plan is as up-to-date as it can get. Its many unique features include: a greenhouse, 78 square feet, off the country kitchen, a media room for all the modern electronic equipment, a hobby/laundry room with a washroom and a deluxe master bath.

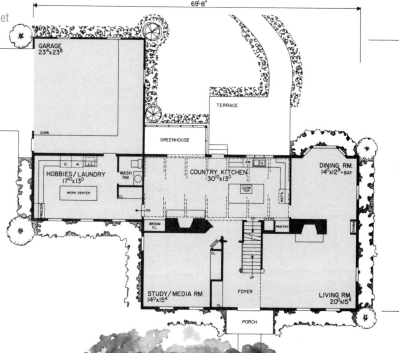

Design V22399

First Floor: 1,301 square feet
Second Floor: 839 square feet
Total: 2,140 square feet

First Floor Plan:

62'-0"
40'-0"

TERRACE

GATHERING RM.
26'-8" x 16'-0"

KITCHEN
10'-0" x 8'-0"

GARAGE
23'-4" x 23'-4"

RAISED HEARTH

NOOK
10'-0" x 8'-0"

BATH

LIVING RM.
13'-4" x 19'-0"

ENTRANCE HALL

BED RM.
10'-0" x 12'-4"

PORCH

Second Floor Plan:

ATTIC STORAGE

BATH

VANITY

DRESSING

WALK IN CLOSET

BATH

LINEN

MASTER BED RM.
13'-4" x 16'-0"

STAIR HALL

BED RM.
12'-0" x 13'-0"

● From Early Colonial America comes this Salt Box. Narrow, horizontal siding, muntined windows, a massive centered chimney, carriage lamps and a classic front entrance set the exterior character. Inside, three bedrooms, three baths and two living areas. And much more.

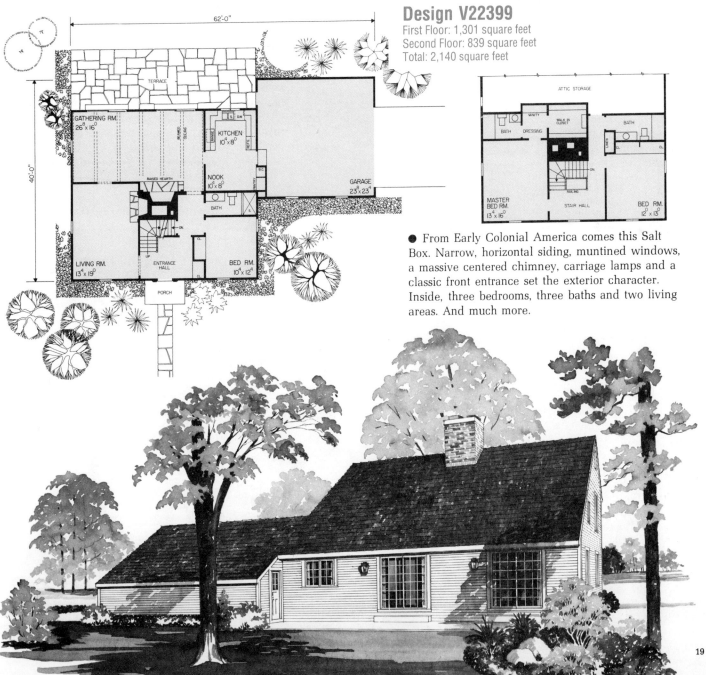

19

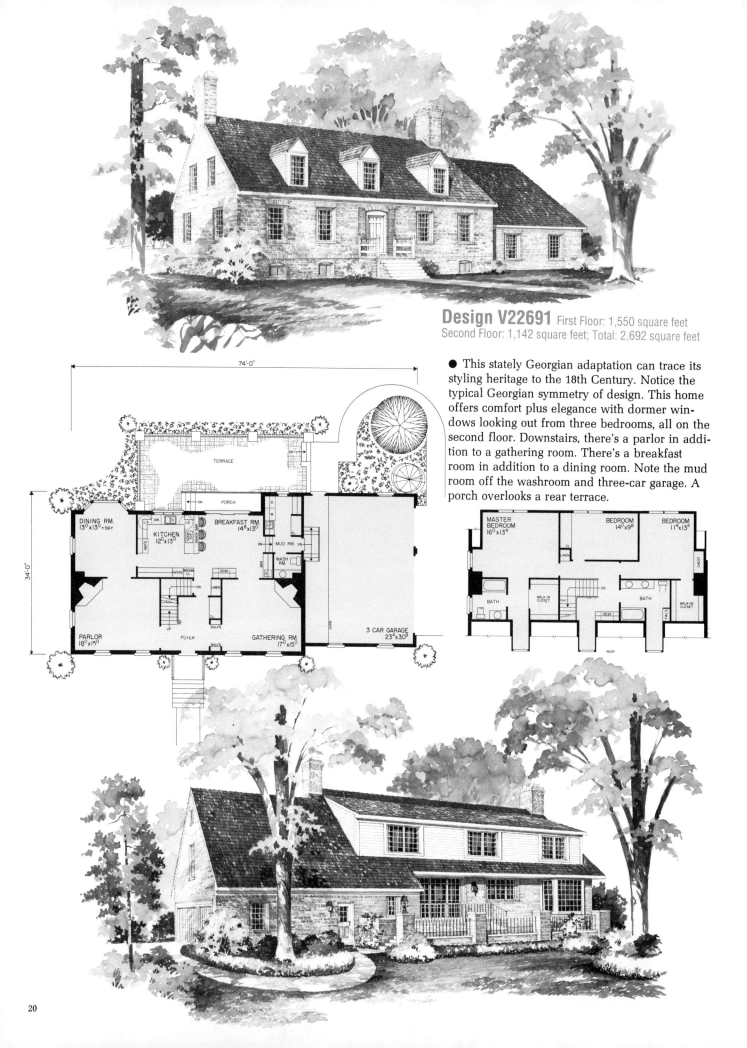

Design V22691 First Floor: 1,550 square feet
Second Floor: 1,142 square feet; Total: 2,692 square feet

74'-0"

34'-0"

TERRACE

DN

PORCH

DN

DINING RM.
13⁰x13⁰ +BAY

KITCHEN
12⁰x13⁰

BREAKFAST RM.
14⁸x13⁰

DN   MUD RM.

WASH
RM.

OVENS

DESK

LINEN

DN

UP

SHLV'S

FOYER

SHLV'S

PARLOR
18⁰x15⁰

GATHERING RM.
17⁰x15⁰

3 CAR GARAGE
23⁴x30⁸

● This stately Georgian adaptation can trace its styling heritage to the 18th Century. Notice the typical Georgian symmetry of design. This home offers comfort plus elegance with dormer windows looking out from three bedrooms, all on the second floor. Downstairs, there's a parlor in addition to a gathering room. There's a breakfast room in addition to a dining room. Note the mud room off the washroom and three-car garage. A porch overlooks a rear terrace.

MASTER
BEDROOM
16⁰x13⁴

BEDROOM
14⁰x9⁸

BEDROOM
11⁴x13⁴

LINEN

BATH

WALK-IN
CLOSET

DN

DESK

BATH

WALK-IN
CLOSET

CHEST

ROOF

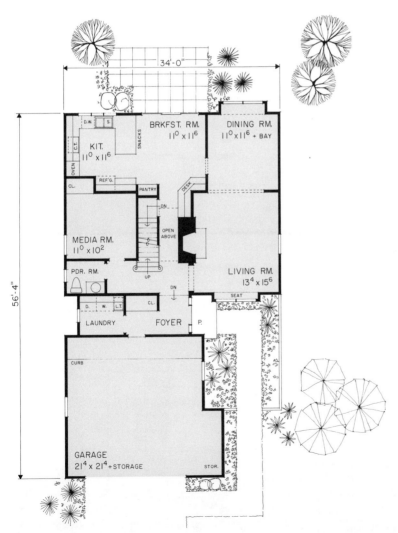

Design V23379 First Floor: 1,086 square feet
Second Floor: 902 square feet; Total: 1,988 square feet

● Colonial styling is perfect in this two-story, narrow-lot plan. With the garage facing toward the front, the home is protected from street noise and works well on a lot that allows very little clearance on the sides. Living areas are concentrated in the formal living and dining rooms and the media room with nearby powder room. The kitchen holds a large snack bar counter through to the breakfast room. Sliding glass doors here allow easy access to the rear terrace. The bedrooms are on the second floor and include a master with fireplace and garden whirlpool and two family bedrooms. One of the secondary bedrooms includes a large walk-in closet.

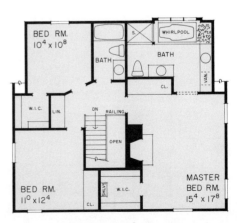

Design V22253 First Floor: 1,503 square feet; Second Floor: 1,291 square feet; Total: 2,794 square feet

● The overhanging second floor sets the character of this Early American design. Study the features, both inside and out.

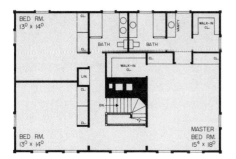

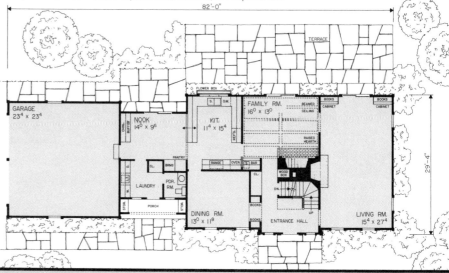

Design V21179 First Floor: 1,378 square feet; Second Floor: 1,040 square feet; Total: 2,418 square feet

● Loads of livability. This home could be called upon to serve as a five bedroom design. It will function admirably however you choose.

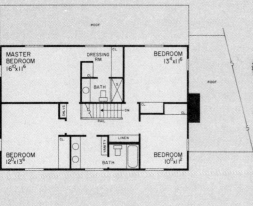

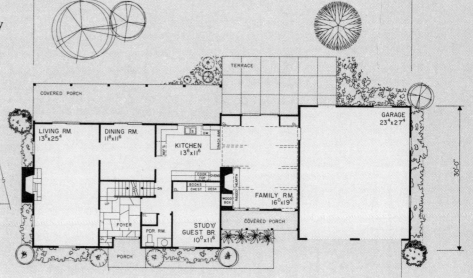

Design V21700 First Floor: 1,836 square feet; Second Floor: 1,232 square feet; Total: 3,068 square feet

● Good zoning, fine traffic circulation, efficient work center, first floor laundry are among convenient living features.

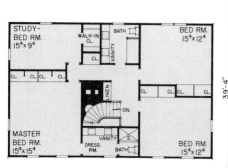

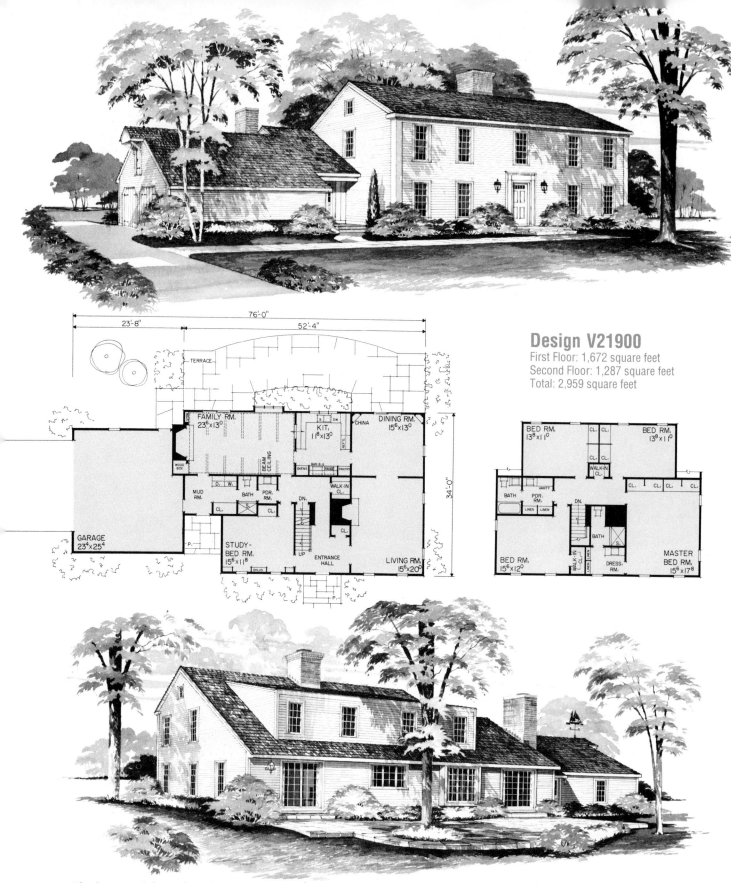

Design V21900
First Floor: 1,672 square feet
Second Floor: 1,287 square feet
Total: 2,959 square feet

● The history of the Colonial Salt Box goes back some 200 years. This unusually authentic adaptation captures all the warmth and charm of the early days both inside as well as outside. To reflect today's living patterns, an up-dating of the floor plan was inevitable. The result is a room arrangement which will serve the active family wonderfully. Formal living and dining take place at one end of the house which is free of cross-room traffic. Informal living activities will center around the family room and expand through sliding glass doors to the terrace. The mud room area is strategically located and includes the laundry and a full bath. An extra study/bedroom supplements four bedrooms upstairs. Count the closets and the other storage areas.

Design V22654

First Floor: 1,152 square feet
Second Floor: 844 square feet
Total: 1,996 square feet

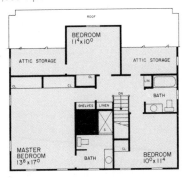

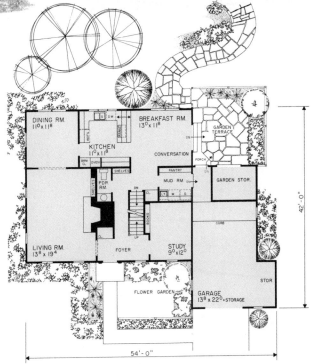

● This is certainly an authentic traditional salt-box. It features a symmetrical design with a center fireplace, a wide, paneled doorway and multi-paned, double-hung windows. Tucked behind the one-car garage is a garden shed which provides work and storage space. The breakfast room features French doors which open onto a flagstone terrace. The U-shaped kitchen has built-in counters which make efficient use of space. The upstairs plan houses three bedrooms.

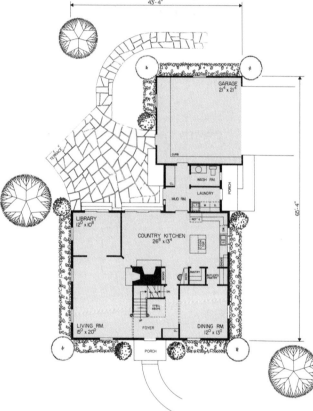

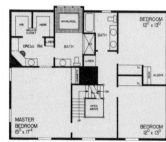

Design V22978 First Floor: 1,451 square feet
Second Floor: 1,268 square feet; Third Floor: 746 square feet
Total: 3,465 square feet

● The Nathaniel Hawthorne house in Salem, Mass. was the inspiration for this New England gambrel-roofed design. It was originally constructed around 1730. This 20th Century version offers a heap of living potential. The family's favorite spot will be in front of the fireplace in the spacious country kitchen. However, there are other places to retire to such as the formal living room, the adjacent library, the bedrooms, or the areas on the third floor. The full basement offers the potential for the development of additional recreational space. Don't overlook the mud room strategically located with access from the garage and both yards.

Design V22659 First Floor: 1,023 square feet
Second Floor: 1,008 square feet; Third Floor: 476 square feet
Total: 2,507 square feet

● The facade of this three-storied, pitch-roofed house has a symmetrical placement of windows and a restrained but elegant central entrance. The central hall, or foyer, expands midway through the house to a family kitchen. Off the foyer are two rooms, a living room with fireplace and a study. The windowed third floor attic can be used as a study and studio. Three bedrooms are housed on the second floor.

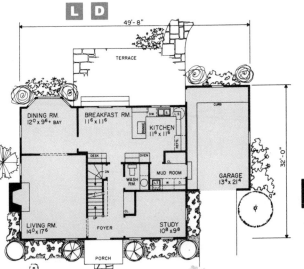

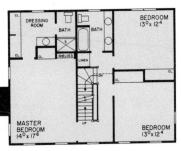

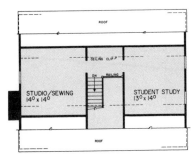

Design V22799 First Floor: 1,196 square feet
Second Floor: 780 square feet; Total: 1,976 square feet

● This two-story traditional design's facade with its narrow clapboards, punctuated by tall multi-paned windows, appears deceptively expansive. Yet the entire length of the house, including the garage, is 66 feet.

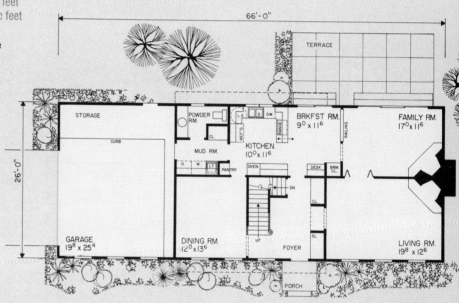

56'-0"

TERRACE

CURB

STOR.

STOR.

CL.

FAMILY RM.
11⁰x18⁸

PASS THRU

S. D.W.
KITCHEN
10⁰x9⁰

REF'G

DINING RM.
10⁰x13⁶

PANTRY | COOK TOP | OVENS

DN

CHINA

CL.

GARAGE
23⁸x23⁴

P

PDR. RM.

CL.

UP

FOYER

LIVING RM.
16⁸x12⁶

PORCH

31'-0"

Design V21719
First Floor: 864 square feet
Second Floor: 896 square feet; Total: 1,760 square feet

BEDROOM
11⁰x10⁰

CL.

BATH

vanity

BEDROOM
10⁰x11⁴

CL.

LINEN

WALK-IN CLOSET

LINEN

DN

CL. CL.

WALK-IN CLOSET

BEDROOM
11⁰x13⁸

S. BATH

MASTER BEDROOM
13⁴x13⁴

● What an appealing low-cost Colonial adaptation. Most of the livability features generally found in the largest of homes are present to cater to family needs.

Design V22870
First Floor: 900 square feet
Second Floor Left Suite: 467 square feet
Second Floor Right Suite: 493 square feet
Total: 1,860 square feet

54'-0"

TERRACE

DINING RM.
11⁰x10⁰

BRKFST.
8⁸x8⁰

SNACK BAR

S. DW

KITCHEN
11⁴x10⁰

RANGE

PANTRY | BRM CL.

REF'G.

CL.

PDR. RM.

DN

CURB

STORAGE | STORAGE

UP

30'-0"

LIVING RM.
13⁶x17⁰

FOYER

STUDY
10⁰x9²

GARAGE
21⁸x23⁴

PORCH

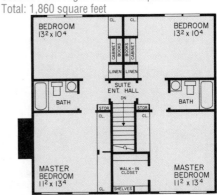

BEDROOM
13²x10⁴

CL. CL.

CABINET | BOOKS | CABINET

LINEN | LINEN

BEDROOM
13²x10⁴

BATH

SUITE ENT. HALL

STOR. | STOR.

DN

CL. CL.

BATH

MASTER BEDROOM
11²x13⁴

SHELVES

WALK-IN CLOSET

MASTER BEDROOM
11²x13⁴

● This colonial home was designed to provide comfortable living space for two families. The first floor is the common living area, with all of the necessary living areas; the second floor has two two-bedroom-one-bath suites. Built-ins are featured in the smaller bedroom.

29

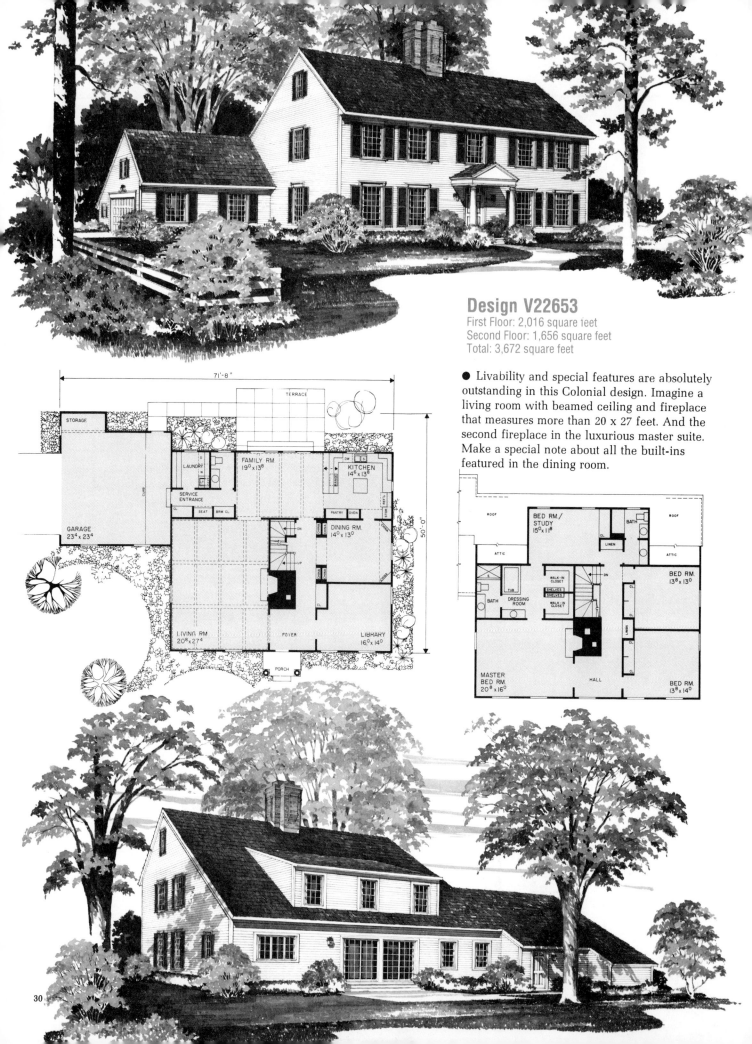

Design V22653

First Floor: 2,016 square feet
Second Floor: 1,656 square feet
Total: 3,672 square feet

● Livability and special features are absolutely
outstanding in this Colonial design. Imagine a
living room with beamed ceiling and fireplace
that measures more than 20 x 27 feet. And the
second fireplace in the luxurious master suite.
Make a special note about all the built-ins
featured in the dining room.

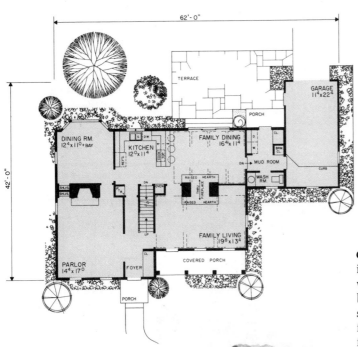

Design V22681

First Floor: 1,350 square feet
Second Floor: 1,224 square feet
Total: 2,574 square feet

● The charm of Early America is exemplified in this delightful design. Note the three areas which are highlighted by a fireplace. The three-bedroom second floor is nicely planned. Make special note of the master bedroom's many fine features. Study the rest of this design's many fine qualities.

Design V22625

First Floor: 1,640 square feet
Second Floor: 1,072 square feet
Total: 2,712 square feet

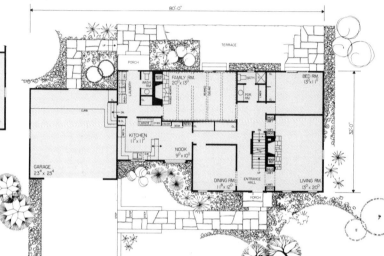

● A 19th-Century Farmhouse! So it might seem. But one with contemporary features . . . like the U-shaped kitchen with a built-in desk and appliances as well as a separate dining nook. Or the 20' by 13' family room. There, a beamed ceiling and raised-hearth fireplace add traditional warmth to a modern convention.

Design V21763
First Floor: 1,246 square feet; Apartment: 624 square feet
Second Floor: 1,054 square feet; Total: 2,924 square feet

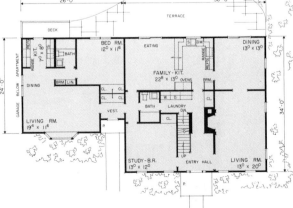

● A charming New England saltbox designed to satisfy the needs of the large family, plus provide facilities for a live-in relative! Many houses can be a problem in adapting to the living requirements of an in-residence relative. But, not this one. Your family will have all the space it needs, while your relative will enjoy all his or her privacy and independence. This apartment area may also function as a doctor's suite.

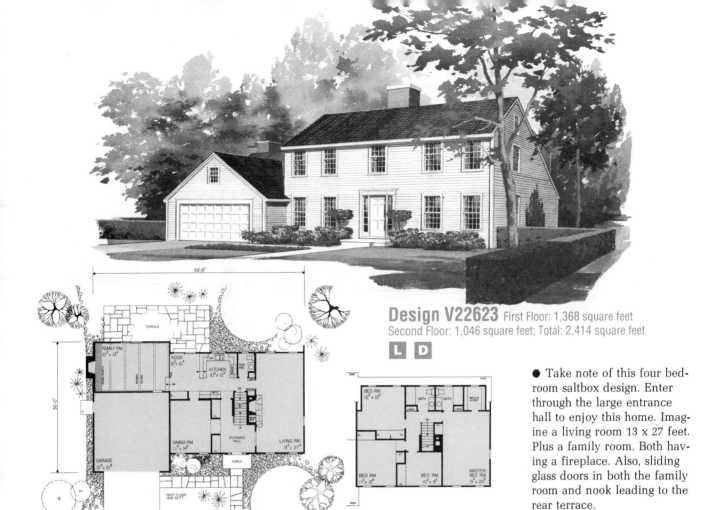

Design V22623 First Floor: 1,368 square feet
Second Floor: 1,046 square feet; Total: 2,414 square feet

L **D**

● Take note of this four bed-room saltbox design. Enter through the large entrance hall to enjoy this home. Imagine a living room 13 x 27 feet. Plus a family room. Both having a fireplace. Also, sliding glass doors in both the family room and nook leading to the rear terrace.

Design V21814
First Floor: 1,471 square feet
Second Floor: 1,052 square feet
Total: 2,523 square feet

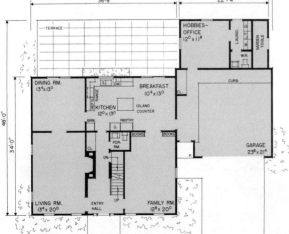

● A saltbox design that has all of the usual traditional exterior features. The interior shows what up-to-date floor planning can do inside the charm of yesteryear's exterior. A central entrance hall routes traffic directly to all major areas. The work area can be made to capture that cozy country kitchen atmosphere.

Design V22641

First Floor: 1,672 square feet
Second Floor: 1,248 square feet
Total: 2,920 square feet

● This Georgian adaptation is from the early 18th-Century and has plenty of historical background. The classical details are sedately stated. The plan promises up-to-date livability. The size of your site need not be large, either.

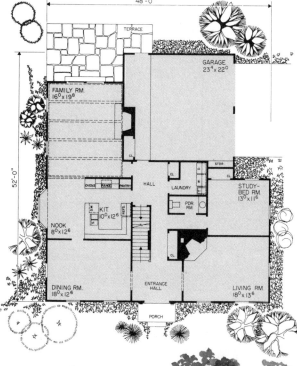

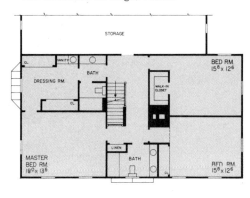

Design V22102

First Floor: 1,682 square feet
Second Floor: 1,344 square feet
Total: 3,026 square feet

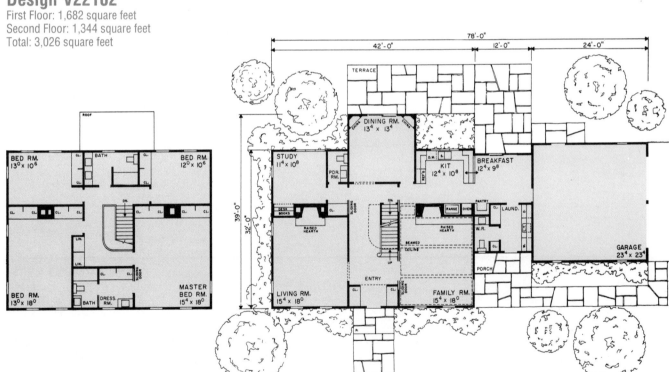

● This Early Colonial adaptation has its roots deep in the past. While it is long on history, it is equally long on 20th-Century livability features. The narrow horizontal siding, the appealing window treatment, the exquisite door detailing, the hip-roof, the mas- sive chimneys and the cupola are exterior architectural features which set the character. It would certainly be difficult by today's living stand- ards to ask for more than what this floor plan offers. From the first floor laundry with its adjacent washroom to the study with its adjacent powder room, the interior is replete with con- venient living appointments. There is a wealth of "little" features such as the built-ins, the raised hearths, the pantry, the pass-through to breakfast room and the beamed ceiling.

● Small house with big house features and livability. Some of the features include two full baths and extra storage upstairs; laundry, washroom and two fireplaces, each with a wood box on the first floor. Two sets of sliding glass doors lead to the terrace.

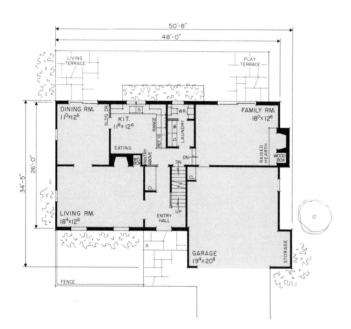

Design V21856
First Floor: 1,023 squarc feet
Second Floor: 784 square feet
Total: 1,807 square feet

D

● The appeal of this Colonial home will be virtually everlasting. It will improve with age and service the growing family well. Imagine your family living here. There are four bedrooms, 2½ baths, plus plenty of first floor living space.

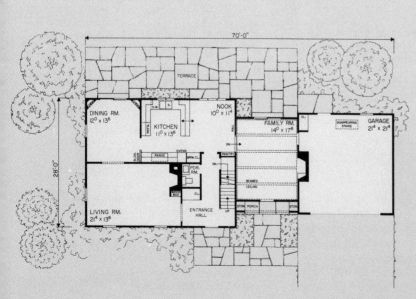

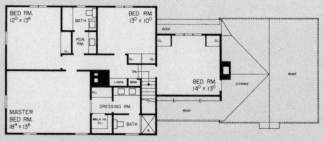

Design V22211 First Floor: 1,214 square feet
Second Floor: 1,146 square feet; Total: 2,360 square feet

L D

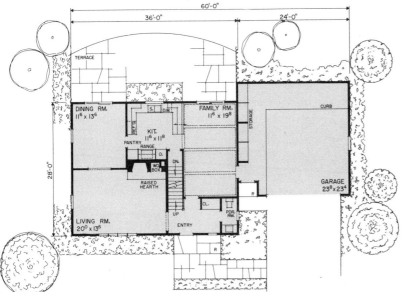

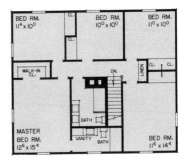

● A Garrison type adaptation that projects all the romance of yesteryear. The narrow horizontal siding, the wide corner boards, the window detailing, the overhanging second floor and the massive, centered chimney help set this home apart.

Design V21849

First Floor: 1,008 square feet
Second Floor: 1,080 square feet
Total: 2,088 square feet

37

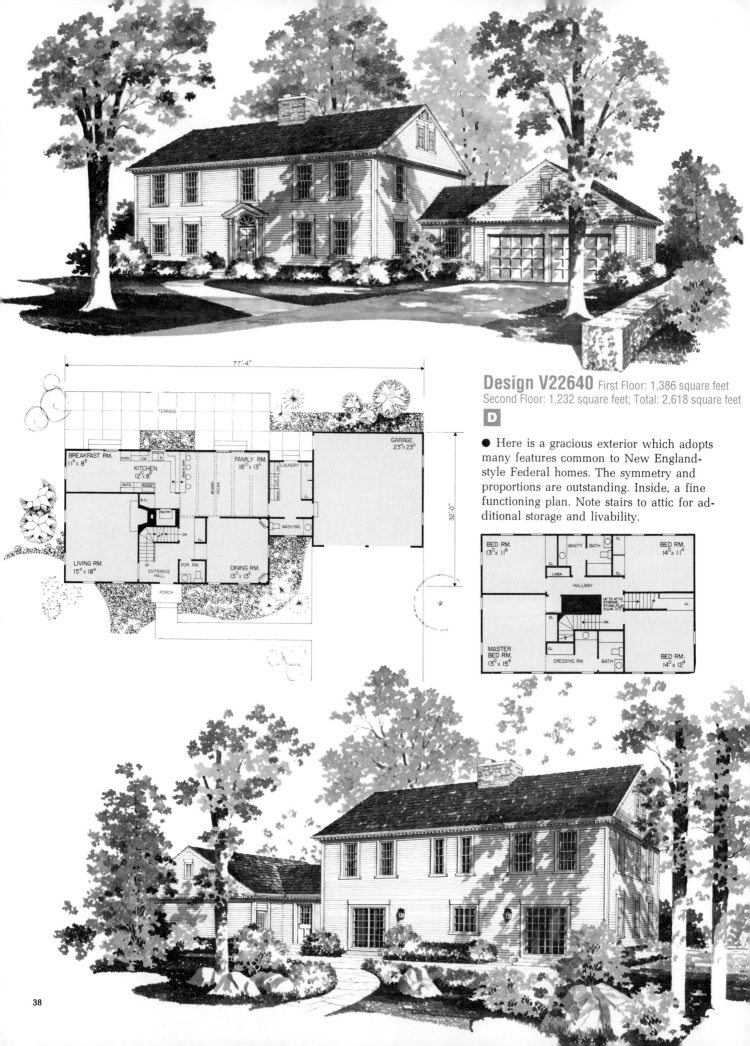

Design V22640 First Floor: 1,386 square feet
Second Floor: 1,232 square feet; Total: 2,618 square feet

D

● Here is a gracious exterior which adopts many features common to New England-style Federal homes. The symmetry and proportions are outstanding. Inside, a fine functioning plan. Note stairs to attic for additional storage and livability.

Floor plan labels (first floor):

TERRACE

BREAKFAST RM. 11⁶ x 8⁸

KITCHEN 12¹⁰ x 8⁸

FAMILY RM. 18¹⁰ x 13⁶

LAUNDRY

GARAGE 23⁴ x 23⁴

PANTRY

WASH RM.

LIVING RM. 15⁴ x 18⁴

ENTRANCE HALL

PDR. RM.

DINING RM. 13⁰ x 13⁶

PORCH

77'-4"

32'-0"

Floor plan labels (second floor):

BED RM. 13⁰ x 11⁶

VANITY

BATH

BED RM. 14⁰ x 11⁴

LINEN

HALLWAY

MASTER BED RM. 13⁰ x 15⁶

DRESSING RM.

BATH

BED RM. 14⁰ x 12⁴

UP TO ATTIC STORAGE, STUDIO, PLAY ROOM, ETC.

Design V22649

First Floor: 1,501 square feet
Second Floor: 1,280 square feet
Total: 2,781 square feet

● This design's front exterior is highlighted by four pedimented nine-over-nine windows, five second-story eyebrow windows and a massive central chimney. Note the spacious kitchen of the interior. It is large in size and features an island range, pantry and broom closets, breakfast room with sliding glass doors to the rear porch and an adjacent laundry room which has access to the garage.

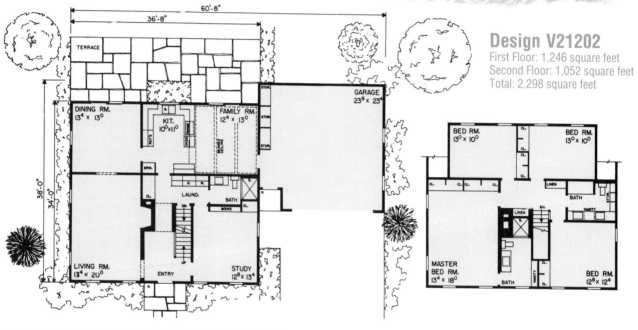

Design V21202

First Floor: 1,246 square feet
Second Floor: 1,052 square feet
Total: 2,298 square feet

60'-8"
36'-8"
38'-0"
34'-0"

TERRACE

DINING RM.
13⁴ x 13⁰

KIT.
10⁰ x 11⁰

FAMILY RM.
12⁴ x 13⁰

GARAGE
23⁸ x 23⁴

STOR.
STOR.
STOR.

REF'S
OVEN
RANGE

BRM.

D. W.

LAUND.

BATH

BOOKS

CL.

CL.

LIVING RM.
13⁴ x 20⁰

ENTRY

STUDY
12⁸ x 13⁴

BED RM.
13⁰ x 10⁰

BED RM.
13⁰ x 10⁰

CL.
CL.
CL.
CL.
CL.

LINEN

BATH

VANITY

STR.

LINEN

MASTER
BED RM.
13⁴ x 18⁰

BATH

VANITY

BED RM.
12⁸ x 12⁴

Design V21266

First Floor: 1,374 square feet
Second Floor: 1,094 square feet
Total: 2,468 square feet

BED RM.
12⁸ x 10⁰

BED RM.
12⁸ x 10⁰

CL.

CL.
CL.
CL.
CL.

LINEN

BATH

VANITY

LINEN

DN.

LIN.

LIN.

CL.

MASTER
BED RM.
13⁴ x 18⁸

BATH

VANITY

BED RM.
12⁸ x 13⁴

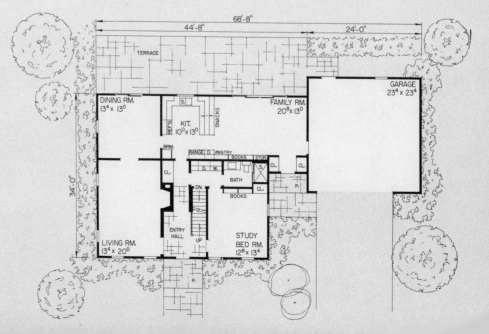

68'-8"
44'-8"
24'-0"
34'-0"

TERRACE

DINING RM.
13⁴ x 13⁰

KIT.
10⁰ x 13⁰

REFG.

S.

SNACKS

FAMILY RM.
20⁸ x 13⁰

GARAGE
23⁴ x 23⁴

BRM.

RANGE
O.

PANTRY

BOOKS

STOR.

CL.
CL.

CL.

D. W.

BATH

BOOKS

CL.

P.

LIVING RM.
13⁴ x 20⁰

ENTRY
HALL

UP

DN.

STUDY
BED RM.
12⁸ x 13⁴

P.

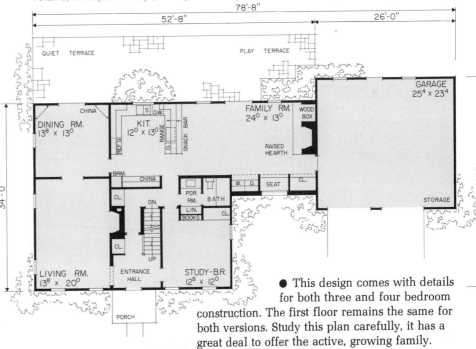

Design V21142 First Floor: 1,525 square feet; Second Floor: 952 square feet
Total: 2,477 square feet (2,578 square feet Optional Four Bedroom)

● This design comes with details for both three and four bedroom construction. The first floor remains the same for both versions. Study this plan carefully, it has a great deal to offer the active, growing family.

Design V22999

First Floor: 2,547 square feet
Second Floor: 2,128 square feet
Guest Apartment: 1,186 square feet
Total: 5,861 square feet

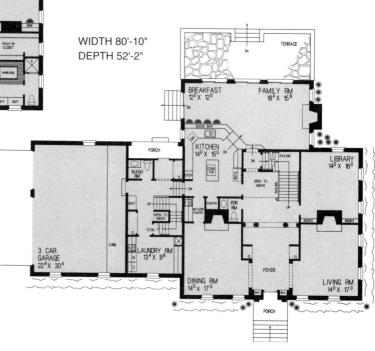

WIDTH 80'-10"
DEPTH 52'-2"

● Recalling the grandeur of its Maryland ancestors, this manor house is replete with exterior details that make it special: keystoned lintels, fluted pilasters, a dormered attic and pedimented doorway. The centerhall floor plan allows formal living and dining areas to the front of the plan. Complementing these are the cozy library and large family room/breakfast room area. A service entrance off the garage holds a laundry room and wash room. Upstairs bedrooms allow more than adequate space. Over the garage is a complete guest apartment with living area, office, bedroom, bath and kitchen.

Design V22992

First Floor: 1,541 square feet
Second Floor: 1,541 square feet
Third Floor: 1,016 square feet
Total: 4,098 square feet

L D

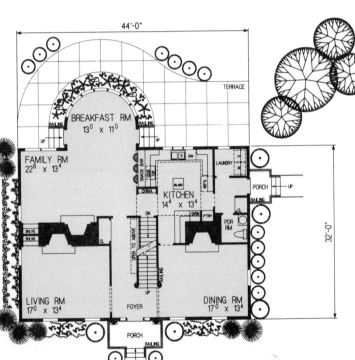

44'-0"

TERRACE

BREAKFAST RM
13⁰ x 11⁰

FAMILY RM
22⁶ x 13⁴

LAUNDRY

KITCHEN
14⁴ x 13⁴

SNACK BAR

PORCH
RAILING

32'-0"

OPEN TO ABOVE

PDR RM

SHLVS
SHLVS

LIVING RM
17⁰ x 13⁴

FOYER

DINING RM
17⁰ x 13⁴

PORCH
RAILING

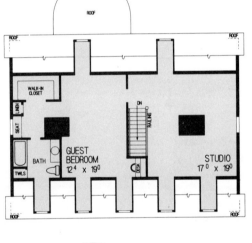

ROOF

ROOF

WALK-IN CLOSET

LINEN

SEAT

BATH

GUEST BEDROOM
12⁴ x 19⁰

STUDIO
17⁰ x 19⁰

RAILING

TWLS

ROOF

ROOF

ROOF

MASTER BEDROOM
21⁴ x 13⁴

BEDROOM
13⁰ x 13⁴

BATH

LINEN

WALK-IN CLOSET

LINEN

WALK-IN CLOSET

OPEN TO BELOW

RAILING

WHIRLPOOL

VANITY

MASTER BATH

SEAT   SEAT

BEDROOM
17⁰ x 13⁴

● The Dalton house, built between 1750 and
1760 in Newburyport, Massachusetts, inspired
our plan shown here. Its lovely proportion and
graceful exterior give way to a floor plan designed
for the times. Left of the entry foyer is the formal
living room; to the right formal dining. Both
rooms have warming hearths. A family room to
the rear of the plan connects with a unique
glass-enclosed breakfast room. Nearby is the
kitchen with pass-through snack bar. The second floor holds three bedrooms — the master
suite and two family bedrooms. On the third
floor is a guest bedroom with private bath and
studio.

Design V22733 First Floor: 1,177 square feet; Second Floor: 1,003 square feet; Total: 2,180 square feet

L D

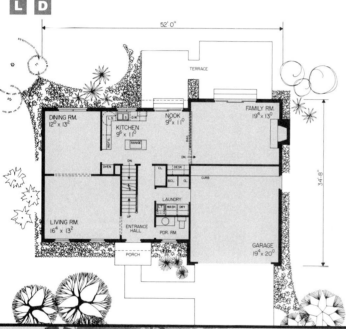

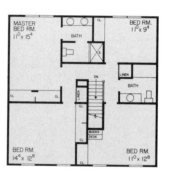

● This is definitely a four bedroom Colonial with charm galore. The kitchen features an island range and other built-ins. All will enjoy the sunken family room with fireplace, which has sliding glass doors leading to the terrace. Also a basement for recreational activities with laundry remaining on first floor for extra convenience.

CUSTOMIZABLE
Custom Alterations? See page 413 for customizing this plan to your specifications.

Design V22598

First Floor: 1,016 square feet
Second Floor: 890 square feet
Total: 1,906 square feet

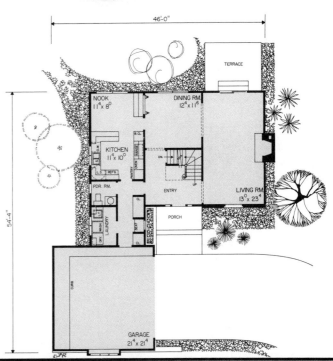

● An impressive, Early Colonial adaptation with a projecting two-car garage and front drive court. It will not demand a large, expensive piece of property. In days of high-cost building, this relatively modest-sized two-story will be a great investment. Note the huge living room. The basement lends itself to recreational facilities.

Design V22622

First Floor: 624 square feet
Second Floor: 624 square feet
Total: 1,248 square feet

L **D**

● Appealing design can envelope little packages, too. Here is a charming, Early Colonial adaptation with an attached two-car garage to serve the young family with a modest building budget.

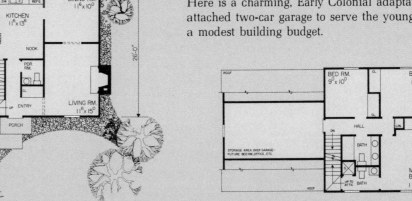

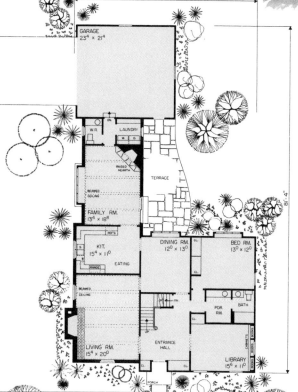

Design V22308

First Floor: 1,807 square feet
Second Floor: 1,195 square feet
Total: 3,002 square feet

● If yours is a corner lot you might want to give this attractive Colonial adaptation your consideration. Or, perhaps more significantly, if you have a large family this may be the design to solve your housing problem. Certainly you won't have to invest in a huge piece of property to enjoy the livability this home has to offer. In addition to the formal living room and informal family room, there is the separate dining room and kitchen eating space. Further, in addition to the three upstairs bedrooms, there is a fourth downstairs. The library could function as the fifth, if desired.

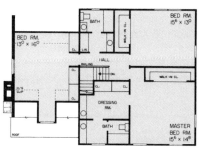

Design V22103

First Floor: 1,374 square feet
Second Floor: 1,056 square feet
Total: 2,430 square feet

D

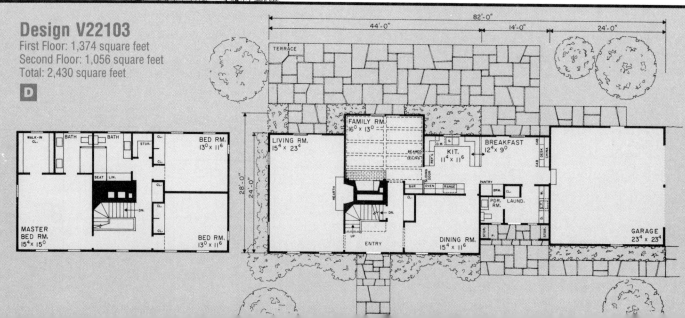

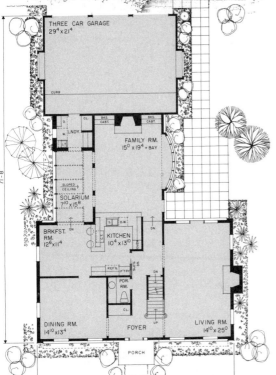

Design V23552

First Floor: 1,784 square feet
Second Floor: 1,192 square feet
Total: 2,976 square feet

● Smart exterior features mark this home as a classic: second-story pop-outs with half-round windows above multi-paned windows, charming lintels, and a combination of horizontal wood siding and brick. Its interior floor plan contains both formal and informal areas, two fireplaces, a cozy solarium and three bedrooms with a sitting room. A three-car garage provides all the space necessary for the family vehicles and plenty of additional paraphernalia.

Design V22610

First Floor: 1,505 square feet
Second Floor: 1,344 square feet
Total: 2,849 square feet

● This full two-story traditional will be worthy of note wherever built. It strongly recalls images of a New England of yesteryear. And well it might; for the window treatment is delightful. The front entrance detail is inviting. The narrow horizontal siding and the corner boards are appealing as are the two massive chimneys. The center entrance hall is large with a handy powder room nearby. The study has built-in bookshelves and offers a full measure of privacy. The interior kitchen has a pass-thru to the family room and enjoys all that natural light from the bay window of the nook. A beamed ceiling, fireplace and sliding glass doors are features of the family room. The mud room highlights a closet, laundry equipment and an extra wash room. Study the upstairs with those four bedrooms, two baths and plenty of closets. An excellent arrangement for all.

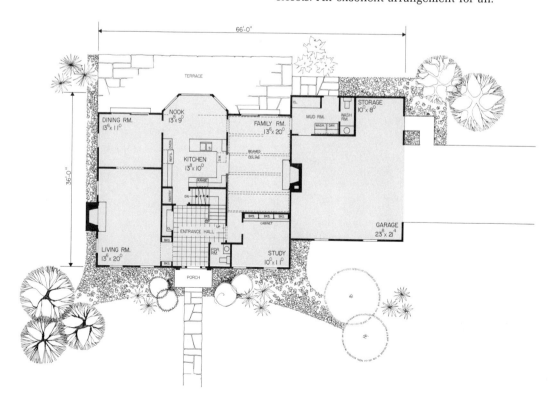

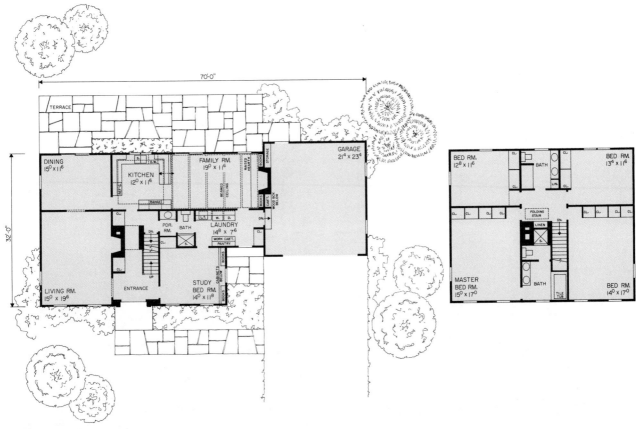

Design V22188

First Floor: 1,440 square feet
Second Floor: 1,280 square feet
Total: 2,720 square feet

● This design is characteristic of early America and its presence will create an atmosphere of that time in our heritage. However, it will be right at home wherever located. Along with exterior charm, this design has outstanding livability to offer its occupants. Beginning with the first floor, there are formal and informal areas plus the work centers. Note the center bath which has direct access from three adjacent areas. Built-in book shelves are the feature of both the family room and the study/bedroom. Built-ins are also featured in the garage. Ascending up to the second floor, one will be in the private sleeping area. This area consists of the master suite, three bedrooms and full bath. Folding stairs are in the upstairs hall for easy access to the attic.

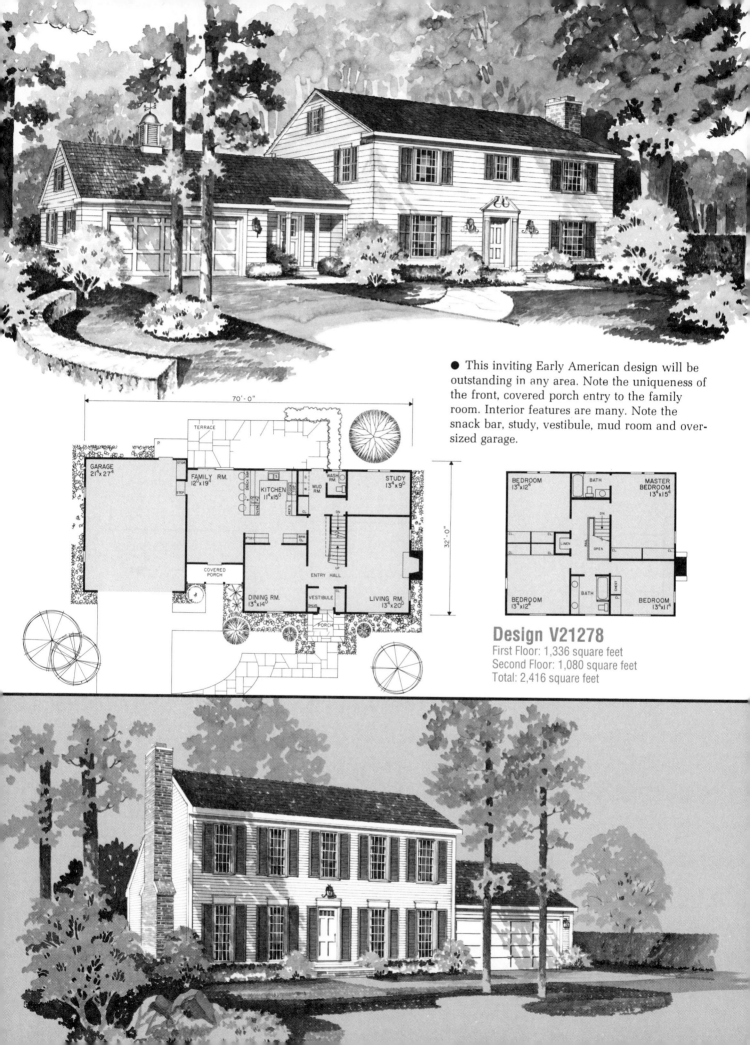

● This inviting Early American design will be outstanding in any area. Note the uniqueness of the front, covered porch entry to the family room. Interior features are many. Note the snack bar, study, vestibule, mud room and oversized garage.

70'-0"

TERRACE

GARAGE
21⁴x27⁴

FAMILY RM.
12'x19⁰

KITCHEN
11⁴x15⁰

MUD RM.

WASH RM.

STUDY
13⁴x9⁰

32'-0"

COVERED PORCH

ENTRY HALL

DINING RM.
13⁴x14⁰

VESTIBULE

LIVING RM.
13⁴x20⁰

PORCH

BEDROOM
13⁴x12⁴

BATH

MASTER BEDROOM
13⁴x15⁴

LINEN

OPEN

BEDROOM
13⁴x12⁴

BATH

BEDROOM
13⁴x11⁴

Design V21278
First Floor: 1,336 square feet
Second Floor: 1,080 square feet
Total: 2,416 square feet

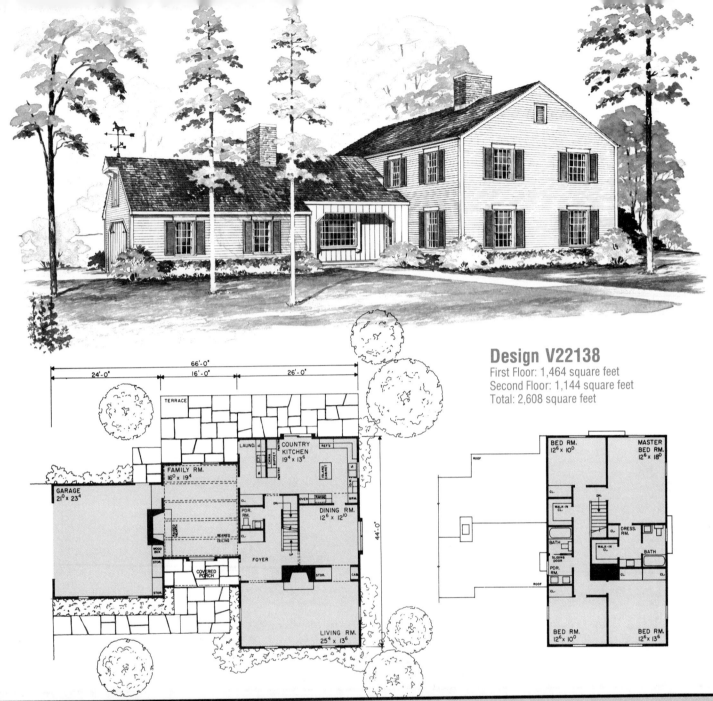

Design V22138

First Floor: 1,464 square feet
Second Floor: 1,144 square feet
Total: 2,608 square feet

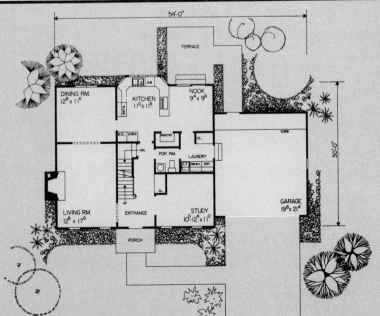

Design V22731 First Floor: 1,039 square feet

Second Floor: 973 square feet; Total: 2,012 square feet

L **D**

● The multi-paned windows with shutters of this two-story highlight the exterior delightfully. Inside the livability is ideal. Formal and informal areas are sure to serve your family with ease. Note efficient U-shaped kitchen with handy first-floor laundry. Sleeping facilities on second floor.

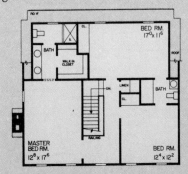

Design V22295

First Floor: 1,947 square feet
Second Floor: 1,092 square feet
Total: 3,039 square feet

● This L-shaped two-story will make efficient use of your building site. The floor plan and how it functions is extremely interesting and practical. Study it carefully.

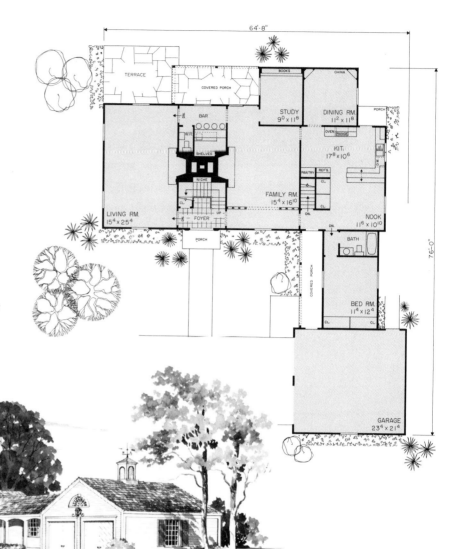

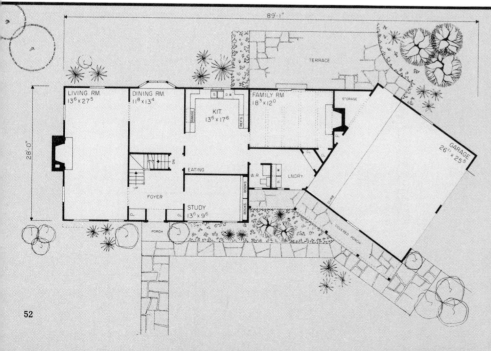

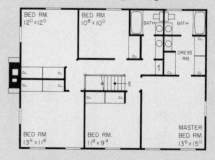

● Angular in its configuration, this inviting home offers loads of livability. There are five bedrooms, study, family room and a 27 foot long living room.

Design V22322

First Floor: 1,480 square feet
Second Floor: 1,172 square feet
Total: 2,652 square feet

Design V22346

First Floor: 1,510 square feet
Second Floor: 1,009 square feet
Total: 2,519 square feet

● A fine mixture of exterior materials, window treatment, and roof planes help set the character here. Envision your family enjoying all that this design has to offer.

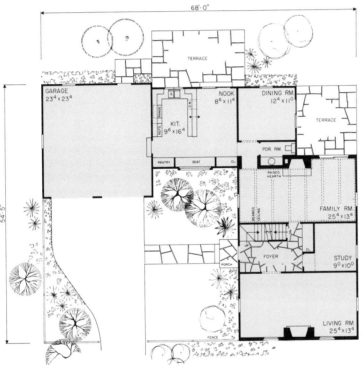

Design V22539

First Floor: 1,450 square feet
Second Floor: 1,167 square feet
Total: 2,617 square feet

● This appealingly proportioned gambrel exudes an aura of coziness. The beauty of the main part of the house is delightfully symmetrical and is enhanced by the attached garage and laundry room. The center entrance routes traffic directly to all major zones of the house.

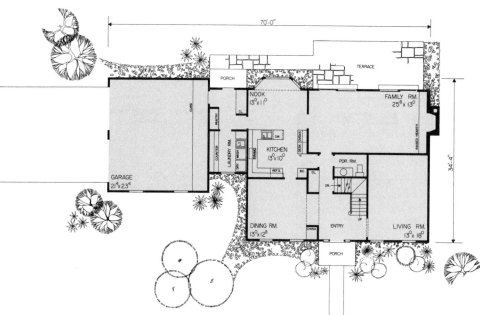

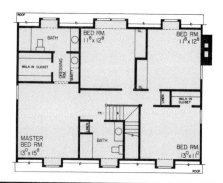

Design V21141

First Floor: 1,360 square feet
Second Floor: 939 square feet; Total: 2,299 square feet

● A 27-foot end living room, a fireplace in the breakfast room and master bedroom and a generous area over the garage for possible future development are highlights of this design. Don't overlook the many other features which include the family room, extra washroom, dining room, etc.

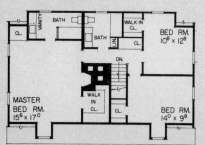

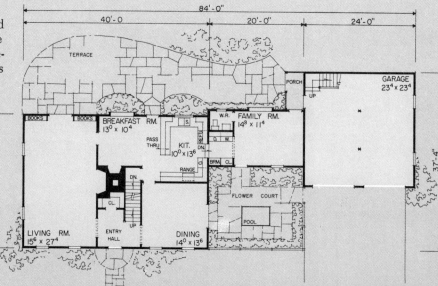

Design V22538

First Floor: 1,503 square feet
Second Floor: 1,095 square feet
Total: 2,598 square feet

L **D**

● This saltbox is charming, indeed. The livability it has to offer to the large and growing family is great. The entry is spacious and is open to the second floor balcony. For living areas, there is the study in addition to the living and family rooms.

Expandable Cape Ann Cottage

Design V22983 First Floor (Basic Plan): 776 square feet
First Floor (Expanded Plan): 1,072 square feet
Second Floor (Both Plans): 652 square feet
Total: 1,428 (Basic Plan); 1,724 (Expanded Plan)

● This charming gambrel-roofed Colonial cottage is reminiscent of the simple houses built and occupied by seafarers on Cape Ann, Mass. in the 17th and 18th Centuries. However, this adaptation offers a new twist. It is designed to expand as your need and/or budget grows. Of course, building the expanded version first will deliver the bonus livability promised by the formal dining room and quiet study, plus the convenience of the attached garage.

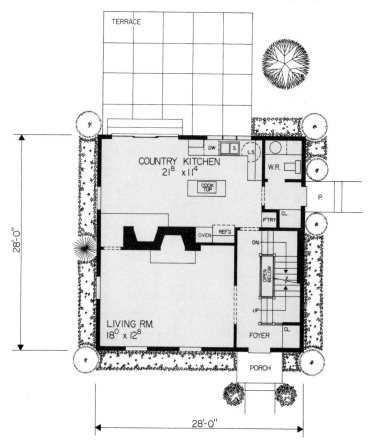

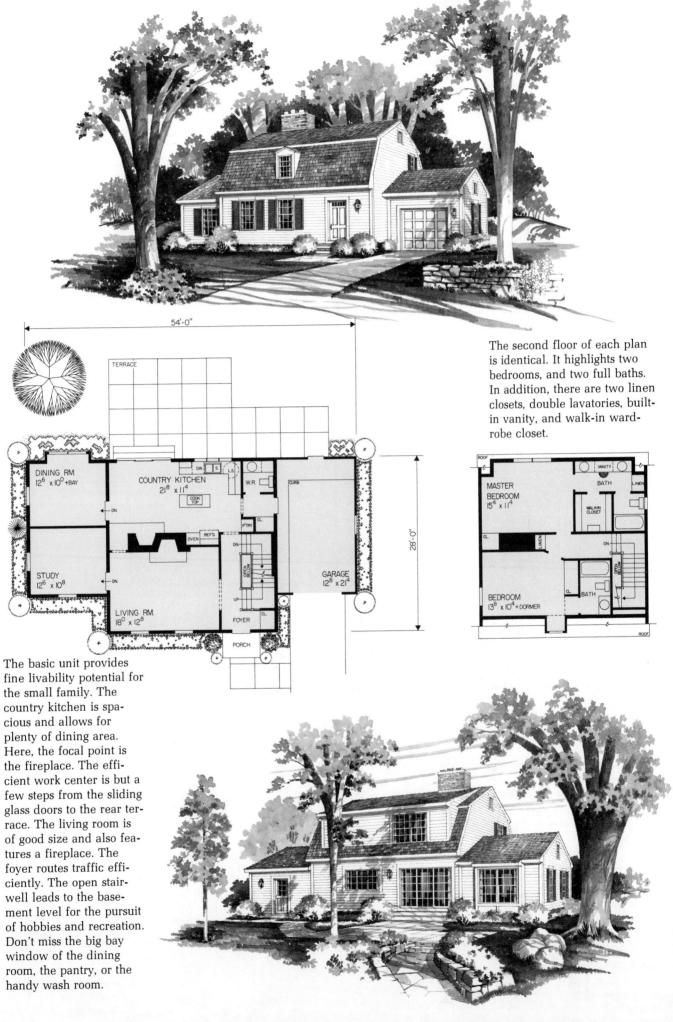

54'-0"

TERRACE

DINING RM.
12⁶ x 10⁰ +BAY

COUNTRY KITCHEN
21⁸ x 11⁴

COOK TOP

DW S L.S.

W.R.

CURB

DN.

P'TRY CL.

OVEN REF'G

STUDY
12⁶ x 10⁸

DN.

OPEN BELOW

UP

DN.

GARAGE
12⁸ x 21⁴

28'-0"

LIVING RM.
18⁰ x 12⁸

FOYER

CL.

PORCH

The second floor of each plan is identical. It highlights two bedrooms, and two full baths. In addition, there are two linen closets, double lavatories, built-in vanity, and walk-in wardrobe closet.

ROOF

VANITY

MASTER BEDROOM
15⁴ x 11⁴

BATH

LINEN

WALK-IN CLOSET

CL.

LINEN

DN.

BEDROOM
13⁸ x 10⁴ +DORMER

CL. BATH

OPEN

ROOF

The basic unit provides fine livability potential for the small family. The country kitchen is spacious and allows for plenty of dining area. Here, the focal point is the fireplace. The efficient work center is but a few steps from the sliding glass doors to the rear terrace. The living room is of good size and also features a fireplace. The foyer routes traffic efficiently. The open stairwell leads to the basement level for the pursuit of hobbies and recreation. Don't miss the big bay window of the dining room, the pantry, or the handy wash room.

Design V21986 First Floor: 896 square feet
Second Floor: 1,148 square feet; Total: 2,044 square feet

L

● This design with its distinctive Gambrel roof will spell charm wherever it may be situated - far out in the country, or on a busy thoroughfare. Compact and economical to build, it will be easy on the budget. Note the location of the family room. It is over the garage on the second floor.

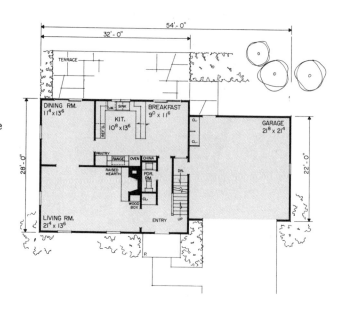

Design V21777 First Floor: 1,142 square feet
Second Floor: 1,010 square feet; Total: 2,152 square feet

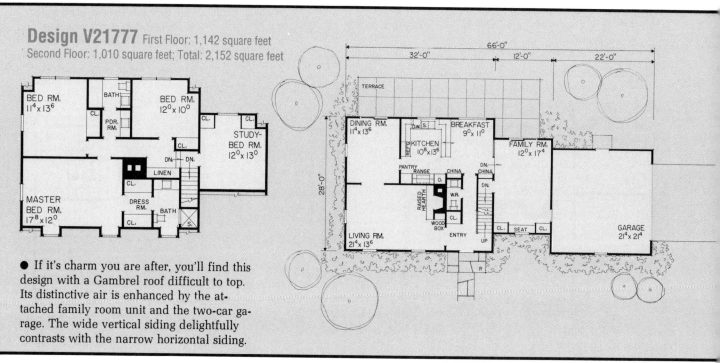

● If it's charm you are after, you'll find this design with a Gambrel roof difficult to top. Its distinctive air is enhanced by the attached family room unit and the two-car garage. The wide vertical siding delightfully contrasts with the narrow horizontal siding.

Design V22531 First Floor: 1,353 square feet
Second Floor: 1,208 square feet; Total: 2,561 square feet

● This design has its roots in the early history of New England. While its exterior is decidedly and purposely dated, the interior reflects an impressive 20th-Century floor plan. All of the elements are present to guarantee outstanding living patterns for today's large, active family.

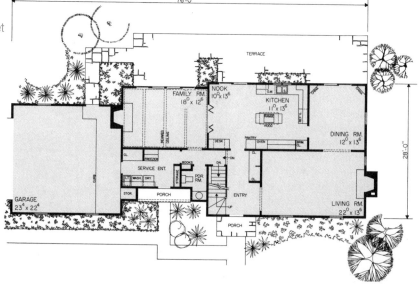

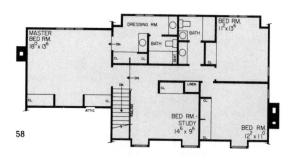

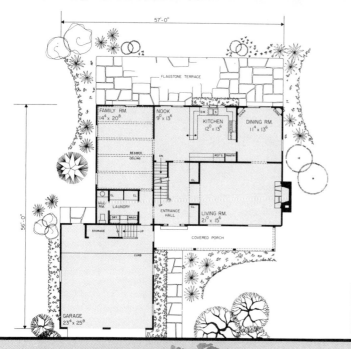

FAMILY RM. 14⁴ x 20⁸ NOOK 9⁰ x 13⁶ KITCHEN 12⁰ x 13⁶ DINING RM. 11⁴ x 13⁶

BEAMED CEILING

LAUNDRY ENTRANCE HALL LIVING RM. 21⁰ x 15⁰

COVERED PORCH

GARAGE 23⁴ x 25⁸

● Efficiently planned, this two-story house will serve the family with ease. Four bedrooms are on the second floor, along with two full baths. Note the attic storage over the projecting garage.

DRESSING BATH BATH WALK-IN CLOSET BED RM. 15⁴ x 10⁴

MASTER BED RM. 14⁴ x 12¹⁰ STAIR HALL

BED RM. 11⁶ x 10² BED RM. 11⁶ x 11⁰

ATTIC STORAGE 17⁴ x 25⁸

Design V22364

First Floor: 1,440 square feet
Second Floor: 1,206 square feet
Total: 2,646 square feet

Design V21827

First Floor: 1,442 square feet
Second Floor: 1,098 square feet
Total: 2,540 square feet

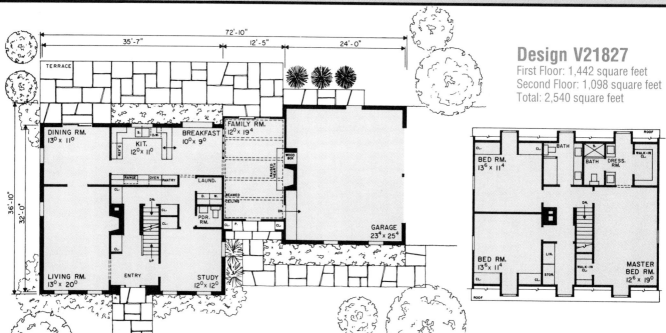

72'-10"
35'-7" 12'-5" 24'-0"

TERRACE

DINING RM. 13⁰ x 11⁰ KIT. 12⁰ x 11⁰ BREAKFAST 10⁰ x 9⁰ FAMILY RM. 12⁰ x 19⁴

RANGE OVEN PANTRY LAUND. PDR. RM.

BEAMED CEILING WOOD BOX

GARAGE 23⁴ x 25⁴

LIVING RM. 13⁰ x 20⁰ ENTRY STUDY 12⁰ x 12⁰

36'-10"
32'-0"

BATH WALK-IN CL.

BED RM. 13⁶ x 11⁴ BATH DRESS. RM.

BED RM. 13⁶ x 11⁴ MASTER BED RM. 12⁶ x 19⁰

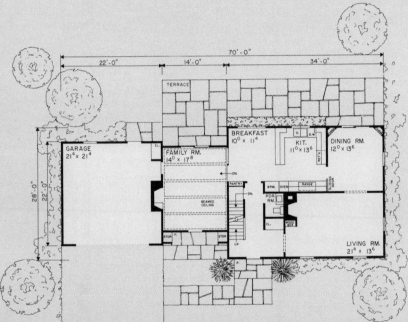

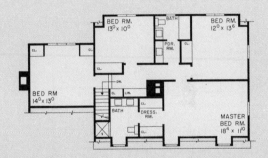

Design V22131

First Floor: 1,214 square feet
Second Floor: 1,097 square feet
Total: 2,311 square feet

L D

● The gambrel-roof home is often the very embodiment of charm from the Early Colonial Period in American architectural history. Fine proportion and excellent detailing were the hallmarks of the era.

Design V22988

First Floor: 1,458 square feet
Second Floor: 1,075 square feet
Total: 2,533 square feet
Optional Loft: 462 square feet

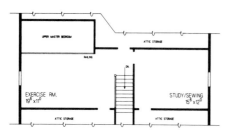

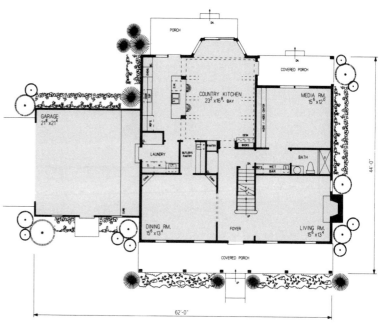

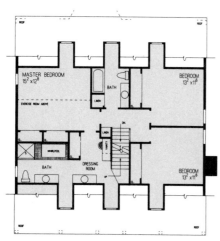

● The Joseph Guyon farmhouse, built in 1740, served as inspiration for this beautiful modern version. Three floors of living space encompass a country kitchen, living room, media room and dining room on the first floor; three bedrooms and two baths on the second floor; and an exercise room and study or sewing room on the third floor. Don't miss the covered porches front and rear, full guest bath near the media room and built-in wet bar.

Design V22995

First Floor: 2,465 square feet
Second Floor: 617 square feet
Total: 3,082 square feet

● This New England Colonial delivers beautiful proportions and great livability on 1½ levels. The main area of the house, the first floor, holds a living room, library, family room, dining room and gourmet kitchen. The master bedroom, also on this floor, features a whirlpool tub and sloped ceiling. A long rear terrace stretches the full width of the house. Two bedrooms on the second floor share a full bath; each has a built-in desk.

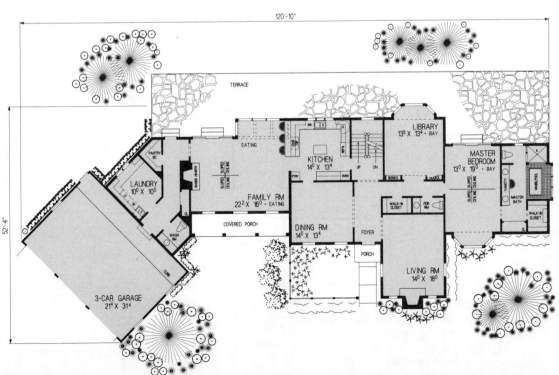

Design V22891

First Floor: 1,405 square feet
Second Floor: 1,226 square feet
Total: 2,631 square feet

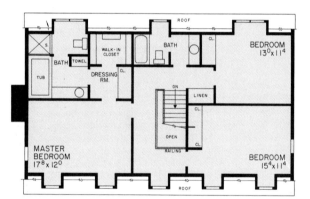

● Here is a charming two-story house with a Gambrel roof that is very appealing. Entering this home, you will find a large dining room to the right which precedes an efficient kitchen. The adjacent breakfast room makes serving meals easy. The nice sized living room has a fireplace as does the family room. A wet bar and sliding glass doors are also in the family room. A powder room and laundry are on the first floor, too. Upstairs, you will find two bedrooms, a bath and a master bedroom suite with walk-in closet, tub and shower. Note that the second floor hall is open to the first floor.

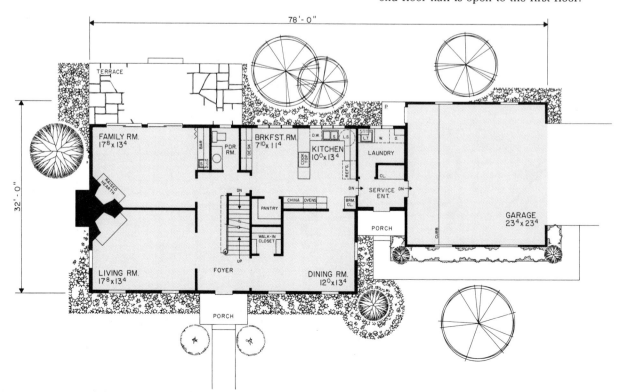

Design V22897

First Floor: 1,648 square feet
Second Floor: 1,140 square feet
Total: 2,788 square feet

● Second-story dormers pierce the gambrel roof for comfortable window seats in the sleeping area of this comfortable home. An upper family room and all three bedrooms – including a luxurious master bedroom suite, are located upstairs. There's plenty of livability downstairs with a living room, formal dining room, breakfast area, study, and family room with raised hearth. Good zoning allows smooth traffic flow throughout the house.

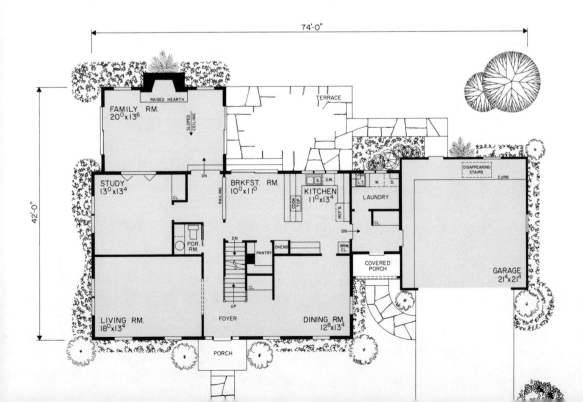

Design V21914 First Floor: 1,470 square feet; Second Floor: 888 square feet; Total: 2,358 square feet

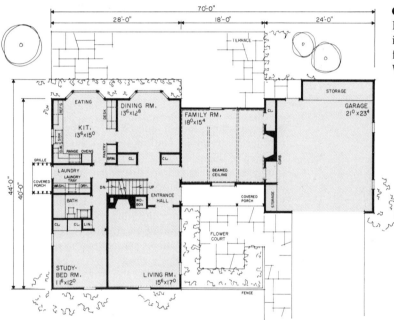

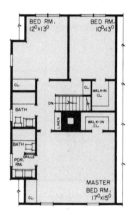

● What an interesting facade for passers-by to enjoy. Here, the delightful configuration of the Gambrel roof is fully visible from the road. The interior has all the features to help assure living convenience at its best. What are your favorite features?

Design V21745 First Floor: 1,440 square feet; Second Floor: 1,124 square feet; Total: 2,564 square feet

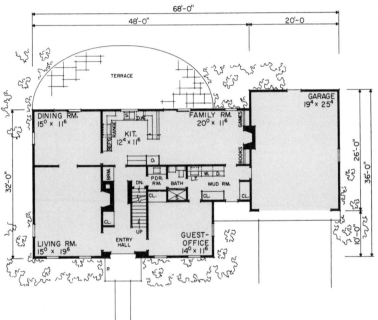

● A picture of charm. For sheer exterior appeal this house would be difficult to top. And inside there is an abundance of livability. Imagine, four bedrooms, three baths, guest room, family room, separate dining room and first floor laundry.

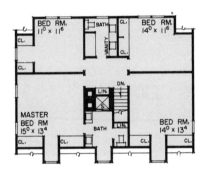

Design V22224 First Floor: 1,567 square feet
Second Floor: 1,070 square feet; Total: 2,637 square feet

L

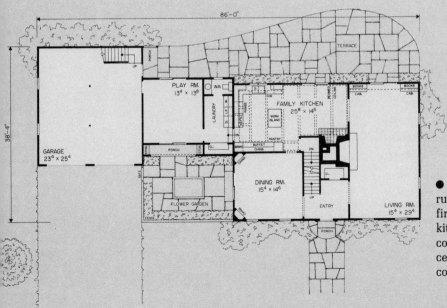

● Certainly reminiscent of the charm of rural New England. The focal point of the first floor is easily the spacious family-kitchen. Formerly referred to as the country-kitchen, this area with its beamed ceiling and fireplace will have a warm and cozy atmosphere, indeed.

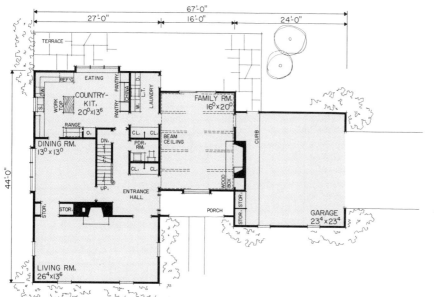

Design V21887
First Floor: 1,518 square feet
Second Floor: 1,144 square feet
Total: 2,662 square feet

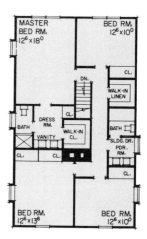

● This Gambrel roof Colonial is steeped in history. And well it should be, for its pleasing proportions are a delight to the eye. The various roof planes, the window treatment, and the rambling nature of the entire house revive a picture of rural New England. The covered porch protects the front door which opens into a spacious entrance hall. Traffic then flows in an orderly fashion to the end living room, the separate dining room, the cozy family room, and to the spacious country-kitchen. There is a first floor laundry, plenty of coat closets, and a handy powder room. Two fireplaces enliven the decor of the living areas. Upstairs there is an exceptional master bedroom layout, and abundant storage. Note the walk-in closets.

Design V22320 First Floor: 1,856 square feet; Second Floor: 1,171 square feet; Total: 3,027 square feet

● A charming Colonial adaptation with a Gambrel roof front exterior and a Salt Box rear. The focal point of family activities will be the spacious family kitchen with its beamed ceiling and fireplace. Blueprints include details for both three and four bedroom options. In addition to the family kitchen, note the family room with beamed ceiling and fireplace. Don't miss the study with built-in bookshelves and cabinets.

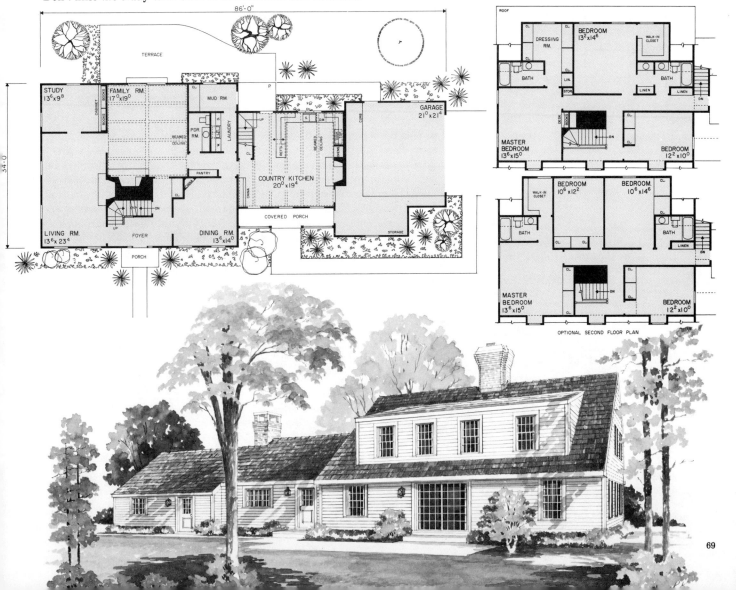

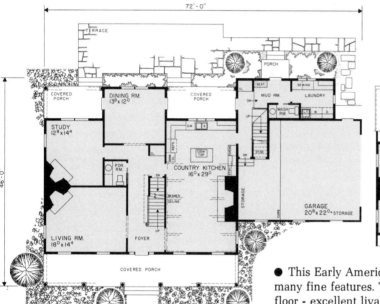

Design V22680 First Floor: 1,707 square feet
Second Floor: 1,439 square feet; Total: 3,146 square feet

D

● This Early American, Dutch Colonial not only has charm, but offers many fine features. The foyer allows easy access to all rooms on the first floor - excellent livability. Note the large country kitchen with beamed ceiling, fireplace and island cook top. A large, formal dining room and powder room are only a few steps away. A fireplace also will be found in the study and living room. The service area, mud room, wash room and laundry are tucked near the garage. Two bedrooms, full bath and master bedroom suite will be found on the second floor. A fourth bedroom and bath are accessible through the master bedroom or stairs in the service entrance.

CAPE COD DESIGNS . . .

dramatically capture the warmth and charm of an early period of our country's architectural history. The low profile of these 1½- and two-story houses is the result of the necessity of the 17th-Century structures of Cape Cod to be able to withstand the lashing winds that frequently swept across the Cape. The Cape Cod house can be found in three recognizable types: The half house with two windows to one side of the front door; the three-quarter house with two windows to one side and one to the other; the full Cape with a center door flanked by two windows on either side. From these basic main structures, appendages were often added to accommodate the growing family.

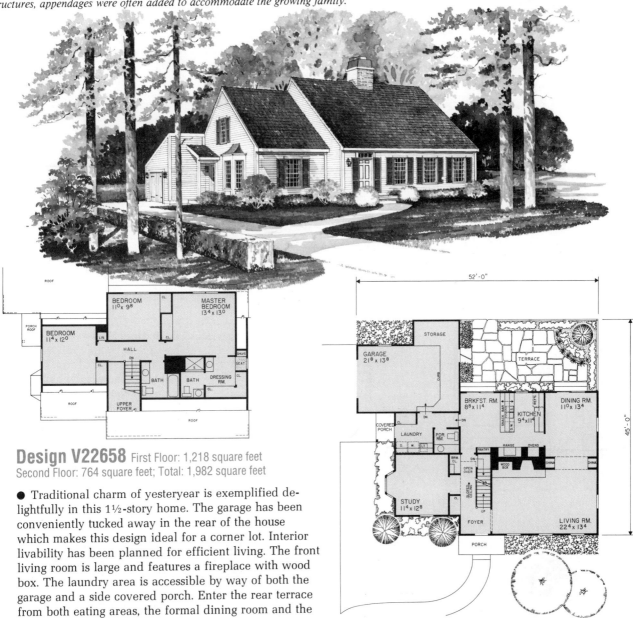

Design V22658 First Floor: 1,218 square feet
Second Floor: 764 square feet; Total: 1,982 square feet

● Traditional charm of yesteryear is exemplified delightfully in this 1½-story home. The garage has been conveniently tucked away in the rear of the house which makes this design ideal for a corner lot. Interior livability has been planned for efficient living. The front living room is large and features a fireplace with wood box. The laundry area is accessible by way of both the garage and a side covered porch. Enter the rear terrace from both eating areas, the formal dining room and the informal breakfast room.

Expanding the Half-House

Design V22682
First Floor (Basic Plan): 976 square feet
First Floor (Expanded Plan): 1,230 square feet
Second Floor (Both Plans): 744 square feet
Total: 1,720 Basic Plan; 1,974 Expanded Plan

L D

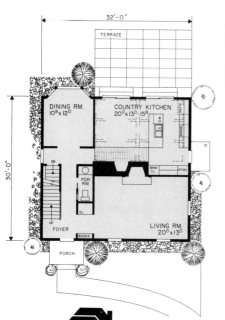

● Here is an expandable Colonial with a full measure of Cape Cod Charm. For those who wish to build the basic house, there is an abundance of low-budget livability. Twin fireplaces serve the formal living room and the informal country kitchen. Note the spaciousness of both areas. A dining room and powder room are also on the first floor of this basic plan. Upstairs three bedrooms and two full baths.

CUSTOMIZABLE
Custom Alterations? See page 413 for customizing this plan to your specifications.

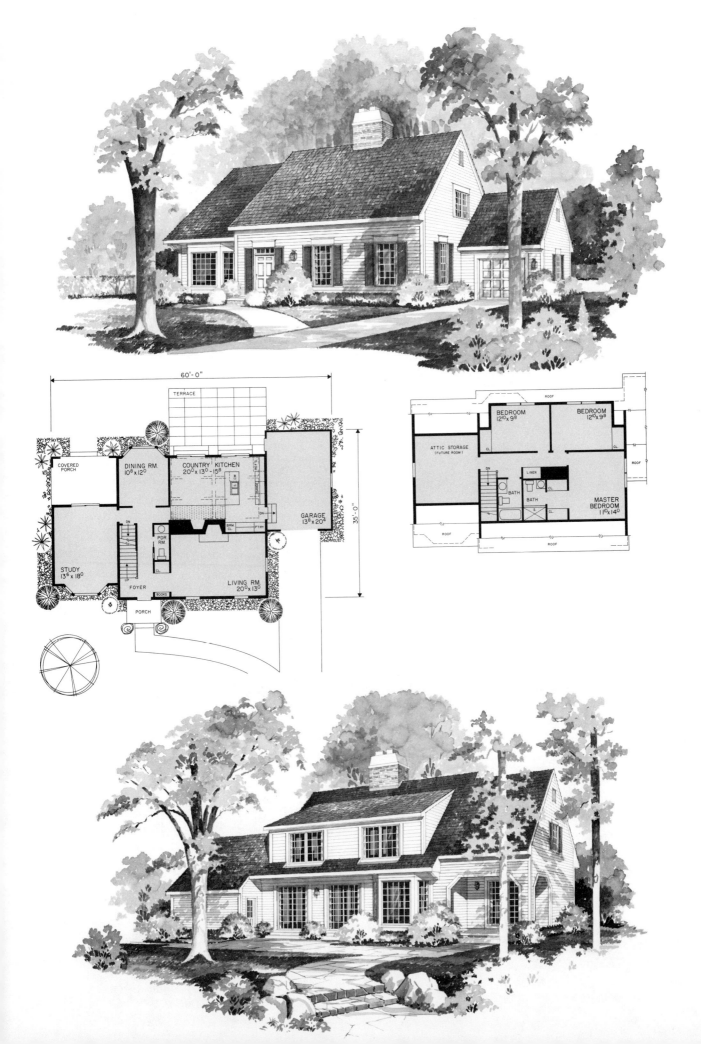

60'-0"

TERRACE

COVERED PORCH

DINING RM.
10⁸ x 12⁰

COUNTRY KITCHEN
20⁰ x 13⁰ - 15⁸

GARAGE
13⁸ x 20⁴

35'-0"

STUDY
13⁶ x 18⁰

DN

PDR. RM.

BRM. CL.

PTRY.

FOYER

BOOKS

LIVING RM.
20⁰ x 13⁰

PORCH

BEDROOM
12⁰ x 9⁸

BEDROOM
12⁰ x 9⁸

ROOF

ROOF

ATTIC STORAGE
(FUTURE ROOM)

DN

LINEN

CL.

BATH

BATH

CL.

MASTER BEDROOM
11⁰ x 14⁰

ROOF

ROOF

73

Design V22563 First Floor: 1,500 square feet
Second Floor: 690 square feet; Total: 2,190 square feet

L **D**

● You'll have all kinds of fun deciding just how your family will function in this dramatically expanded half-house. There is a lot of attic storage, too. Observe the three-car garage.

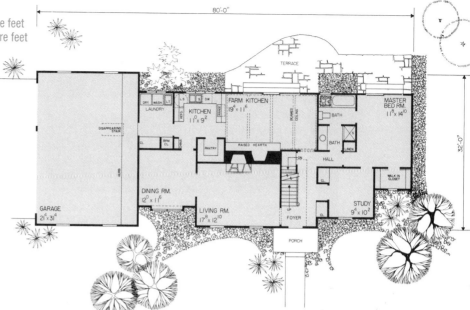

Design V22395

First Floor: 1,481 square feet
Second Floor: 861 square feet
Total: 2,342 square feet

● New England revisited. The appeal of this type of home is ageless. As for its livability, it will serve its occupants admirably for generations to come. With two bedrooms downstairs, you may want to finish off the second floor at a later date.

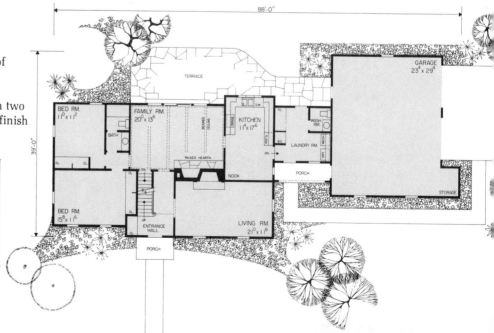

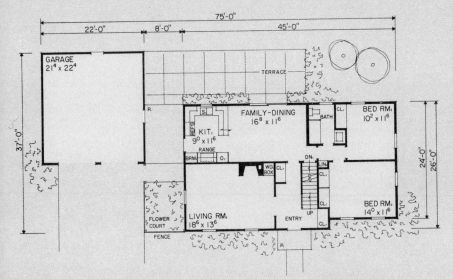

Design V23126

First Floor: 1,141 square feet
Second Floor: 630 square feet
Total: 1,771 square feet

L **D**

● This New England adaptation has a lot to offer. There is the U-shaped kitchen, family-dining room, four bedrooms, two full baths, fireplace, covered porch and two-car garage. A delightful addition to any neighborhood.

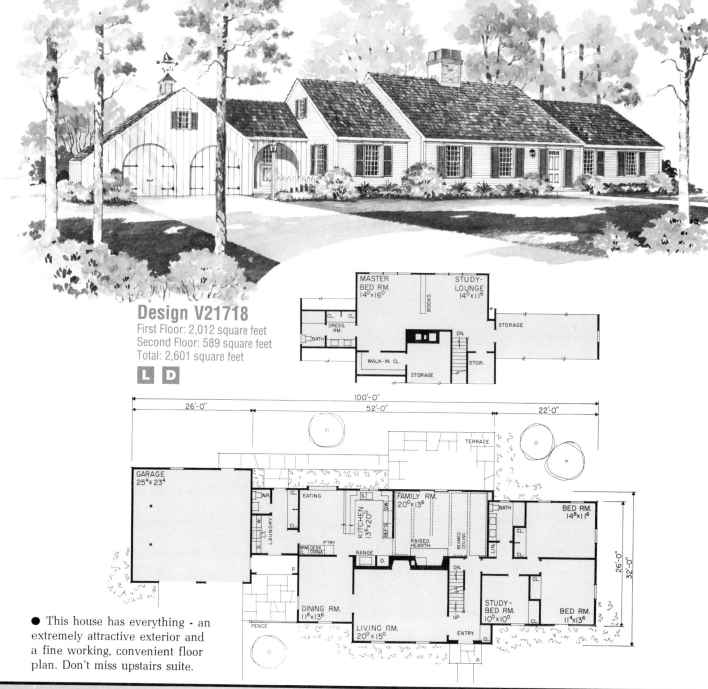

Design V21718

First Floor: 2,012 square feet
Second Floor: 589 square feet
Total: 2,601 square feet

L **D**

MASTER BED RM.
14⁰x16⁰

STUDY-LOUNGE
14⁰x11⁶

CL. CL.

DRESS. RM.

BATH

BOOKS

DN.

STORAGE

WALK-IN CL.

STORAGE

STOR.

100'-0"

26'-0" 52'-0" 22'-0"

TERRACE

GARAGE
25⁴x23⁴

W.R.

CL.

EATING

CL.

LAUNDRY

D. W.

BRM DESK CL. CHINA

P'TRY

RANGE

KITCHEN
13⁶x20⁰

S.

DW

REF'G

FAMILY RM.
20⁰x13⁶

RAISED HEARTH

BEAMED CEILING

BATH

LIN.

BED RM.
14⁸x11⁶

CL.

CL.

26'-0"
32'-0"

O.

DN.

CL.

DINING RM.
11⁸x13⁶

LIVING RM.
20⁰x15⁰

UP

ENTRY

STUDY-BED RM.
10⁰x10⁰

CL.

BED RM.
11⁴x13⁶

CL.

FENCE

P.

CL.

P.

● This house has everything - an extremely attractive exterior and a fine working, convenient floor plan. Don't miss upstairs suite.

Design V21902 First Floor: 1,312 square feet
Second Floor: 850 square feet; Total: 2,162 square feet

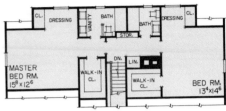

● This design has a great deal to offer the prospective home owner. The main living unit has a formal living room with fireplace and wood box, U-shaped kitchen with adjacent dining room, family room with beamed ceiling and sliding glass doors to the terrace, a study with built-in book shelves (or a second bedroom) and a bedroom. Later development of the second floor will create an additional two bedrooms and two full baths. This home offers a lot of livability and many years of enjoyable living.

Design V21987 First Floor: 1,632 square feet
Second Floor: 980 square feet; Total: 2,612 square feet

L D

● The comforts of home will be endless and enduring when experienced and enjoyed in this Colonial adaptation. What's your favorite feature?

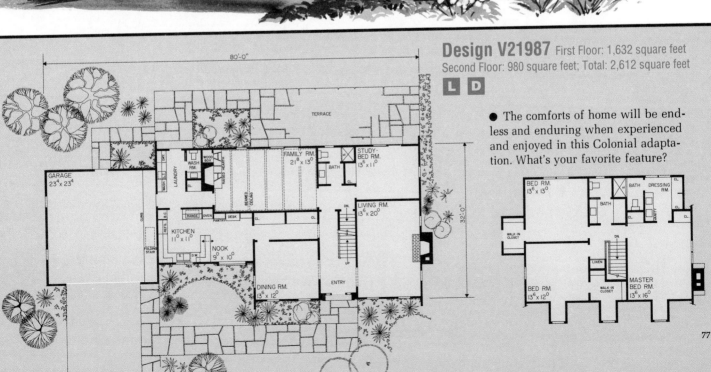

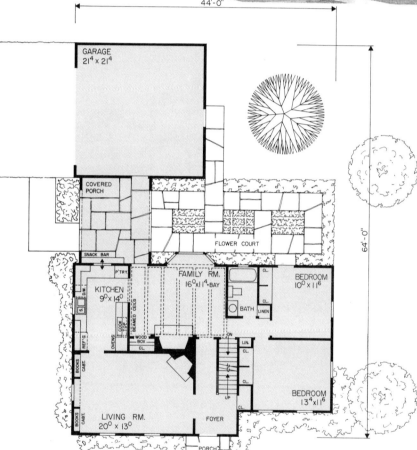

44'-0"

64'-0"

GARAGE
21⁴ x 21⁴

COVERED PORCH

FLOWER COURT

SNACK BAR

KITCHEN
9⁰ x 14⁰

P'TRY

FAMILY RM.
16⁰ x 11⁴ +BAY

BEAMED CEIL'G

WOOD BOX

COOK TOP

OVENS

CL.

REF'G

BOOKS CABT.

BOOKS CABT.

LIVING RM.
20⁰ x 13⁰

FOYER

UP

CL.

CL.

CL.

BEDROOM
10⁰ x 11⁶

BATH

LINEN

CL.

DN

BEDROOM
13⁴ x 11⁶

PORCH

Design V22145

First Floor: 1,182 square feet
Second Floor: 708 square feet
Total: 1,890 square feet

L

● Historically referred to as a "half house", this authentic adaptation has its roots in the heritage of New England. With completion of the second floor, the growing family doubles their sleeping capacity. Notice that the overall width of the house is only 44 feet. Take note of the covered porch leading to the garage and the flower court.

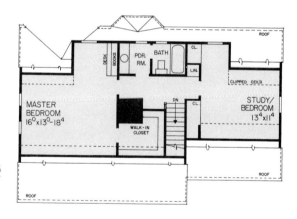

DESK

BOOKS

PDR. RM.

BATH

CL.

LIN.

ROOF

CLIPPED CEIL'G.

MASTER BEDROOM
16⁰ x 13⁰-18⁴

WALK-IN CLOSET

DN

CL.

STUDY/ BEDROOM
13⁴ x 11⁴

ROOF

ROOF

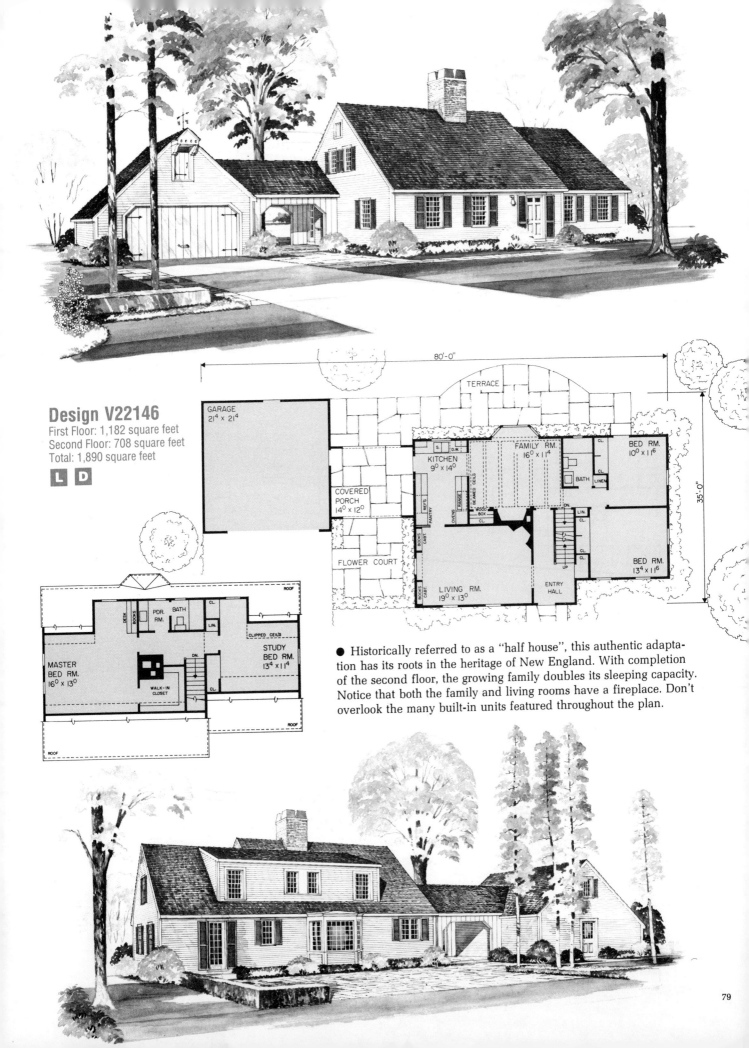

Design V22146

First Floor: 1,182 square feet
Second Floor: 708 square feet
Total: 1,890 square feet

L **D**

GARAGE
21⁴ x 21⁴

COVERED
PORCH
14⁰ x 12⁰

FLOWER COURT

TERRACE

KITCHEN
9⁰ x 14⁰

FAMILY RM.
16⁰ x 11⁴

BED RM.
10⁰ x 11⁶

BATH

LINEN

S.
D.W.

REF'G.

PANTRY

OVENS

RANGE

BEAMED CEIL'G

WOOD
BOX

CL.

BOOKS
CAB'T.

DN.

LIN.

CL.

UP

CL.

CL.

BED RM.
13⁴ x 11⁶

LIVING RM.
19⁰ x 13⁰

ENTRY
HALL

BOOKS
CAB'T.

80'-0"

35'-0"

MASTER
BED RM.
16⁰ x 13⁰

DESK

BOOKS

PDR.
RM.

BATH

CL.

LIN.

CLIPPED CEIL'G

STUDY
BED RM.
13⁴ x 11⁴

WALK-IN
CLOSET

DN.

CL.

ROOF

ROOF

ROOF

● Historically referred to as a "half house", this authentic adaptation has its roots in the heritage of New England. With completion of the second floor, the growing family doubles its sleeping capacity. Notice that both the family and living rooms have a fireplace. Don't overlook the many built-in units featured throughout the plan.

Design V21791
First Floor: 1,157 square feet
Second Floor: 875 square feet; Total: 2,032 square feet

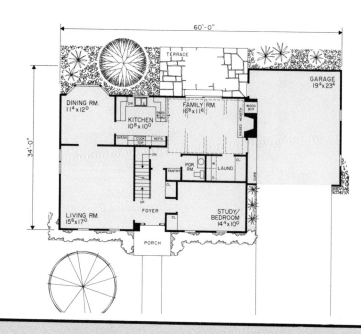

● Wherever you build this moderately sized house an aura of Cape Cod is sure to unfold. The symmetry is pleasing, indeed. The authentic center entrance seems to project a beckoning call.

Design V21870
First Floor: 1,136 square feet
Second Floor: 936 square feet; Total: 2,072 square feet

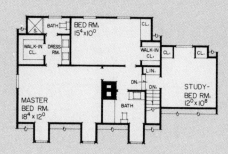

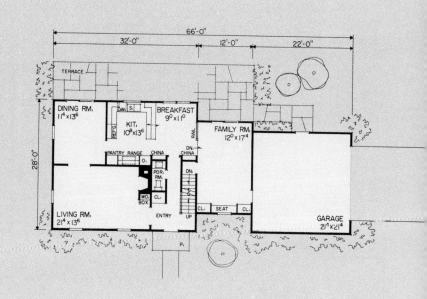

● Besides an enchanting exterior, this home has formal dining and living rooms, plus informal family and breakfast rooms. Built-ins are located in both of these informal rooms. U-shaped, the kitchen will efficiently service both of the dining areas. Study the sleeping facilities of the second floor.

Design V22396
First Floor: 1,616 square feet
Second Floor: 993 square feet; Total: 2,609 square feet

● Another picturesque facade right from the pages of our Colonial heritage. The authentic features are many. Don't miss the stairs to area over the garage.

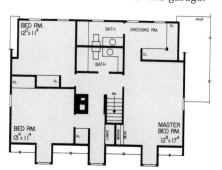

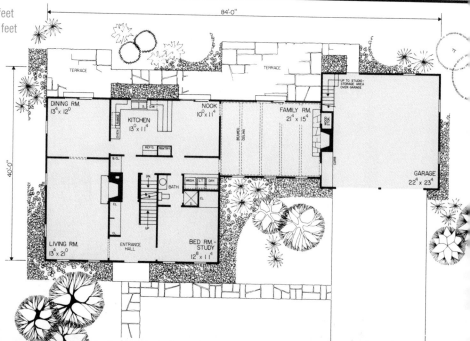

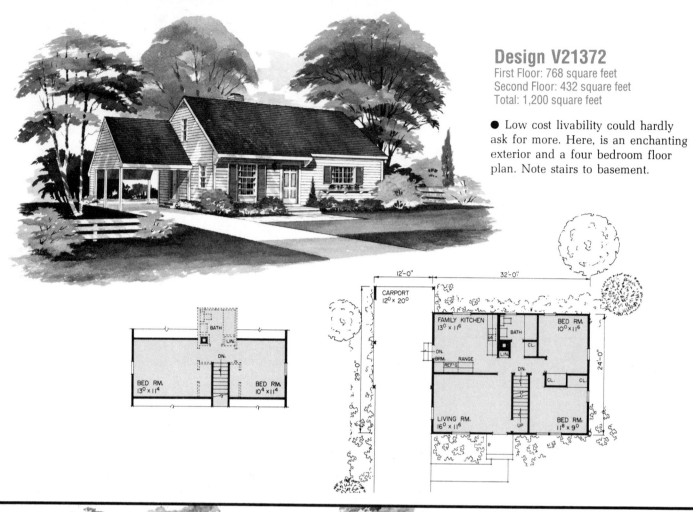

Design V21372

First Floor: 768 square feet
Second Floor: 432 square feet
Total: 1,200 square feet

● Low cost livability could hardly ask for more. Here, is an enchanting exterior and a four bedroom floor plan. Note stairs to basement.

CARPORT 12⁰ x 20⁰

FAMILY KITCHEN 13⁰ x 11⁶

BED RM. 10⁰ x 11⁶

BATH

LIVING RM. 16⁰ x 11⁶

BED RM. 11⁸ x 9⁰

BED RM. 13⁰ x 11⁴

BATH

BED RM. 10⁴ x 11⁴

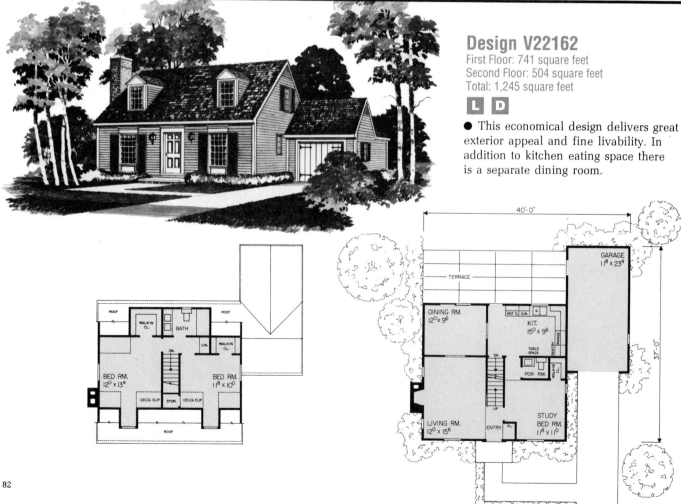

Design V22162

First Floor: 741 square feet
Second Floor: 504 square feet
Total: 1,245 square feet

L D

● This economical design delivers great exterior appeal and fine livability. In addition to kitchen eating space there is a separate dining room.

GARAGE 11⁸ x 23⁴

TERRACE

DINING RM. 12⁰ x 9⁶

KIT. 15⁰ x 9⁶

TABLE SPACE

PDR. RM.

LIVING RM. 12⁰ x 15⁶

ENTRY

STUDY BED RM. 11⁸ x 11⁰

WALK-IN CL.

BATH

WALK-IN CL.

BED RM. 12⁰ x 13⁴

BED RM. 11⁸ x 10⁰

CEIL'G. CLIP.

STOR.

CEIL'G. CLIP.

ROOF

Design V21394

First Floor: 832 square feet
Second Floor: 512 square feet
Total: 1,344 square feet

L D

● The growing family with a restricted building budget will find this a great investment - a convenient living floor plan inside an attractively designed facade.

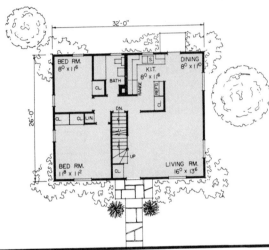

Design V22510

First Floor: 1,191 square feet
Second Floor: 533 square feet
Total: 1,724 square feet

L D

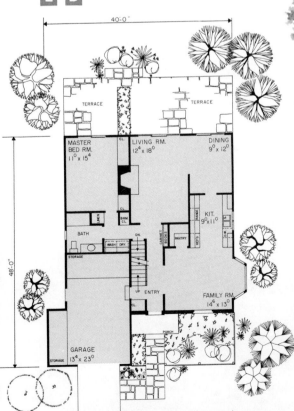

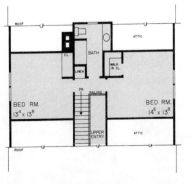

● The pleasant in-line kitchen is flanked by a separate dining room and a family room. The master bedroom is on the first floor with two more bedrooms upstairs.

Design V22655

First Floor: 893 square feet
Second Floor: 652 square feet
Total: 1,545 square feet

● Wonderful things can be enclosed in small packages. This is the case for this two-story design. The total square footage is a mere 1,545 square feet yet its features are many, indeed. Its exterior appeal is very eye-pleasing with horizontal lines and two second story dormers. Livability will be enjoyed in this plan. The front study is ideal for a quiet escape. Nearby is a powder room also convenient to the kitchen and breakfast room. Two bedrooms and two full baths are located on the second floor.

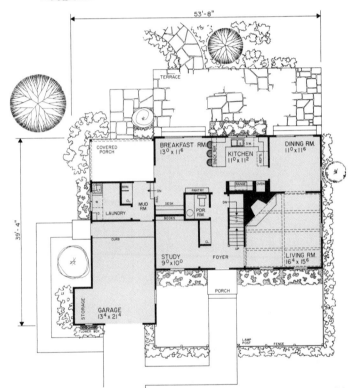

Design V22656 First Floor: 1,122 square feet
Second Floor: 884 square feet; Total: 2,006 square feet

L **D**

● This charming Cape cottage possesses a great
sense of shelter through its gambrel roof. Dormers at
front and rear pierce the gambrel roof to provide
generous, well-lit living space on the second floor
which houses three bedrooms. This design's first
floor layout is not far different from that of the
Cape cottages of the 18th century. The large kitchen
and adjoining dining room recall cottage keeping
rooms both in function and in location at the rear of
the house.

Design V22852 First Floor: 919 square feet
Second Floor: 535 square feet; Total: 1,454 square feet

L D

● Compact enough for even the smallest lot, this cozy design provides comfortable living space for a small family. At the heart of the plan is a spacious country kitchen. It features a cooking island - snack bar and a dining area that opens to a house-wide rear terrace. The nearby dining room also opens to the terrace. At the front of the plan is the living room, warmed by a fireplace. Across the centered foyer is a cozy study. Two second floor bedrooms are serviced by two baths. Note the first floor powder room and storage closet located next to the side entrance. This home will be a delight.

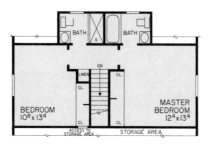

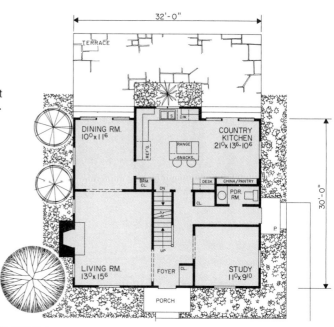

Design V22571 First Floor: 1,137 square feet
Second Floor: 795 square feet; Total: 1,932 square feet

L D

● Cost-efficient space! That's the bonus with this attractive Cape Cod. Start in the living room. It is spacious and inviting with full-length paned windows. In the formal dining room, a bay window adds the appropriate touch. For more living space, a delightfully appointed family room. The efficient kitchen has a snack bar for casual meals. Three bedrooms are on the second floor.

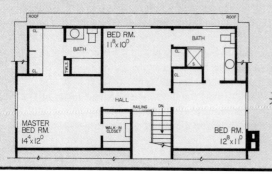

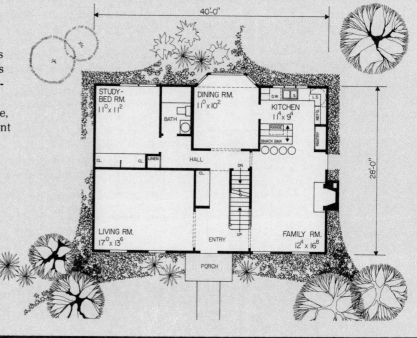

Design V23189 First Floor: 884 square feet
Second Floor: 598 square feet; Total: 1,482 square feet

D

● A large kitchen/dining area and living room are the living areas of this design. Four bedrooms, two up and two down, compose the sleeping zone. Each floor also has a full bath. A full basement and an attached garage will provide plenty of storage areas.

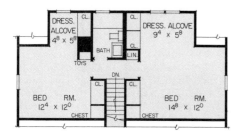

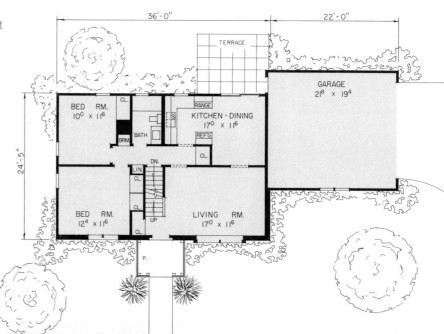

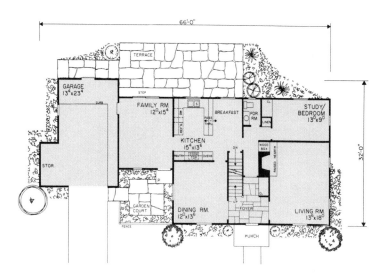

● Colonial charm could hardly be more appealingly captured than it is by this winsome design. List the features and study the living patterns.

Design V21901
First Floor: 1,200 square feet
Second Floor: 744 square feet
Total: 1,944 square feet

Design V21104
First Floor: 1,396 square feet
Second Floor: 574 square feet
Total: 1,970 square feet

● Here is a home whose front elevation makes one think of early New England. The frame exterior is highlighted by authentic double-hung windows with charming shutters. The attractive front entrance detail, flanked by the traditional side lites, and the projecting two-car garage with its appealing double doors are more exterior features.

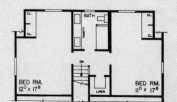

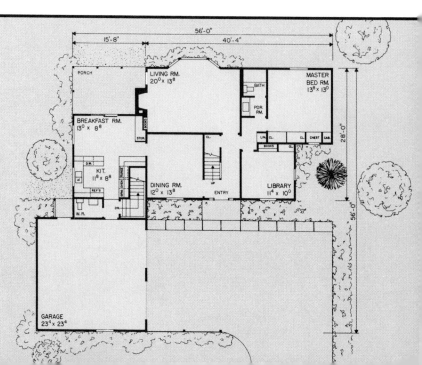

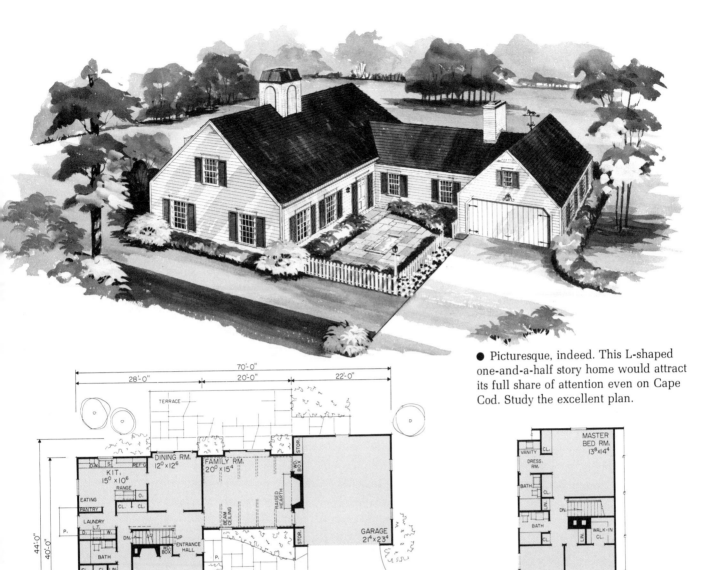

● Picturesque, indeed. This L-shaped one-and-a-half story home would attract its full share of attention even on Cape Cod. Study the excellent plan.

First floor plan labels:

TERRACE

DINING RM. 12⁰×12⁶

FAMILY RM. 20⁰×15⁴

KIT. 15⁰×10⁶

RANGE

REF'G.

EATING

PANTRY

LAUNDRY

BATH

CL. CL. LIN.

DN.

UP

ENTRANCE HALL

WD. BOX

RAISED HEARTH

BEAM CEILING

STOR.

WD. BOX

STOR.

GARAGE 21⁴×23⁴

POOL

FLOWER COURT

FENCE

BED RM. 11⁶×14⁰

LIVING RM. 15⁶×18⁰

Dimensions: 28'-0", 20'-0", 22'-0", 70'-0", 44'-0", 40'-0"

Second floor plan labels:

MASTER BED RM. 13⁸×14⁴

VANITY

CL.

DRESS. RM.

BATH

CL.

BATH

CL.

DN.

WALK-IN CL.

BED RM. 10⁰×12⁰

BED RM. 11⁰×14⁴

CL.

Design V21903

First Floor: 1,460 square feet
Second Floor: 854 square feet
Total: 2,314 square feet

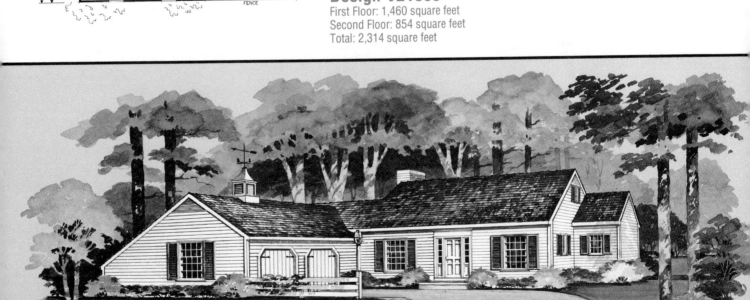

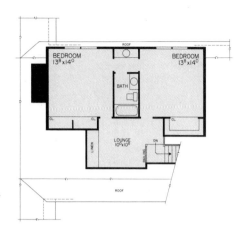

Design V22921

First Floor: 3,215 square feet
Second Floor: 711 square feet
Total: 3,926 square feet

● This popular traditionally styled house features bay windows, shutters, a fanlight and a cupola on the roof. Interior planning was designed for "empty-nesters," whose children are grown and moved out on their own. Open planning is geared for entertaining and relaxing rather than child-rearing. The major focal point of the interior will be the country kitchen. It has a work island with cook-top and snack bar and a spacious dining area with numerous built-ins. A sun room, 296 sq. ft. not included in the total above, is in the rear corner of the house, adjacent to the kitchen. Its sloped ceiling and glass walls open this room to the outdoors. Also adjacent to the kitchen, there is a "clutter room." It includes a workshop, laundry, pantry and washroom.

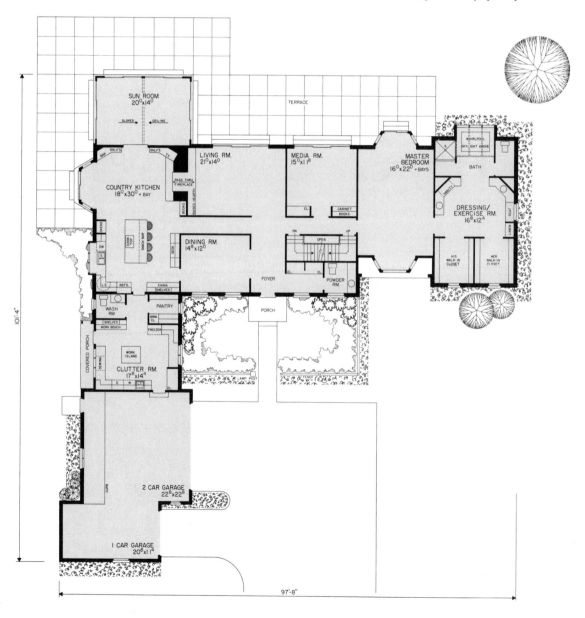

A Trend House for "Empty Nesters"

Design V23372

First Floor: 1,259 square feet
Second Floor: 942 square feet
Total: 2,201 square feet

L **D**

● Charm is the key word for this delightful plan's exterior, but don't miss the great floor plan inside. Formal living and dining rooms flank the entry foyer to the front; a family room and breakfast room with beamed ceilings are to the rear. The kitchen and service areas function well together and are near the garage and service entrance for convenience. Upstairs are the sleeping accommodations: two family bedrooms and a master suite of nice proportion.

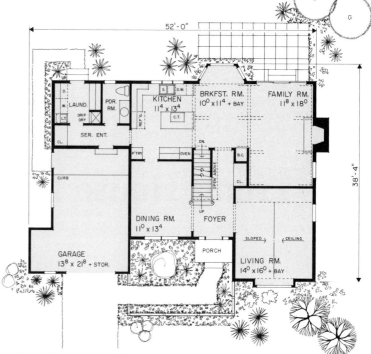

Design V21196

First Floor: 1,008 square feet
Second Floor: 648 square feet; Total: 1,656 square feet

● This cozy home is ideal for a small family. Upon entering this house, you will find a nice sized living room with a fireplace. Adjacent, the formal dining area has sliding glass doors leading to the terrace. The kitchen and informal eating area are just a few steps away. A full bath and an optional bedroom/study also are on this floor. A full bath and two good sized bedrooms, each with its own dressing area, are on the second floor.

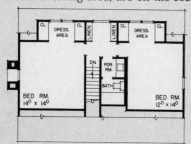

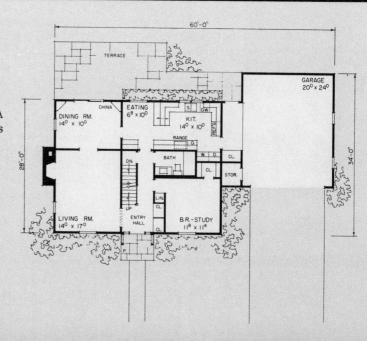

Design V21241

First Floor: 1,064 square feet
Second Floor: 898 square feet
Total: 1,962 square feet

L D

● You don't need a mansion to live graciously. What you do need is a practical floor plan which takes into consideration the varied activities of the busy family. This plan does that! This story-and-a-half design will not require a large piece of property while it returns the maximum per construction dollar. Its living potential is tremendous.

Design V22644

First Floor: 1,349 square feet
Second Floor: 836 square feet
Total: 2,185 square feet

D

● What a delightful, compact two-story this is! This design has many fine features tucked within its framework. The bowed roofline of this house stems from late 17th-Century architecture.

Design V22661

First Floor: 1,020 square feet
Second Floor: 777 square feet
Total: 1,797 square feet

L **D**

● Any other starter house or retirement home couldn't have more charm than this design. Its compact frame houses a very livable plan. An outstanding feature of the first floor is the large country kitchen. Its fine attractions include a beamed ceiling, raised hearth fireplace, built-in window seat and a door leading to the outdoors. A living room is in the front of the plan and has another fireplace which shares the single chimney. The rear dormered second floor houses the sleeping and bath facilities.

CUSTOMIZABLE
Custom Alterations? See page 413 for customizing this plan to your specifications.

95

Design V23553

First Floor: 2,471 square feet
Second Floor: 1,071 square feet
Total: 3,542 square feet

● Delightful Colonial design makes a fine statement for two-story living. The bay windows, columned front porch and charming dormers are big attractions on the exterior. Inside, a wide entry foyer directs traffic to the left to living areas and to the right to the master bedroom suite and a cozy study. The family room and living room both have fireplaces. The L-shaped kitchen is enhanced by an island cooktop and breakfast room with sliding glass doors to the rear porch. Upstairs are three secondary bedrooms and two full baths.

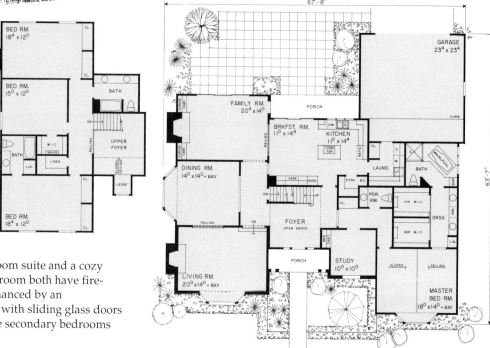

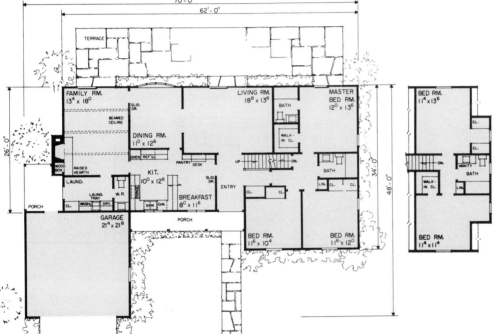

Design V21967

First Floor: 1,804 square feet
Second Floor: 496 square feet
Total: 2,300 square feet

● You'll always want that first impression your guests get of your new home to be a lasting one. There will be much that will linger in the memories of most of your visitors after their visit to this home. Of course, the impressive exterior will long be remembered. And little wonder with its distinctive projecting garage and bedroom wing, its recessed front porch, its horizontal siding and its interesting roof lines. Inside, there is much to behold. The presence of five bedrooms and three full baths will not be forgotten soon. Formal and informal areas will serve every family occasion.

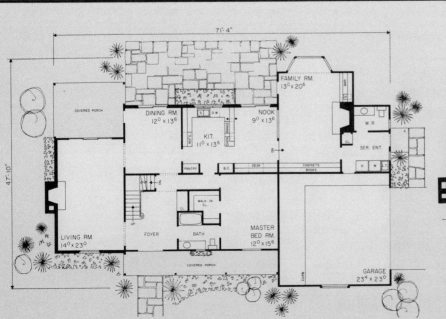

Design V22500

First Floor: 1,851 square feet
Second Floor: 762 square feet
Total: 2,613 square feet

 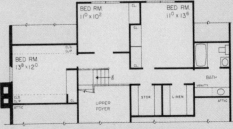

● The large family will enjoy the wonderful living patterns offered by this charming home. Don't miss the covered rear porch and the many features of the family room.

Design V22657

First Floor: 1,217 square feet
Second Floor: 868 square feet
Total: 2,085 square feet

● Deriving its design from the traditional Cape Cod style, this facade features clapboard siding, small-paned windows and a transom-lit entrance flanked by carriage lamps. A central chimney services two fireplaces, one in the country-kitchen and the other in the formal living room which is removed from the disturbing flow of traffic. The master suite is located to the left of the upstairs landing. A full bathroom services two additional bedrooms on the second floor.

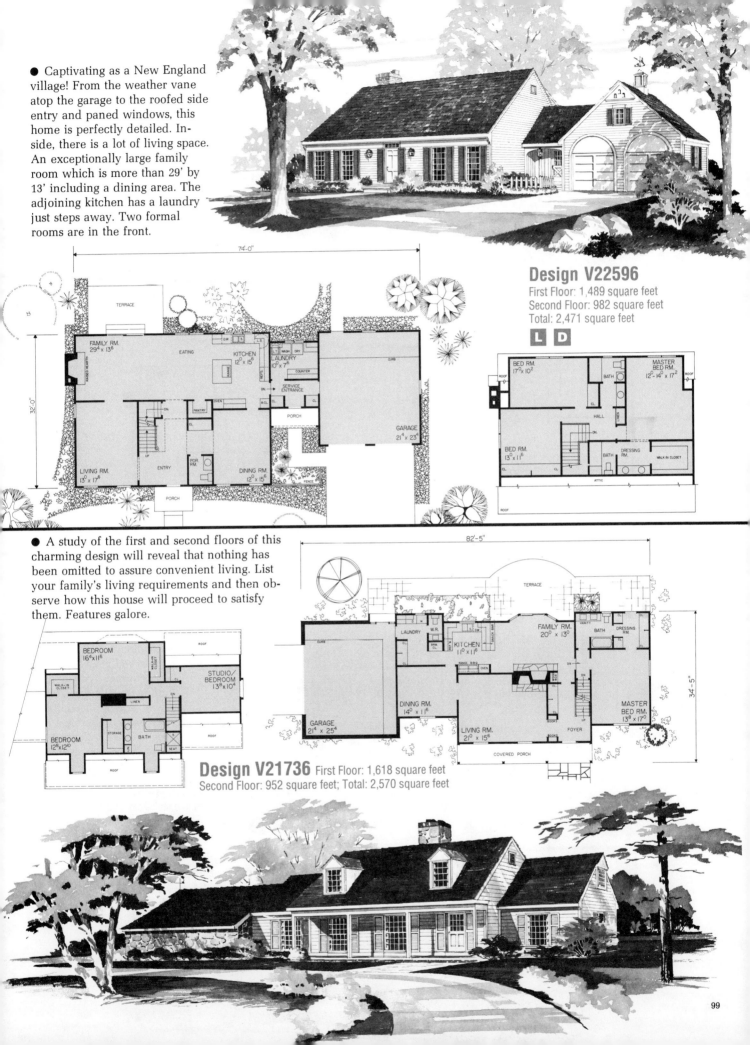

● Captivating as a New England village! From the weather vane atop the garage to the roofed side entry and paned windows, this home is perfectly detailed. Inside, there is a lot of living space. An exceptionally large family room which is more than 29' by 13' including a dining area. The adjoining kitchen has a laundry just steps away. Two formal rooms are in the front.

Design V22596

First Floor: 1,489 square feet
Second Floor: 982 square feet
Total: 2,471 square feet

L D

● A study of the first and second floors of this charming design will reveal that nothing has been omitted to assure convenient living. List your family's living requirements and then observe how this house will proceed to satisfy them. Features galore.

Design V21736
First Floor: 1,618 square feet
Second Floor: 952 square feet; Total: 2,570 square feet

● This cozy home has over 2,600 square feet of livable floor area! And the manner in which this space is put to work to function conveniently for the large family is worth studying. Imagine five bedrooms, three full baths, living, dining and family rooms. Note large kitchen.

Design V21766 First Floor: 1,638 square feet
Second Floor: 1,006 square feet; Total: 2,644 square feet

D

● Surely your list of favorite features will be fun to compile. It certainly will be a long one. The center entry hall helps establish excellent traffic patterns and good zoning. The formal living and dining rooms function well together, as do the kitchen and family room. Note laundry and study.

Design V22124 First Floor: 1,176 square feet
Second Floor: 922 square feet; Total: 2,098 square feet

L **D**

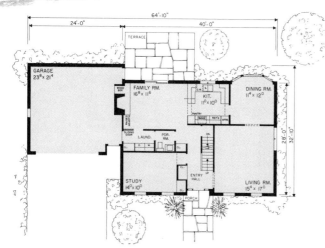

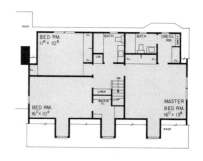

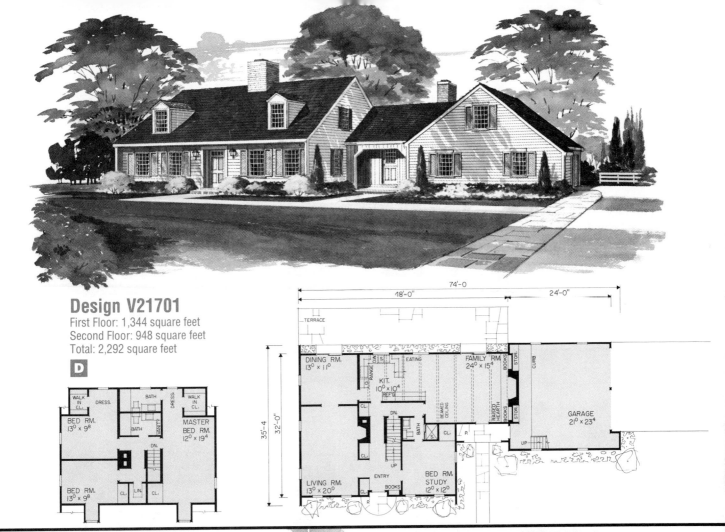

Design V21701

First Floor: 1,344 square feet
Second Floor: 948 square feet
Total: 2,292 square feet

D

Design V21793 First Floor: 1,986 square feet; Second Floor: 944 square feet; Total: 2,930 square feet

D

● A great plan! The large family will find its living requirements satisfied admirably all throughout those active years of growing up. This would make a fine expansible house. The upstairs may be finished off as the size of the family increases and budget permits. Complete living requirements can be obtained on the first floor.

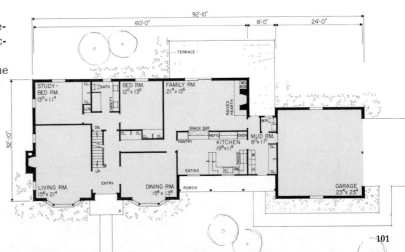

Design V22569
First Floor: 1,102 square feet
Second Floor: 764 square feet; Total: 1,866 square feet

L D

● What an enchanting updated version of the popular Cape Cod cottage. There are facilities for both formal and informal living pursuits. Note the spacious family area, the formal dining/living room, the first floor laundry and the efficient kitchen. The second floor houses the three bedrooms and two economically located baths.

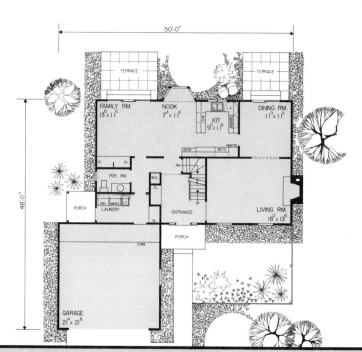

Design V22559
First Floor: 1,388 square feet
Second Floor: 809 square feet; Total: 2,197 square feet

D

● Imagine, a 26 foot living room with fireplace, a quiet study with built-in bookshelves and excellent dining facilities. All of this, plus much more, is within an appealing, traditional exterior. Study the rest of this plan and list its numerous features.

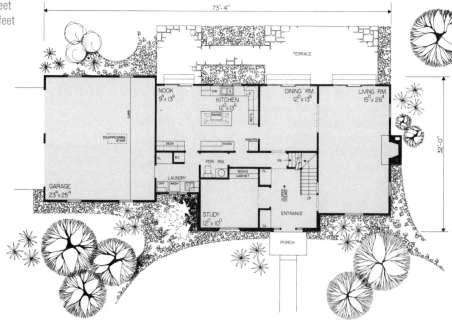

Design V21365

First Floor: 975 square feet
Second Floor: 583 square feet
Total: 1,558 square feet

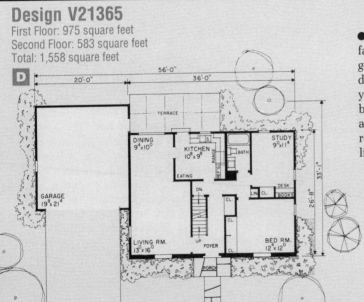

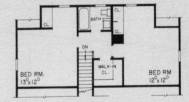

● This cozy, story-and-a-half home will suit a small family nicely. Upon entering this home, you will find a good sized living room. A few steps away is the formal dining area which has an excellent view of the backyard. Adjacent is the nice sized kitchen. A bedroom, bath and a study with a built-in desk and bookshelves also will be found on this floor. There are two bedrooms upstairs and a full bath. This home is big on livability; light on your building budget.

Design V22631

First Floor: 1,634 square feet
Second Floor: 1,011 square feet
Total: 2,645 square feet

L **D**

● Two fireplaces and much more! Notice how all the rooms are accessible from the main hall. That keeps traffic in each room to a minimum, saving you work by preserving your furnishings. There's more. A large family room featuring a beamed ceiling, a fireplace with built-in wood box and double doors onto the terrace. An exceptional U-shaped kitchen is ready to serve you. It has an adjacent breakfast nook. Built-ins, too . . a desk, storage pantry, oven and range. Plus a first floor laundry close at hand.

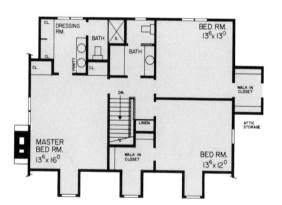

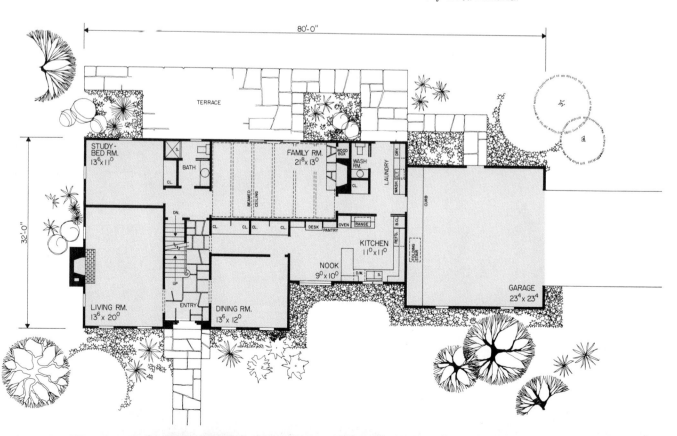

Design V21970

First Floor: 1,664 square feet
Second Floor: 1,116 square feet
Total: 2,780 square feet

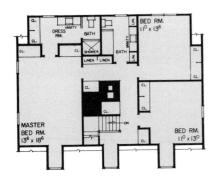

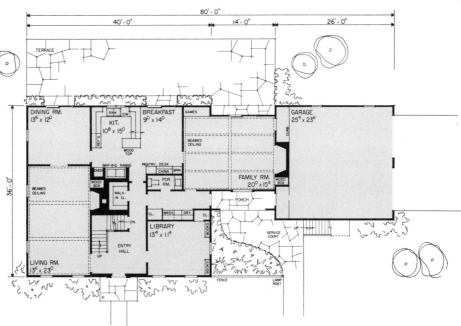

● The prototype of this Colonial house was an integral part of the 18th-Century New England landscape; the updated version is a welcome addition to any suburban scene. The main entry wing, patterned after a classic Cape Cod cottage design, is two stories high but has a pleasing groundhugging look. The steeply pitched roof, triple dormers, and a massive central chimney anchor the house firmly to its site. Entry elevation is symmetrically balanced; doorway, middle dormer, and chimney are in perfect alignment. The one story wing between the main house and the garage is a spacious, beam-ceilinged family room with splay-walled entry porch at the front elevation and sliding glass windows at the rear opening to terrace, which is the full length of the house.

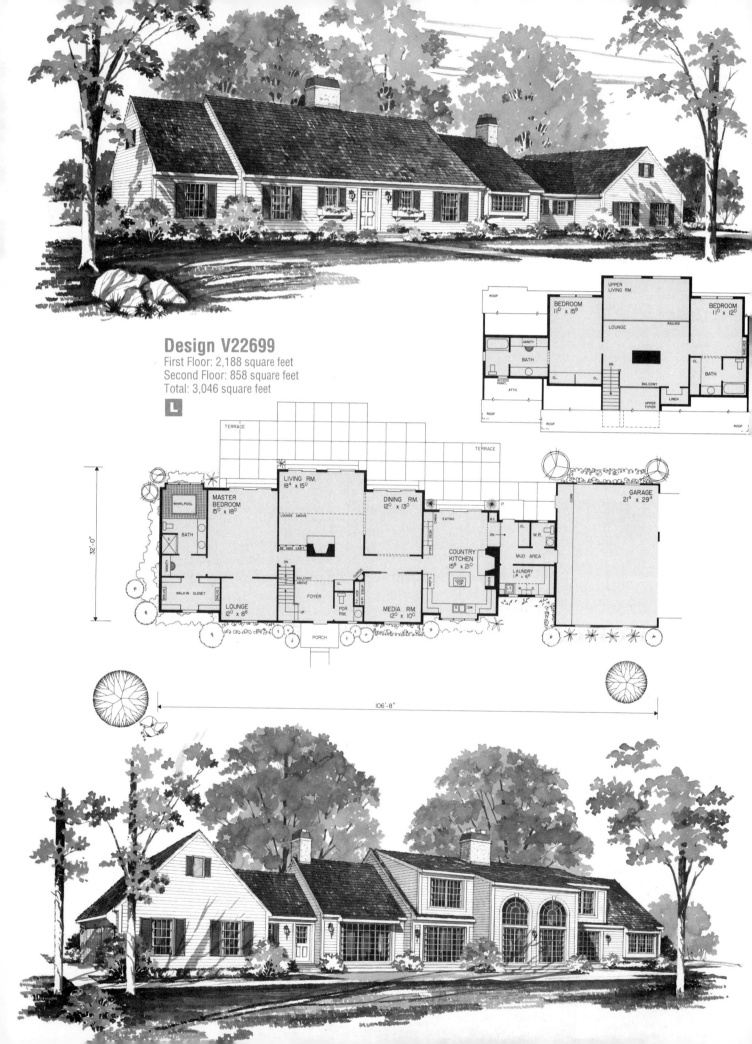

Design V22699
First Floor: 2,188 square feet
Second Floor: 858 square feet
Total: 3,046 square feet

L

BEDROOM 11⁰ x 15⁸
BEDROOM 11⁰ x 12⁰
UPPER LIVING RM.
LOUNGE
RAILING
VANITY
BATH
BATH
ACCESS PANEL
ATTIC
CL.
CL.
DN.
BALCONY
UPPER FOYER
LINEN
SHELVES
CL.
ROOF
ROOF
ROOF
ROOF

TERRACE
TERRACE
LIVING RM. 18⁴ x 15⁰
DINING RM. 12⁰ x 13⁰
EATING
GARAGE 21⁴ x 29⁴
WHIRLPOOL
MASTER BEDROOM 15⁰ x 18⁰
LOUNGE ABOVE
BATH
CHINA
DESK
B.C.
CL.
W.R.
MUD AREA
36" HIGH CAB'T
VANITY
DN.
BALCONY ABOVE
CL.
COUNTRY KITCHEN 15⁸ x 21⁰
REF'G
COOK TOP
OVEN
LAUNDRY 11⁸ x 6⁰
WALK-IN CLOSET
SHELVES
LOUNGE 12⁰ x 8⁸
FOYER
UP
PDR. RM.
TV-VCR HI-FI EQUIP
MEDIA RM. 12⁰ x 10⁰
DW.
PORCH

32'-0"
106'-8"

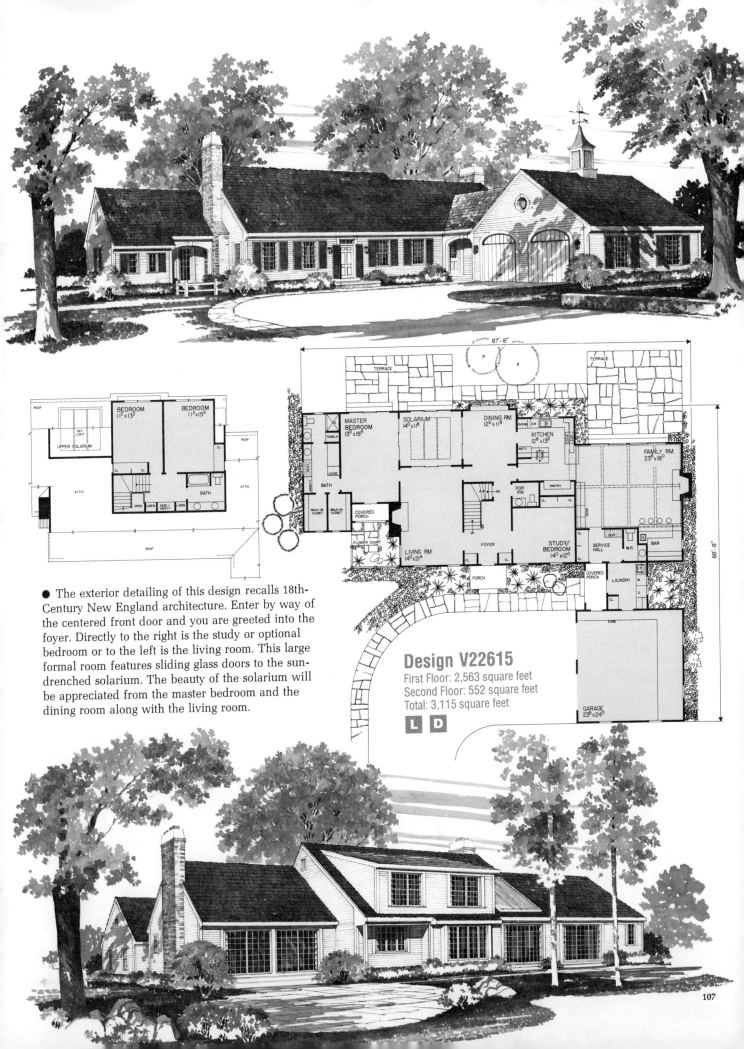

● The exterior detailing of this design recalls 18th-Century New England architecture. Enter by way of the centered front door and you are greeted into the foyer. Directly to the right is the study or optional bedroom or to the left is the living room. This large formal room features sliding glass doors to the sun-drenched solarium. The beauty of the solarium will be appreciated from the master bedroom and the dining room along with the living room.

Design V22615

First Floor: 2,563 square feet
Second Floor: 552 square feet
Total: 3,115 square feet

L D

Design V23351

First Floor: 1,794 square feet
Second Floor: 887 square feet
Total: 2,681 square feet

L D

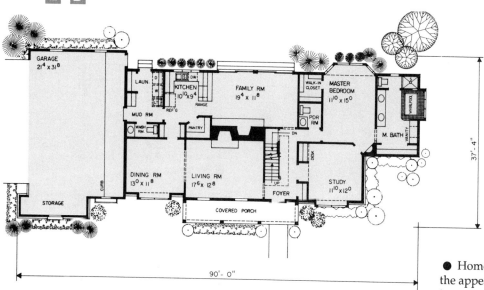

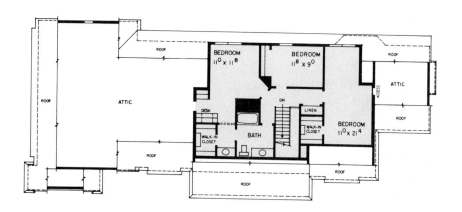

● Home-grown comfort is the key to the appeal of this traditionally styled home. From the kitchen with attached family room to the living room with fireplace and attached formal dining room, this plan has it all. Notice the first-floor master bedroom with whirlpool tub and adjacent study. A nearby powder room turns the study into a convenient guest room. On the second floor are three more bedrooms with ample closet space and a full bath. The two-car garage has a large storage area.

● Another 1¾-story home - a type of house favored by many of Cape Cod's early whalers. The compact floor plan will be economical to build and surely an energy saver. An excellent house to finish-off in stages.

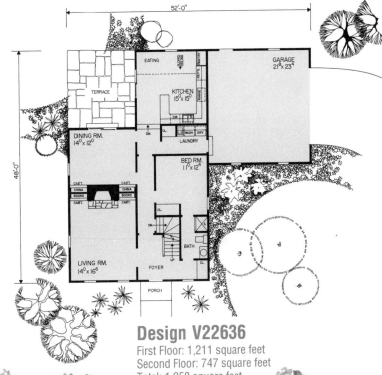

Design V22636

First Floor: 1,211 square feet
Second Floor: 747 square feet
Total: 1,958 square feet

Design V22521

First Floor: 1,272 square feet
Second Floor: 1,139 square feet
Total: 2,411 square feet

● Here is a house to remind one of the weather-beaten facades of Nantucket. The active family plan is as up-to-date as tomorrow. Along with formal and informal areas on the first floor, there is a music alcove. If a music alcove is not needed, this area would make an ideal intimate sitting area.

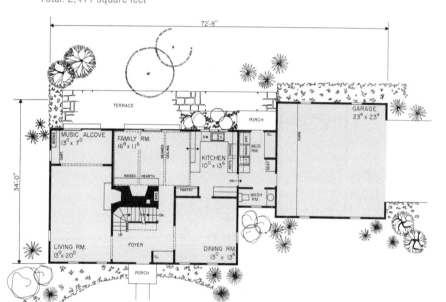

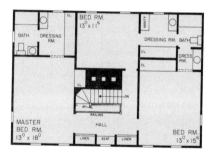

THE FARMHOUSE THEME . . . *is one that can be found in*

abundance throughout the country. It can take many forms and project a limitless variety of faces. It can be a full two-story or feature a partial half-story second floor. It can feature an exterior of wood, stone, brick or a combination of all three materials. Perhaps its most predominant feature is the covered porch. And, of course, this can be executed in numerous ways. The wrap-around porch is once again becoming the favorite of many.

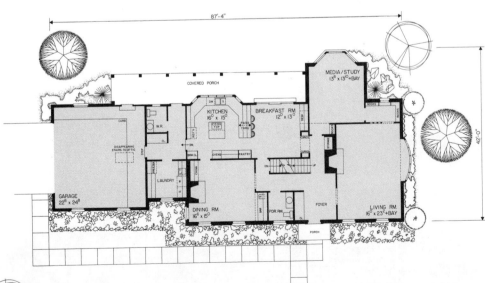

Design V22963

First Floor: 2,046 square feet
Second Floor: 1,644 square feet
Total: 3,690 square feet

● Featuring a gracious foyer and stairway at the entry, this home in the Colonial tradition is actually a modified version of the center-hall classic. Unlike the classic standard, the entrance here is off-center in the facade, with three windows to the left and two to the right of the entry door. Yet the design offers the dignity and grace so readily associated with its center-hall cousin. In addition, the rambling proportions of the house reflect Colonial precedents–as families grew, so did their houses. Both the dining and living rooms boast large fireplaces. Family meals are likely to be served in the cozy nook attached to the kitchen. Ample cabinet, shelf, and pantry space is provided wherever storage space is most needed. To retreat from the clamor of an active household, family members can read a good book in the study tucked in behind the living room, where generous provision is made for an entire library. Upstairs, four bedrooms provide a comfortable arrangement for each family member.

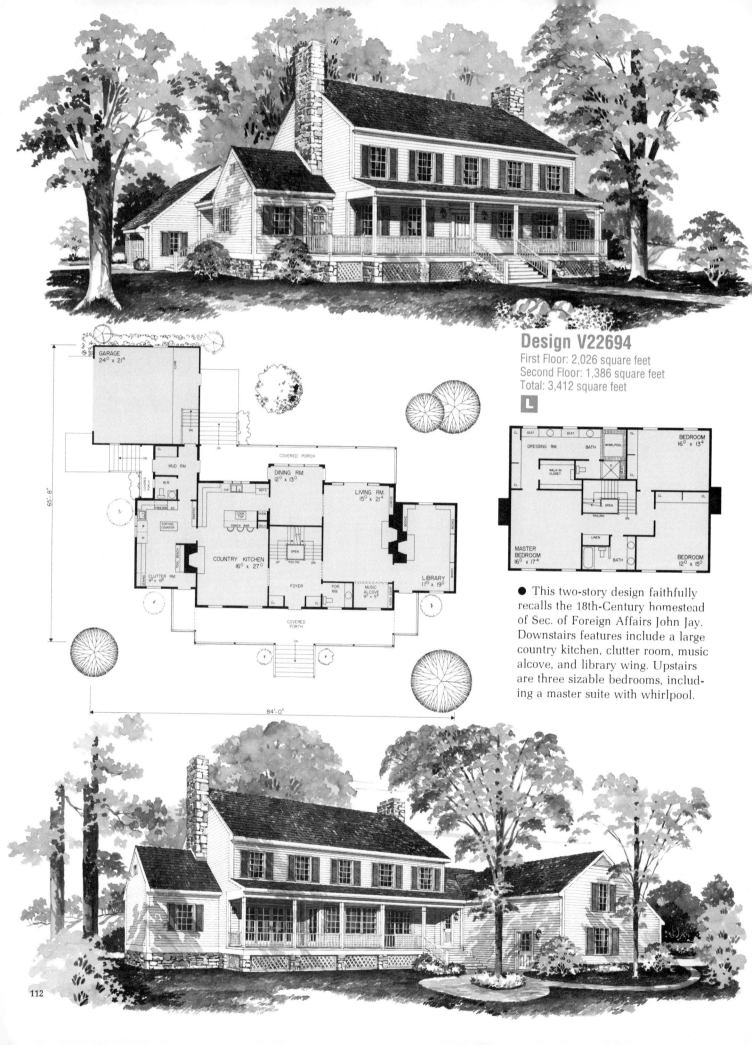

Design V22694

First Floor: 2,026 square feet
Second Floor: 1,386 square feet
Total: 3,412 square feet

L

Floor plan labels

GARAGE 24⁰ x 21⁴

MUD RM

W.R.

FREEZER

SORTING COUNTER

COUNTRY KITCHEN 16⁰ x 27⁰

TOOL BENCH

CLUTTER RM 9⁹ x 19⁰

COOK TOP

OVEN

SNACK BAR

SHLV

DINING RM. 12⁰ x 13⁰

FOYER

OPEN RAILING UP

DN

PDR. RM.

MUSIC ALCOVE 9⁹ x 5⁴

LIVING RM. 15⁰ x 21⁴

LIBRARY 11⁰ x 19⁰

COVERED PORCH

COVERED PORCH

65' - 8"

84' - 0"

Second floor labels

DRESSING RM

BATH

WHIRLPOOL

WALK-IN CLOSET

SEAT

SEAT

CL

BEDROOM 16⁰ x 13⁴

MASTER BEDROOM 16⁰ x 17⁴

LINEN

BATH

BEDROOM 12⁰ x 15⁰

OPEN

RAILING DN

● This two-story design faithfully recalls the 18th-Century homestead of Sec. of Foreign Affairs John Jay. Downstairs features include a large country kitchen, clutter room, music alcove, and library wing. Upstairs are three sizable bedrooms, including a master suite with whirlpool.

Design V22981
First Floor: 2,104 square feet
Second Floor: 2,015 square feet
Total: 4,119 square feet

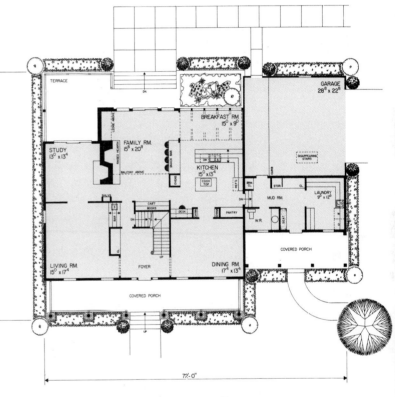

● This formal two-story recalls a Louisiana plantation house, Land's End, built in 1857. The Ionic columns of the front porch and the pediment gable echo the Greek Revival style. Highlighting the interior is the bright and cheerful spaciousness of the informal family room area. It features a wall of glass stretching to the second story sloping ceiling. Enhancing the drama of this area is the adjacent glass area of the breakfast room. Note the "His/Her" areas of the master bedroom.

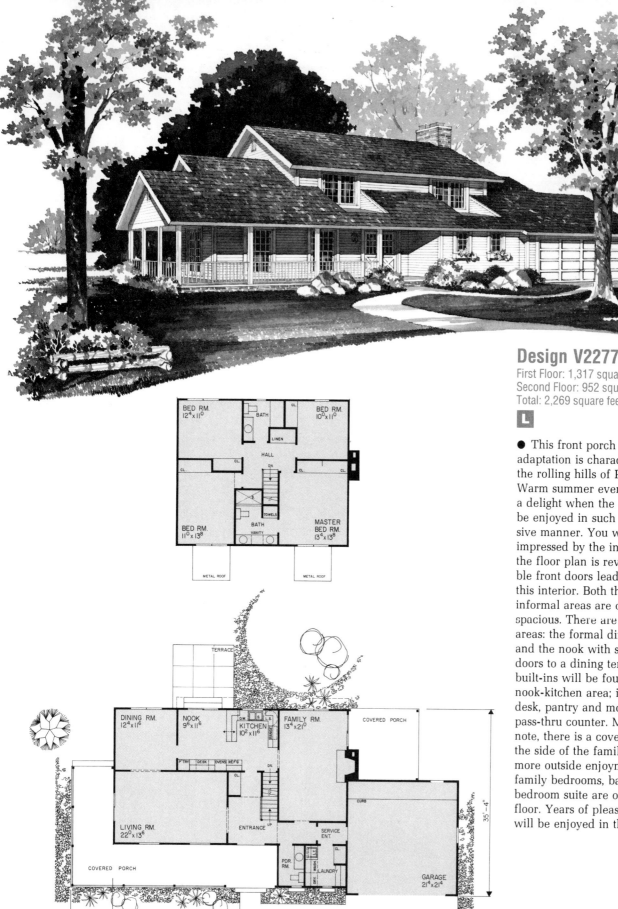

Design V22775

First Floor: 1,317 square feet
Second Floor: 952 square feet
Total: 2,269 square feet

L

● This front porch Farmhouse adaptation is characteristic of the rolling hills of Pennsylvania. Warm summer evenings will be a delight when the outdoors can be enjoyed in such an impressive manner. You will also be impressed by the interior after the floor plan is reviewed. Double front doors lead the way into this interior. Both the formal and informal areas are outstandingly spacious. There are two eating areas: the formal dining room and the nook with sliding glass doors to a dining terrace. Many built-ins will be found in the nook-kitchen area; including a desk, pantry and more. Notice pass-thru counter. Make special note, there is a covered porch to the side of the family room for more outside enjoyment. Three family bedrooms, bath and master bedroom suite are on the second floor. Years of pleasurable living will be enjoyed in this home.

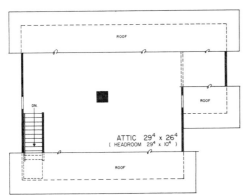

ROOF

ROOF

DN.

ATTIC 29⁴ x 26⁴
(HEADROOM 29⁴ x 10⁴)

ROOF

BEDROOM/
STUDY
11⁰x13²

BATH   DRESS. RM.

VANITY

MASTER
BEDROOM
13⁰x13²

CL.

BATH

CL.

DN.

LIN.

CL.

CL.

CL.

BEDROOM
10⁰x10⁶

UP TO
ATTIC

CL.

BEDROOM
13⁰x10⁶

Design V22774

First Floor: 1,370 square feet
Second Floor: 969 square feet
Total: 2,339 square feet

L **D**

● Another Farmhouse adaptation with all the most up-to-date features expected in a new home. Beginning with the formal areas, this design offers pleasures for the entire family. There is the quiet corner living room which has an opening to the sizable dining room. This room will enjoy plenty of natural light from the delightful bay window overlooking the rear yard. It is also conveniently located with the efficient U-shaped kitchen just a step away. The kitchen features many built-ins with pass-thru to the beamed ceiling breakfast room. Sliding glass doors to the terrace are fine attractions in both the sunken family room and breakfast room. The service entrance to the garage is flanked by a clothes closet and a large, walk-in pantry. There is a secondary entrance thru the laundry room. Recreational activities and hobbies can be pursued in the basement area. Four bedrooms, two baths upstairs.

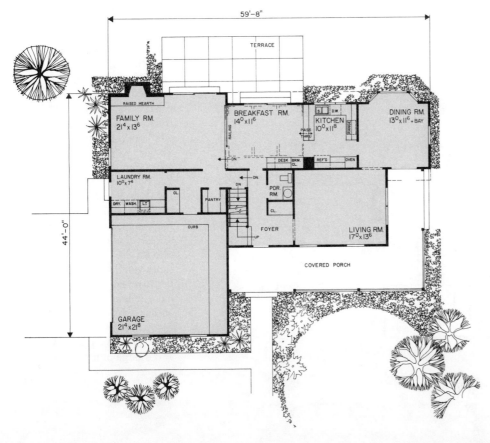

59'-8"

TERRACE

RAISED HEARTH

FAMILY RM.
21⁴ x 13⁶

BREAKFAST RM.
14⁰x11⁶

KITCHEN
10⁰x11⁰

DINING RM.
13⁰x11⁶ + BAY

RANGE

PASS-THRU

RAILING

DN.

DESK   BRM.   REF'G   OVEN
CL.

LAUNDRY RM.
10⁰x7⁶

DRY. WASH. LT.

CL.

PANTRY

DN.

DN.

PDR.
RM.

CL.

44'-0"

CURB

FOYER

UP

LIVING RM.
17⁰x13⁶

GARAGE
21⁴x21⁸

COVERED PORCH

CUSTOMIZABLE

Custom Alterations? See page 413 for customizing this plan to your specifications.

115

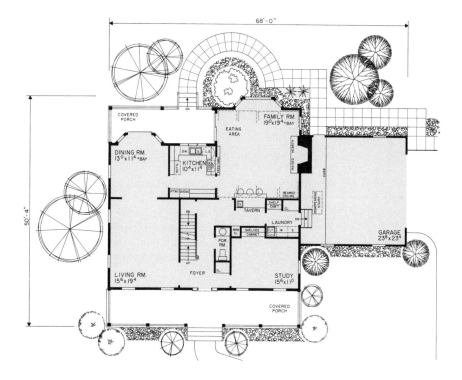

Design V22890

First Floor: 1,612 square feet
Second Floor: 1,356 square feet
Total: 2,968 square feet

 D

● An appealing Farmhouse that is complimented by an inviting front porch. Many memorable summer evenings will be spent here. Entering this house, you will notice a nice-sized study to your right and spacious living room to the left. The adjacent dining room is enriched by an attractive bay window. Just a step away, an efficient kitchen will be found. Many family activities will be enjoyed in the large family room. The tavern/snack bar will make entertaining guests a joy. A powder room and laundry are also on the first floor. Upstairs you'll find a master bedroom suite featuring a bath with an oversized tub and shower and a dressing room. Also on this floor; two bedrooms, full bath and a large attic.

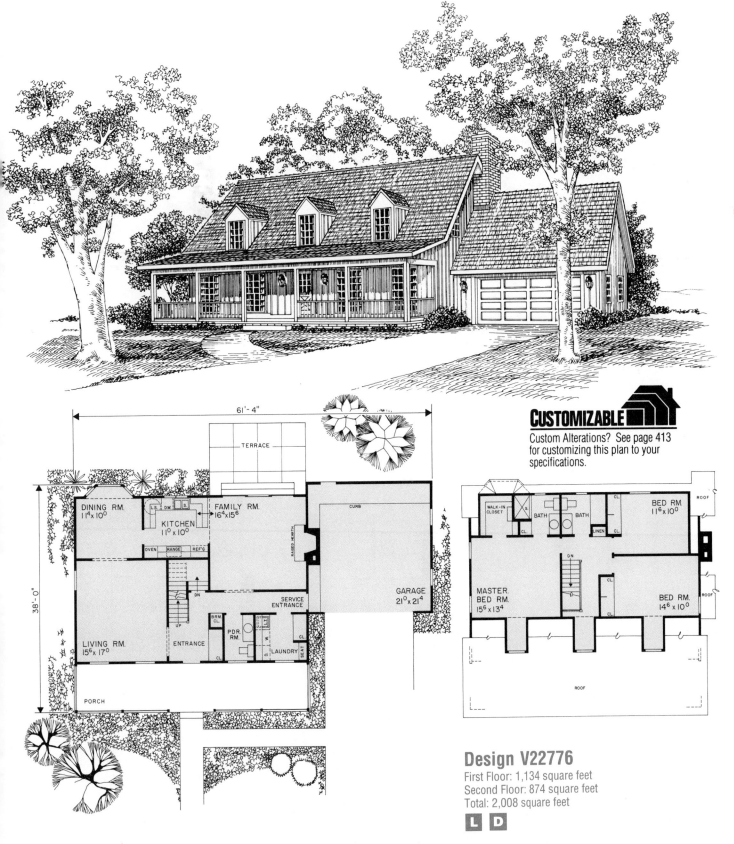

TERRACE

DINING RM.
11⁴ x 10⁰

KITCHEN
11⁰ x 10⁰

FAMILY RM.
16⁴ x 15⁶

CURB

GARAGE
21⁰ x 21⁴

RAISED HEARTH

OVEN | RANGE | REF'G

SERVICE
ENTRANCE

LIVING RM.
15⁶ x 17⁰

ENTRANCE

PDR.
RM.

LAUNDRY

PORCH

61'-4"

38'-0"

WALK-IN
CLOSET

BATH | BATH

LINEN

BED RM.
11⁶ x 10⁰

ROOF

MASTER.
BED RM.
15⁶ x 13⁴

BED RM.
14⁶ x 10⁰

ROOF

ROOF

Design V22776

First Floor: 1,134 square feet
Second Floor: 874 square feet
Total: 2,008 square feet

L **D**

● This board-and-batten farmhouse design has all of the country charm of
New England. The large front covered
porch surely will be appreciated during
the beautiful warm weather months.
Immediately off the front entrance is
the delightful corner living room. The

dining room with bay window will be
easily served by the U-shaped kitchen.
Informal family living enjoyment will
be obtained in the family room which
features a raised hearth fireplace, sliding glass doors to the rear terrace and
easy access to the work center of powd-

er room, laundry and service entrance.
The second floor houses all of the
sleeping facilities. There is a master bedroom with a private bath and walk-in
closet. Two other bedrooms share a
bath. This is an excellent one-and-a-
half story design.

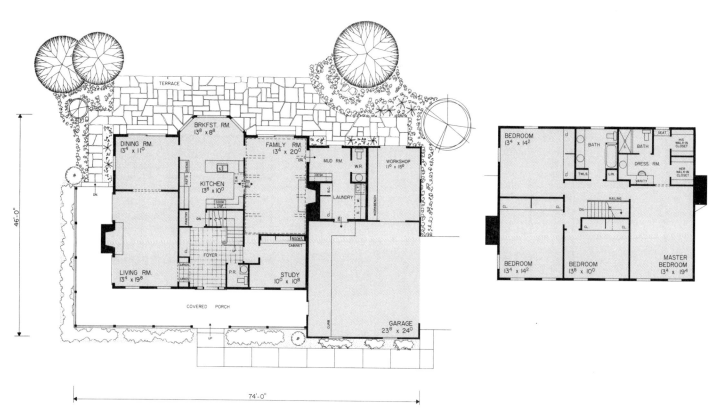

Design V22946 First Floor: 1,590 square feet; Second Floor: 1,344 square feet; Total: 2,934 square feet

L D

● Here's a traditional design that's made for down-home hospitality, the pleasures of casual conversation, and the good grace of pleasant company. The star attractions are the large covered porch and terrace, perfectly relaxing gathering points for family and friends. Inside, though, the design is truly a hard worker; separate living room and family room, each with its own fireplace; formal dining room; large kitchen and breakfast area with bay windows; separate study; workshop with plenty of room to maneuver; mud room; and four bedrooms up, including a master suite. Not to be overlooked are the curio niches, the powder room, the built-in bookshelves, the kitchen pass-thru, the pantry, the planning desk, the workbench, and the stairs to the basement.

Design V22865

First Floor: 1,703 square feet
Second Floor: 1,044 square feet
Total: 2,747 square feet

D

● Here's a cozy traditional farmhouse with a big wrap-around covered porch. Up front, flanking the entry foyer, are a living room with fireplace, and formal dining room. To the rear are a study, that could be used as a guest room, and the family room with another fireplace. The kitchen/breakfast room combination is conveniently located near the service entrance off the garage. Note three bedrooms with dormer windows upstairs.

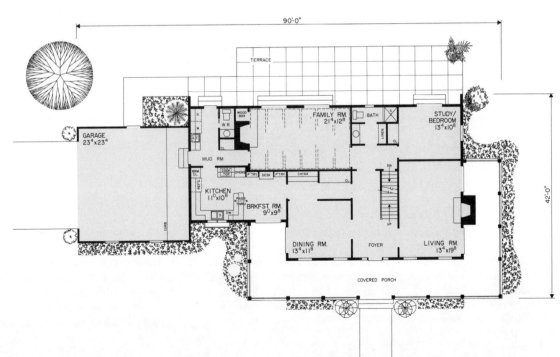

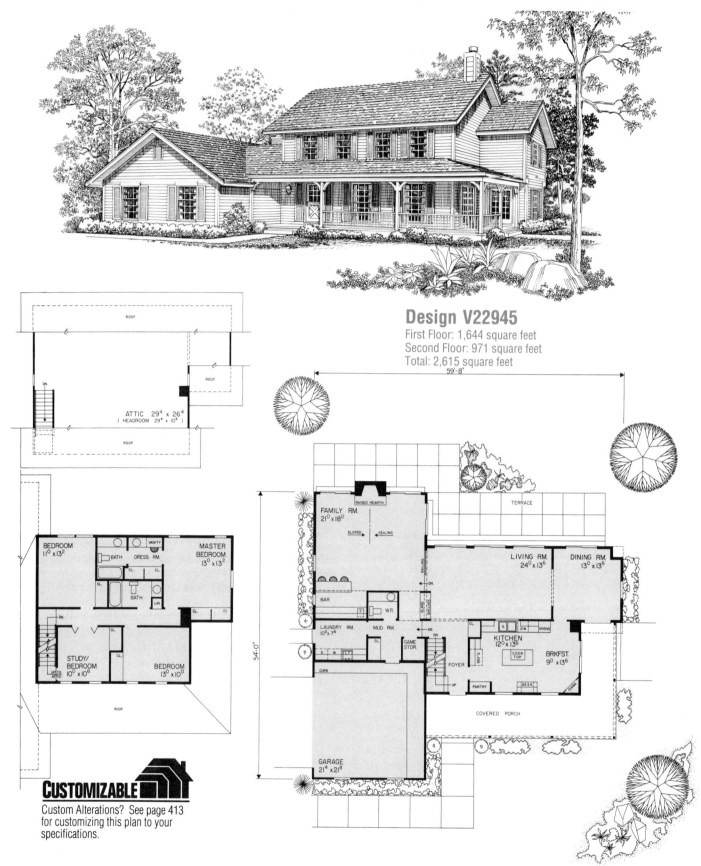

Design V22945

First Floor: 1,644 square feet
Second Floor: 971 square feet
Total: 2,615 square feet

59'-8"

ROOF

ATTIC 29⁴ x 26⁴
(HEADROOM 29⁴ x 10⁴)

ROOF

ROOF

BEDROOM 11⁰ x 13²

VANITY

BATH   DRESS. RM.

MASTER BEDROOM 13⁰ x 13²

BATH

LIN

STUDY/BEDROOM 10⁰ x 10⁶

BEDROOM 13⁰ x 10⁰

UP TO ATTIC

ROOF

CUSTOMIZABLE

Custom Alterations? See page 413 for customizing this plan to your specifications.

FAMILY RM. 21⁰ x 18⁰

RAISED HEARTH

SLOPED ← → CEILING

TERRACE

LIVING RM. 24⁰ x 13⁶

DINING RM. 13⁰ x 13⁶

BAR

W.R.

LAUNDRY RM. 10⁰ x 7⁶

MUD RM.

GAME STOR.

KITCHEN 12⁰ x 13⁶

OVENS

FOYER

COOK TOP

BRKFST. 9⁰ x 13⁶

CURB

PANTRY

DESK

COVERED PORCH

54'-0"

GARAGE 21⁴ x 21⁸

● Here is a new floor plan designed to go with the almost identical exterior of one of Home Planners' most popular houses. A masterfully affordable design, this plan manages to include all the basics - and then adds a little more. Note the wraparound covered porch, large family room with raised-hearth fireplace and wet bar, spacious kitchen with island cook top, formal dining room, rear terrace, and extra storage on the first floor. Upstairs, the plan's as flexible as they come: three or four bedrooms (the fourth could easily be a study or playroom) and lots of unfinished attic just waiting for you to transform it into living space. This could make a fine studio, sewing room, home office, or just a place for the safe, dry storage of the family's paraphernalia, Christmas decorations, etc.

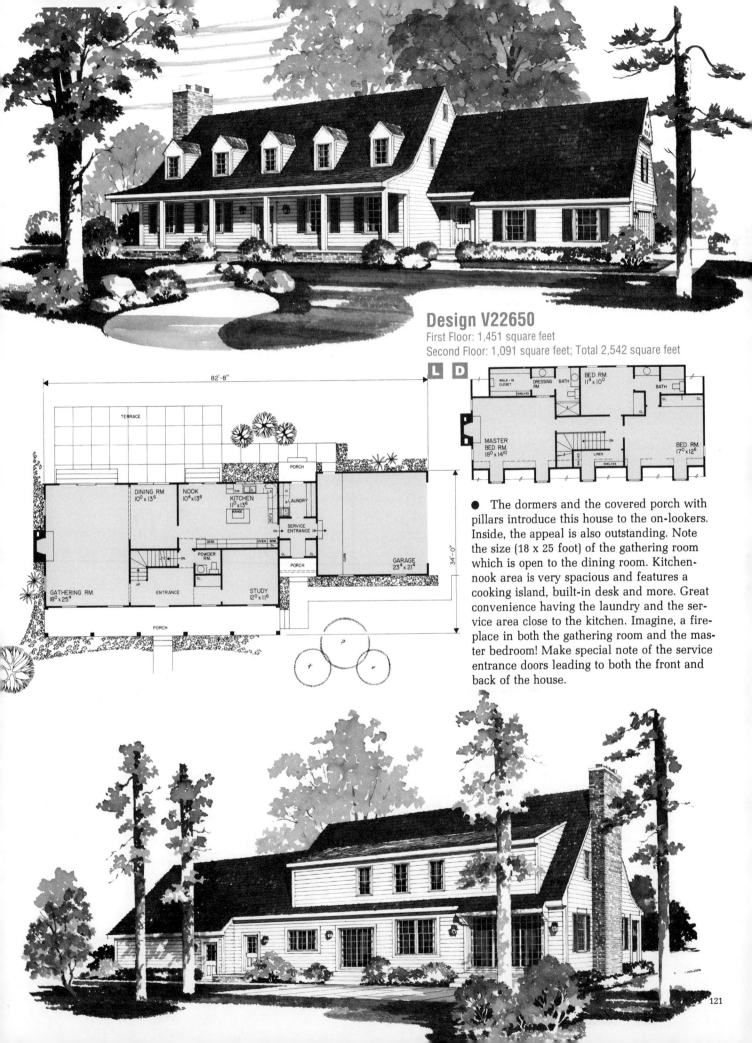

Design V22650

First Floor: 1,451 square feet
Second Floor: 1,091 square feet; Total 2,542 square feet

L **D**

Floor plan labels (first floor):

82'-8"

TERRACE

PORCH

DINING RM. 10⁰ x 13⁶

NOOK 10⁴ x 13⁶

KITCHEN 11⁰ x 13⁶

RANGE

LAUNDRY

SERVICE ENTRANCE

DESK

OVEN

POWDER RM.

GATHERING RM. 18⁰ x 25⁴

ENTRANCE

UP

STUDY 12⁰ x 11⁶

PORCH

GARAGE 23⁴ x 21⁴

34'-0"

PORCH

Floor plan labels (second floor):

WALK-IN CLOSET

DRESSING RM.

BATH

BED RM. 11⁴ x 10¹⁰

BATH

SHELVES

MASTER BED RM. 18⁰ x 14¹⁰

LINEN

SHELVES

BED RM. 17⁰ x 12⁶

SHELVES

● The dormers and the covered porch with pillars introduce this house to the on-lookers. Inside, the appeal is also outstanding. Note the size (18 x 25 foot) of the gathering room which is open to the dining room. Kitchen-nook area is very spacious and features a cooking island, built-in desk and more. Great convenience having the laundry and the service area close to the kitchen. Imagine, a fireplace in both the gathering room and the master bedroom! Make special note of the service entrance doors leading to both the front and back of the house.

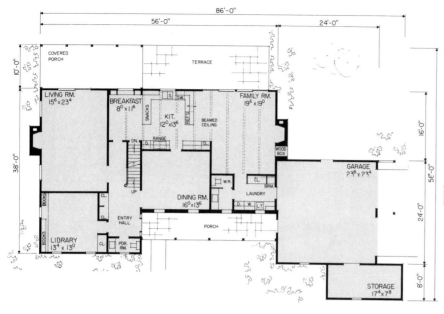

Design V21239

First Floor: 1,822 square feet
Second Floor: 1,419 square feet
Total: 3,241 square feet

Design V21955

First Floor: 1,192 square feet
Second Floor: 1,192 square feet
Total: 2,384 square feet

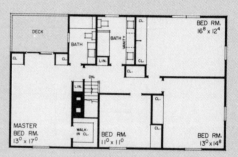

● Here is a design with all of the features a home-owner would want most in a new house. It abounds in exterior appeal and will be a neighborhood show place. Picture yourself relaxing on the front, covered porch after a hard day of work.

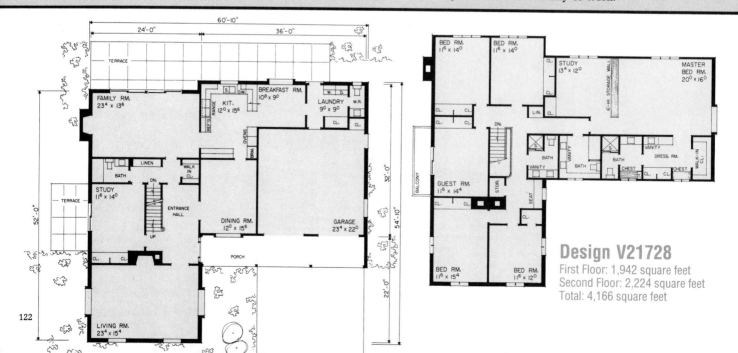

Design V21728

First Floor: 1,942 square feet
Second Floor: 2,224 square feet
Total: 4,166 square feet

123

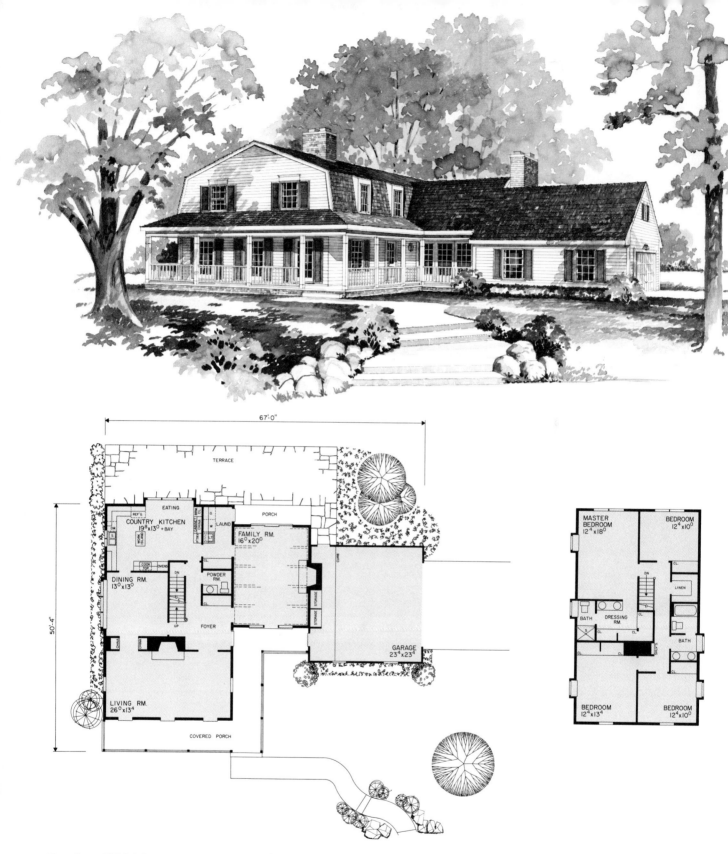

Design V22907 First Floor: 1,546 square feet; Second Floor: 1,144 square feet; Total: 2,690 square feet

● This traditional L-shaped farmhouse is charming, indeed, with gambrel roof, dormer windows, and covered porch supported by slender columns and side rails. A spacious country kitchen with a bay provides a cozy gathering place for family and friends, as well as convenient place for food preparation with its central work island and size. There's a formal dining room also adjacent to the kitchen. A rear family room features its own fireplace, as does a large living room in the front. All four bedrooms are isolated upstairs, away from other household activity and noise. Included is a larger master bedroom suite with its own bath, dressing room, and abundant closet space. This is a comfortable home for the modern family who can appreciate the tradition and charm of the past.

BEDROOM 12⁰x13⁴ BEDROOM 12⁸x10⁰

MASTER BEDROOM 18⁰x13⁴

DRESSING RM.

WALK-IN CLOSET

Design V22908

First Floor: 1,427 square feet
Second Floor: 1,153 square feet
Total: 2,580 square feet

L D

● This Early American farmhouse offers plenty of modern comfort with its covered front porch with pillars and rails, double chimneys, building attachment, and four upstairs bedrooms. The first floor attachment includes a family room with bay window. It leads from the main house to a two-car garage. The family room certainly is the central focus of this fine design, with its own fireplace and rear entrance to a laundry and sewing room behind the garage. Disappearing stairs in the building attachment lead to attic space over the garage. The upstairs also is accessible from stairs just off the front foyer. Included is a master bedroom suite. Downstairs one finds a modern kitchen with breakfast room, dining room, and front living room.

CUSTOMIZABLE

Custom Alterations? See page 413 for customizing this plan to your specifications.

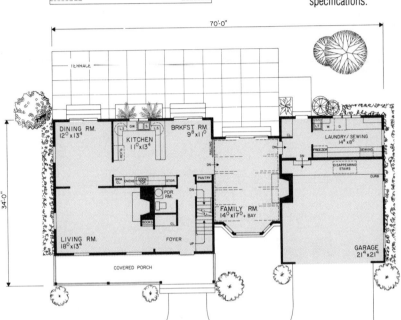

70'-0"

TERRACE

DINING RM. 12⁰x13⁴

KITCHEN 11⁰x13⁴

BRKFST RM. 9⁸x11⁰

LAUNDRY/SEWING 14⁸x8⁰

FREEZER   SEWING

DISAPPEARING STAIRS

PANTRY

34'-0"

PDR. RM.

FAMILY RM. 14⁰x17⁰+ BAY

LIVING RM. 18⁰x13⁴

FOYER

GARAGE 21⁴x21⁴

COVERED PORCH

Design V21996

First Floor: 1,056 square feet
Second Floor: 1,040 square feet
Total: 2,096 square feet

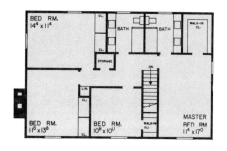

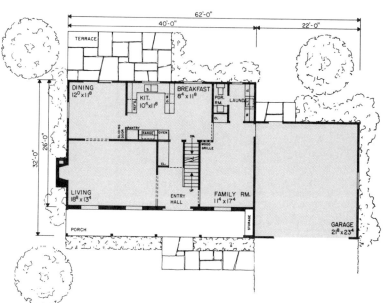

Design V21304

First Floor: 1,120 square feet
Second Floor: 1,120 square feet
Total: 2,240 square feet

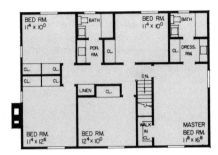

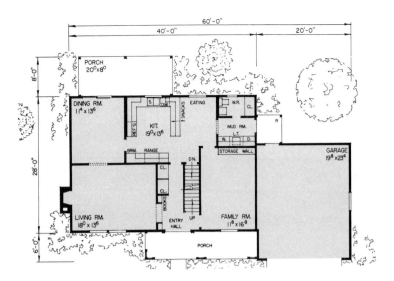

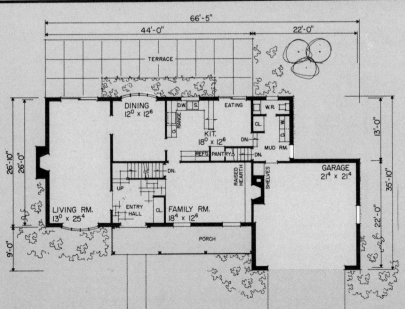

Design V21339

First Floor: 1,292 square feet
Second Floor: 1,232 square feet
Total: 2,524 square feet

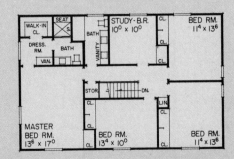

Design V21354

First Floor: 644 square feet
Second Floor: 572 square feet
Total: 1,216 square feet

● Livability galore for the 50 foot building site. The homemaker will enjoy the U-shaped work center with the extra washroom, laundry equipment nearby.

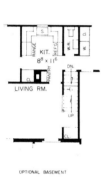

OPTIONAL BASEMENT

Design V21361

First Floor: 965 square feet
Second Floor: 740 square feet
Total: 1,705 square feet

● An abundance of livability is in this charming, traditional adaptation. It will be most economical to build. Count the numerous features.

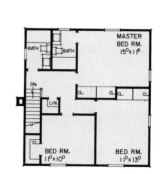

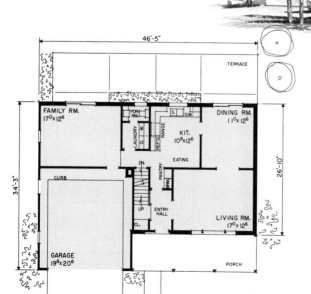

Design V21723

First Floor: 888 square feet
Second Floor: 970 square feet
Total: 1,858 square feet

● You'll not need a large parcel of property to accommodate this home. Neither will you need too large a building budget. Note fourth bedroom.

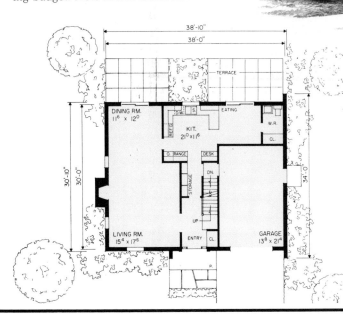

Design V21368

First Floor: 728 square feet
Second Floor: 728 square feet
Total: 1,456 square feet

● Study this outstanding layout. All of the elements are present for fine family living. Four bedrooms, family room, first floor laundry and more are available.

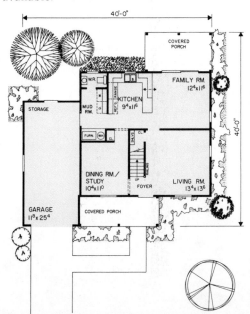

OPTIONAL BASEMENT

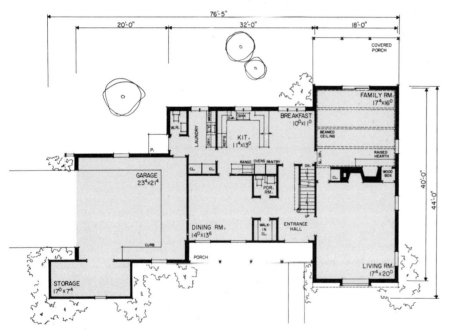

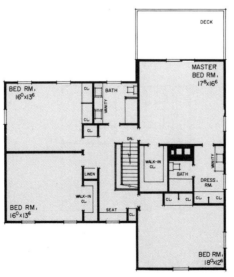

Design V21905
First Floor: 1,596 square feet
Second Floor: 1,574 square feet
Total: 3,170 square feet

● A pleasing Farmhouse adaptation that just looks like it should be catering to the needs of a big, active family. What makes this house so interesting are the various roof lines and projecting wings. The covered front porch and the double front doors add their full measure of charm, too. The traffic patterns of this plan will be a favorite feature for a long time. One whole wing is devoted to living activities. Off the formal entrance hall is the quiet living room. Behind, and functioning with the covered rear porch, is the beamed ceiling family room. It has fine blank wall space and a raised hearth fireplace. The kitchen looks out upon the rear yard and efficiently serves the eating areas. Observe the laundry area with the powder room. Upstairs, four bedrooms!

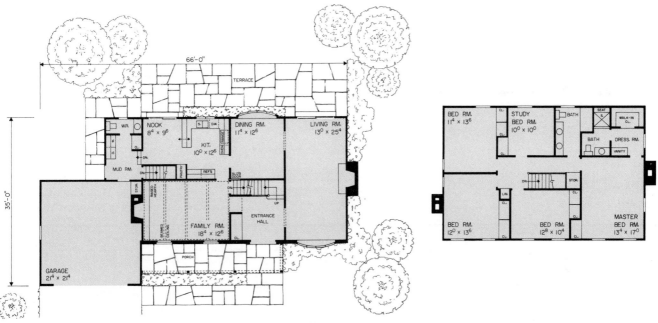

Design V22223 First Floor: 1,266 square feet; Second Floor: 1,232 square feet; Total: 2,498 square feet

L **D**

● The appealing double front doors of this home open wide to fine livability for the large, growing family. The spacious entrance hall is flanked by the formal, end living room and the all-purpose, beamed ceiling family room. Both rooms have a commanding fire- place. The U-shaped kitchen overlooks the rear yard and is but a step, or two, from the breakfast nook and the for- mal dining room. The mud room controls the flows of traffic during the inclement weather. Observe the laun- dry equipment and the washroom. Five bedrooms, two full baths, and plenty of closets are what make the second floor truly outstanding. There are a number of other convenient living features that make this design distinctive. How many of these can you list?

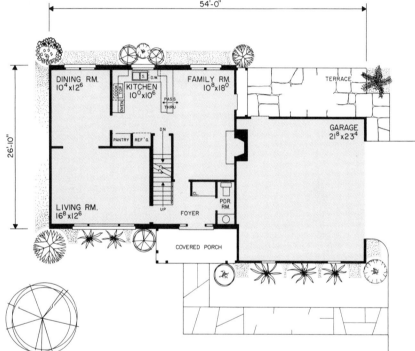

54'-0"

26'-10"

DINING RM.
10⁴x12⁶

KITCHEN
10⁰x10⁶

COOK TOP

OVEN

S D.W.

FAMILY RM.
10⁸x18⁰

PASS THRU

TERRACE

PANTRY REF'G.

DN

GARAGE
21⁸x23⁴

LIVING RM.
16⁸x12⁶

CL.

PDR. RM.

UP

FOYER

COVERED PORCH

BEDROOM
10⁰x11⁰

CL.

BEDROOM
8⁶x10⁰

BEDROOM
10⁰x10⁰

CL.

CL.

CL.

ROOF

CL.

CL.

LINEN

CL.

CL.

DN

BATH

MASTER BEDROOM
11⁴x13¹⁰

BATH

S

BEDROOM
10⁸x12⁴

ROOF

Design V21318

First Floor: 854 square feet
Second Floor: 896 square feet
Total: 1,750 square feet

● Imagine! Five bedrooms, 2½ baths, informal family room, formal living and dining rooms, excellent kitchen, snack bar and a big two-car garage.

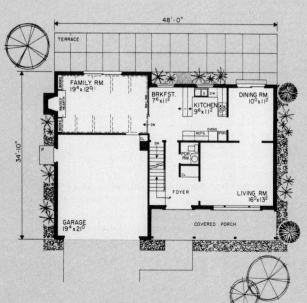

48'-0"

34'-10"

TERRACE

FAMILY RM.
19⁴x12⁹

BRKFST.
7⁶x11²

KITCHEN
9⁶x11²

S D.W.

DINING RM.
10⁰x11²

OVENS

REFG.

PDR RM

CL.

DN

CL.

FOYER

LIVING RM.
16⁰x13²

GARAGE
19⁴x21⁰

COVERED PORCH

BEDROOM
9⁴x9⁴

BATH

S

MASTER BEDROOM
10⁰x15⁰

CL.

BATH

LINEN

DN

BEDROOM
10⁰x10⁰

BEDROOM
11⁴x10⁰

BATH

MASTER BEDROOM
14⁸x11⁸

BATH

LINEN

DN

BEDROOM
10⁰x10⁰

BEDROOM
11⁴x13⁴

OPTIONAL 3 BEDROOM PLAN

CUSTOMIZABLE
Custom Alterations? See page 413 for customizing this plan to your specifications.

Design V21956

First Floor: 990 square feet
Second Floor: 728 square feet
Total: 1,718 square feet

L D

● The blueprints for this home include details for both the three bedroom and four bedroom options. The first floor livability does not change.

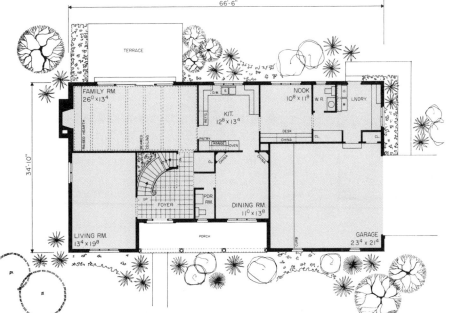

66'-6"

34'-10"

TERRACE

FAMILY RM. 26⁰ x 13⁴

KIT. 12⁸ x 13⁴

NOOK 10⁸ x 11⁸

LNDRY.

W.R.

D.W.

REF.

DESK

CHINA

CL.

PNTRY

RANGE OVEN

CL.

CHINA

CHINA

UP

FOYER

PDR. RM.

DINING RM. 11⁰ x 13⁸

LIVING RM. 13⁴ x 19⁸

PORCH

CURB

GARAGE 23⁴ x 21⁴

Design V22172
First Floor: 1,618 square feet
Second Floor: 1,205 square feet
Total: 2,823 square feet

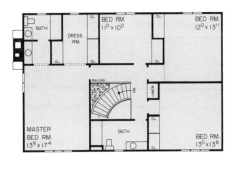

BATH

DRESS. RM.

BED RM. 11⁰ x 10⁰

CL.

CL.

BED RM. 12⁰ x 13¹¹

CL.

RAILING

DN.

LINEN

MASTER BED RM. 13⁹ x 17⁴

BATH

CL.

BED RM. 13⁰ x 13⁶

Design V21868

First Floor: 1,190 square feet
Second Floor: 1,300 square feet
Total: 2,490 square feet

● A five-bedroom Farmhouse adaptation that is truly a home for family living. The big family room will be everyone's favorite area. Note the master bedroom suite, located over the garage.

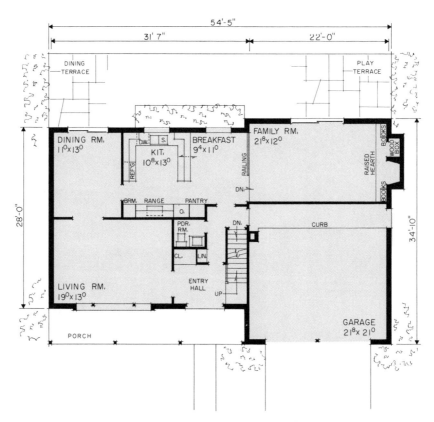

Design V21285

First Floor: 1,202 square feet
Second Floor: 896 square feet
Total: 2,098 square feet

L D

● Such a pretty traditional Farmhouse design — and with so much to offer in the way of floor planning. From the front entry, turn left into a good-sized living room with attached dining room. A right turn leads to a well-placed powder room and laundry or farther back to the beamed-ceiling family room (note the fireplace with wood box here). The kitchen and adjacent breakfast nook will make mealtimes a pleasure. Upstairs, four symmetrically laid-out bedrooms share space with two baths.

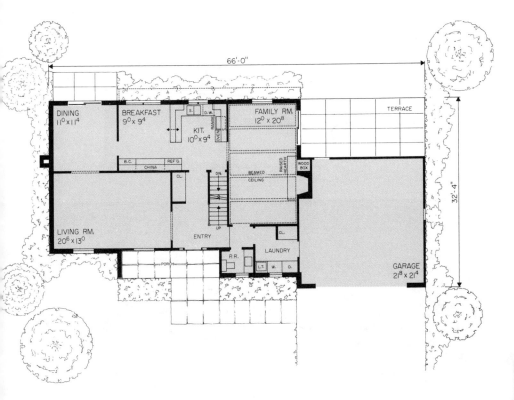

Design V21933

First Floor: 1,184 square feet
Second Floor: 884 square feet
Total: 2,068 square feet

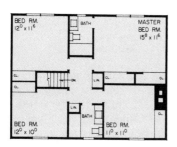

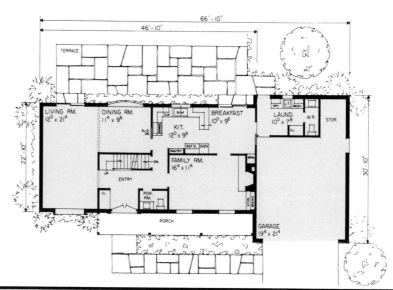

Design V21269

First Floor: 1,232 square feet
Second Floor: 1,232 square feet
Total: 2,464 square feet

Design V21082

First Floor: 1,254 square feet
Second Floor: 1,096 square feet
Total: 2,350 square feet

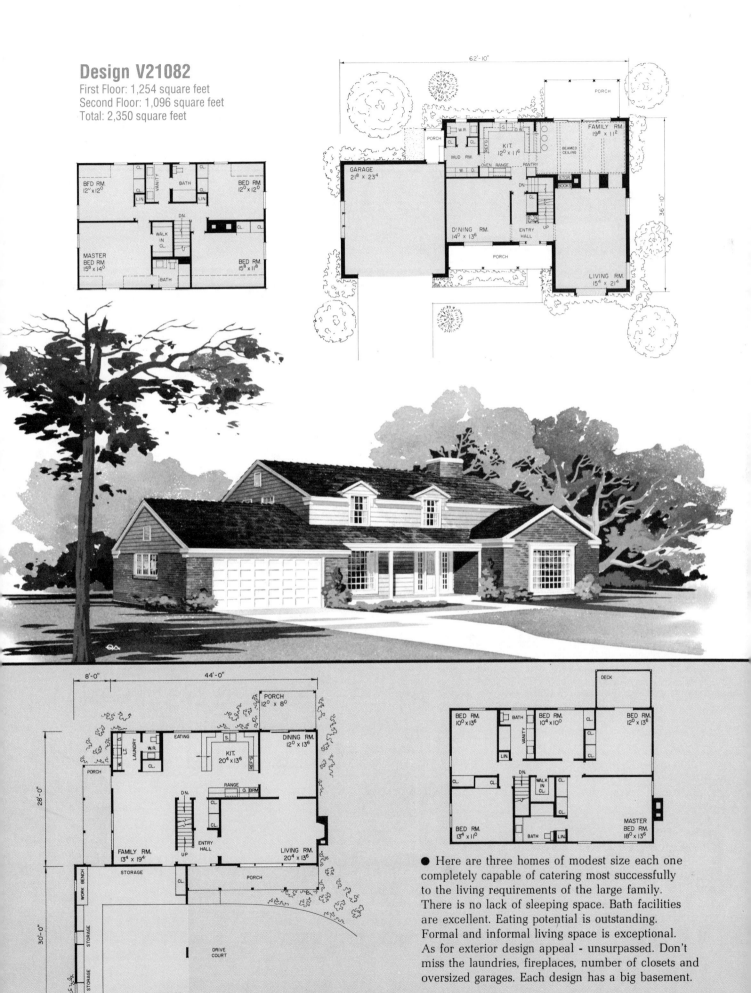

BED RM. 12' x 12⁰

BATH

BED RM. 12⁰ x 12⁰

MASTER BED RM. 15⁸ x 14⁰

WALK IN CL.

BED RM. 15⁸ x 11⁸

62'-0"

PORCH

W.R.

FAMILY RM. 19⁸ x 11²

BEAMED CEILING

KIT. 12⁰ x 11⁶

MUD RM.

OVEN RANGE

PANTRY

STOR.

BOOKS

GARAGE 21⁸ x 23⁴

36'-0"

D'NING RM. 14⁰ x 13⁶

ENTRY HALL

UP

LIVING RM. 15⁴ x 21⁴

PORCH

8'-0"   44'-0"

PORCH 12⁰ x 8⁰

EATING

DINING RM. 12⁰ x 13⁶

LAUNDRY

W.R.

KIT. 20⁴ x 13⁶

PORCH

RANGE

DN.

FAMILY RM. 13⁴ x 19⁴

ENTRY HALL

UP

LIVING RM. 20⁴ x 13⁶

28'-0"

STORAGE

PORCH

WORK BENCH

30'-0"

STORAGE

STORAGE

DRIVE COURT

GARAGE 23⁴ x 29⁸

DECK

BED RM. 10⁰ x 13⁶

BATH

VANITY

BED RM. 10⁴ x 10⁰

BED RM. 12⁰ x 13⁶

DN.

WALK IN CL.

BED RM. 13⁴ x 11⁰

BATH

MASTER BED RM. 18⁰ x 13⁶

● Here are three homes of modest size each one completely capable of catering most successfully to the living requirements of the large family. There is no lack of sleeping space. Bath facilities are excellent. Eating potential is outstanding. Formal and informal living space is exceptional. As for exterior design appeal - unsurpassed. Don't miss the laundries, fireplaces, number of closets and oversized garages. Each design has a big basement.

Design V21787

First Floor: 2,656 square feet
Second Floor: 744 square feet
Total: 3,400 square feet

D

● Can't you picture this dramatic home sitting on your property? The curving front drive is impressive as it passes the walks to the front door and the service entrance. The roof masses, the centered masonry chimney, the window symmetry and the 108 foot expanse across the front are among the features that make this a distinctive home. Of interest are the living and family rooms — both similar in size and each having its own fireplace.

STUDY - LOUNGE
16⁴ x 12⁴

BOOKS

DN.

STORAGE

LIN.

MASTER BED. RM.
15⁰ x 21⁶

DRESSING RM.

BATH

CL.

CL.

108'-0"

24'-0"   20'-0"   36'-0"   28'-0"

STOR.

COOKING

POOL HOUSE

STOR.

GATE

POOL
36⁰ x 20⁰

TERRACE

16'-0"

16'-0"

64'-5"

28'-0"

BED. RM.
11⁸ x 12⁰

CL.

BED. RM.
11⁰ x 15⁸

CL.

STORAGE

CL.

LAUNDRY

W.   D.

BREAKFAST
11⁰ x 10⁰

D.W.   S.

KIT.
11⁴ x 15⁰

REF.

FAMILY RM.
23⁸ x 14⁴

UP.

BATH

BATH

BED. RM.
11⁰ x 13⁶

CL.

PDR. RM.

DN.

PORCH

STOR.

PANTRY

BAR-B-Q   RANGE

CHINA

O.

WOOD BOX

RAISED HEARTH

STORAGE

CL.

ENTRY HALL

LIN.   CL.   CHEST

CL.

GARAGE
23⁴ x 27⁴

DINING RM.
11⁸ x 14⁴

LIVING RM.
23⁴ x 14⁰

PORCH

CL.

BED. RM.
17⁰ x 11⁴

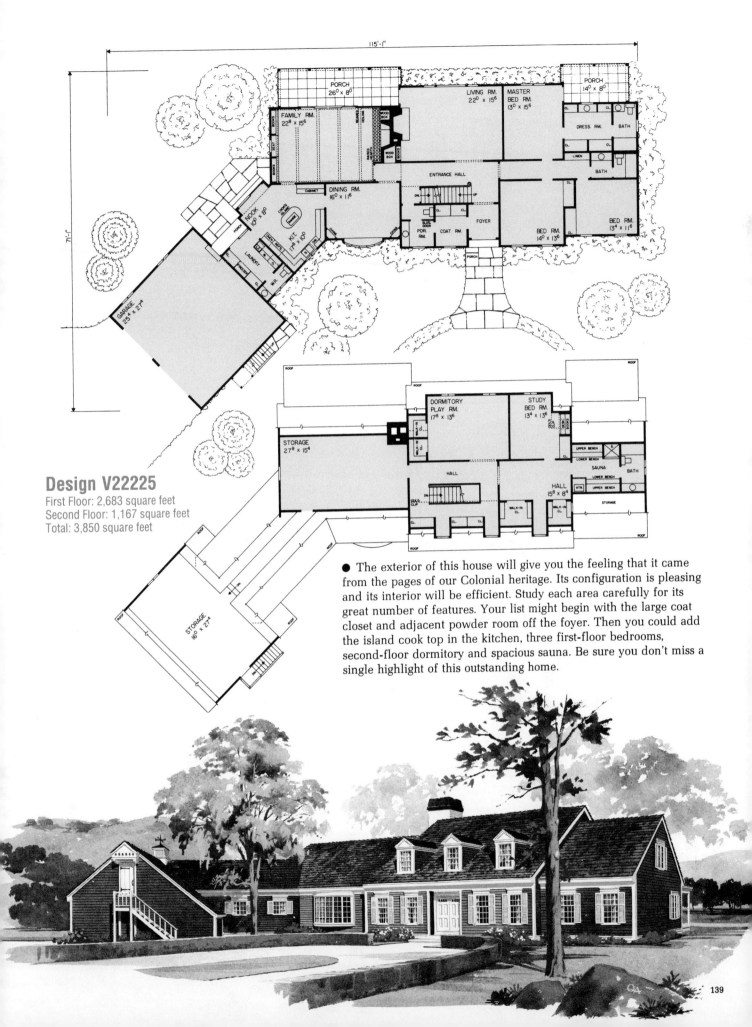

115'-1"

PORCH
26⁰ x 8⁰

PORCH
14⁰ x 8⁰

LIVING RM.
22⁰ x 15⁶

MASTER
BED RM.
13⁰ x 15⁶

FAMILY RM.
22⁸ x 15⁶

WOOD
BOX

DRESS. RM.

BATH

CL

LINEN

BATH

CABINET

DINING RM.
16⁰ x 11⁶

ENTRANCE HALL

NOOK
10⁰ x 8⁰

KIT.
17⁸ x 10⁰

DN.

UP.

CL

BED RM.
13⁴ x 11⁶

71'-1"

LAUNDRY

WR.

CL

SLDG.
DOOR

PDR.
RM.

COAT
RM.

FOYER

BED RM.
14⁰ x 13⁶

CL

GARAGE
25⁴ x 27⁴

PORCH

ROOF

ROOF

DORMITORY
PLAY RM.
17⁸ x 13⁶

STUDY
BED RM.
13⁴ x 13⁶

STORAGE
27⁸ x 15⁴

UPPER BENCH

LOWER BENCH

SAUNA

BATH

HALL

LOWER BENCH

UPPER BENCH

HALL
15⁸ x 8⁴

STORAGE

WALK-IN
CL.

WALK-IN
CL.

DN.

CL.

CL.

CL.

ROOF

ROOF

Design V22225
First Floor: 2,683 square feet
Second Floor: 1,167 square feet
Total: 3,850 square feet

ROOF

ROOF

STORAGE
16⁰ x 27⁴

ROOF

UP.

● The exterior of this house will give you the feeling that it came from the pages of our Colonial heritage. Its configuration is pleasing and its interior will be efficient. Study each area carefully for its great number of features. Your list might begin with the large coat closet and adjacent powder room off the foyer. Then you could add the island cook top in the kitchen, three first-floor bedrooms, second-floor dormitory and spacious sauna. Be sure you don't miss a single highlight of this outstanding home.

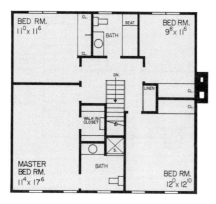

BED RM.
11^0 x 11^6

BATH

SEAT

BED RM.
9^8 x 11^6

DN.

LINEN

CL.

CL.

WALK-IN CLOSET

MASTER BED RM.
11^4 x 17^6

BATH

BED RM.
12^0 x 12^{10}

Design V22752

First Floor: 1,209 square feet
Second Floor: 960 square feet
Total: 2,169 square feet

● This impressive two-story home is sure to catch the eye of even the most casual of on-lookers. The extended one-story wing adds great appeal to the exterior. The covered porch with pillars also is a charming feature. Now take a walk through the efficient floor plan. The living/dining room is L-shaped with the dining room being convenient to the kitchen. The U-shaped kitchen has a pass-thru to the breakfast nook plus has many built-ins to help ease kitchen duties. The nook, along with the family room, has sliding glass doors to the terrace. Also on the first floor is a powder room and laundry. The second floor houses the three family bedrooms, bath and the master bedroom suite with all the extras. Note the extra curb area in the garage.

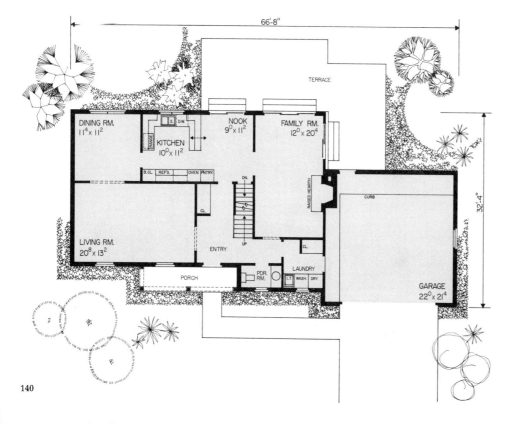

66'-8"

TERRACE

DINING RM.
11^4 x 11^2

KITCHEN
10^0 x 11^2

S. D.W.

GARB.

B.G.L. REF'S. OVEN PNTRY.

CL.

LIVING RM.
20^8 x 13^2

NOOK
9^0 x 11^2

FAMILY RM.
12^0 x 20^4

RAISED HEARTH

DN.

UP

CL.

ENTRY

PORCH

PDR. RM.

LAUNDRY
L.T. WASH. DRY.

CURB

GARAGE
22^0 x 21^4

32'-4"

Design V22585

First Floor: 990 square feet
Second Floor: 1,011 square feet
Total: 2,001 square feet

L **D**

● An elegant Colonial! This is a version of a front porch type house. The exterior is highlighted with seven large paned-glass windows and pillars. Note that the second floor overhangs in the front to extend the size of the master bedroom. After entering through the front door one can either go directly to the formal area of the living room and dining room or to the informal area which is the front family room with fireplace. No matter which direction you choose, satisfaction will be found. The U-shaped kitchen will serve the nook area orderly and is just a step away from the wash room. Upstairs one will find all of the sleeping facilities.

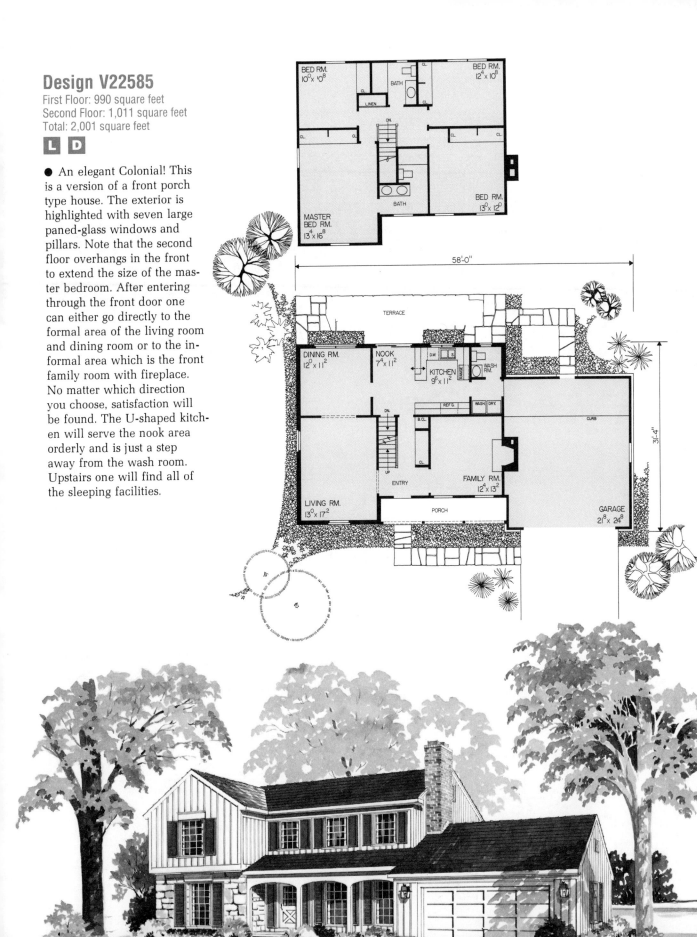

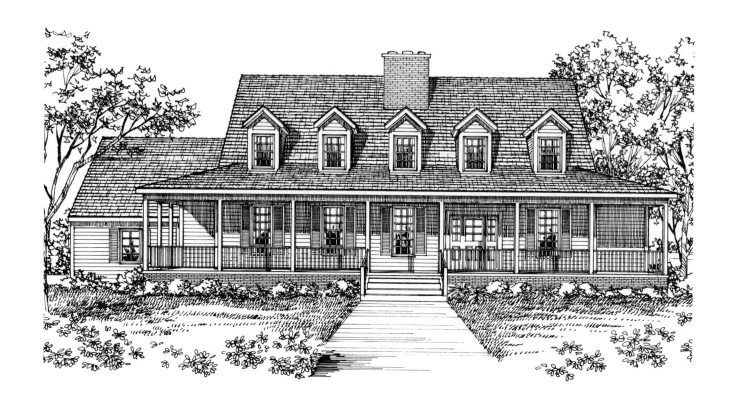

Design V23397

First Floor: 1,855 square feet
Second Floor: 1,241 square feet
Total: 3,096 square feet

L D

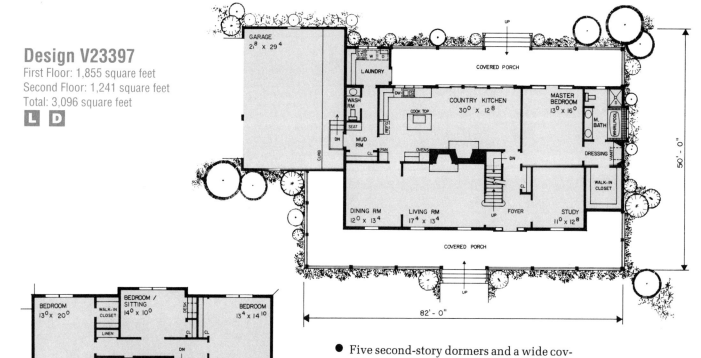

● Five second-story dormers and a wide covered front porch add to the charm of this farmhouse design. Inside, the entry foyer opens to the left to a formal living room with fireplace and attached dining room. To the right is a private study. The back of the plan is dominated by a huge country kitchen featuring an island cook top. On this floor is the master suite with a large walk-in closet. The second floor holds three bedrooms (or two and a sitting room) with two full baths.

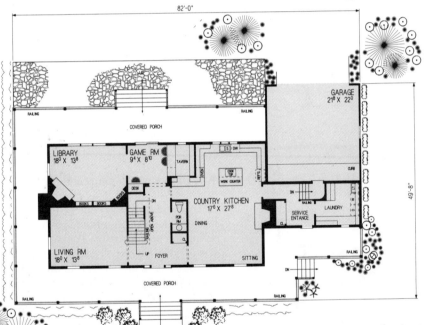

Design V23399

First Floor: 1,716 square feet
Second Floor: 2,102 square feet
Total: 3,818 square feet

L D

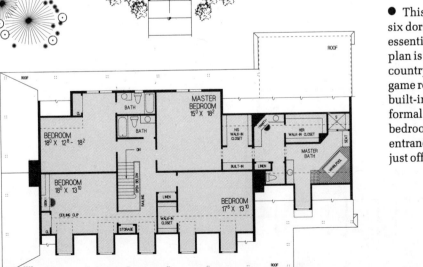

● This is the ultimate in farmhouse living — six dormer windows and a porch that stretches essentially around the entire house. Inside, the plan is open and inviting. Besides the large country kitchen with fireplace, there is a small game room with attached tavern, a library with built-in bookshelves and a fireplace, and a formal living room. The second floor has four bedrooms and three full baths. The service entrance features a laundry area conveniently just off the garage.

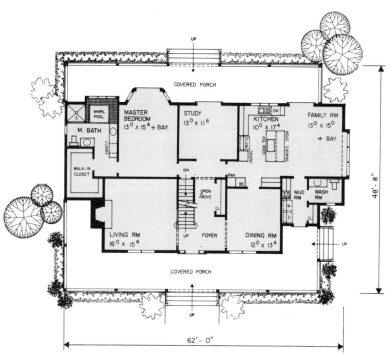

COVERED PORCH

UP

MASTER BEDROOM
13⁰ x 15⁴ + BAY

STUDY
13⁰ x 11⁶

KITCHEN
10⁰ x 17⁴

FAMILY RM
13⁰ x 15⁰
+ BAY

WHIRL POOL

M. BATH

VANITY

WALK-IN CLOSET

REF G

OVENS

COOK TOP

SNACK'S

STO R

DS

DW

DN

PAN

BC

OPEN ABOVE

CL

MUD RM

WASH RM

W

D

CL

LIVING RM
16⁰ x 15⁴

UP

FOYER

DINING RM
12⁰ x 13⁴

UP

COVERED PORCH

UP

62' - 0"

48' - 8"

BEDROOM
13⁰ x 11⁰

BATH

DRESSING

CL

LIN

LIN

CL

BEDROOM
13⁸ x 12⁰

DN

LIN

RAILING

OPEN

BEDROOM
14⁴ x 15⁰

CL

CL

Design V23396
First Floor: 1,829 square feet
Second Floor: 947 square feet
Total: 2,776 square feet

L **D**

● Rustic charm abounds in this pleasant farm-house rendition. Covered porches to the front and rear enclose living potential for the whole family. Flanking the entrance foyer are the living and dining rooms. To the rear is the L-shaped kitchen with island cook top and snack bar. A small family room/breakfast nook is attached. A private study is tucked away on this floor next to the master suite. On the second floor are three bedrooms and a full bath. Two of the bedrooms have charming dormer windows.

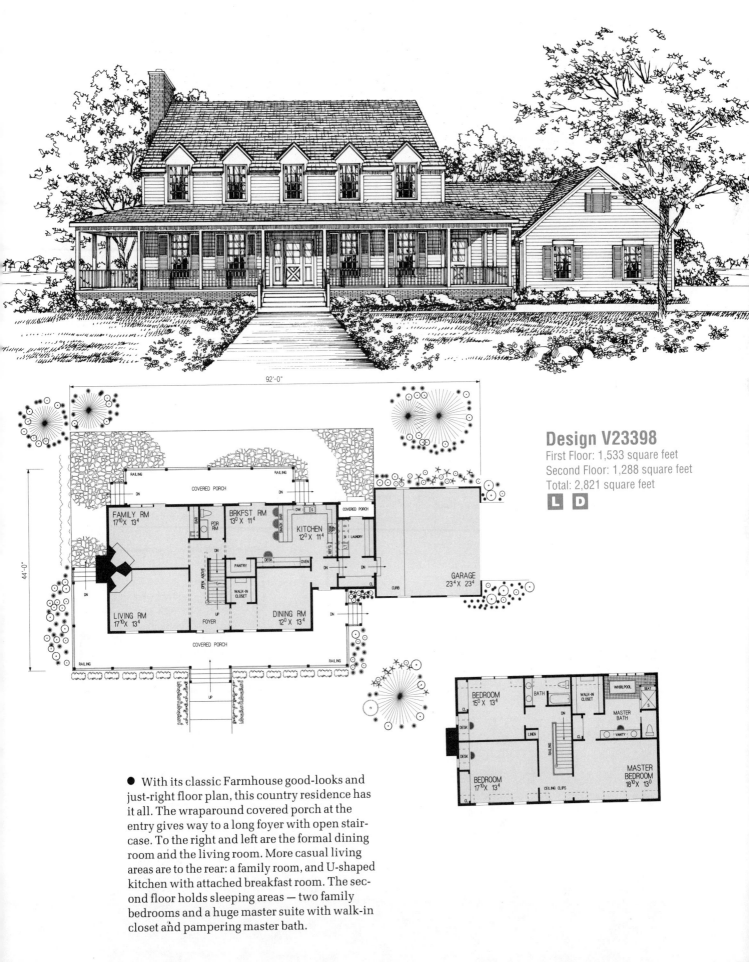

Design V23398
First Floor: 1,533 square feet
Second Floor: 1,288 square feet
Total: 2,821 square feet

L **D**

● With its classic Farmhouse good-looks and just-right floor plan, this country residence has it all. The wraparound covered porch at the entry gives way to a long foyer with open staircase. To the right and left are the formal dining room and the living room. More casual living areas are to the rear: a family room, and U-shaped kitchen with attached breakfast room. The second floor holds sleeping areas — two family bedrooms and a huge master suite with walk-in closet and pampering master bath.

Design V22633

First Floor: 1,338 square feet
Second Floor: 1,200 square feet
Third Floor: 506 square feet
Total: 3,044 square feet

● This is certainly a pleasing Georgian. Its facade features a front porch with a roof supported by 12'' diameter wooden columns. The garage wing has a sheltered service entry and brick facing which complements the design. Sliding glass doors link the terrace and family room, providing an indoor/outdoor area for entertaining as pictured in the rear elevation. The floor plan has been designed to serve the family efficiently. The stairway in the foyer leads to four second-floor bedrooms. The third floor is windowed and can be used as a studio and study.

GEORGIAN HOUSES . . .

are noted for the many fine characteristics that first graced these popular homes: perfect proportions, eye-pleasing symmetry, massive chimneys, tasteful detailing, and classic entries. The well-designed Georgian epitomizes quiet strength, restrained beauty, and gracious living.

Design V21858

First Floor: 1,794 square feet
Second Floor: 1,474 square feet
Studio: 424 square feet
Total: 3,692 square feet

D

● You'll never regret your choice of this Georgian design. Its stately facade seems to foretell all of the exceptional features to be found inside. From the delightful spacious front entry hall, to the studio or maid's room over the garage, this home is unique all along the way. Imagine four fireplaces, three full baths, two extra washrooms, a family room, plus a quiet library. Don't miss the first floor laundry. Note the separate set of stairs to the studio or maid's room. The center entrance leads to the vestibule and entry hall. All the major areas are but a step or two from this formal hall. The kitchen is well planned and strategically located between the separate dining room and the breakfast room. Sliding glass doors permit easy access to the functional rear terraces.

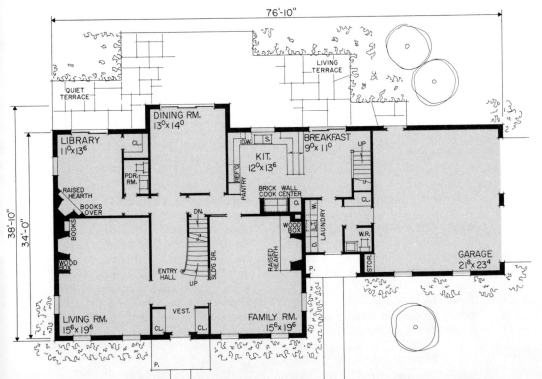

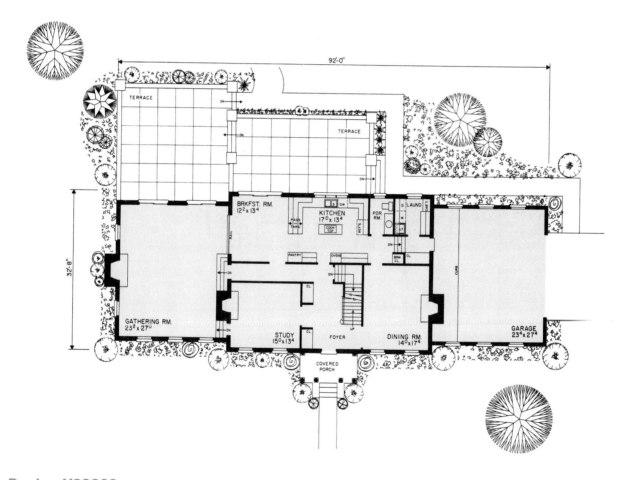

Design V22683 First Floor: 2,126 square feet; Second Floor: 1,882 square feet; Total: 4,008 square feet

L D

● This historical Georgian home has its roots in the 18th Century. Dignified symmetry is a hallmark of both front and rear elevations. The full two-story center section is delightfully complemented by the 1½-story wings. Interior livability has been planned to serve today's active family. The elegant gathering room, three steps down from the rest of the house, has ample space for entertaining on a grand scale. It fills an entire wing and is dead-ended so that traffic does not pass through it. Guests and family alike will enjoy the two rooms flanking the foyer, the study and formal dining room. Each of these rooms will have a fireplace as its highlight. The breakfast room, kitchen, powder room and laundry are arranged for maximum efficiency. This area will always have that desired light and airy atmosphere with the sliding glass door and the triple window over the kitchen sink. The second floor houses the family bedrooms. Take special note of the spacious master bedroom suite. It has a deluxe bath, fireplace and sunken lounge with dressing room and walk-in closet. Surely an area to be appreciated.

Georgian Elegance from the Past

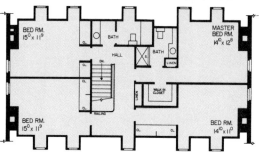

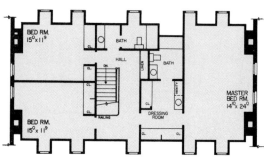

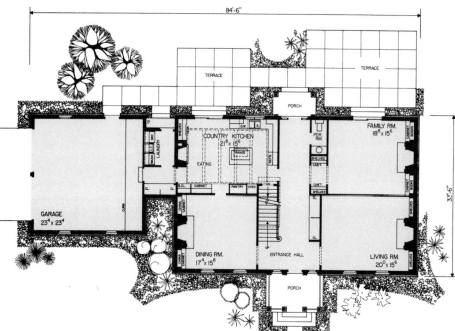

84'-6"

TERRACE

TERRACE

PORCH

FAMILY RM.
18⁸ x 15⁶

COUNTRY KITCHEN
21⁸ x 15⁶

EATING

RANGE

GARAGE
23⁴ x 23⁴

LAUNDRY

PANTRY

OVEN

DINING RM.
17⁴ x 15⁶

ENTRANCE HALL

UP

LIVING RM.
20⁰ x 15⁶

PORCH

33'-6"

Design V22638

First Floor: 1,836 square feet
Second Floor: 1,323 square feet
Total: 3,159 square feet

● The brick facade of this two-story re-presents the mid-18th-Century design concept. Examine its fine exterior. It has a steeply pitched roof which is broken by two large chimneys at each end and by pedimented dormers. Inside Georgian details lend elegance. Turned balusters and a curved banister orna-ment the formal staircase. Blueprints include details for both three and four bedroom options.

Design V22132

First Floor: 1,958 square feet
Second Floor: 1,305 square feet
Total: 3,263 square feet

L

● Another Georgian adaptation with a great heritage dating back to 18th-Century America. Exquisite and symmetrical detailing set the character of this impressive home. Don't overlook such features as the two fireplaces, the laundry, the beamed ceiling, the built-in china cabinets and the oversized garage.

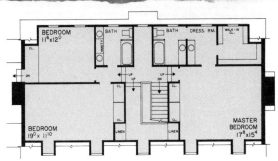

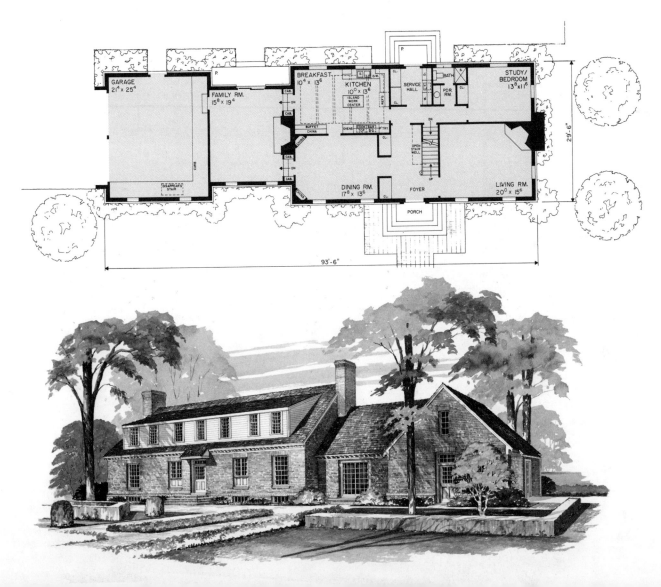

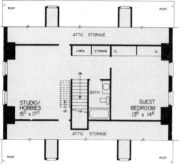

ATTIC STORAGE

LINEN | STORAGE | CL. | CL.

STUDIO/
HOBBIES
15⁰ x 17⁰

BATH

DN

GUEST
BEDROOM
13⁸ x 14⁶

ATTIC STORAGE

ROOF | ROOF

WHIRLPOOL

BATH

DRESSING RM.

HER WALK IN CLOSET

HIS WALK IN CLOSET

LINEN

BATH

OPEN BELOW

RAILING

BEDROOM
15⁴ x 12⁰

CL.

MASTER
BEDROOM
15⁰ x 18⁰

BEDROOM
14⁰ x 14⁴

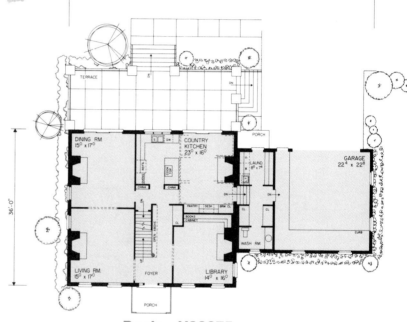

72'-0"

36'-0"

TERRACE

DN

PORCH

DINING RM.
15⁰ x 17⁰

COUNTRY
KITCHEN
23⁰ x 16⁰

REF.

COOK TOP

CHINA

CHINA

LAUND.
6⁰ x 7⁸

DW

CL.

CL.

GARAGE
22⁴ x 22⁸

CURB

PANTRY

DESK

BRM. CL.

BOOKS CABINET

CL.

DN

WASH RM.

LIVING RM.
15⁰ x 17⁰

FOYER

LIBRARY
14⁰ x 16⁰

OPEN ABOVE

PORCH

Design V22975 First Floor: 1,656 square feet
Second Floor: 1,440 square feet; Third Floor: 715 square feet
Total: 3,811 square feet

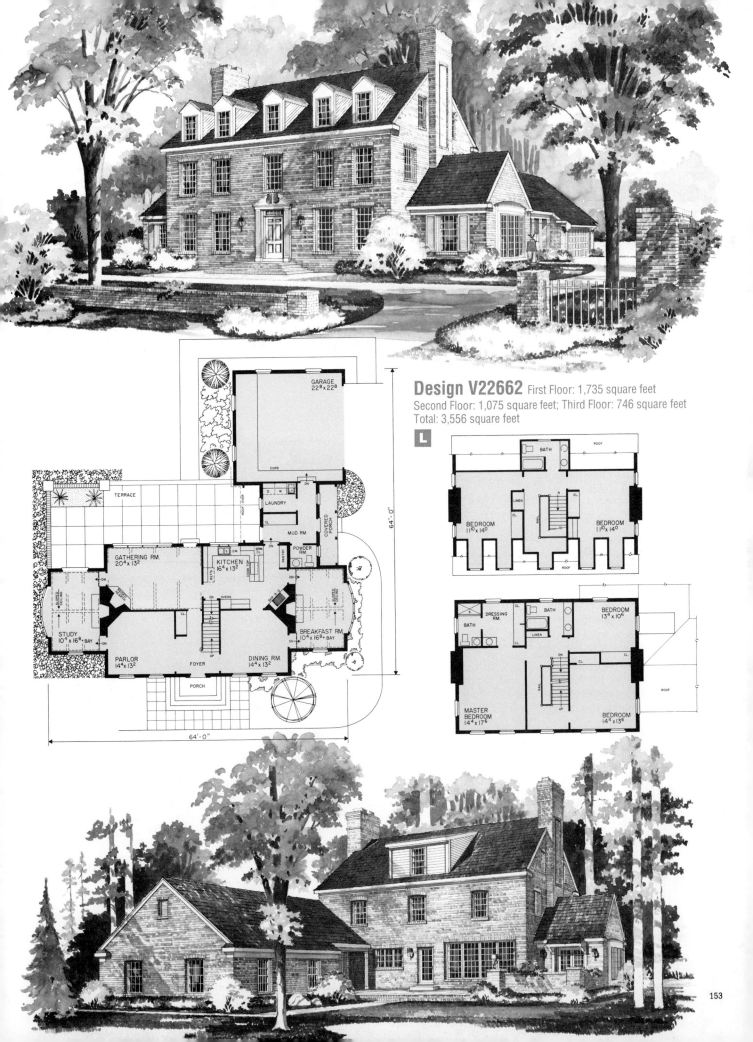

Design V22662 First Floor: 1,735 square feet
Second Floor: 1,075 square feet; Third Floor: 746 square feet
Total: 3,556 square feet

L

First Floor plan labels:
GARAGE 22⁸ x 22⁸
TERRACE
LAUNDRY
MUD RM.
COVERED PORCH
GATHERING RM. 20⁴ x 13²
KITCHEN 16⁴ x 13²
POWDER RM.
PANTRY
STUDY 10⁴ x 16⁸+ BAY
OVENS
BREAKFAST RM. 10⁴ x 16⁸+ BAY
PARLOR 14⁴ x 13²
FOYER
DINING RM. 14⁴ x 13²
PORCH
64'-0"

Third Floor plan labels:
BATH
ROOF
LINEN
CL.
BEDROOM 11¹⁰ x 14⁰
BEDROOM 11¹⁰ x 14⁰

Second Floor plan labels:
BATH
DRESSING RM.
BATH
LINEN
BEDROOM 13⁴ x 10⁶
MASTER BEDROOM 14⁴ x 17⁶
BEDROOM 14⁴ x 13⁶
ROOF

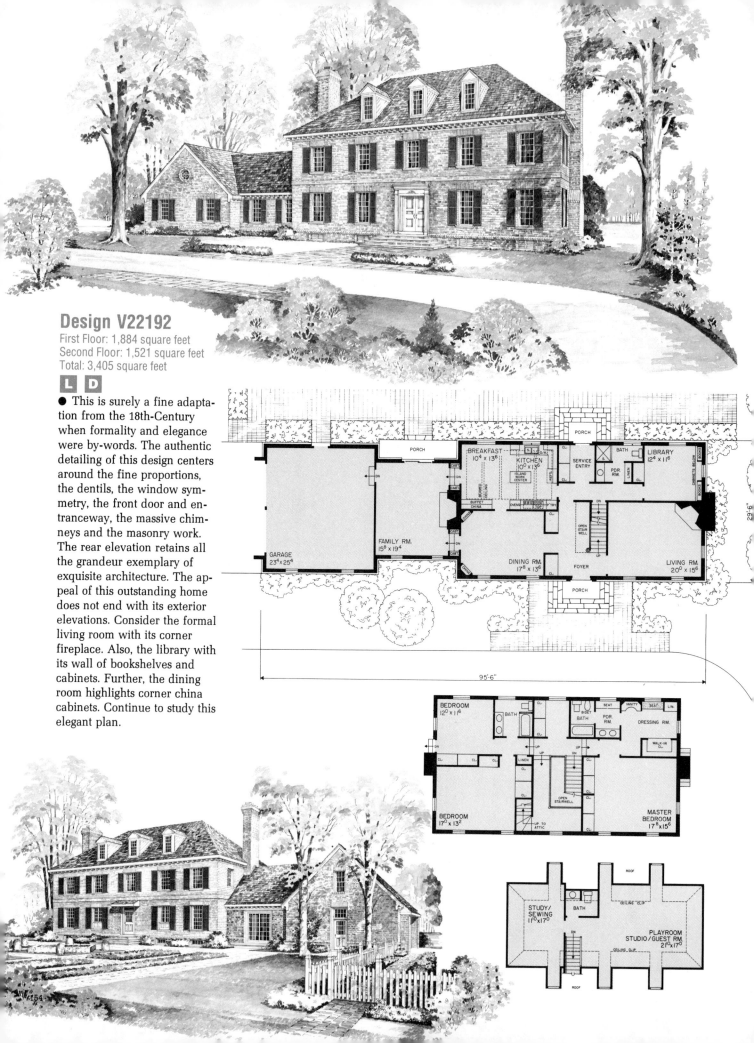

Design V22192

First Floor: 1,884 square feet
Second Floor: 1,521 square feet
Total: 3,405 square feet

L D

● This is surely a fine adaptation from the 18th-Century when formality and elegance were by-words. The authentic detailing of this design centers around the fine proportions, the dentils, the window symmetry, the front door and entranceway, the massive chimneys and the masonry work. The rear elevation retains all the grandeur exemplary of exquisite architecture. The appeal of this outstanding home does not end with its exterior elevations. Consider the formal living room with its corner fireplace. Also, the library with its wall of bookshelves and cabinets. Further, the dining room highlights corner china cabinets. Continue to study this elegant plan.

154

Design V22982

First Floor: 1,584 square feet
Second Floor: 1,513 square feet
Total: 3,097 square feet

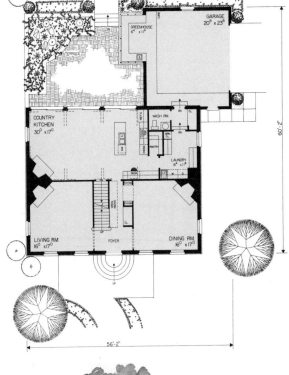

● An early 18th Century Georgian so common to Williamsburg, Va. and environs. Observe the massive twin chimneys, the cornice ornamentation, and the wrought iron balcony sheltering the front panelled door. The rectangular shape of this house will lead to economical construction costs. The 30 foot, beamed-ceiling country kitchen with its commanding corner fireplace and rear yard access is outstanding. Notice the fireplaces for the country kitchen, living, dining and master bedrooms.

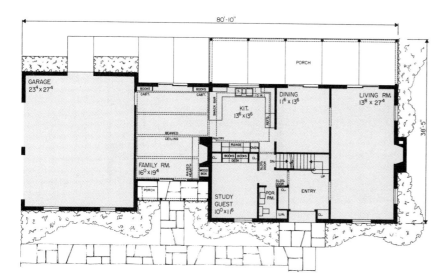

● A big, end living room featuring a fireplace and sliding glass doors is the focal point of this Georgian design. Adjacent is the formal dining room strategically located but a couple of steps from the efficient kitchen. Functioning closely with the kitchen is the family room.

Design V22176

First Floor: 1,485 square feet
Second Floor: 1,175 square feet
Total: 2,660 square feet

Design V21767

First Floor: 1,510 square feet
Second Floor: 1,406 square feet
Total: 2,916 square feet

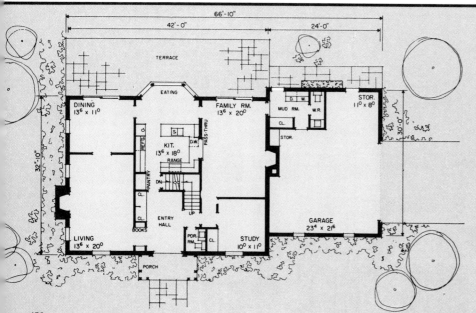

Design V22139

First Floor: 1,581 square feet
Second Floor: 991 square feet
Total: 2,572 square feet

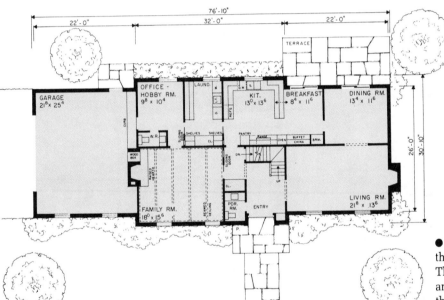

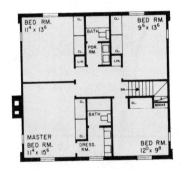

● Four bedrooms and two baths make-up the second floor of this two-story design. The first floor has all of the living areas and work center. Note the convenience of the powder room at the entry.

● A Georgian Colonial adaptation on the grand scale. The authentic front entrance is delightfully detailed. Two massive end chimneys, housing four fireplaces, are in keeping with the architecture of its day.

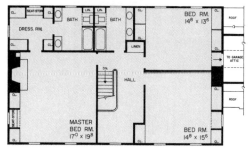

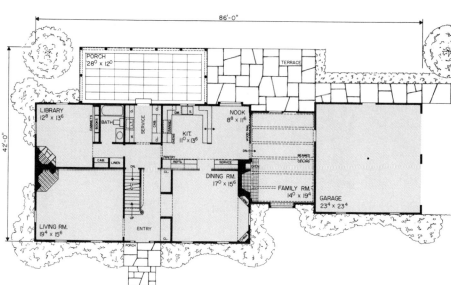

Design V22221 First Floor: 1,726 square feet
Second Floor: 1,440 square feet; Total: 3,166 square feet

Design V21852 First Floor: 1,802 square feet
Second Floor: 1,603 square feet; Total: 3,405 square feet

● This is an impressive Georgian adaptation. The front entrance detailing, the window treatment and the masses of brick help put this house in a class of its own.

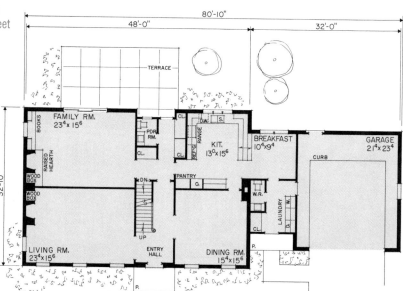

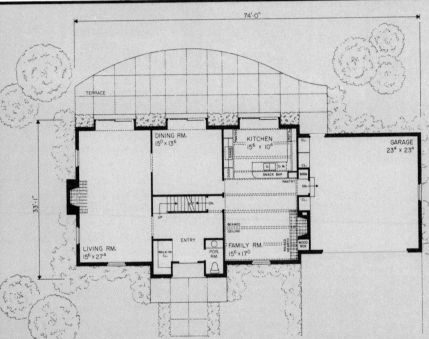

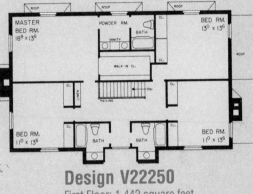

● This stately home, whose roots go back to an earlier period in American architecture, will forever retain its aura of distinction. The spacious front entry effectively separates the formal and informal living zones. Four bedrooms on second floor.

Design V22250

First Floor: 1,442 square feet
Second Floor: 1,404 square feet
Total: 2,846 square feet

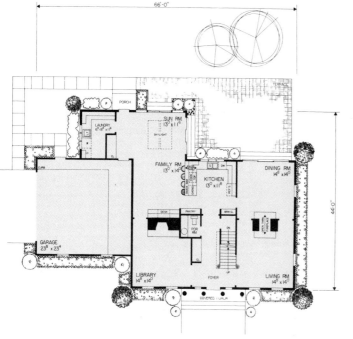

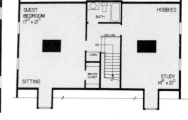

Design V22980 First Floor: 1,648 square feet
Second Floor: 1,368 square feet; Third Floor: 567 square feet
Total: 3,583 square feet

● This late Georgian adaptation is reminiscent of the Cowles house built in Farmington, Conn. around 1786. The formal symmetry and rich ornamentation were typical of houses of this period. Ionic columns, a Palladian window, and a pedimented gable are among the details that set the character of this historic house. Inside there are three floors of livability. And, of course, there is no hint of antiquity here. The centered foyer is flanked by wonderfully spacious living areas which flow around the fireplaces. Note the sun room, laundry, and bonus space of the third floor where there is all kinds of livability.

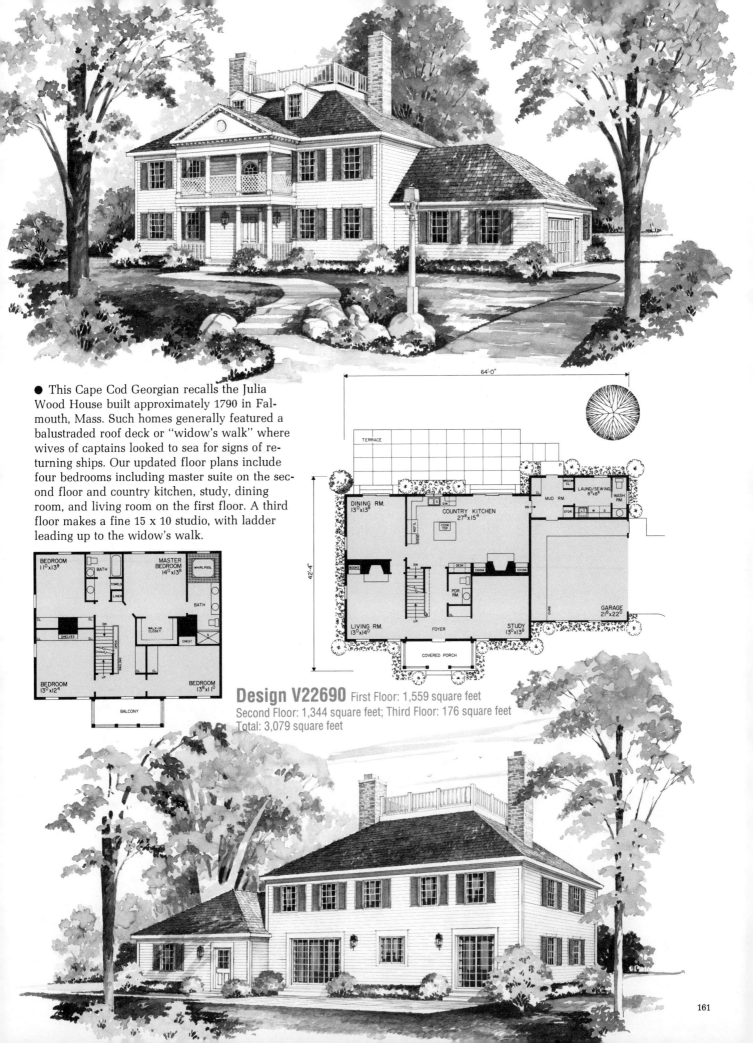

● This Cape Cod Georgian recalls the Julia Wood House built approximately 1790 in Falmouth, Mass. Such homes generally featured a balustraded roof deck or "widow's walk" where wives of captains looked to sea for signs of returning ships. Our updated floor plans include four bedrooms including master suite on the second floor and country kitchen, study, dining room, and living room on the first floor. A third floor makes a fine 15 x 10 studio, with ladder leading up to the widow's walk.

Design V22690 First Floor: 1,559 square feet
Second Floor: 1,344 square feet; Third Floor: 176 square feet
Total: 3,079 square feet

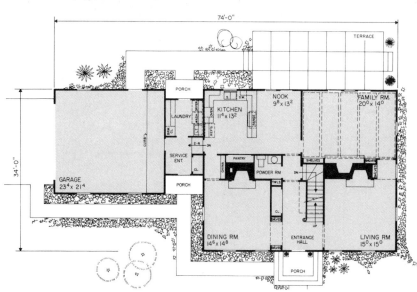

● Here is a New England Georgian adaptation with an elevated doorway highlighted by pilasters and a pediment. It gives way to a second-story Palladian window, capped in turn by a pediment projecting from the hipped roof. The interior is decidely up-to-date with even an upstairs lounge.

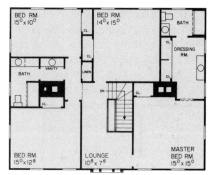

Design V22639 First Floor. 1,556 square feet; Second Floor: 1,428 square feet; Total: 2,984 square feet

L D

Design V23349

First Floor: 2,807 square feet
Second Floor: 1,363 square feet
Total: 4,170 square feet

L **D**

● Grand traditional design comes to the forefront in this elegant two-story. From the dramatic front entry with curving double stairs to the less formal gathering room with fireplace and terrace access, this plan accommodates family lifestyles. Notice the split-bedroom plan with the master suite on the first floor and family bedrooms upstairs. A four-car garage handles the largest of family fleets.

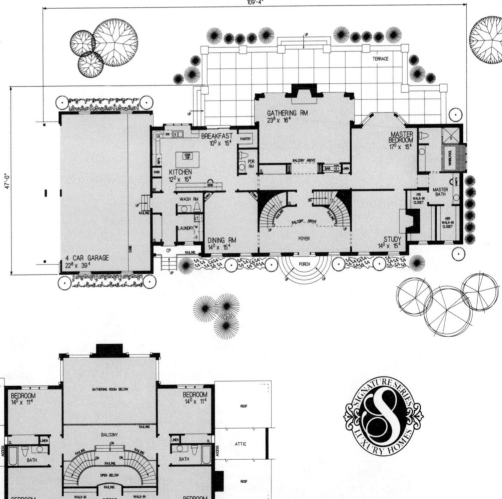

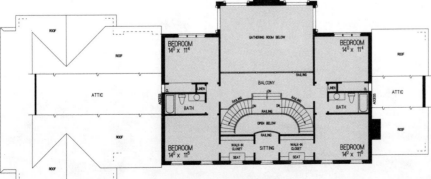

STORAGE
18⁴ x 18⁸

POTENTIAL PLAYROOM, STUDIO, GUEST ROOM
22⁸ x 18⁸

ROOF

BED RM - SITTING RM. 15⁴ x 10²

BATH

DRESSING RM.

BED RM. 16⁰ x 10²

VANITY

BATH

MASTER BED RM. 18⁴ x 12¹⁰

HALL

BED RM. 16⁰ x 12¹⁰

78'-4"

Design V22556

First Floor: 1,675 square feet
Second Floor: 1,472 square feet
Total: 3,147 square feet

44'-4"

TERRACE

PORCH

FAMILY RM. 18⁴ x 15⁶

NOOK 12² x 13²

KITCHEN 14⁶ x 13²

RANGE

LAUNDRY

PORCH

RAISED HEARTH

CABINET
BOOKS
BOOKS
CABINET

PDR. RM.

PANTRY

CHINA CABINET

SERV. ENT.

GARAGE 23⁴ x 21⁴

LIVING RM. 18⁴ x 12¹⁰

ENTRY

DINING RM. 16⁰ x 12¹⁰

PORCH

Design V22600

First Floor: 1,408 square feet
Second Floor: 1,408 square feet
Total: 2,816 square feet

● Here are two full stories of excellently planned living space. A third floor is available if the extra space is needed.

67'-8"

TERRACE

DINING RM.
13'⁰ x 13'⁴

BREAKFAST RM.
10'⁰ x 11'⁰

KITCHEN
12'⁰ x 11'⁰

LAUNDRY

GARAGE
23' x 23'⁴

40'-0"

PANTRY

RANGE

OVENS

PDR. RM.

HALL

WOOD BOX

LIVING RM.
17'⁴ x 15'⁴

ENTRANCE HALL

BEAMED CEILING

FAMILY RM.
15' x 20'²

PORCH

MASTER BED RM.
17'⁴ x 14'⁴

VANITY

BATH

BATH

LINEN

BED RM.
12'⁰ x 14'⁴

ATTIC STORAGE

BOOKS

CABINET

WALK-IN CLOSET

BED RM.
17'⁴ x 12'⁰

STAIR HALL

BED RM.
15'⁴ x 13'⁴

Design V23367

First Floor: 3,634 square feet
Second Floor: 1,450 square feet
Total: 5,084 square feet

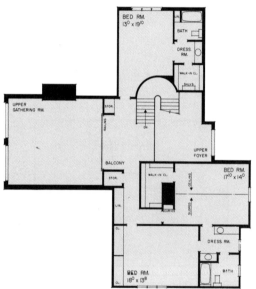

● This may be the perfect plan for you if your proposed building site is narrow but quite deep. Notice that the entire width of the home is only 64', while the depth is over 100'. The floor plan loses nothing to this unusual scheme. First-floor living areas include a two-story gathering room, more casual keeping room (note fireplaces in both rooms), media room (another fireplace!), dining room with bow window, and kitchen with butler's pantry. The handy service entrance off the garage has a huge walk-in closet, washroom, and laundry area. The master bedroom on this level has a sloped ceiling and His and Hers walk-ins. Three family bedrooms are upstairs. One of these has its own private bath; the other two share a full bath.

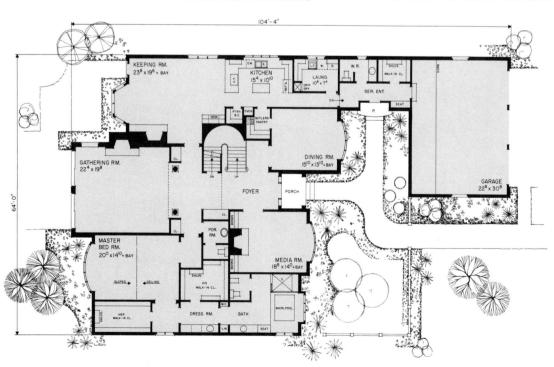

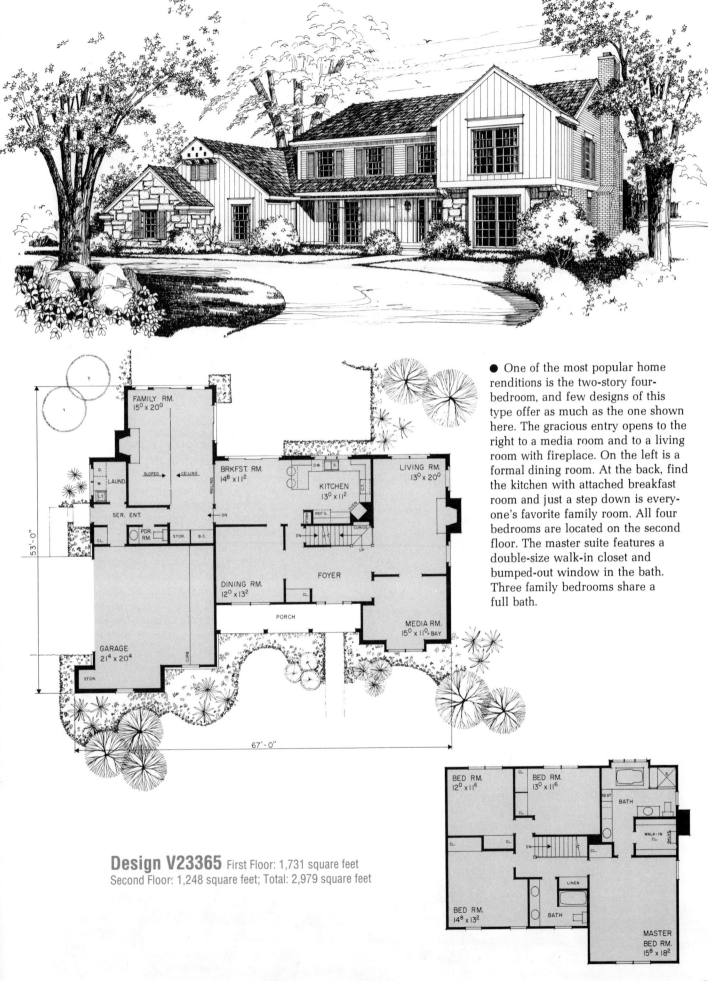

One of the most popular home renditions is the two-story four-bedroom, and few designs of this type offer as much as the one shown here. The gracious entry opens to the right to a media room and to a living room with fireplace. On the left is a formal dining room. At the back, find the kitchen with attached breakfast room and just a step down is everyone's favorite family room. All four bedrooms are located on the second floor. The master suite features a double-size walk-in closet and bumped-out window in the bath. Three family bedrooms share a full bath.

FAMILY RM.
15⁰ x 20⁰

LAUND.

SLOPED ← CEILING

BRKFST. RM.
14⁸ x 11²

KITCHEN
13⁰ x 11²

LIVING RM.
13⁰ x 20⁰

SER. ENT.

PDR. RM.

STOR.

B.C.

CURIOS

DINING RM.
12⁰ x 13²

FOYER

PORCH

MEDIA RM.
15⁰ x 11⁰+ BAY

GARAGE
21⁴ x 20⁴

STOR.

53'-0"

67'-0"

Design V23365 First Floor: 1,731 square feet
Second Floor: 1,248 square feet; Total: 2,979 square feet

BED RM.
12⁰ x 11⁶

BED RM.
13⁰ x 11⁶

BATH

WALK-IN CL.

BED RM.
14⁸ x 13²

LINEN

BATH

MASTER BED RM.
15⁸ x 18²

Design V22695 First Floor: 2,058 square feet
Second Floor: 1,181 square feet; Total: 3,239 square feet

● This is a house style that was common to Tidewater, Virginia during the 18th Century. The gambrel roof, projecting dormers, and end chimneys were highly indentifiable architectural features of the period. This house takes a huge leap from the past with the addition of a first floor master bedroom suite. With three bedrooms upstairs, one with private bath, the first floor could accommodate a live-in relative in fine fashion. The projecting rear bay windows add an extra measure of light and livability.

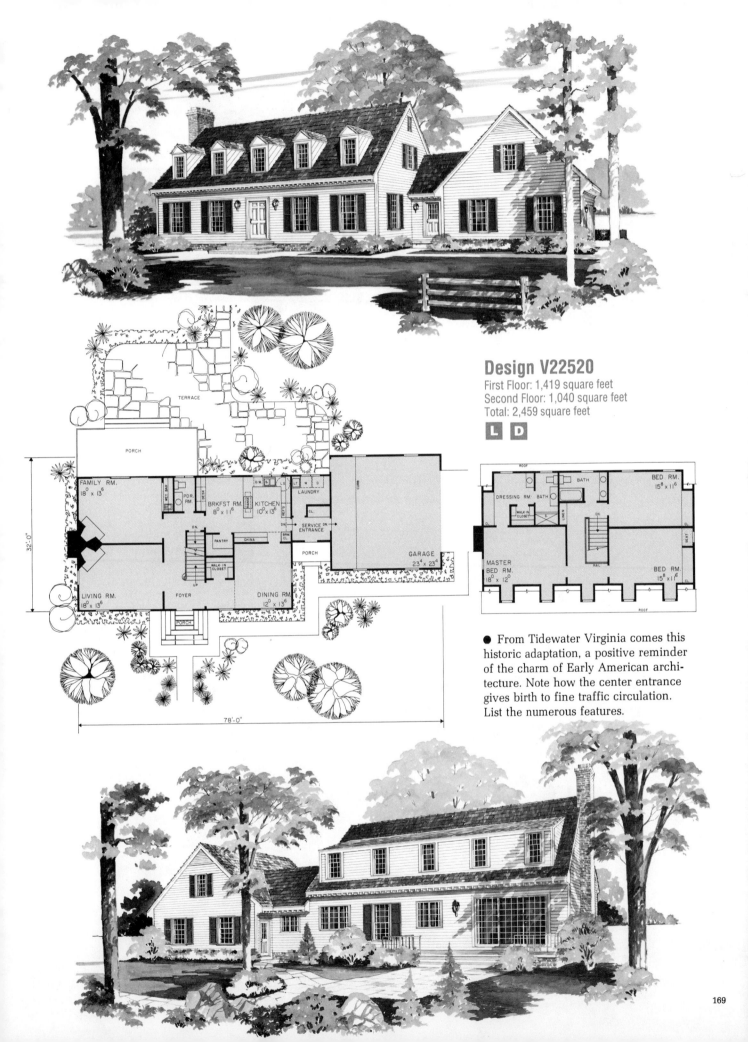

Design V22520
First Floor: 1,419 square feet
Second Floor: 1,040 square feet
Total: 2,459 square feet

L **D**

● From Tidewater Virginia comes this historic adaptation, a positive reminder of the charm of Early American architecture. Note how the center entrance gives birth to fine traffic circulation. List the numerous features.

169

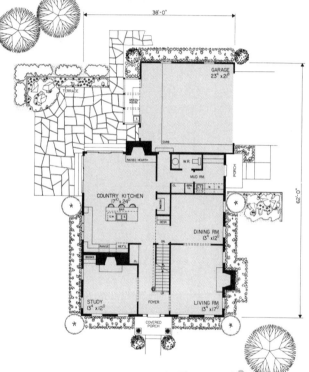

● The memory of Noah Webster's house, built in 1823, in New Hampshire is recalled by this Greek Revival adaptation. A picture home for a narrow site, it delivers big-house livability. In addition to the formal living and dining rooms, there is the huge country kitchen and handy mud room. There is also a study. Upstairs, four bedrooms and three full baths. Don't miss the four fireplaces or the outdoor balcony of the master bedroom. A basement provides additional space for recreation and the pursuit of hobbies.

Design V22979 First Floor: 1,440 square feet
Second Floor: 1,394 square feet; Total: 2,834 square feet

SOUTHERN COLONIAL VERSIONS . . .

and more Georgian adaptations are featured in this section. Stately Greek Revival columns supporting projecting pediment gables have become symbols of gracious living. Other variations of this theme are hardly less dramatic as evidenced by winged two-story houses. (The formal Georgian designs are enhanced by the massive twin chimneys, symmetrical window arrangement, and appealing front entrance detailing. Brick quoins, dentils, carriage lamps, recessed entrances, and cupolas are among the other attractive features.)

Design V22889
First Floor: 2,529 square feet
Second Floor: 1,872 square feet
Total: 4,401 square feet

L D

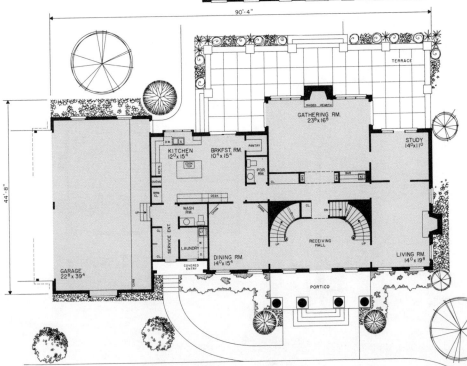

● This is truly classical, Georgian design at its best. Some of the exterior highlights of this two-story include the pediment gable with cornice work and dentils, the beautifully proportioned columns, the front door detailing and the window treatment. These are just some of the features which make this design so unique and appealing. Behind the facade of this design is an equally elegant interior. Imagine greeting your guests in the large receiving hall. It is graced by two curving staircases and opens to the formal living and dining rooms. Beyond the living room is the study. It has access to the rear terrace. Those large, informal occasions for family get-togethers or entertaining will be enjoyed in the spacious gathering room. It has a centered fireplace flanked by windows on each side, access to the terrace and a wet bar. Your appreciation for this room will be never-ending. The work center is efficient: the kitchen with island cook top, breakfast room, washroom, laundry and service entrance. The second floor also is outstanding. Three family bedrooms and two full baths are joined by the feature-filled master bedroom suite. Study this area carefully. If you like this basic floor plan but would prefer a French exterior, see Design V22543 on page 215.

Design V22987

First Floor: 2,822 square feet
Second Floor: 1,335 square feet
Total: 4,157 square feet

● Andrew Jackson's dream of white-pillared splendor resulted in the building of The Hermitage. The essence of that grand dream is recaptured in this modern variation. One wing of the first floor contains a luxurious master suite which accommodates everyone's needs gracefully. The opposite wing features a country kitchen, laundry, washroom and two-car garage. The family room, dining room and living room are centrally located. On the second floor are three bedrooms (one a guest room) and one and a half baths.

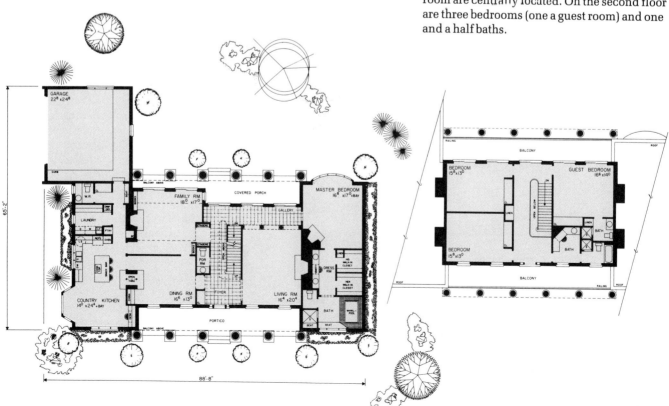

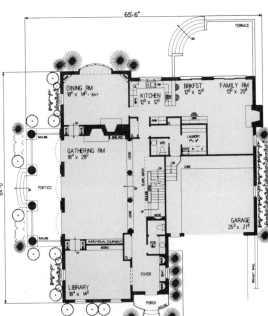

Design V22993

First Floor: 2,440 square feet
Second Floor: 2,250 square feet
Total: 4,690 square feet

● This dramatically columned home delivers beautiful proportions and great livability on two levels. The main area of the house, the first floor, holds a gathering room, library, family room, dining room and gourmet kitchen. The master bedroom features a whirlpool tub and through fireplace. Two family bedrooms on the second floor share a full bath. A fourth bedroom is the perfect guest bedroom with its own private bath.

Design V22984

First Floor: 3,116 square feet
Second Floor: 1,997 square feet
Total: 5,113 square feet

● An echo of Whitehall, built in
1765 in Anne Arundel County,
Maryland, resounds in this home.
Its classic symmetry and columned
facade herald a grand interior.
There's no lack of space whether
entertaining formally or just enjoying a family get-together, and all
are kept cozy with fireplaces in
the gathering room, study, and
family room. An island kitchen
with attached breakfast room
handily serves the nearby dining
room. Four second floor bedrooms
include a large master suite with
another fireplace, a whirlpool, and
His and Hers closets in the bath.
Three more full baths are found
on this floor.

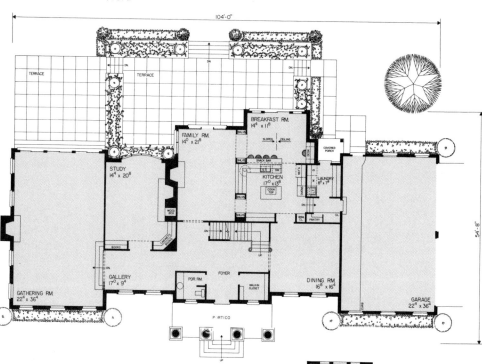

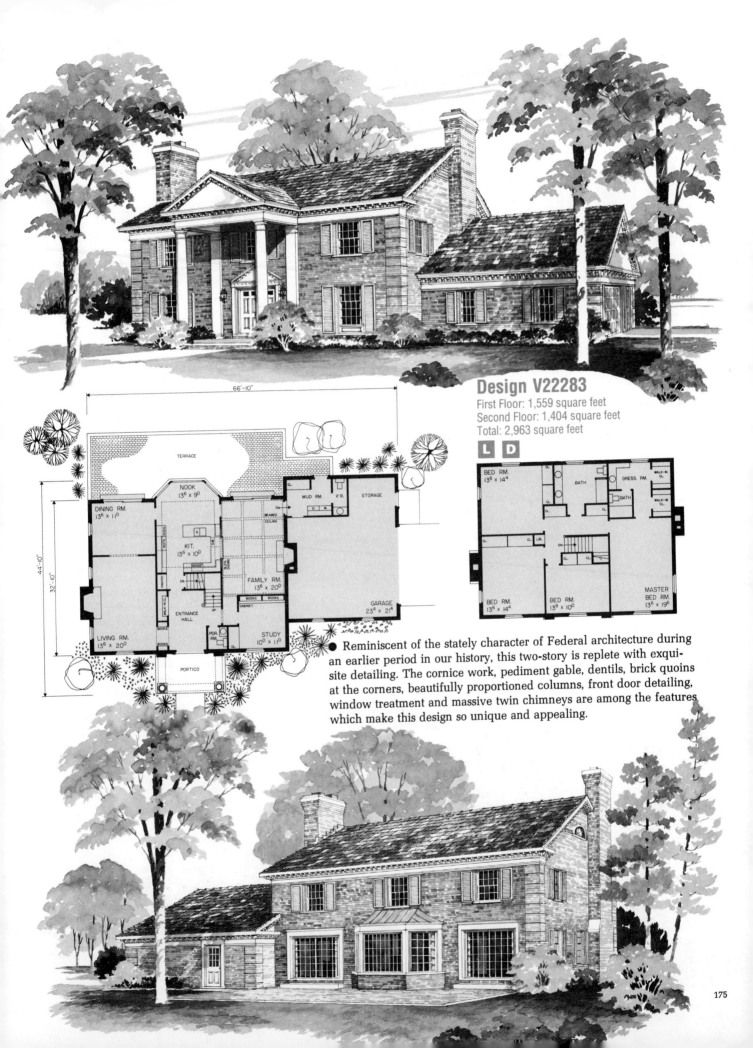

Design V22283
First Floor: 1,559 square feet
Second Floor: 1,404 square feet
Total: 2,963 square feet

L D

● Reminiscent of the stately character of Federal architecture during an earlier period in our history, this two-story is replete with exqui-site detailing. The cornice work, pediment gable, dentils, brick quoins at the corners, beautifully proportioned columns, front door detailing, window treatment and massive twin chimneys are among the features which make this design so unique and appealing.

Floor plan labels (first floor):
66'-10"
44'-10"
32'-10"
TERRACE
NOOK 13⁶ x 9⁰
DINING RM. 13⁶ x 11⁰
MUD RM.
V'R.
STORAGE
BEAMED CEILING
KIT. 13⁶ x 10⁰
RANGE
FAMILY RM. 13⁶ x 20⁰
GARAGE 23⁴ x 21⁴
ENTRANCE HALL
BOOKS
CABINET
PDR. RM.
STUDY 10⁰ x 11⁰
LIVING RM. 13⁶ x 20⁰
PORTICO

Floor plan labels (second floor):
BED RM. 13⁶ x 14⁴
BATH
DRESS. RM.
WALK-IN
BATH
WALK-IN
BED RM. 13⁶ x 14⁴
BED RM. 13⁸ x 10⁰
MASTER BED RM. 13⁶ x 19⁶

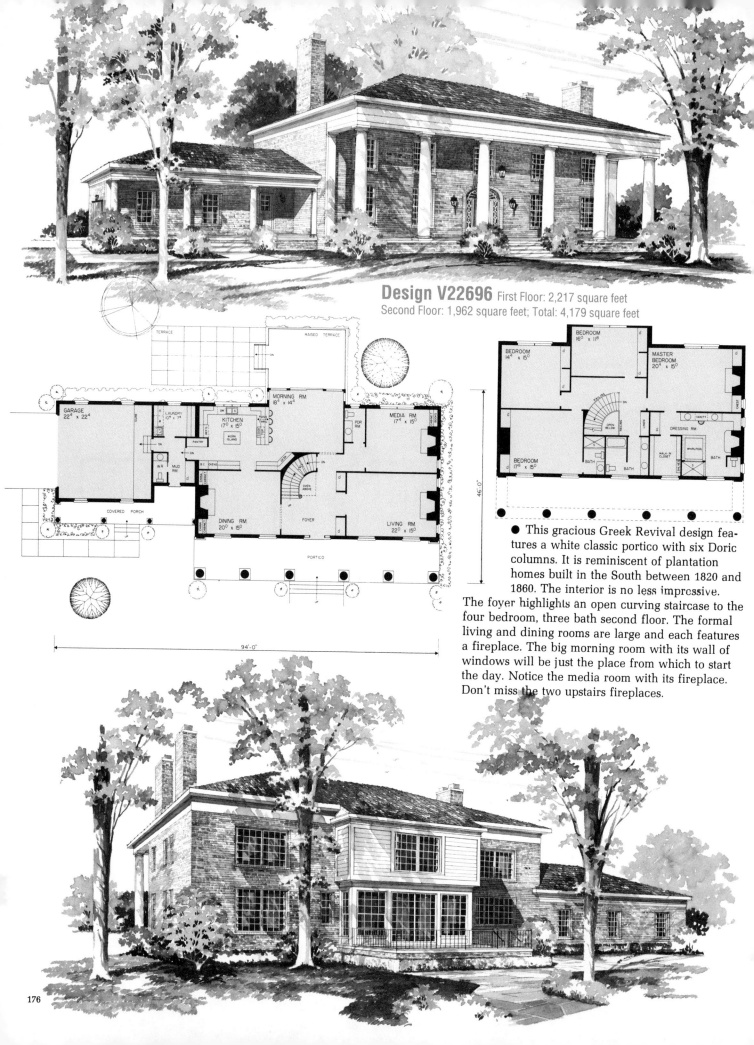

Design V22696 First Floor: 2,217 square feet
Second Floor: 1,962 square feet; Total: 4,179 square feet

● This gracious Greek Revival design features a white classic portico with six Doric columns. It is reminiscent of plantation homes built in the South between 1820 and 1860. The interior is no less impressive. The foyer highlights an open curving staircase to the four bedroom, three bath second floor. The formal living and dining rooms are large and each features a fireplace. The big morning room with its wall of windows will be just the place from which to start the day. Notice the media room with its fireplace. Don't miss the two upstairs fireplaces.

Design V22230

First Floor: 2,288 square feet
Second Floor: 1,863 square feet
Total: 4,151 square feet

● The gracefulness and appeal of this southern adaptation will be everlasting. The imposing two-story portico is truly dramatic. Notice the authentic detailing of the tapered Doric columns, the balustraded roof deck, the denticulated cornice, the front entrance and the shuttered windows. The architecture of the rear is no less appealing with its formal symmetry and smaller Doric portico. The impressive exterior of this two-story houses a total of 4,151 square feet. The spacious, formal front entrance hall provides a fitting introduction to the scale and elegance of the interior.

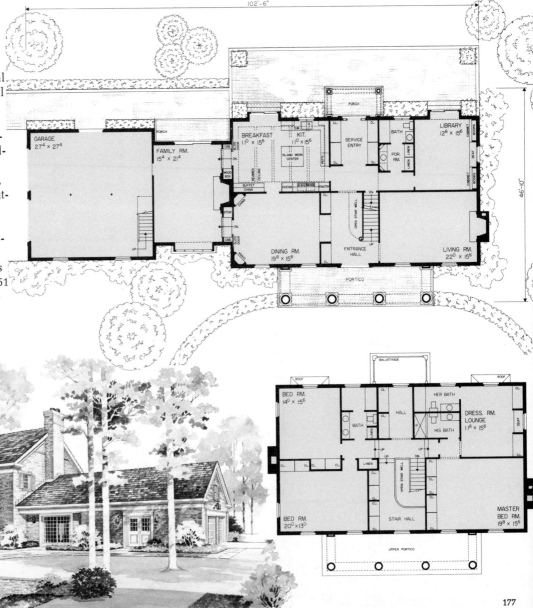

Design V23320

First Floor: 2,337 square feet
Second Floor: 1,232 square feet
Total: 3,569 square feet

● What a grand impression this home makes! A spacious two-story foyer with circular staircase greets visitors and leads to the dining room, media room and two-story gathering room with fireplace. The well-equipped kitchen includes a snack bar for informal meals. A luxurious master suite downstairs and four bedrooms upstairs complete this impressive plan.

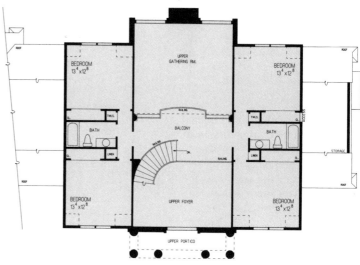

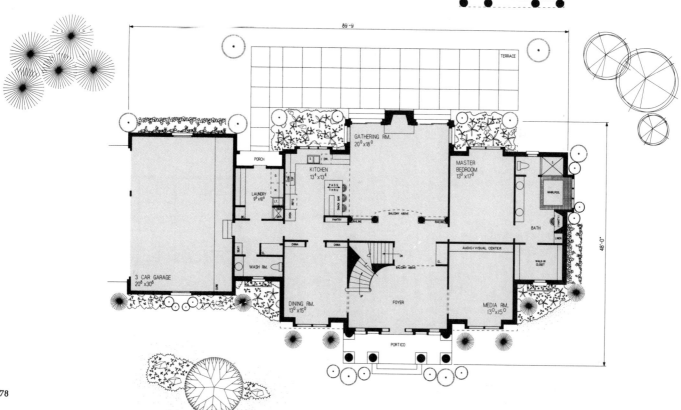

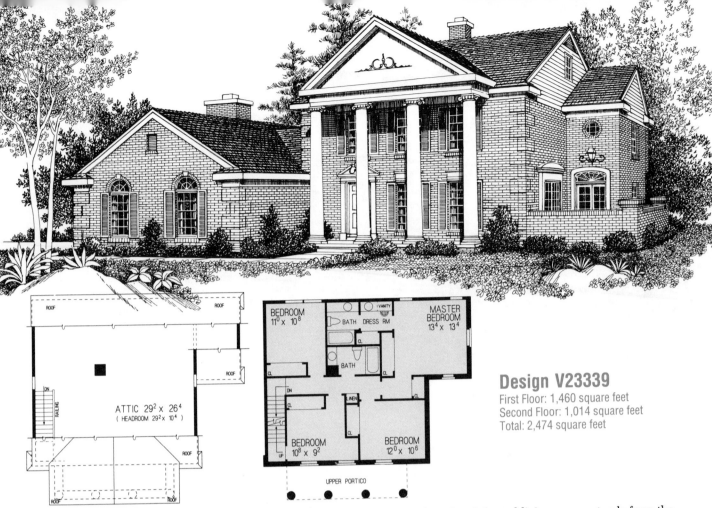

ATTIC 29² x 26⁴
(HEADROOM 29² x 10⁴)

ROOF | ROOF

DN

RAILING

ROOF

ROOF | ROOF

BEDROOM 11⁰ x 10⁸

VANITY

BATH DRESS RM

MASTER BEDROOM 13⁴ x 13⁴

BATH

CL

DN

LINEN

CL

BEDROOM 10⁸ x 9²

UP

BEDROOM 12⁰ x 10⁶

UPPER PORTICO

Design V23339

First Floor: 1,460 square feet
Second Floor: 1,014 square feet
Total: 2,474 square feet

● This Colonial four-bedroom features the livable kind of plan you're looking for. A formal living room extends from the front foyer and leads to the formal dining area and nearby kitchen. A sunken family room has a raised-hearth fireplace. Three family bedrooms share a bath and are joined by the master bedroom with its own full bath.

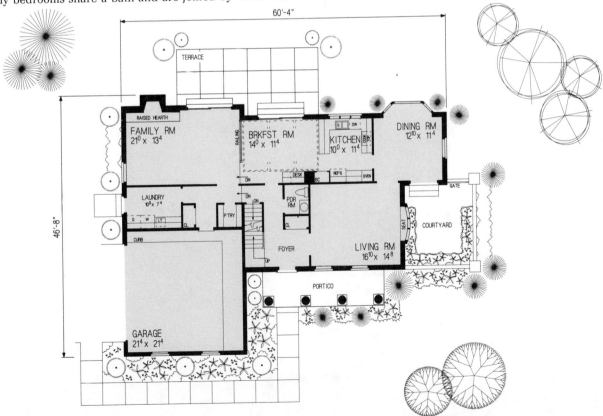

60'-4"

46'-8"

TERRACE

RAISED HEARTH

FAMILY RM 21⁰ x 13⁴

RAILING

BRKFST RM 14⁴ x 11⁴

KITCHEN 10⁰ x 11⁴

DW

DINING RM 12¹⁰ x 11⁴

DESK

REF'G

OVEN

BC

LAUNDRY 10⁰ x 7⁴

DN

DN

PDR RM

GATE

SEAT

COURTYARD

CURB

P'TRY

CL

FOYER

UP

LIVING RM 16¹⁰ x 14⁸

GARAGE 21⁴ x 21⁴

PORTICO

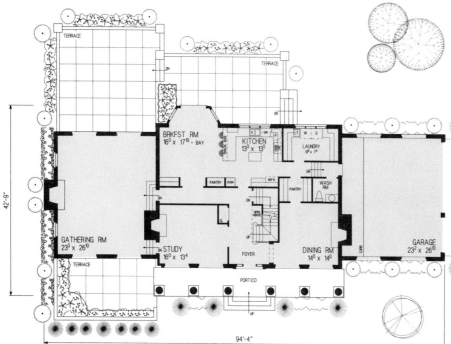

Design V23337

First Floor: 2,167 square feet
Second Floor: 1,992 square feet
Total: 4,159 square feet

● The elegant facade of this design with its columned portico, fanlights, and dormers houses an amenity-filled interior. The gathering room, study and dining room, each with fireplace, provide plenty of room for relaxing and entertaining. A large work area contains a kitchen with breakfast room and snack bar, laundry room and pantry. The four-bedroom upstairs includes a master suite with a sumptuous bath and an exercise room.

Design V23303

First Floor: 2,563 square feet
Second Floor: 1,496 square feet
Total: 4,059 square feet

● With its stately columns and one-story wings, this design is a fine representation of 18th Century adaptations. Formal living and dining areas flank the entry foyer at the front of the home. Look for a fireplace in the living room, china cabinet built-ins in the dining room. More casual living dominates the back section in a family room and kitchen/breakfast room combination that features access to the rear terrace and plenty of space for cooking and informal dining. The left wing garage is connected to the main structure by a service entrance adjacent to the laundry. The right wing contains the private master suite. Four second floor bedrooms share two full baths and each has its own walk-in closet.

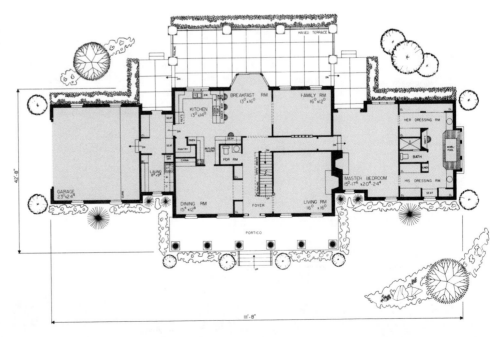

A Mount Vernon Reminiscence

● This magnificent manor's streetview illustrates a centralized mansion connected by curving galleries to matching wings. What a grand presentation this home will make! The origin of this house dates back to 1787 and George Washington's stately Mount Vernon. The underlying aesthetics for this design come from the rational balancing of porticoes, fenestration and chimneys. The rear elevation of this home also deserves mention. Six two-story columns, along with four sets of French doors, highlight this view. Study all of the intricate detailing that is featured all around these exteriors.

The flanking wings create a large formal courtyard where guests of today can park their cars. This home, designed from architecture of the past, is efficient and compact enough to fit many suburban lots. Its interior has been well planned and is ready to serve a family of any size.

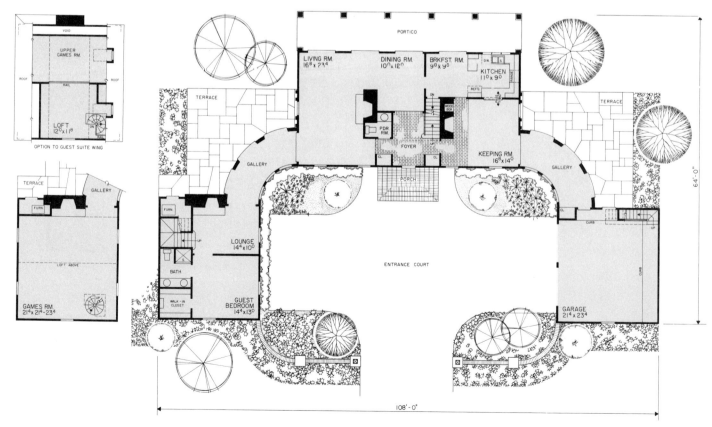

Design V22665 First Floor: 1,152 square feet; Second Floor: 1,152 square feet
Total: 2,304 square feet (Excludes Guest Suite and Galleries)

● The main, two-story section of this home houses the living areas. First - there is the large, tiled foyer with two closets and powder room. Then there is the living room which is the entire width of the house. This room has a fireplace and leads into the formal dining room. Three sets of double French doors lead to the rear portico from this formal area. The kitchen and breakfast room will function together. There is a pass-thru from the kitchen to the keeping room. All of the sleeping facilities, four bedrooms, are on the second floor. The gallery on the right leads to the garage; the one on the left, to a lounge and guest suite with studio above. The square footage quoted above does not include the guest suite or gallery areas. The first floor of the guest suite contains 688 sq. ft.; the second floor studio, 306 sq. ft. The optional plan shows a game room with a loft above having 162 sq. ft.

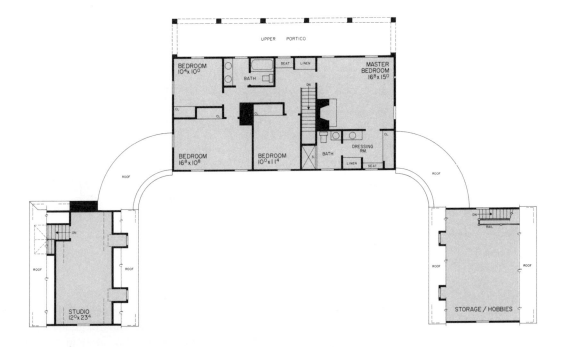

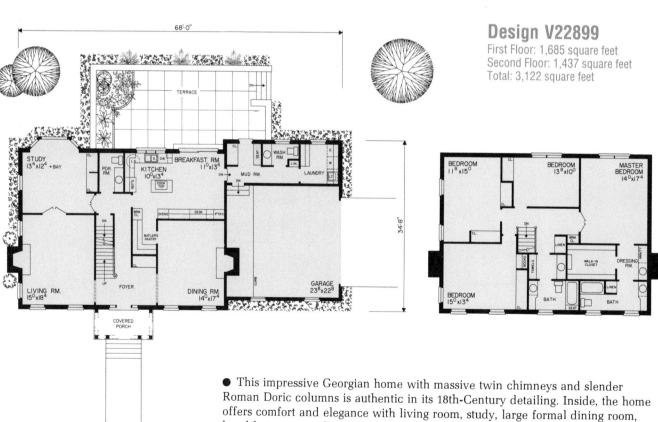

Design V22899

First Floor: 1,685 square feet
Second Floor: 1,437 square feet
Total: 3,122 square feet

First Floor (dimensions and rooms):

68'-0"
34'-8"

TERRACE

STUDY 13⁴x12⁴ +BAY
PDR. RM.
KITCHEN 10⁰x13⁴
COOK TOP
BREAKFAST RM. 11⁰x13⁴
MUD RM.
WASH RM.
SEAT
LAUNDRY
BRM CL.
OVENS
DESK
P'TRY
BUTLER'S PANTRY
LIVING RM. 15⁰x18⁴
FOYER
DINING RM. 14⁰x17⁴
GARAGE 23⁸x22⁸
COVERED PORCH

Second Floor:

BEDROOM 11⁸x15⁰
BEDROOM 13⁸x10⁰
MASTER BEDROOM 14⁰x17⁴
LINEN
BOOKS
TOWELS
BRM CL.
WALK-IN CLOSET
DRESSING RM.
VANITY
BATH
SEAT
BATH
LINEN
BEDROOM 15⁰x13⁴

● This impressive Georgian home with massive twin chimneys and slender Roman Doric columns is authentic in its 18th-Century detailing. Inside, the home offers comfort and elegance with living room, study, large formal dining room, breakfast room, and even a butler's pantry. Smooth traffic flow is enhanced by a central foyer that opens to stairs leading to the second story. Downstairs there's also a mud room adjacent to the laundry. Upstairs is thoughtfully zoned, too, with a central bath to accommodate a master bedroom and three other bedrooms there.

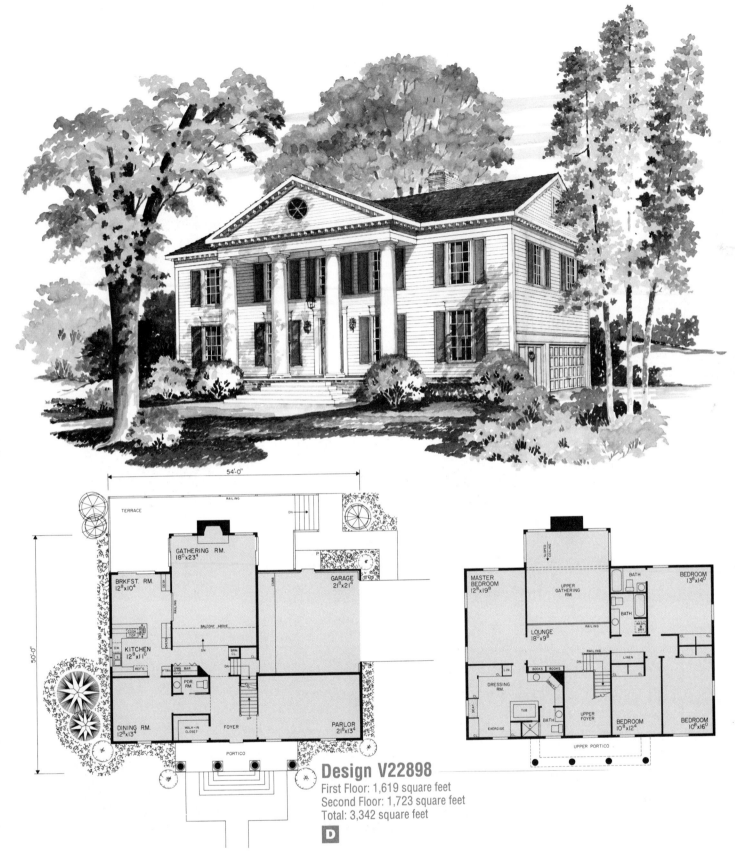

Design V22898

First Floor: 1,619 square feet
Second Floor: 1,723 square feet
Total: 3,342 square feet

D

● Four soaring Doric columns highlight the exterior of this Greek Revival dwelling. The elevation reflects a balanced design that incorporates four bedrooms and a two-car garage in one central unit. The stylish heart of this dwelling is a two-story gathering room. A balcony lounge on the second floor offers a quiet aerie overlooking this living area. Both of these areas will have sunlight streaming through the high windows. A second living area is the parlor. It could serve as the formal area whereas the gathering room could be considered informal. Entrance to all of these areas will be through the foyer. It has an adjacent powder room and spacious walk-in closet. The U-shaped kitchen will conveniently serve the breakfast and dining rooms. Second floor livability is outstanding. Study all of the features in the master bedroom: dressing room, tub and shower, large vanity and exercise area. Three more bedrooms, another has a private bath which would make it an ideal guest room.

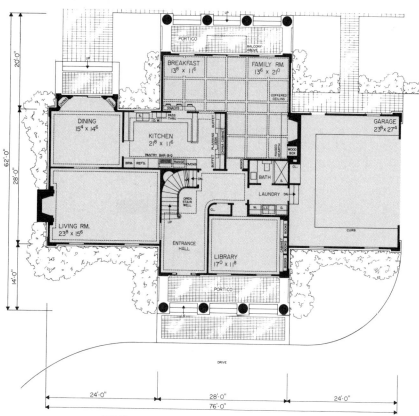

DINING
15⁴ x 14⁶

BREAKFAST
13⁸ x 11⁶

FAMILY RM.
13⁶ x 21⁰

COFFERED CEILING

KITCHEN
21⁸ x 11⁶

GARAGE
23⁸ x 27⁴

LIVING RM.
23⁸ x 15⁶

BATH

LAUNDRY

OPEN STAIR WELL

CURB

ENTRANCE HALL

LIBRARY
17⁰ x 11⁸

PORTICO

PORTICO

BALCONY ABOVE

DRIVE

24'-0"   28'-0"   24'-0"
76'-0"

20'-0"
62'-0"
28'-0"
14'-0"

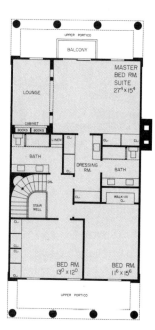

UPPER PORTICO
BALCONY

LOUNGE

MASTER BED RM. SUITE
27⁴ x 15⁴

CABINET
BOOKS   BOOKS

LINEN

BATH

DRESSING RM.

BATH

STAIR WELL

WALK-IN CL.

BED RM.
13⁰ x 12⁰

BED RM.
11⁶ x 15⁶

UPPER PORTICO

Design V22184
First Floor: 1,999 square feet
Second Floor: 1,288 square feet
Total: 3,287 square feet

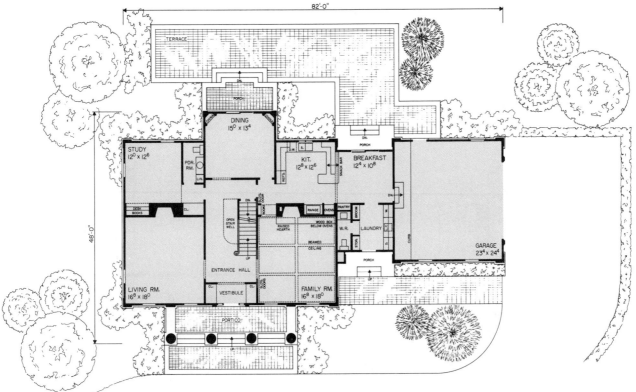

Design V22185 First Floor: 1,916 square feet
Second Floor: 1,564 square feet; Total: 3,480 square feet

● The elements of Greek Revival architecture when adapted to present day standards can be impressive, indeed. A study of this floor plan will reveal its similarity to that on the opposite page. There is a vestibule which leads to a wonderfully spacious entrance hall. The open stairwell is most dramatic. As it affords a view of the four bedroom, two bath second floor. The study and family room will be favorite spots for family relaxation. Both the dining and living rooms can be made to function as formally as you wish.

Design V22668 First Floor: 1,206 square feet
Second Floor: 1,254 square feet; Total: 2,460 square feet

● This elegant exterior houses a very livable plan. Every bit of space has been put to good use. The front country kitchen is a good place to begin. It is efficiently planned with its island cook top, built-ins and pass-thru to the dining room. The large great room will be the center of all family activities. Quiet times can be enjoyed in the front library. Study the second floor sleeping areas.

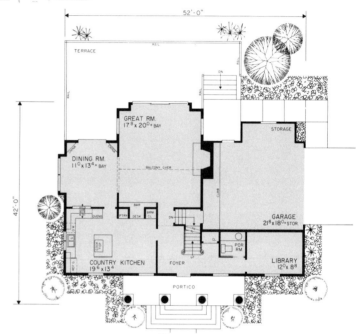

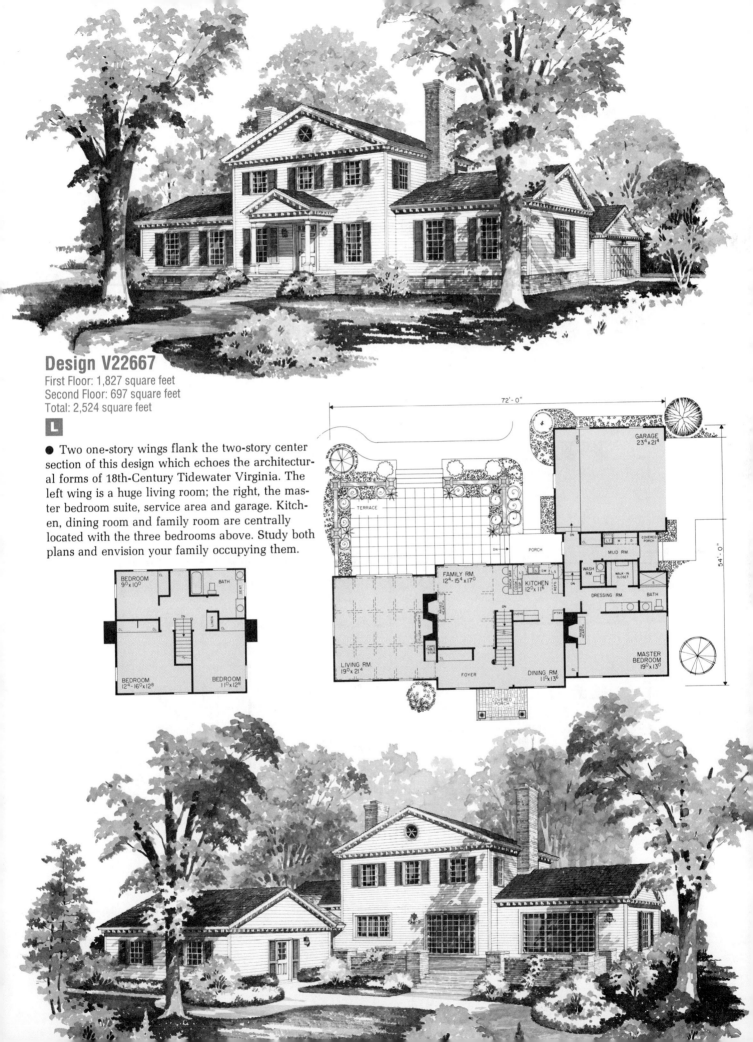

Design V22667

First Floor: 1,827 square feet
Second Floor: 697 square feet
Total: 2,524 square feet

L

● Two one-story wings flank the two-story center section of this design which echoes the architectural forms of 18th-Century Tidewater Virginia. The left wing is a huge living room; the right, the master bedroom suite, service area and garage. Kitchen, dining room and family room are centrally located with the three bedrooms above. Study both plans and envision your family occupying them.

BEDROOM 9⁰ x 10⁰
BATH
BEDROOM 12⁴-16⁰ x 12⁸
BEDROOM 11⁰ x 12⁸

72'-0"

54'-0"

GARAGE 23⁴ x 21⁴
COVERED PORCH
MUD RM.
WASH RM.
WALK-IN CLOSET
TERRACE
PORCH
FAMILY RM. 12⁴-15⁴ x 17⁰
KITCHEN 12⁰ x 11⁶
DRESSING RM.
BATH
OVENS
LIVING RM. 19⁰ x 21⁴
FOYER
DINING RM. 11⁰ x 13⁶
MASTER BEDROOM 19⁰ x 13⁰
COVERED PORCH

Design V22924

First Floor: 1,520 square feet
Second Floor: 1,352 square feet
Total: 2,872 square feet

MASTER BEDROOM
21⁰ x 13⁰

OPEN BELOW

WALK-IN CLOSET

BATH

WHIRLPOOL

RAILING

DN.

STORAGE

CL.

BEDROOM
15⁰ x 12⁰

CL.

LINEN

CL.

CL.

BATH

BEDROOM
13⁰ x 13⁰

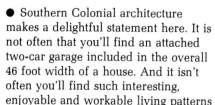

BALCONY

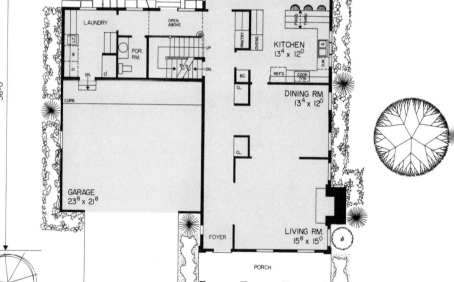

46'-0"

56'-0"

TERRACE

FAMILY RM.
21⁰ x 15⁴

LAUNDRY

OPEN ABOVE

PASS THRU

PANTRY

OVENS

KITCHEN
13⁴ x 12⁰

POR. RM.

UP

REF'G

COOK TOP

DN.

B.C.

DINING RM.
13⁴ x 12⁰

CURB

CL.

GARAGE
23⁸ x 21⁸

CL.

FOYER

LIVING RM.
15⁸ x 15⁰

PORCH

UP

● Southern Colonial architecture makes a delightful statement here. It is not often that you'll find an attached two-car garage included in the overall 46 foot width of a house. And it isn't often you'll find such interesting, enjoyable and workable living patterns as those found here. There are formal and informal living areas, a separate formal dining room and an informal snack bar. Then there is the fine laundry room with the handy powder room. A curving open stairway leads to the upstairs. Here three large bedrooms are to be found. The master bath has an impressive whirlpool plus a stall shower. A second bath with twin lavatories serve the two children's bedrooms. The master bedroom has its own fireplace. This design also has a basement for recreation space.

Design V23333
First Floor: 1,584 square feet
Second Floor: 1,344 square feet
Total: 2,928 square feet

● This Southern Colonial adaptation boasts an up-to-date floor plan which caters to the needs of today's families. The entrance hall is flanked by formal and informal living areas: to the left a spacious living room and connecting dining room, to the right a cozy study and family room. A large kitchen with bay-windowed morning room is convenient to both the dining and family rooms. The upstairs sleeping area includes four bedrooms.

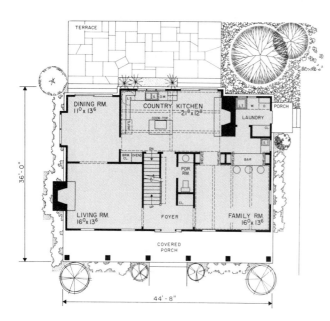

TERRACE

DINING RM.
11⁰ x 13⁶

COUNTRY KITCHEN
21⁸ x 12⁸

COOK-TOP

LAUNDRY

PORCH

36' - 0"

BRM OVEN CL.

DN

PDR. RM.

BAR

LIVING RM.
16⁰ x 13⁶

UP

FOYER

FAMILY RM.
16⁰ x 13⁶

COVERED PORCH

44' - 8"

● The exterior of this full two-story is highlighted by the covered porch and balcony. Many enjoyable hours will be spent at these outdoor areas. The interior is highlighted by a spacious country kitchen. Be sure to notice its island cook-top, fireplace and the beamed ceiling. A built-in bar is in the family room.

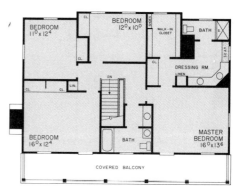

BEDROOM
11⁰ x 12⁴

BEDROOM
12⁰ x 10⁰

WALK-IN CLOSET

BATH

DRESSING RM.

LINEN

DN

BEDROOM
16⁰ x 12⁴

BATH

MASTER BEDROOM
16⁰ x 13⁶

COVERED BALCONY

Design V22664 First Floor: 1,308 square feet
Second Floor: 1,262 square feet; Total: 2,570 square feet

D

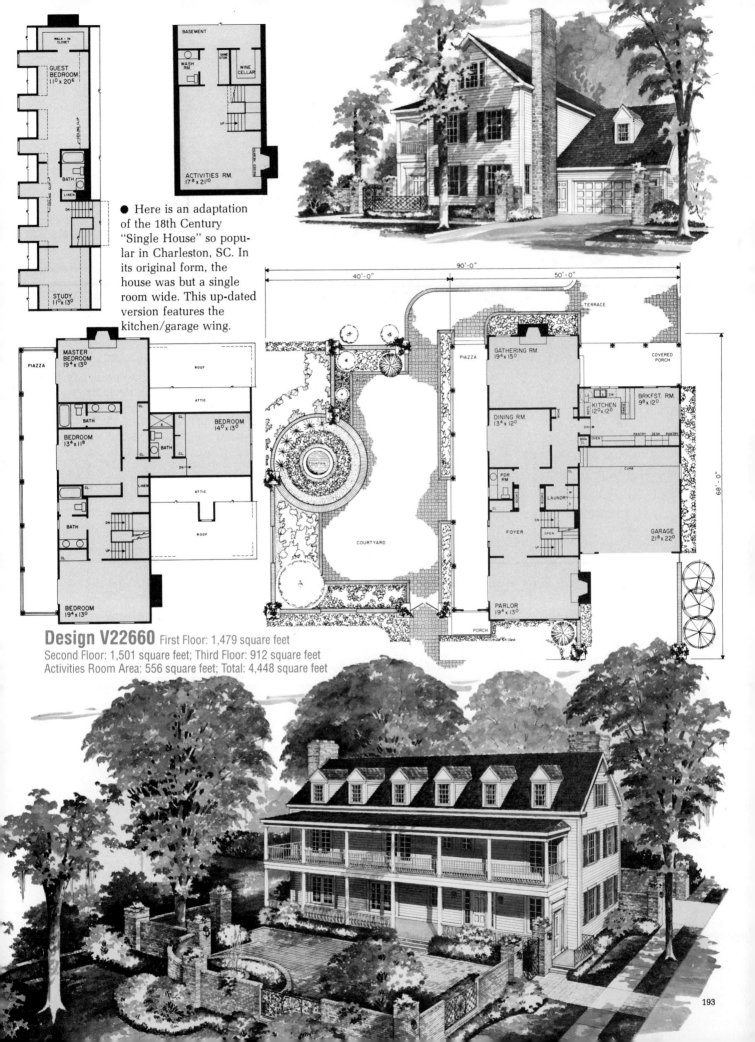

WALK-IN CLOSET

GUEST BEDROOM
11⁰ x 20⁶

BATH

LINEN

DN

STUDY
11⁰ x 13⁰

BASEMENT

WASH RM.

GAME STOR.

WINE CELLAR

UP

RAISED HEARTH

ACTIVITIES RM.
17⁸ x 21¹⁰

● Here is an adaptation of the 18th Century "Single House" so popular in Charleston, SC. In its original form, the house was but a single room wide. This up-dated version features the kitchen/garage wing.

PIAZZA

MASTER BEDROOM
19⁴ x 13⁰

ROOF

ATTIC

BATH

CL

CL

BEDROOM
14⁰ x 13⁰

BEDROOM
13⁴ x 11⁸

BATH

LINEN

CL

DN

ATTIC

BATH

CL

DN

UP

ROOF

BEDROOM
19⁴ x 13⁰

40'-0"

90'-0"

50'-0"

TERRACE

PIAZZA

GATHERING RM.
19⁴ x 15⁰

COVERED PORCH

FOUNTAIN

DINING RM.
13⁴ x 12⁰

NICHE

KITCHEN
12⁰ x 12⁰

BRKFST. RM.
9⁸ x 12⁰

OVEN

PANTRY   DESK   PANTRY

PDR RM.

CL

BOOKS

BOOKS

LAUNDRY

CURB

COURTYARD

FOYER

OPEN

DN

UP

GARAGE
21⁸ x 22⁰

68'-0"

PARLOR
19⁴ x 13⁰

PORCH

Design V22660 First Floor: 1,479 square feet
Second Floor: 1,501 square feet; Third Floor: 912 square feet
Activities Room Area: 556 square feet; Total: 4,448 square feet

● A Southern Colonial adaptation under 2,000 square feet. The two projecting, one-story wings are devoted to the living room and garage. The two-story portion houses three bedrooms, 2½ baths, study, laundry, dining room and kitchen with eating area.

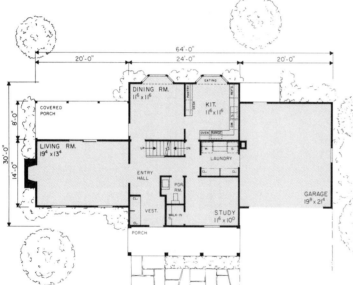

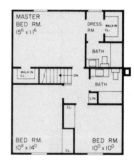

Design V22107
First Floor: 1,020 square feet
Second Floor: 720 square feet
Total: 1,740 square feet

Design V21773

First Floor: 1,546 square feet
Second Floor: 1,040 square feet
Total: 2,586 square feet

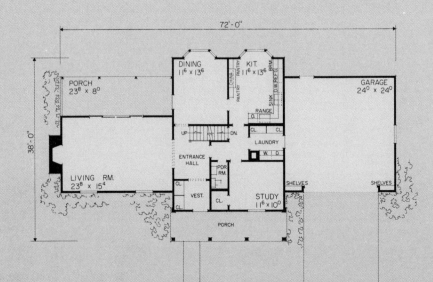

Design V21208

First Floor: 1,170 square feet
Second Floor: 768 square feet
Total: 1,938 square feet

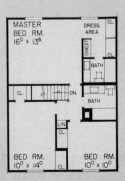

Design V22996 First Floor: 2,191 square feet
Second Floor: 1,928 square feet; Total: 4,119 square feet

● Covered porches upstairs and down are charming additions to the well appointed two-story. Four chimney stacks herald four hearths inside: living room, dining room, family room and study. The second floor holds four bedrooms including a master suite with its own fireplace and a huge walk-in closet.

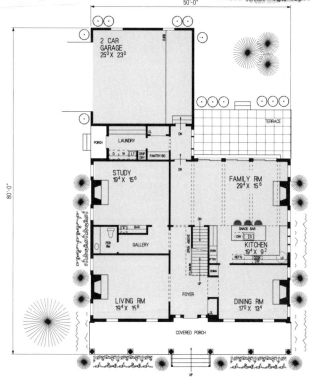

Design V22762

First Floor: 2,345 square feet
Second Floor: 1,016 square feet
Total: 3,361 square feet

● This home features a full apartment to the side to accommodate a live-in relative. The main house has all the features to ensure happiness for years to come. The three-car garage is sure to come in handy.

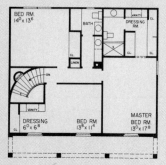

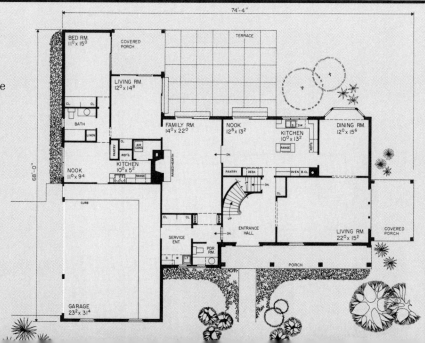

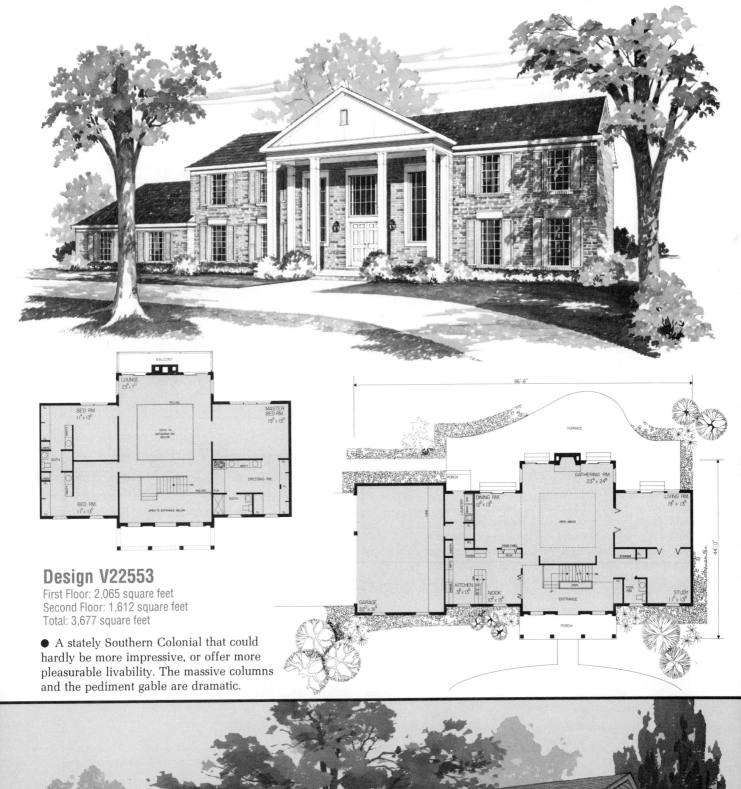

Design V22553

First Floor: 2,065 square feet
Second Floor: 1,612 square feet
Total: 3,677 square feet

● A stately Southern Colonial that could hardly be more impressive, or offer more pleasurable livability. The massive columns and the pediment gable are dramatic.

Design V22673

First Floor: 1,895 square feet
Second Floor: 1,661 square feet
Total: 3,556 square feet

● A two-story pillared entrance portico and tall multi-paned windows, flanking the double front doors, together accentuate the facade of this Southern Colonial design. This brick home is stately and classic in its exterior appeal. The three-car garage opens to the side so it does not disturb the street view. This is definitely a charming home that will stand strong for many years into the future. Not only is the exterior something to talk about, but so is the interior. Enter into the extremely spacious foyer and begin to discover what this home has to offer in the way of livability. Front, living and dining rooms are at each end of this foyer. The living room is complimented by a music room, or close it off and make it a bedroom. A full bath is nearby. The formal dining room will be easily served by the kitchen as will the breakfast room and snack bar. The family room is spacious and features a built-in wet bar which can be closed off by doors. An open, staircase leads to the second floor, four bedroom sleeping area.

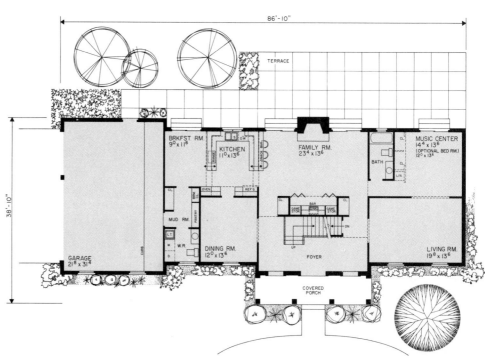

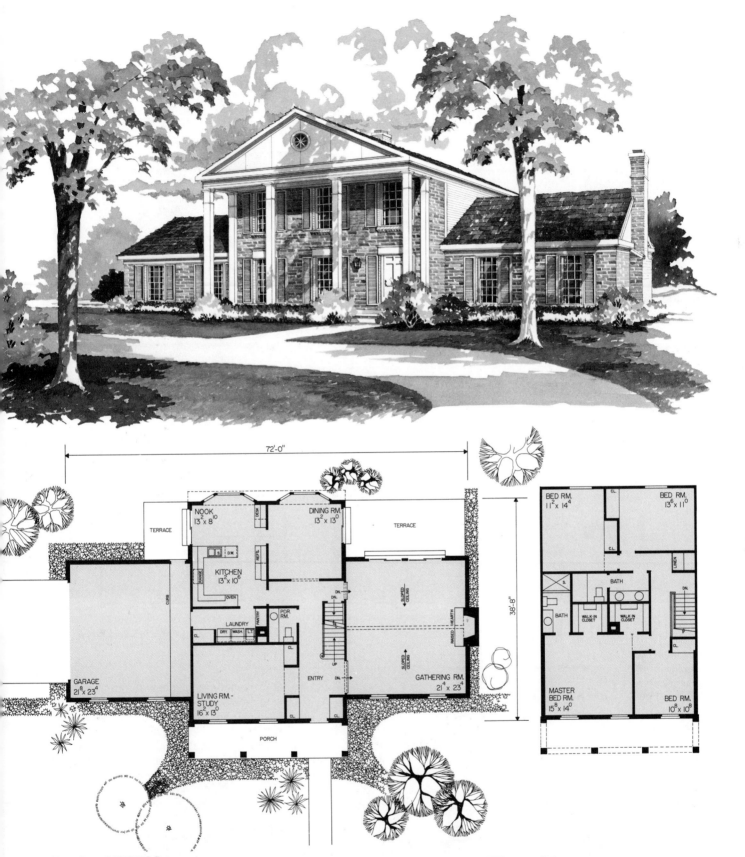

Design V22700 First Floor: 1,640 square feet; Second Floor: 1,129 square feet; Total: 2,769 square feet

● Southern Colonial grace! And much more. An elegant gathering room, more than 21' by 23' large. . . with sloped ceilings and a raised-hearth fireplace. Plus two sets of sliding glass doors that open onto the terrace. Correctly appointed formal rooms! A living room with full length paned windows. And a formal dining room that features a large bay window. Plus a contemporary kitchen. A separate dining nook that includes another bay window. Charming and sunny! Around the corner, a first floor laundry offers more modern conveniences. Four large bedrooms! Including a master suite with two walk-in closets and private bath. This home offers all the conveniences that make life easy! And its eminently suited to a family with traditional tastes. List your favorite features.

199

Design V22839 First Floor: 1,565 square feet; Second Floor: 1,120 square feet; Total: 2,685 square feet

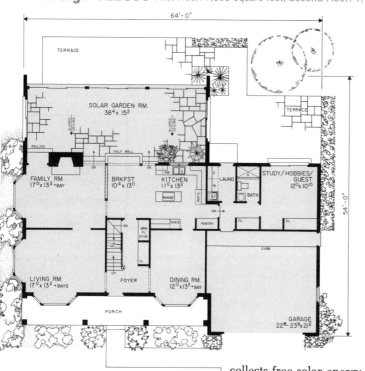

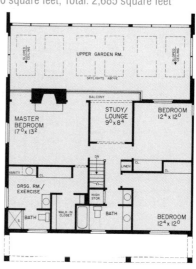

● Bay windows highlight the front and side exteriors of this three-bedroom Colonial. For energy efficiency, this design has an enclosed garden room that collects free solar energy. This area opens to the family room, breakfast room and second floor master suite. The solar garden room includes 576 sq. ft. This figure is not included in the above total.

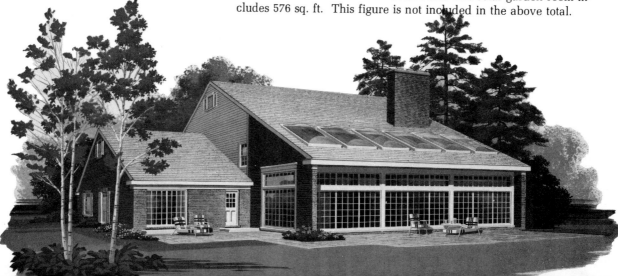

Design V22140 First Floor: 1,822 square feet; Second Floor: 1,638 square feet; Total: 3,460 square feet

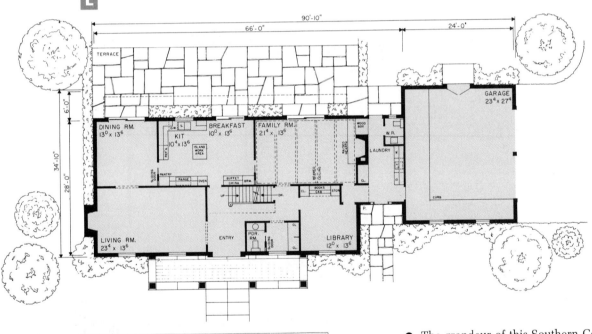

● The grandeur of this Southern Colonial adaptation is almost breathtaking. The stately columns supporting the distinctive pediment gable are truly impressive. The proportions and the symmetry of the windows and the entranceway are delightful. The double front doors enter to a spacious hall. Among the noteworthy features are the library, the powder room and the spacious kitchen area. Also, the second floor has three baths and a lounge or fifth bedroom. An outdoor balcony is accessible from each of the three rear bedrooms. What other features does your family like? Why not make a list?

Design V22693
3,462 square feet

● This elegant Georgian manor is reminiscent of historic Rose Hill, built 1818 in Lexington, Kentucky. It is typical of the classic manors with Greek Revival features built in Kentucky as the 19th Century dawned. Note the classical portico of four Ionic columns plus the fine proportions. Also noteworthy is the updated interior, highlighted by a large country kitchen with fireplace and an efficient work center that includes an island cooktop. The country kitchen leads directly into a front formal dining room, just off the foyer. On the other side of the foyer is a front living room. A large library is located in the back of the house. It features built-in bookcases plus a fireplace, one of four fireplaces.

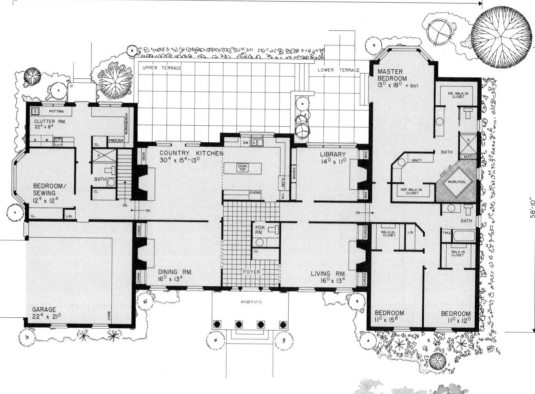

Design V22977 First Floor: 4,104 square feet; Second Floor: 979 square feet; Total: 5,083 square feet

L

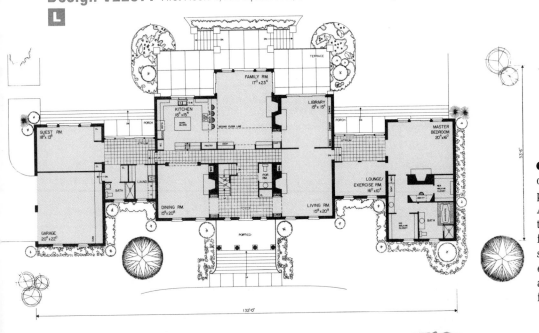

● Both front and rear facades of this elegant brick manor depict classic Georgian symmetry. A columned, Greek entry opens to an impressive two-story foyer. Fireplaces, built-in shelves, and cabinets highlight each of the four main gathering areas: living room, dining room, family room, and library.

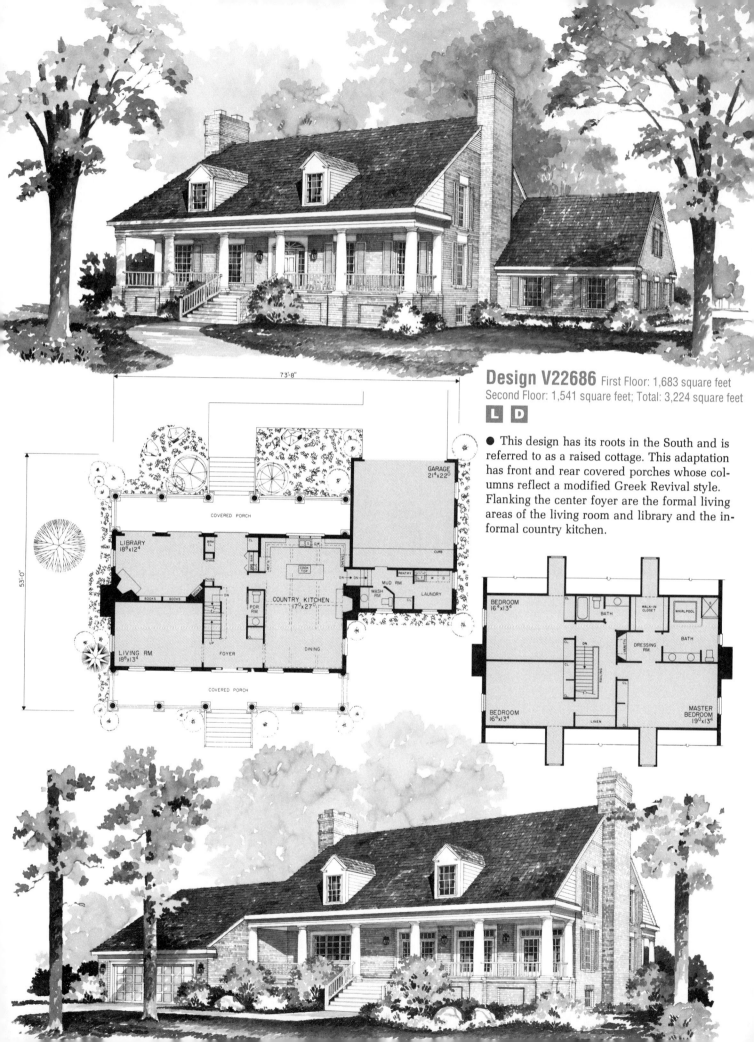

Design V22686 First Floor: 1,683 square feet
Second Floor: 1,541 square feet; Total: 3,224 square feet

L **D**

● This design has its roots in the South and is referred to as a raised cottage. This adaptation has front and rear covered porches whose columns reflect a modified Greek Revival style. Flanking the center foyer are the formal living areas of the living room and library and the informal country kitchen.

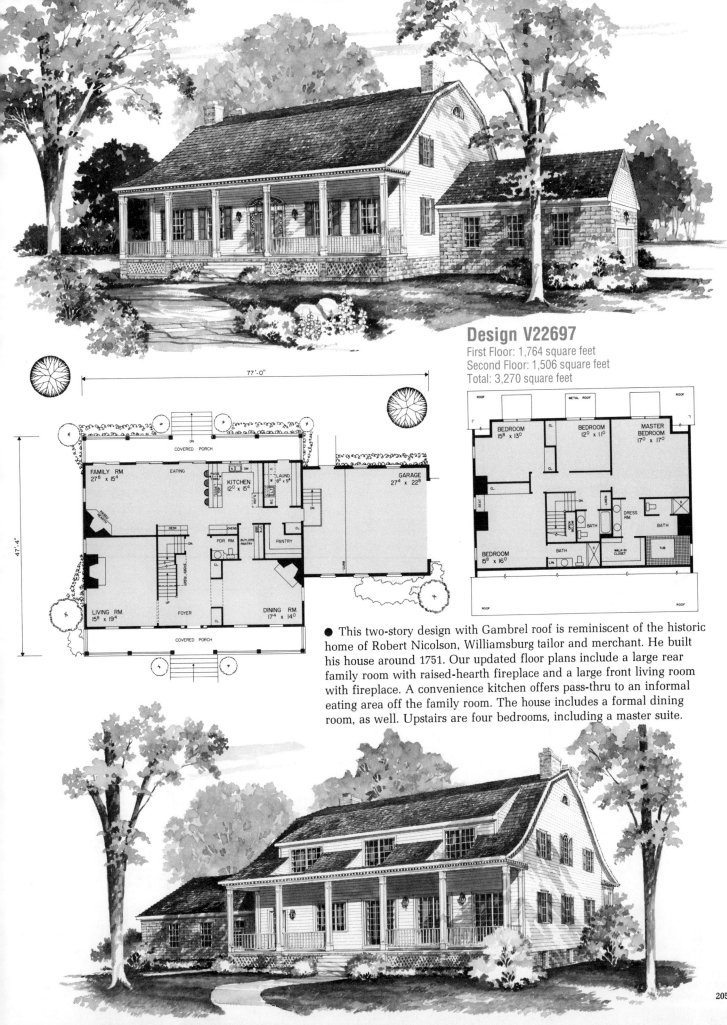

Design V22697

First Floor: 1,764 square feet
Second Floor: 1,506 square feet
Total: 3,270 square feet

● This two-story design with Gambrel roof is reminiscent of the historic home of Robert Nicolson, Williamsburg tailor and merchant. He built his house around 1751. Our updated floor plans include a large rear family room with raised-hearth fireplace and a large front living room with fireplace. A convenience kitchen offers pass-thru to an informal eating area off the family room. The house includes a formal dining room, as well. Upstairs are four bedrooms, including a master suite.

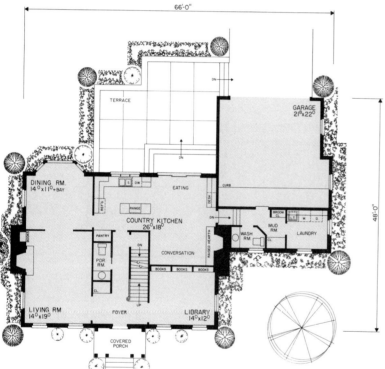

66'-0"

TERRACE

GARAGE
21⁸x22⁰

DINING RM.
14⁰x11⁰+BAY

EATING

CURB

REF.

RANGE

COUNTRY KITCHEN
26⁰x18⁰

PANTRY

CONVERSATION

PDR. RM.

RAISED HEARTH

WASH RM.

MUD RM.

LAUNDRY

BOOKS BOOKS BOOKS

LIVING RM
14⁰x19⁰

FOYER

UP

LIBRARY
14⁰x13⁰

COVERED PORCH

48'-0"

Design V22688 First Floor: 1,588 square feet
Second Floor: 1,101 square feet; Total: 2,689 square feet

● Here are two floors of excellent livability. Start at the country kitchen. It will be the center for family activities. It has an island, desk, raised hearth fireplace, conversation area and sliding glass doors to the terrace. Adjacent to this area is the washroom and laundry. Quieter areas are available in the living room and library. Three bedrooms are housed on the second floor.

ROOF

BEDROOM
13⁰x12⁴

BATH

BATH

DRESSING RM

LINEN

BEDROOM
15⁰x11⁴

MASTER BEDROOM
14⁰x13⁴

ROOF

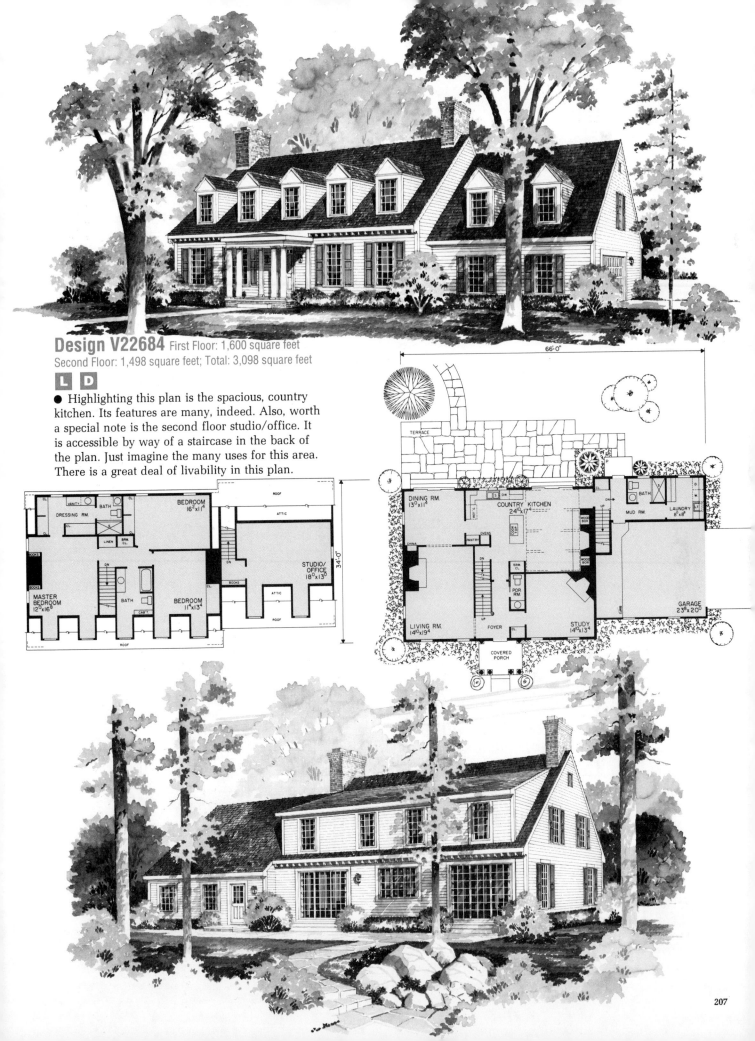

Design V22684 First Floor: 1,600 square feet
Second Floor: 1,498 square feet; Total: 3,098 square feet

L **D**

● Highlighting this plan is the spacious, country kitchen. Its features are many, indeed. Also, worth a special note is the second floor studio/office. It is accessible by way of a staircase in the back of the plan. Just imagine the many uses for this area. There is a great deal of livability in this plan.

Design V22133 First Floor: 3,024 square feet; Second Floor: 826 square feet; Total: 3,850 square feet

L D

● A country-estate home which will command all the attention it truly deserves. The projecting pediment gable supported by the finely proportioned columns lends an aura of elegance. The window treatment, the front door detailing, the massive, capped chimney, the cupola, the brick veneer exterior and the varying roof planes complete the characterization of an impressive home. Inside, there are 3,024 square feet on the first floor. In addition, there is a two bedroom second floor should its development be necessary. However, whether called upon to function as one, or 1-1/2 story home it will provide a lifetime of gracious living. Don't overlook the compartment baths, the big library, the coat room, the beamed ceiling family room, the two fireplaces, the breakfast room and the efficient kitchen. Note pass-thru to breakfast room.

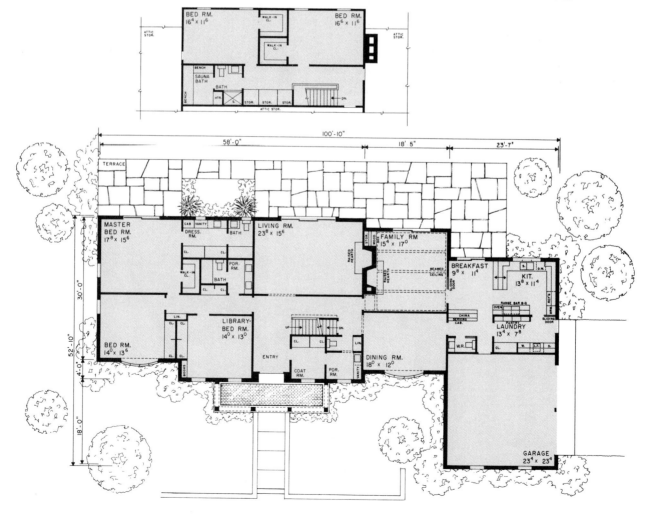

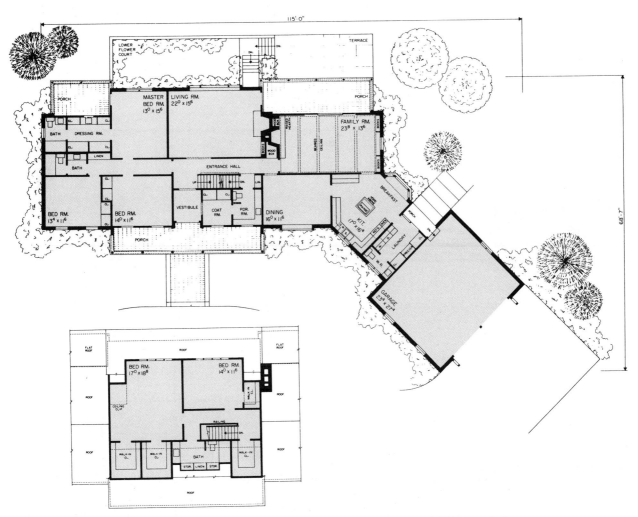

Design V21711 First Floor: 2,580 square feet; Second Floor: 938 square feet; Total: 3,518 square feet

● If the gracious charm of the Colonial South appeals to you, this may be just the house you've been waiting for. There is something solid and dependable in its well-balanced facade and wide, pillared front porch. Much of the interest generated by this design comes from its interesting expanses of roof and angular projection of its kitchen and garage. The feeling of elegance is further experienced upon stepping inside, through double doors, to the spacious entrance hall where there is the separate coat room. Adjacent to this is the powder room, also convenient to the living areas. The work area of the kitchen and laundry room is truly outstanding. Designed as a five bedroom house, each is large. Storage and bath facilities are excellent.

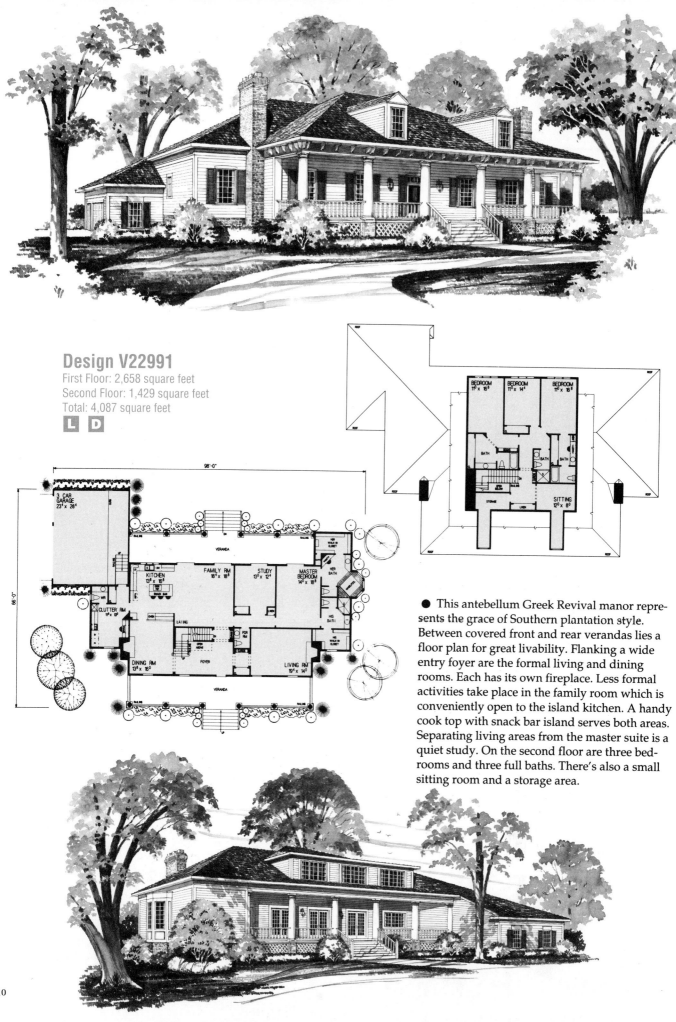

Design V22991

First Floor: 2,658 square feet
Second Floor: 1,429 square feet
Total: 4,087 square feet

L **D**

● This antebellum Greek Revival manor represents the grace of Southern plantation style.
Between covered front and rear verandas lies a
floor plan for great livability. Flanking a wide
entry foyer are the formal living and dining
rooms. Each has its own fireplace. Less formal
activities take place in the family room which is
conveniently open to the island kitchen. A handy
cook top with snack bar island serves both areas.
Separating living areas from the master suite is a
quiet study. On the second floor are three bedrooms and three full baths. There's also a small
sitting room and a storage area.

● This Southern Colonial adaptation is certainly one of a kind. It will forever foster the feeling of distinctiveness as well as individuality. The second floor porches provide the shelter for the porticos. The solidly proportioned pillars of the porticos are delightful, indeed. The center entry introduces one to a very orderly and formal interior, which is planned to assure each room its full measure of privacy. If desired, however, the family room may easily be opened up to function directly with the kitchen-nook area. The library will be a favorite spot for retreat. Four large bedrooms and three full baths are the highlights of the upstairs. Notice the complete accessibility of the two porches. The garage is attached and has a generous bulk storage area. Ideal for garden, lawn equipment.

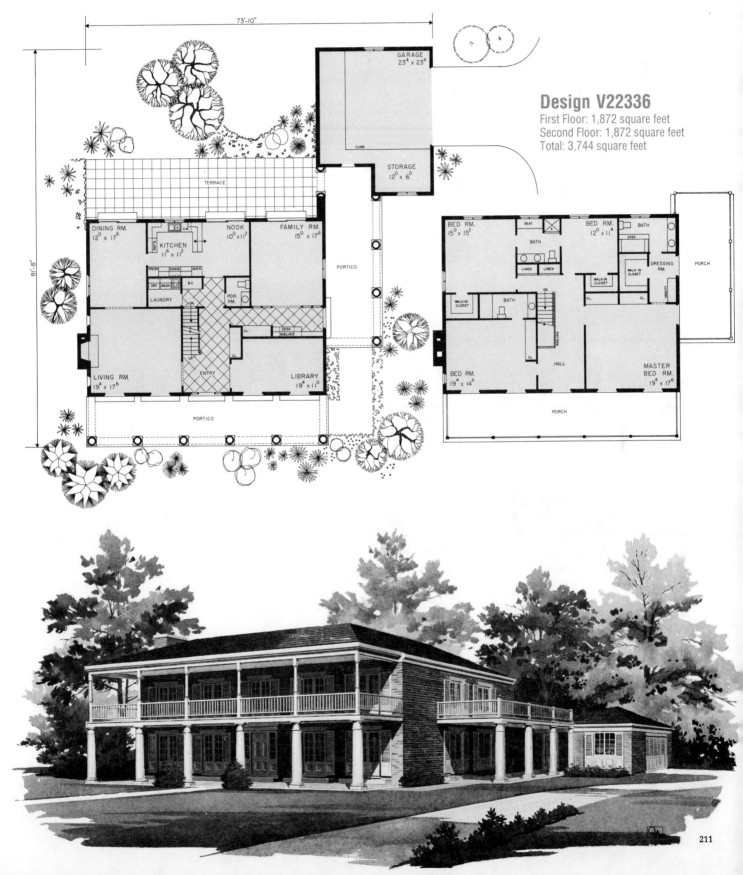

Design V22336
First Floor: 1,872 square feet
Second Floor: 1,872 square feet
Total: 3,744 square feet

Design V21816 First Floor: 2,036 square feet
Second Floor: 1,836 square feet; Total: 3,872 square feet

● The influence of the Colonial South is delightfully apparent in this gracious design. The stately
columns of the front porch set the stage for a
memorable visit. The entry hall is impressive
with its open stairway. The large, country kitchen
will be a sheer delight in which to work and, yes,
even congregate.

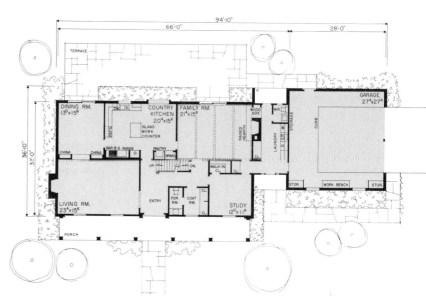

Design V22524 First Floor: 994 square feet
Second Floor: 994 square feet; Total: 1,988 square feet

D

● This small two-story, with a modest investment,
will result in an impressive exterior and an
outstanding interior which will provide exceptional
livability. Your list of features will be long and
surely impressive.

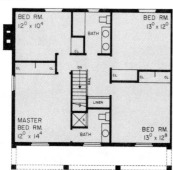

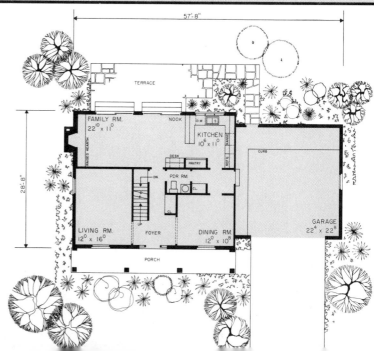

Design V22627 First Floor: 845 square feet
Second Floor: 896 square feet; Total: 1,741 square feet

● This charming, economically built, home with its stately two-story porch columns is reminiscent of the South. The efficient interior features bonus space over garage and in the third-floor attic which may be developed into another livable room. The U-shaped kitchen offers many built-ins and is conveniently located to serve the nook and the dining room with ease. Sliding glass doors in both these eating areas lead to the terrace.

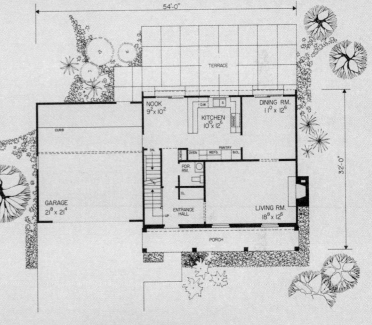

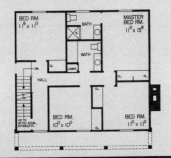

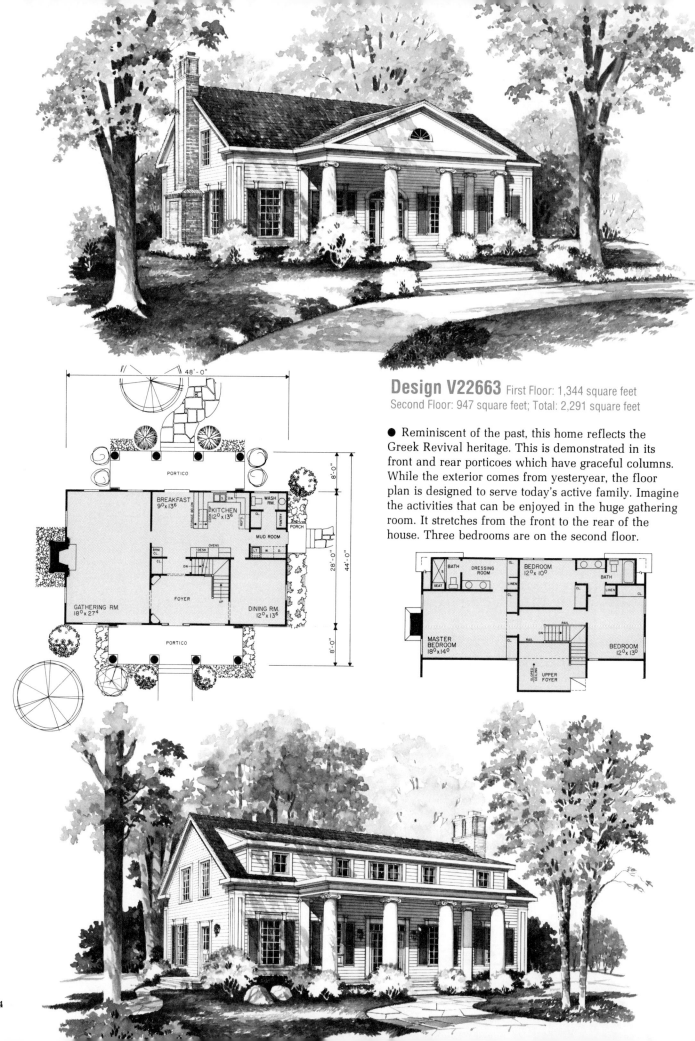

Design V22663 First Floor: 1,344 square feet
Second Floor: 947 square feet; Total: 2,291 square feet

● Reminiscent of the past, this home reflects the Greek Revival heritage. This is demonstrated in its front and rear porticoes which have graceful columns. While the exterior comes from yesteryear, the floor plan is designed to serve today's active family. Imagine the activities that can be enjoyed in the huge gathering room. It stretches from the front to the rear of the house. Three bedrooms are on the second floor.

FRENCH FACADES . . . .

and the pleasing formality they successfully project, are featured in this section by a variety of adaptations. The Mansard roof lends itself to many floor plan configurations. The hip-roof is also highly identifiable with the French style. Brick quoins at the corners, dentils, casement windows, arched window openings and shutters, raised molding doors, carriage lamps, and wrought iron grillwork complete the picture. Center entrances, large foyers, formal living and dining rooms, family rooms and abundant second floor sleeping facilities are among the floor plan features of these French Facades. Don't miss the extra baths, studies, and first floor laundries.

Design V22543 First Floor: 2,345 square feet
Second Floor: 1,687 square feet; Total: 4,032 square feet

L **D**

● Certainly a dramatic French adaptation highlighted by effective window treatment, delicate cornice detailing, appealing brick quoins and excellent proportion. Stepping through the double front doors the drama is heightened by the spacious entry hall with its two curving staircases to the second floor. The upper hall is open and looks down to the hall below. There is a study and a big gathering room which look out on the raised terrace. The work center is outstanding. The garage will accommodate three cars.

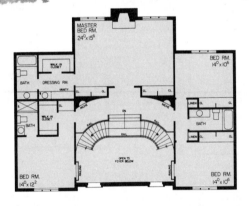

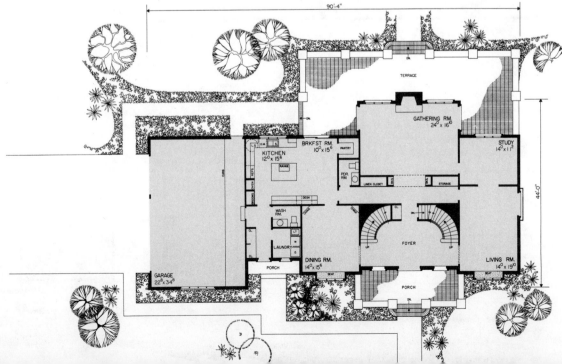

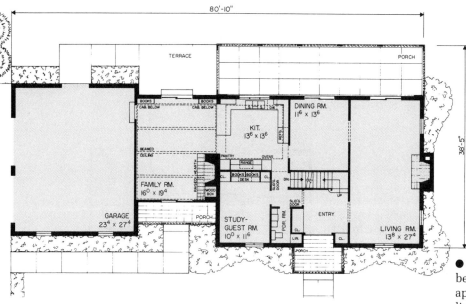

Design V22222

First Floor: 1,485 square feet
Second Floor: 1,175 square feet
Total: 2,660 square feet

● Gracious, formal living could hardly find a better backdrop than this two-story French adaptation. The exterior is truly exquisite. Inside, living patterns will be most enjoyable.

Design V22281 First Floor: 1,961 square feet; Second Floor: 1,472 square feet; Total: 3,433 square feet

D

● Regal in character, this French design is a fine example of excellent proportion and perfect symmetry. The distinctiveness of this home continues right through the front doors into the spacious entrance hall with its curving staircase.

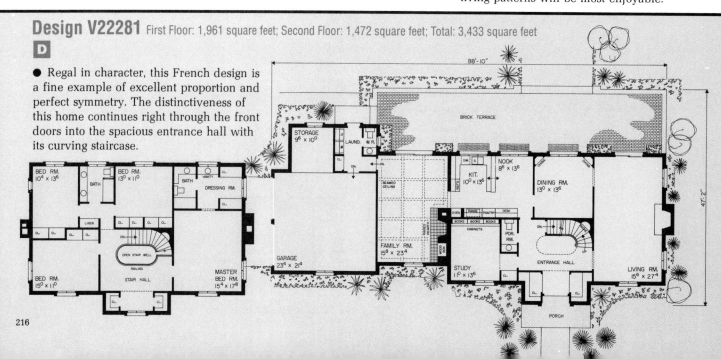

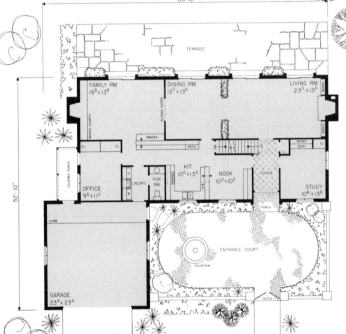

Design V22326

First Floor: 1,674 square feet
Second Floor: 1,107 square feet
Total: 2,781 square feet

● If your family enjoys the view of the backyard, then this is the design for you. The main rooms, family, dining and living, are all in the back of the plan, each having sliding glass doors to the terrace. They are away from the confusion of the work center, yet easily accessible. A study and separate office are also available. Four bedrooms are on the second floor. Be sure to note all of the features in the master bedroom suite.

217

Design V21228

First Floor: 2,583 square feet
Second Floor: 697 square feet
Total: 3,280 square feet

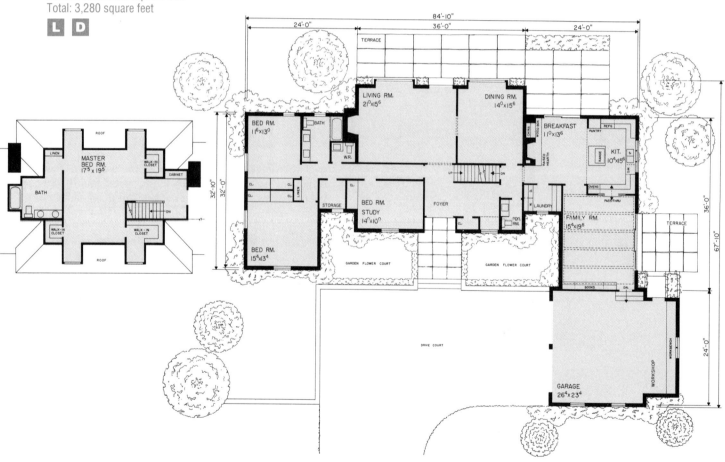

● This beautiful house has a wealth of detail taken from the rich traditions of French Regency design. The roof itself is a study in pleasant dormers and the hips and valleys of a big flowing area. A close examination of the plan shows the careful arrangement of space for privacy as well as good circulation of traffic. The spacious formal entrance hall sets the stage for good zoning. The informal living area is highlighted by the updated version of the old country kitchen. Observe the fireplace, built-in wood box, and china cabinet. While there is a half-story devoted to the master bedroom suite, this home functons more as a one-story country estate design than as a 1½ story.

Design V22342

First Floor: 2,824 square feet
Second Floor: 1,013 square feet
Total: 3,837 square feet

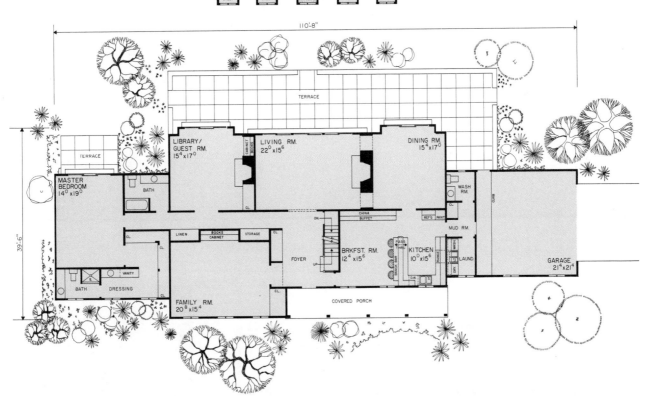

● A distinctive exterior characterized by varying roof planes, appealing window treatment, attractive chimneys and a covered front porch with prominent vertical columns. The main portion of the house is effectively balanced by the master bedroom wing on the one side and the garage wing on the other. As a buffer between house and garage is the mud room and the laundry. The kitchen is U-shaped, efficient and strategically located to serve the breakfast and dining rooms. Notice how the rooms at the rear function through sliding glass doors with the outdoor terrace areas. Fireplaces highlight both the spacious living room and the large library. The big family room features a built-in bookshelf and cabinet. Upstairs, two bedrooms and a study alcove will be found.

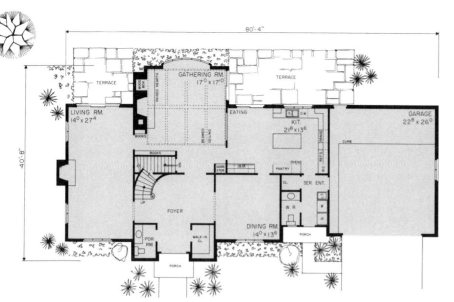

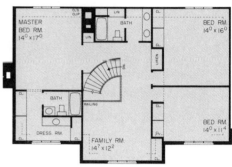

Design V22503
First Floor: 1,847 square feet
Second Floor: 1,423 square feet
Total: 3,270 square feet

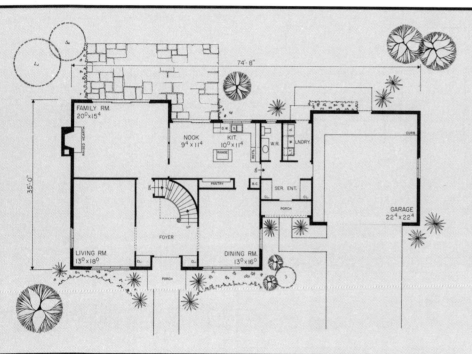

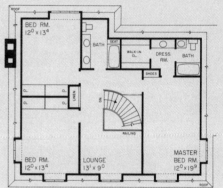

Design V22507
First Floor: 1,529 square feet
Second Floor: 1,206 square feet
Total: 2,735 square feet

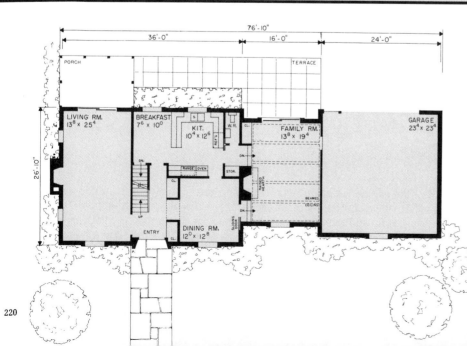

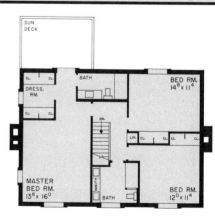

Design V21260
First Floor: 1,318 square feet
Second Floor: 989 square feet
Total: 2,307 square feet

● The elegance of pleasing proportion and delightful detailing has seldom been better exemplified than by this classic French country manor adaptation. Approaching the house across the drive court, the majesty of this multi-roofed structure is breathtaking, indeed. An outstanding feature is the maid's suite. It is located above the garage and is easily reached by use of the covered porch connecting the laundry room's service entrance to the garage. If desired, it would make an excellent studio, quiet retreat or even a game room.

Design V21993

First Floor: 2,658 square feet
Master Suite: 840 square feet
Maid's Suite: 376 square feet
Total: 3,874 square feet

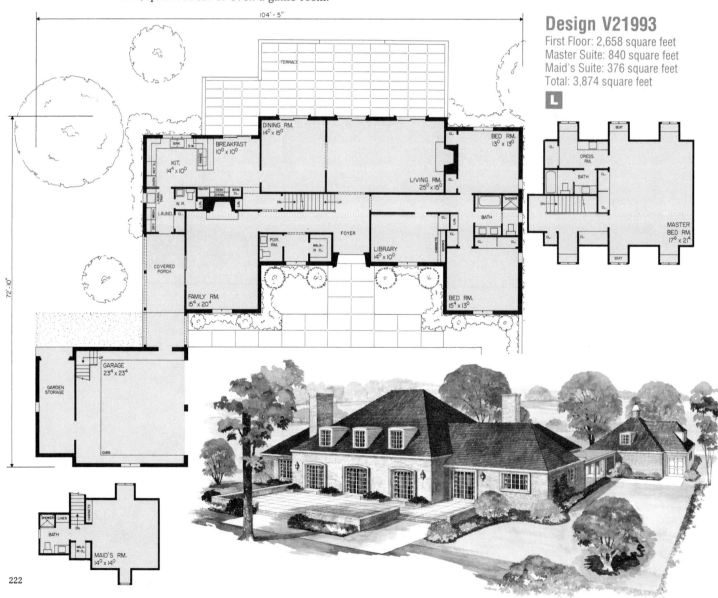

Design V23380

First Floor: 3,350 square feet
Second Floor: 1,298 square feet
Total: 4,648 square feet

● Reminiscent of a Mediterranean villa, this grand manor is a showstopper on the outside and a comfortable residence on the inside. An elegant receiving hall boasts a double staircase and is flanked by the formal dining room and the library. A huge gathering room is found to the back. The master bedroom is found on the first floor for privacy. Upstairs are four additional bedrooms and two full baths.

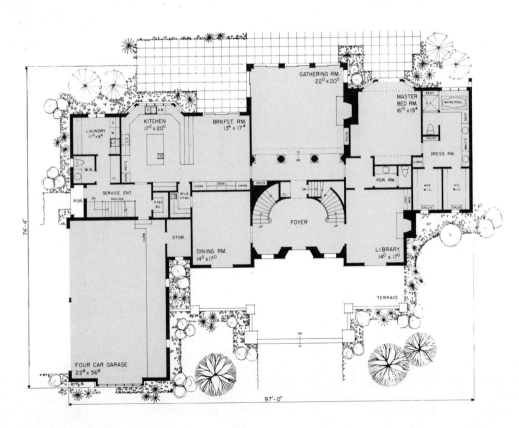

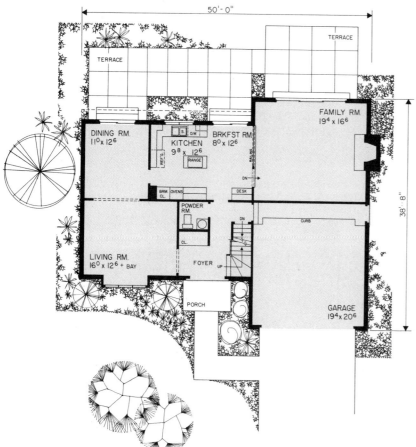

Design V22798
First Floor: 1,149 square feet
Second Floor: 850 square feet
Total: 1,999 square feet

L D

● An island range in the kitchen is a great feature of the work center in this two-story French designed home. The breakfast room has an open railing to the sunken family room so it can enjoy the view of the family room's fireplace.

Sliding glass doors in each of the major rear rooms, dining, breakfast and family rooms, lead to the terrace for outdoor enjoyment. The front, formal living room is highlighted by a bay window. A powder room is conven-

iently located on the first floor near all of the major areas. All of the sleeping facilities are housed on the second floor. Each of the four bedrooms will serve its occupants ideally. A relatively narrow lot can house this design.

VICTORIAN HOUSES . . . *extend from a pointed, exuberant expression of*

America's prominent place in the world late in the 19th Century. Today, they are every bit as lively, dressed in all the spectacular finery so typical of the style. Spindlework details, expansive porches, towers, turrets, grand chimneys, and varied exterior materials combine to create our fine collection of Victorian adaptations.

Design V22971 First Floor: 1,766 square feet
Second Floor: 1,519 square feet; Total: 3,285 square feet

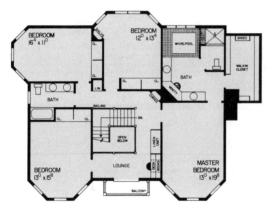

● The stately proportions and the exquisite detailing of Victorian styling are exciting, indeed. Like so many Victorian houses, interesting roof lines set the character with this design. Observe the delightful mixture of gable roof, hip roof, and the dramatic turret. Horizontal siding, wood shingling, wide fascia, rake and corner boards make a strong statement. Of course, the delicate detailing of the windows, railings, cornices and front entry is most appealing to the eye. Inside, a great four-bedroom family living plan.

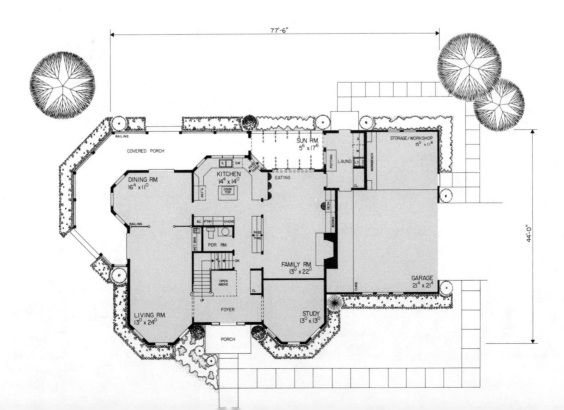

225

Design V22973

First Floor: 1,269 square feet
Second Floor: 1,227 square feet
Total: 2,496 square feet

L

● A most popular feature of the Victorian house has always been its covered porches. In addition to being an appealing exterior design feature, covered porches have their practical side, too. They provide wonderful indoor-outdoor living relationships. Notice sheltered outdoor living facilities for the various formal and informal living and dining areas of the plan. This home has a myriad of features to cater to the living requirements of the growing, active family.

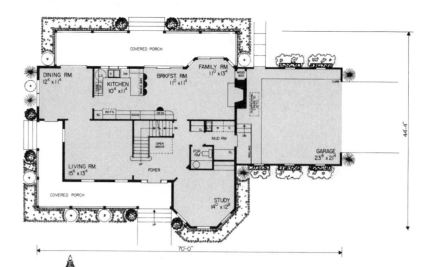

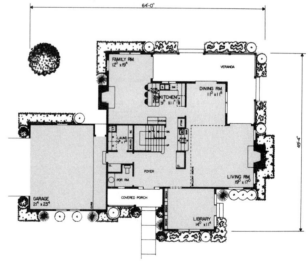

Design V22972

First Floor: 1,432 square feet
Second Floor: 1,108 square feet
Total: 2,540 square feet

L

● The spacious foyer of this Victorian is prelude to a practical and efficient interior. The formal living and dining area is located to one side of the plan. The more informal area of the plan includes the fine U-shaped kitchen which opens to the big family room. Just inside the entrance from the garage is the laundry; a closet and the powder room are a few steps away. The library will enjoy its full measure of privacy. Upstairs is the three-bedroom sleeping zone with a fireplace.

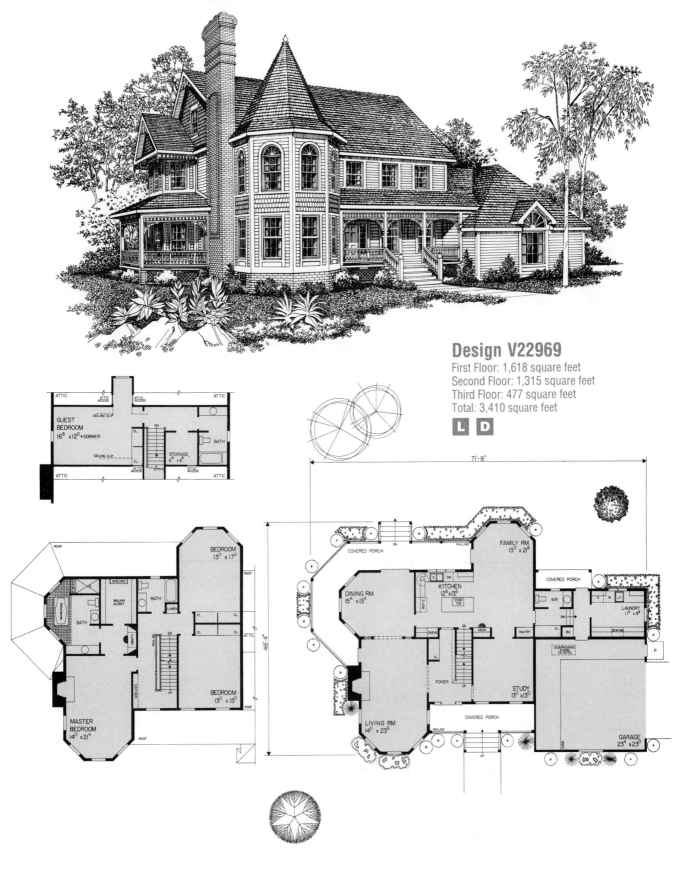

Design V22969

First Floor: 1,618 square feet
Second Floor: 1,315 square feet
Third Floor: 477 square feet
Total: 3,410 square feet

L D

● What could beat the charm of a turreted Victorian with covered porches to the front, side and rear? This delicately detailed exterior houses an outstanding family oriented floor plan. Projecting bays make their contribution to the exterior styling. In addition, they provide an extra measure of livability

to the living, dining and family rooms, plus two of the bedrooms. The efficient kitchen, with its island cooking station, functions well with the dining and family rooms. A study provides a quiet first floor haven for the family's less active pursuits. Upstairs there are three big bedrooms and a fine master bath.

The third floor provides a guest suite and huge bulk storage area (make it a cedar closet if you wish). This house has a basement for the development of further recreational and storage facilities. Don't miss the two fireplaces, large laundry and attached two-car garage. A great investment.

Design V23308

First Floor: 2,515 square feet
Second Floor: 1,708 square feet
Third Floor: 1,001 square feet
Total: 5,224 square feet

L **D**

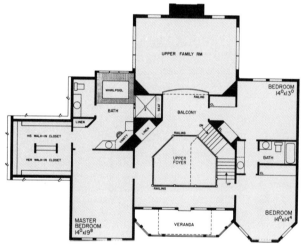

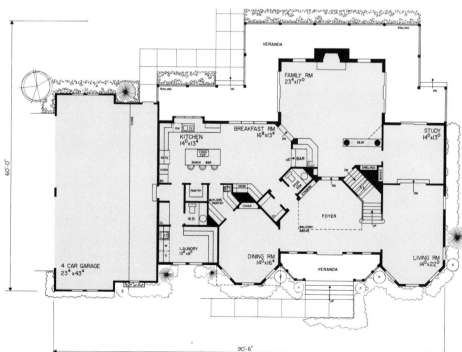

● Uniquely shaped rooms and a cache of amenities highlight this three-story beauty. Downstairs rooms can accommodate both formal and informal entertaining and also provide a liberal share of work space in the kitchen and laundry. Notice the abundance of built-ins and the butler's pantry. A four-car garage easily holds the family fleet. The second floor has two bedrooms and a full bath plus a master suite with His and Hers closets and whirlpool bath. An exercise room on the third floor has its own sauna and bath, while the large guest room on this floor is complemented by a charming alcove and another full bath.

Design V23386

First Floor: 1,683 square feet
Second Floor: 1,388 square feet
Third Floor: 808 square feet
Total: 3,879 square feet

L **D**

● This beautiful Folk Victorian has all the properties of others in its class. Living areas include a formal Victorian parlor, a private study and large gathering room. The formal dining room has its more casual counterpart in a bay-windowed breakfast room. Both are near the well-appointed kitchen. Five bedrooms serve family and guest needs handily. Three bedrooms on the second floor include a luxurious master suite. For outdoor entertaining, there is a covered rear porch leading to a terrace.

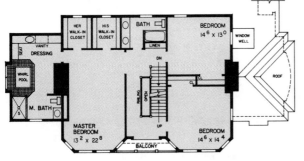

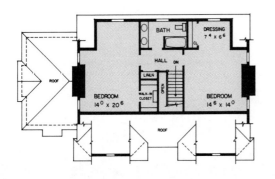

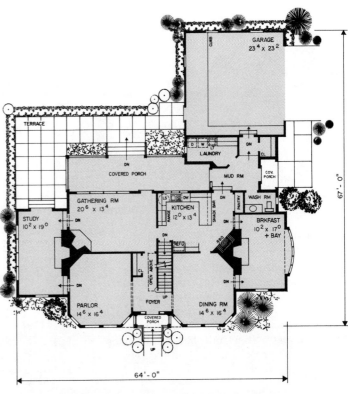

Design V23388

First Floor: 1,517 square feet
Second Floor: 1,267 square feet
Third Floor: 480 square feet
Total: 3,264 square feet

● This delightful home offers the best in
thoughtful floor planning. The home opens to a
well-executed entry foyer. To the left is the
casual family room with fireplace. To the right
is the formal living room which connects to the
formal dining area. The kitchen/breakfast room
combination features an island cook top and
large pantry. Second-floor bedrooms include a
master suite and two family bedrooms served
by a full bath. A guest room dominates the third
floor.

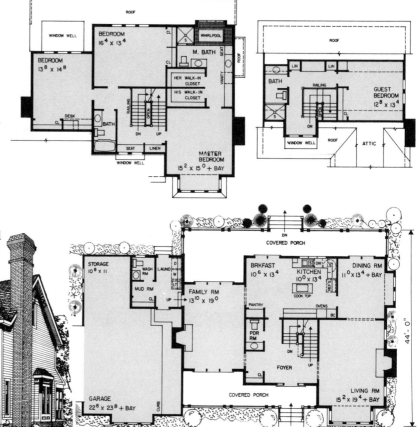

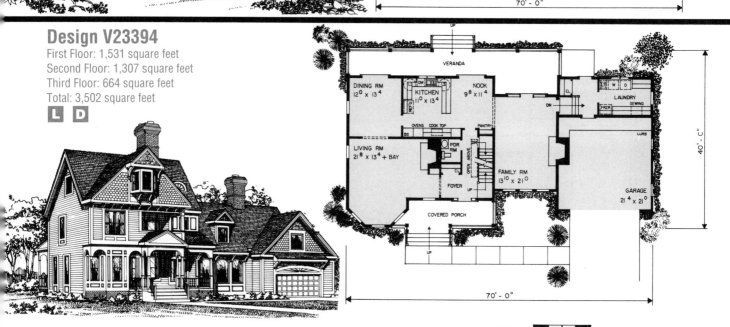

Design V23394

First Floor: 1,531 square feet
Second Floor: 1,307 square feet
Third Floor: 664 square feet
Total: 3,502 square feet

● The Folk Victorian is an important and
delightful interpretation. And this version
offers the finest in modern floor plans. The
formal living areas are set off by a family room
which connects the main house to the service
areas. The second floor holds three bedrooms
and two full baths. A sitting area in the master
suite separates it from family bedrooms. On the
third floor is a guest bedroom with gracious
bath and large walk-in closet.

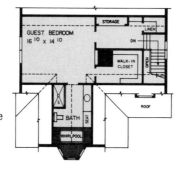

Design V22829 First Floor: 2,044 square feet
Second Floor: 1,962 square feet; Total: 4,006 square feet

L **D**

● The architecture of this design is Post-Modern with a taste of Victorian styling. Detailed with gingerbread woodwork and a handsome double-width chimney, this two-story design is breathtaking. Enter this home to the large, tiled receiving hall and begin to explore this very livable floor plan. Formal areas consist of the front living room and the dining room. Each has features to make it memorable. The living room is spacious, has a fireplace and access to the covered porch; the dining room has a delightful bay window and is convenient to the kitchen for ease in meal serving. The library is tucked between these two formal areas. Now let's go to the informal area. The family room will welcome many an explorer. It will be a great place for many family activities. Note the L-shaped snack bar with cabinets below. Onward to the second floor, where the private area will be found. Start with the two bedrooms that have two full bathrooms joining them together. The older children will marvel at this area's efficiency and privacy. A third family bedroom is nearby. Then, there is the master bedroom suite. Its list of features is long, indeed. Begin with the "his" and "her" baths and see how many features you can list. A guest bedroom and bath are on the first floor.

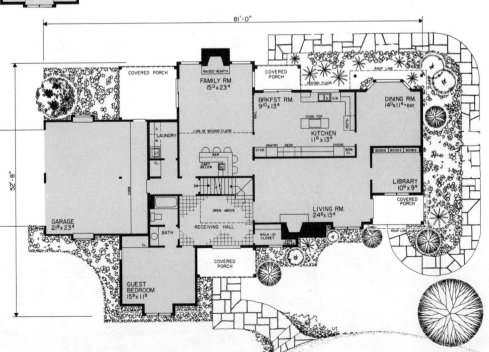

231

Design V22646 First Floor: 1,274 square feet
Second Floor: 1,322 square feet; Total: 2,596 square feet

L D

● What a stylish departure from today's usual architecture. This refreshing exterior may be referred to as Neo-Victorian. Its vertical lines, steep roofs and variety of gables remind one of the old Victorian houses of yesteryear. Inside, there is an efficiently working floor plan that is delightfully spacious.

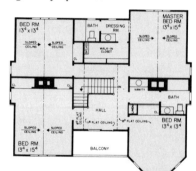

Design V22645
First Floor: 1,600 square feet
Second Floor: 1,305 square feet
Third Floor: 925 square feet
Total: 3,830 square feet

L

Design V22647 First Floor: 2,104 square feet; Second Floor: 1,230 square feet; Total: 3,334 square feet

● Another Neo-Victorian, and what an impressive and unique design it is. Observe the roof lines, the window treatment, the use of contrasting exterior materials and the arched, covered front entrance.

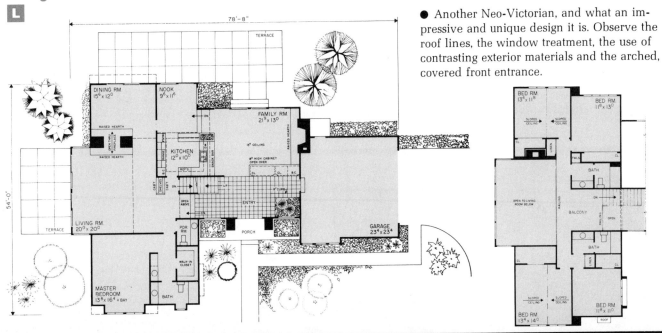

● Reminiscent of the Gothic Victorian style of the mid-19th Century, this delightfully detailed, three-story house has a wraparound veranda for summertime relaxing. The parlor and family room, each with fireplaces, provide excellent formal and informal living facilities. The third floor houses two more great areas plus bath.

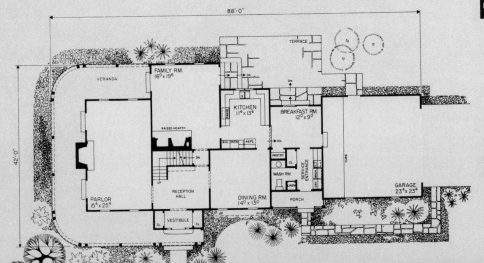

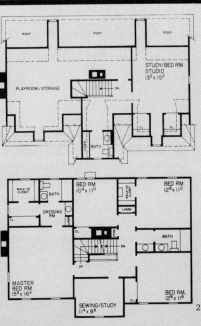

233

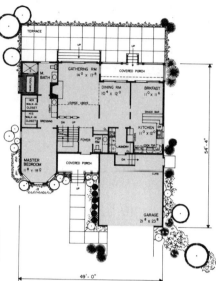

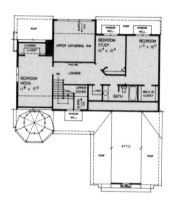

● A grand facade makes this Victorian stand out. Inside, guests and family are well accommodated: gathering room with terrace access, fireplace and attached formal dining room; split-bedroom sleeping arrangements. The master suite contains His and Hers walk-in closets, a separate shower and whirlpool tub and a delightful bay-windowed area. Upstairs there are three more bedrooms (one could serve as a study, one as a media room), a full bath and an open lounge area overlooking the gathering room.

Design V23393

First Floor: 1,449 square feet
Second Floor: 902 square feet
Total: 2,351 square feet

L D

Design V23389

First Floor: 1,161 square feet
Second Floor: 1,090 square feet
Third Floor: 488 square feet
Total: 2,739 square feet

L D

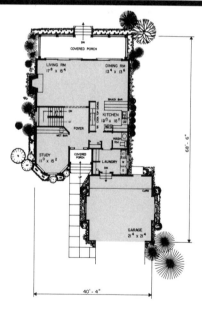

● A Victorian turret accents the facade of this compact three-story. Downstairs rooms include a grand-sized living room/dining room combination. The U-shaped kitchen has a snack-bar pass-through to the dining room. Just to the left of the entry foyer is a private study. On the second floor are three bedrooms and two full baths. The master bedroom has a whirlpool spa and large walk-in closet. The third floor is a perfect location for a guest bedroom with private bath.

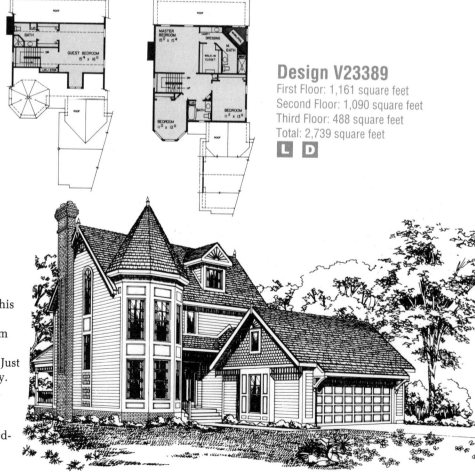

Design V22970 First Floor: 1,538 square feet
Second Floor: 1,526 square feet; Third Floor: 658 square feet
Total: 3,722 square feet

L

● A porch, is a porch, is a porch. But, when it wraps around to a side, or even two sides, of the house, we have called it a veranda. This charming Victorian features a covered outdoor living area on all four sides! It even ends at a screened porch which features a sun deck above. This interesting plan offers three floors of livability. And what livability it is! Plenty of formal and informal living facilities to go along with the potential of five bedrooms. The master suite is just that. It is adjacent to an interesting sitting room. It has a sun deck and excellent bath/personal care facilities. The third floor will make a wonderful haven for the family's student members.

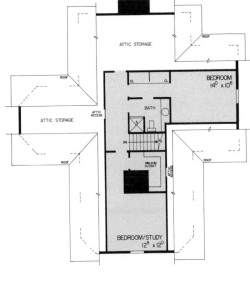

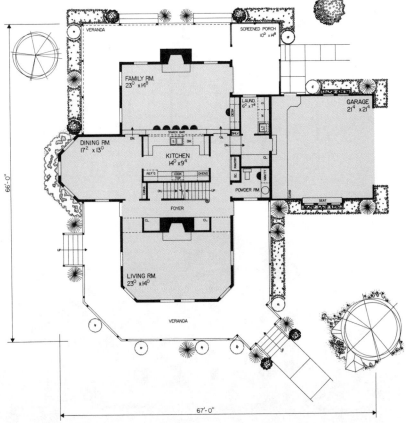

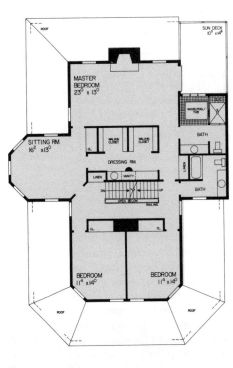

235

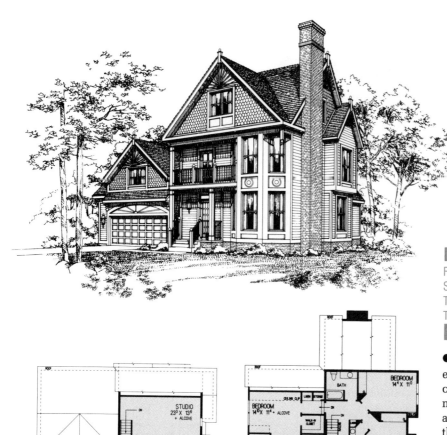

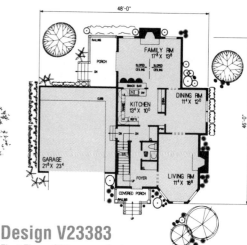

Design V23383

First Floor: 995 square feet
Second Floor: 1,064 square feet
Third Floor: 425 square feet
Total: 2,484 square feet

L **D**

● This delightful Victorian cottage features exterior details that perfectly complement the convenient plan inside. Note the central placement of the kitchen, near to the dining room and the family room. Two fireplaces keep things warm and cozy. Three second-floor bedrooms include a master suite with bay window and two family bedrooms, one with an alcove and walk-in closet. Use the third-floor studio as a study, office or playroom for the children.

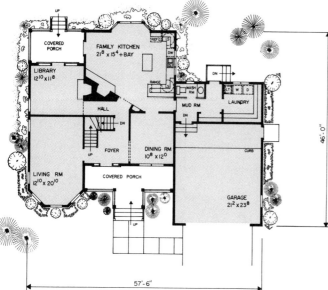

Design V23384

First Floor: 1,399 square feet
Second Floor: 1,123 square feet
Total: 2,522 square feet

L **D**

● Classic Victorian styling comes to the forefront in this Queen Anne. The interior boasts comfortable living quarters for the entire family. On opposite sides of the foyer are the formal dining and living rooms. To the rear is a country-style island kitchen with attached family room. A small library shares a covered porch with this informal gathering area and also has its own fireplace. Three bedrooms on the second floor include a master suite with grand bath. The two family bathrooms share a full bath.

Design V23391

First Floor: 1,230 square feet
Second Floor: 991 square feet
Total: 2,221 square feet

L D

● Detailing is one of the characteristic features of Queen Anne Victorians and this home has no lack of it. Interior rooms add special living patterns. Features include a powder room for guests in the front hallway, a through-fireplace between the ample gathering room and cozy study, an efficient U-shaped kitchen with pantry, and a full-width terrace to the rear. On the second floor are three bedrooms — one a master suite with walk-in closet and amenity-filled bath. An open balcony overlooks the gathering room.

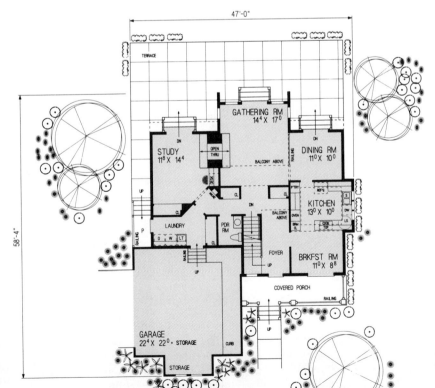

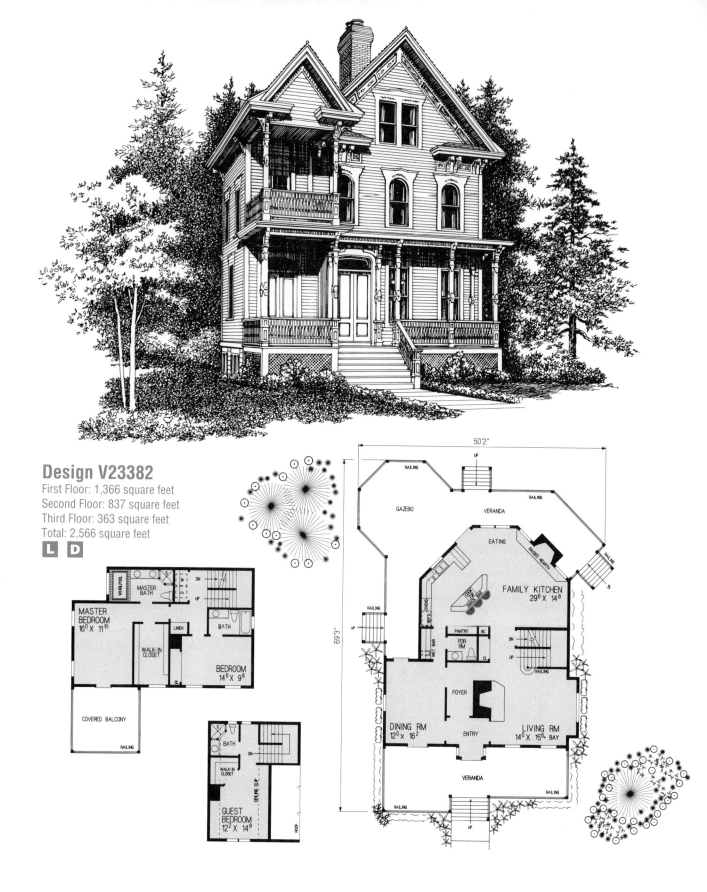

Design V23382

First Floor: 1,366 square feet
Second Floor: 837 square feet
Third Floor: 363 square feet
Total: 2,566 square feet

L **D**

● A simple but charming Queen Anne Victorian, this enchanting three-story home boasts delicately turned rails and decorated columns on its covered front porch. Inside is a floor plan that includes a living room with fireplace and dining room that connects to the kitchen via a wet bar. The adjoining family room contains another fireplace. The second floor holds two bedrooms, one a master suite with grand bath. A tucked-away guest suite on the third floor has a private bath.

Design V22974 First Floor: 911 square feet
Second Floor: 861 square feet; Total: 1,772 square feet

L

● Victorian houses are well known for their orientation on narrow building sites. And when this occurs nothing is lost to captivating exterior styling. This house is but 38 feet wide. Its narrow width belies the tremendous amount of livability found inside. And, of course, the ubiquitous porch/veranda contributes mightily to style as well as livability. The efficient, U-shape kitchen is flanked by the informal breakfast room and formal dining room. The rear living area is spacious and functions in an exciting manner with the outdoor areas. Bonus recreational, hobby and storage space is offered by the basement and the attic.

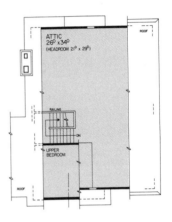

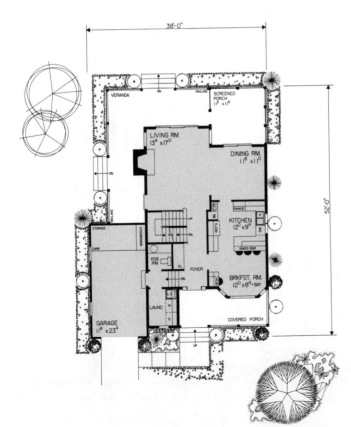

● This two-story farmhouse will be a delight for those who work at home. The second floor has a secluded master bedroom and a studio. A U-shaped kitchen with snack bar and breakfast area with bay window are only the first of the eating areas, which extend to a formal dining room and a covered rear porch for dining al fresco. The two-story living room features a cozy fireplace. A versatile room to the back could serve as a media room or a third bedroom.

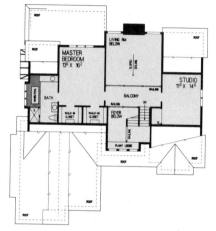

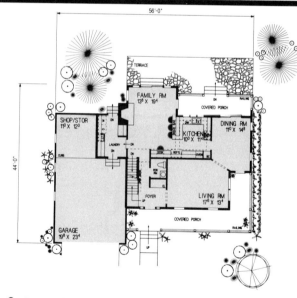

Design V23390

First Floor: 1,508 square feet
Second Floor: 760 square feet
Total: 2,268 square feet

Design V23385

First Floor: 1,096 square feet
Second Floor: 900 square feet
Total: 1,996 square feet

● Covered porches front and rear are complemented by a grand plan for family living. A formal living room and attached dining room provide space for entertaining guests. The large family room with fireplace is a gathering room for everyday use. Four bedrooms occupy the second floor. The master suite features two lavatories, a window seat and three closets. One of the family bedrooms has its own private balcony and could be used as a study.

Design V23307

First Floor: 1,765 square feet
Second Floor: 1,105 square feet
Total: 2,870 square feet

L D

● This charming design brings together the best in historical styling and modern floor planning. Inside, the first-floor plan boasts formal living and dining areas on either side of the entry foyer, a study that could double as a guest room, a large family room with raised-hearth fireplace and snack bar pass-through, and a U-shaped kitchen with attached breakfast room. Two family bedrooms on the second floor share a full bath; the master bedroom has a thoughtfully appointed bath and large walk-in closet.

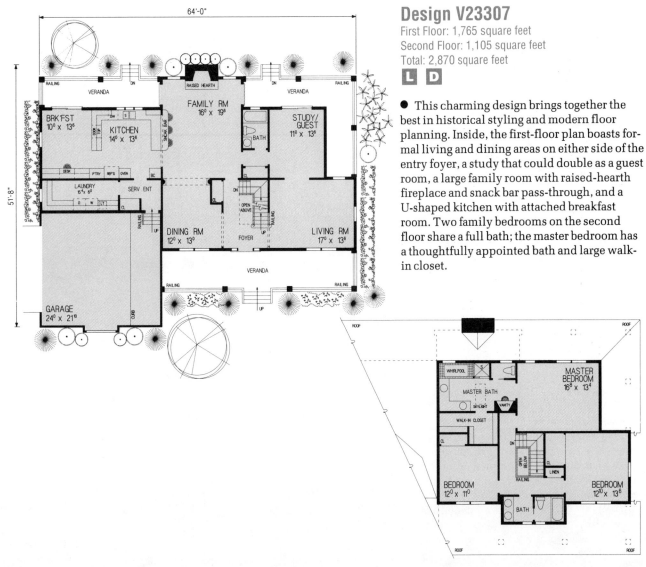

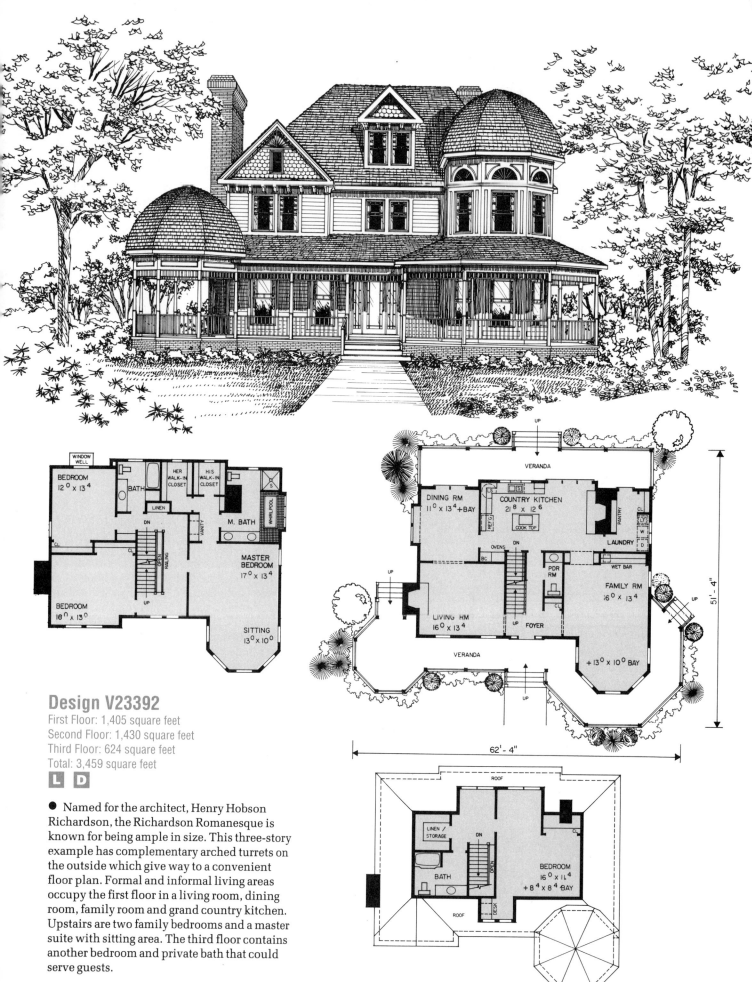

Design V23392

First Floor: 1,405 square feet
Second Floor: 1,430 square feet
Third Floor: 624 square feet
Total: 3,459 square feet

L **D**

● Named for the architect, Henry Hobson Richardson, the Richardson Romanesque is known for being ample in size. This three-story example has complementary arched turrets on the outside which give way to a convenient floor plan. Formal and informal living areas occupy the first floor in a living room, dining room, family room and grand country kitchen. Upstairs are two family bedrooms and a master suite with sitting area. The third floor contains another bedroom and private bath that could serve guests.

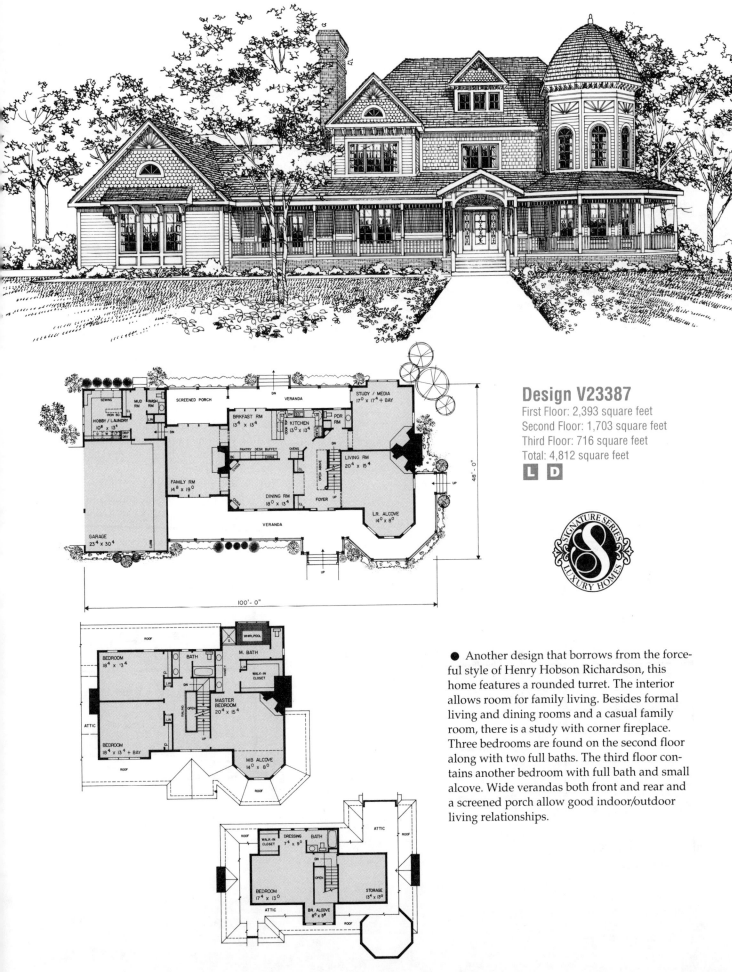

Design V23387

First Floor: 2,393 square feet
Second Floor: 1,703 square feet
Third Floor: 716 square feet
Total: 4,812 square feet

L **D**

● Another design that borrows from the forceful style of Henry Hobson Richardson, this home features a rounded turret. The interior allows room for family living. Besides formal living and dining rooms and a casual family room, there is a study with corner fireplace. Three bedrooms are found on the second floor along with two full baths. The third floor contains another bedroom with full bath and small alcove. Wide verandas both front and rear and a screened porch allow good indoor/outdoor living relationships.

Design V23309

First Floor: 1,375 square feet
Second Floor: 1,016 square feet
Total: 2,391 square feet

L **D**

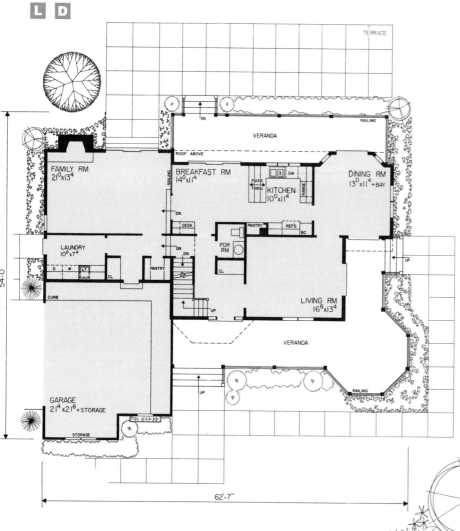

● Covered porches, front and back, are a fine preview to the livable nature of this Victorian. Living areas are defined in a family room with fireplace, formal living and dining rooms, and a kitchen with breakfast room. An ample laundry room, garage with storage area, and powder room round out the first floor. Three second floor bedrooms are joined by a study and two full baths.

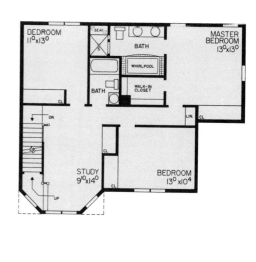

ENGLISH TUDOR HOUSES ...

have enjoyed a long and varied history in America. Recent years have seen a growth in popularity of this pleasing exterior style. From a purist standpoint, what is called Tudor today should really be referred to as Elizabethan. The many variations on the following pages are highlighted by simulated half-timber work, stucco, diamond-paned casement windows, massive sculptured chimneys, brick, stone and frame exterior walls, panelled doors, and varied roof planes. Note wavy siding and extra beam work. Of particular interest are the Cotswold Cottage/1½-story variations which project a low profile and retain a full measure of English charm.

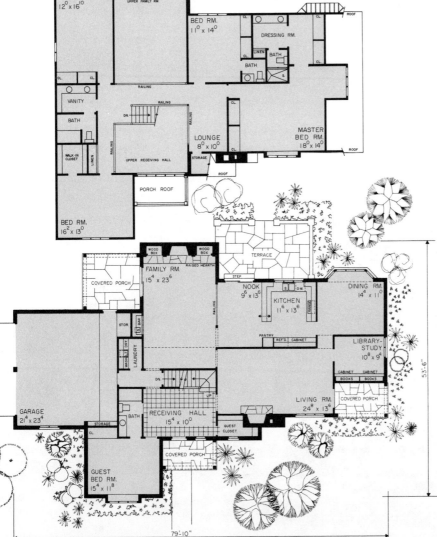

Design V22356

First Floor: 1,969 square feet
Second Floor: 1,702 square feet
Total: 3,671 square feet

L **D**

● Here is truly an exquisite Tudor adaptation. The exterior, with its interesting roof lines, window treatment, stately chimney and its appealing use of brick and stucco, could hardly be more dramatic. Inside, the drama really begins to unfold as one envisions his family's living patterns. The delightfully large receiving hall has a two story ceiling and controls the flexible traffic patterns. The living and dining rooms, with the library nearby, will cater to the formal living pursuits. The guest room offers another haven for the enjoyment of peace and quiet. Observe the adjacent full bath. Just inside the entrance from the garage is the laundry room. For the family's informal activities there are the interactions of the family room - covered porch - nook - kitchen zone. Notice the raised hearth fireplace, the wood boxes, the sliding glass doors, built-in bar and the kitchen pass-thru. Adding to the charm of the family room is its high ceiling. From the second floor hall one can look down and observe the activities below.

245

Design V22794

First Floor: 1,680 square feet
Second Floor: 1,165 square feet
Apartment: 867 square feet
Total: 3,712 square feet

● This exceptionally pleasing Tudor design has a great deal of interior livability to offer its occupants. Use the main entrance, enter into the foyer and begin your journey throughout this design. To the left of the foyer is the study, to the right, the formal living room. The living room leads to the rear, formal dining room. This room has access to the outdoors and is conveniently located adjacent to the kitchen. A snack bar divides the kitchen from the family room which also has access to outdoors plus it has a fireplace as does the living room. The second floor houses the family's four bedrooms. Down six steps from the mud room is the laundry and entrance to the garage, up six steps from this area is a complete apartment. This is an excellent room for a live-in relative. It is completely private by gaining access from the outdoor balcony.

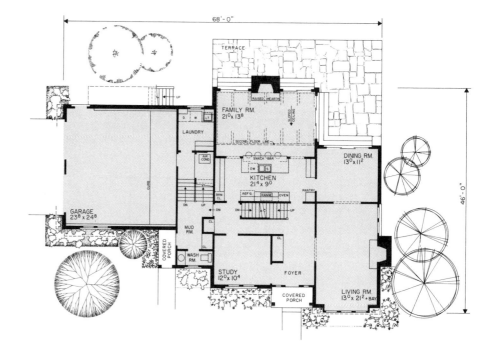

Design V22957

First Floor: 2,557 square feet
Second Floor: 1,939 square feet
Total: 4,496 square feet

L D

● The decorative half timbers and stone wall-cladding on this manor are stately examples of Tudor architecture. A grand double staircase is the highlight of the elegant, two-story foyer that opens to each of the main living areas. The living and gathering rooms are anchored by impressive central fireplaces. Handy built-ins, including a lazy susan and desk, and an island workstation with sink and cooktop, are convenient amenities in the kitchen. The adjacent breakfast room opens to the terrace for a sunny start to the day. Functioning with both the kitchen and the formal dining room is the butler's pantry. It has an abundance of cabinet and cupboard space and even a sink for a wet bar. Accessible from both the gathering and living rooms is the quiet study. If desired this could become a media center, sewing room or home office. The outstanding master suite features a cozy bedroom fireplace, picturesque whirlpool bath, and a convenient walk-in closet. Three additional second-floor bedrooms include a guest suite with dressing room and walk-in closet. Every part of this house speaks elegance, formality and the time-honored values for which Tudor is renowned.

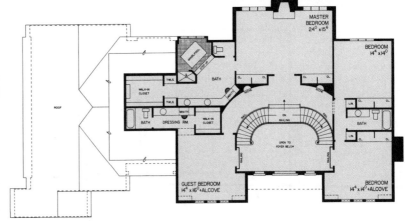

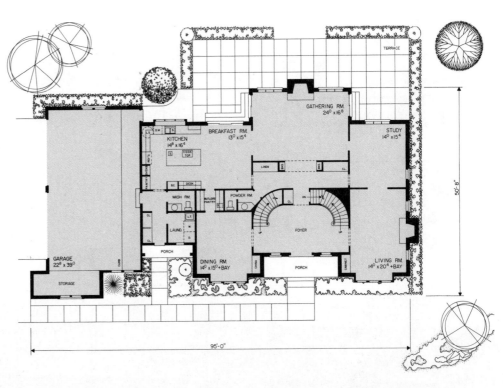

Design V22960

First Floor: 1,372 square feet
Second Floor: 1,245 square feet
Total: 2,617 square feet

● The swooping roof of the projecting front gable results in a sheltered entrance to the foyer of this unique design. It would be difficult to imagine more appealing roof lines than this Tudor has to offer. Roof, exterior wall, and window treatment all blend together to present a harmonious facade. The two chimneys with their massive caps add their appeal, too. Once inside your guests will be impressed again. They will delight to find two such large living areas - one for formal and another for informal living. They will enjoy further the eating facilities - a formal dining room and informal breakfast room. The L-shaped kitchen will be a charm in which to work. It has an island cooking station, plenty of cupboard and counter space and a pantry nearby. The homemaker will love the strategic location of the mud room. It is just inside the entrance from the garage and is directly accessible from the rear yard. The covered porch is a nice feature. And don't miss the two fireplaces - one with a raised hearth. Upstairs there are four bedrooms, two baths and good storage facilities.

 CUSTOMIZABLE

Custom Alterations? See page 413 for customizing this plan to your specifications.

BEDROOM 13⁸ x 13⁴

BEDROOM 12⁰ x 10⁰

BATH

BEDROOM 11⁴ x 13⁶

ATTIC

ATTIC

ROOF

ROOF

ROOF

ACCESS PANEL

DESK

SHELVES

LIN.

RAILING

DN

OPEN

CL

TUB

BATH

VANITY

DRESSING RM.

LINEN

SEAT

MASTER BEDROOM 16⁴ x 17²

ROOF

Design V22855

First Floor: 1,372 square feet
Second Floor: 1,245 square feet
Total: 2,617 square feet

L **D**

● This elegant Tudor house is perfect for the family who wants to move-up in living area, style and luxury. As you enter this home you will find a large living room with a fire-place on your right. Adja-cent, the formal dining room has easy access to both the living room and the kitchen. The kitchen/ breakfast room has an open plan and access to the rear terrace. Sunken a few steps, the spacious family room is highlighted with a fireplace and access to the rear, covered porch. Note the optional planning of the garage storage area. Plan this area according to the needs of your family. Upstairs, your family will enjoy three bedrooms and a full bath, along with a spacious master bedroom suite. Truly a house that will bring many years of pleasure to your family.

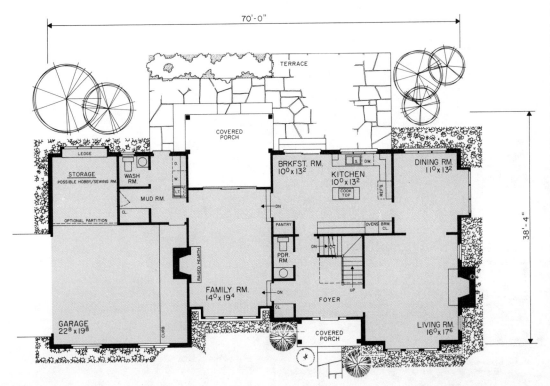

70'-0"

38'-4"

TERRACE

COVERED PORCH

LEDGE

STORAGE
POSSIBLE HOBBY/SEWING RM.

WASH. RM.

MUD RM.

OPTIONAL PARTITION

BRKFST. RM. 10⁰ x 13²

KITCHEN 10⁰ x 13²

COOK TOP

DINING RM. 11⁰ x 13²

REF'S

PANTRY

OVENS

BRM CL

PDR. RM.

DN

DN

UP

RAISED HEARTH

GARAGE 22⁸ x 19⁸

CURB

FAMILY RM. 14⁰ x 19⁴

CL

FOYER

COVERED PORCH

LIVING RM. 16⁰ x 17⁶

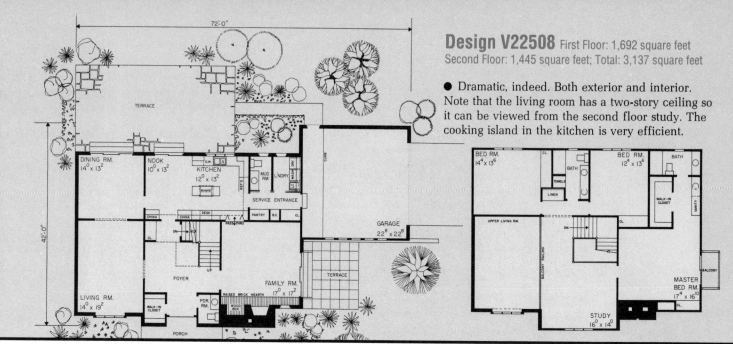

Design V22508 First Floor: 1,692 square feet
Second Floor: 1,445 square feet; Total: 3,137 square feet

● Dramatic, indeed. Both exterior and interior. Note that the living room has a two-story ceiling so it can be viewed from the second floor study. The cooking island in the kitchen is very efficient.

Design V22128 First Floor: 1,152 square feet
Second Floor: 896 square feet; Total: 2,048 square feet

L D

● Here is proof that your restricted building budget can return to you wonderfully pleasing design and loads of livability. This is an English Tudor adaptation that will surely become your subdivision's favorite facade. Its mark of individuality is obvious to all.

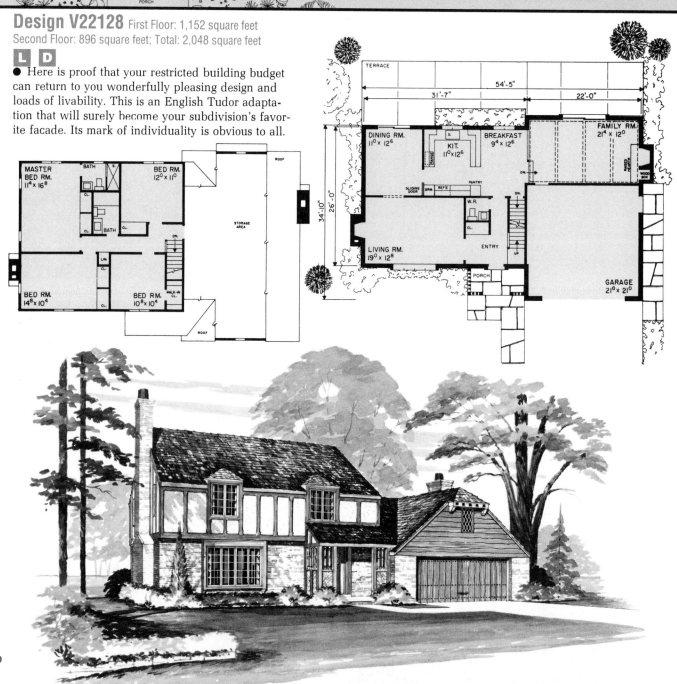

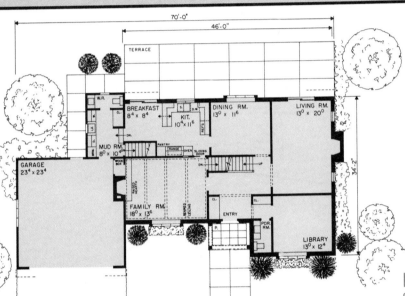

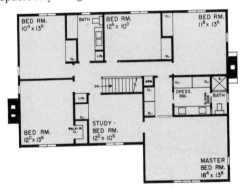

● Imagine, six bedrooms on the second floor. The first floor houses the living areas: family room, living room, dining areas plus a library. Not much more livability could be packed into this spaciously designed home.

Design V22141 First Floor: 1,490 square feet
Second Floor: 1,474 square feet; Total: 2,964 square feet

Design V22967

First Floor: 1,877 square feet
Second Floor: 467 square feet
Total: 2,344 square feet

● Special interior amenities abound in this unique 1½-story Tudor. Living areas include an open gathering room/dining room area with fireplace and pass-through to the breakfast room. Quiet time can be spent in a sloped-ceiling study. Look for plenty of workspace in the island kitchen and workshop/storage area. Sleeping areas are separated for utmost privacy: an elegant master suite on the first floor, two bedrooms and a full bath on the second. Note the unusual curved balcony seat in the stairwell and the second floor ledge—a perfect spot for displaying plants or collectibles.

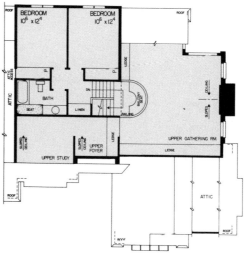

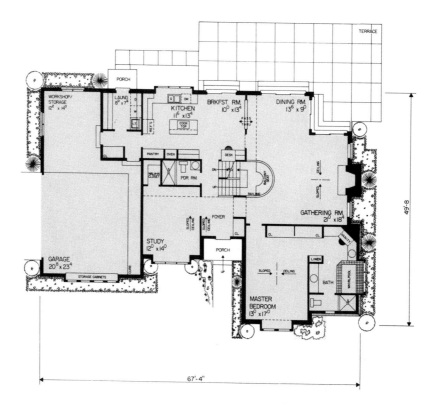

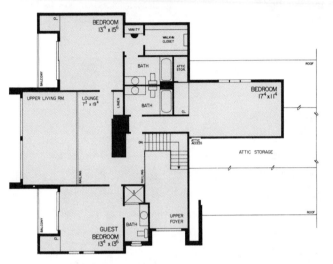

Design V22965

First Floor: 2,313 square feet
Second Floor: 1,314 square feet
Total: 3,627 square feet

● An appealing mix of contrasting exterior materials go well together to help create this distinctive Tudor. Brick, quarried stone and stucco will result in a pleasingly colorful facade. The varying heights of the gabled roof planes add their measure of drama. But that is not all that helps set the character of this stylish house. The window and door treatments add their exquisite appeal too. As one passes through the double front door he is welcomed by a delightfully spacious foyer. It has a sloping two-story ceiling which fosters a view upward to the overlooking balcony and the expanse of window-wall. To the right of the foyer is a fine-functioning kitchen which conveniently opens to the breakfast room. It is strategically located to serve both the formal dining room and the informal family room equally well. The mud room with laundry and washroom is but a step or two away. The sunken living room could hardly be more inviting. It has a high sloping ceiling, a view of the overhanging balcony, a wall of windows, a fireplace and a wet bar. Access to the terrace is through two sets of sliding glass doors. Imagine, four baths serving the four bedrooms. Don't miss the three-car garage.

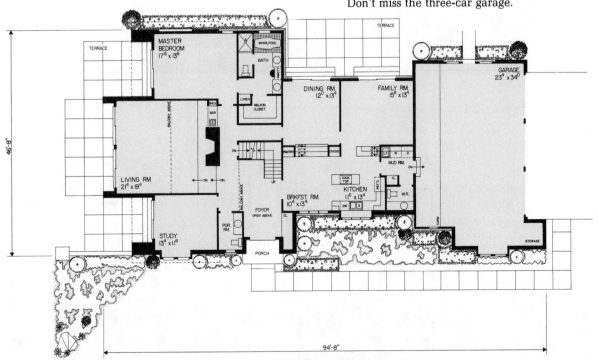

Design V22242 First Floor: 1,327 square feet
Second Floor: 832 square feet; Total: 2,159 square feet

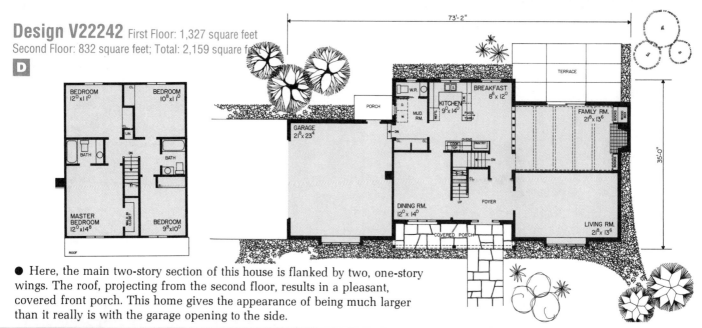

● Here, the main two-story section of this house is flanked by two, one-story wings. The roof, projecting from the second floor, results in a pleasant, covered front porch. This home gives the appearance of being much larger than it really is with the garage opening to the side.

Design V22732

First Floor: 1,071 square feet
Second Floor: 1,022 square feet
Total: 2,093 square feet

● The two-story front entry hall will be dramatic indeed. Note the efficient kitchen adjacent to informal family room, formal dining room. Upstairs, three big bedrooms, two baths.

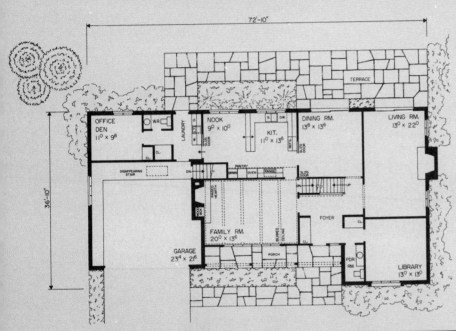

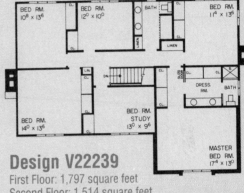

● Not only does the first floor of this plan contain formal and informal living areas, but it also houses a library and a rear office, plus two washrooms and a first floor laundry. Now that is a lot of living space! Imagine a second floor with five bedrooms and a study. Or make it six bedrooms.

Design V22239

First Floor: 1,797 square feet
Second Floor: 1,514 square feet
Total: 3,311 square feet

Design V23335

First Floor: 1,504 square feet
Second Floor: 1,348 square feet
Total: 2,852 square feet

● This is a first-rate Tudor with three bedrooms upstairs and casual and formal living downstairs. Corner fireplaces in the family room and living room will be favorite gathering spots. From the efficient U-shaped kitchen move to a convenient service area and two-car garage.

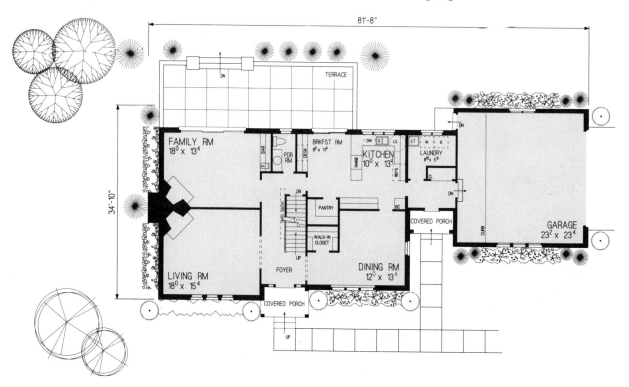

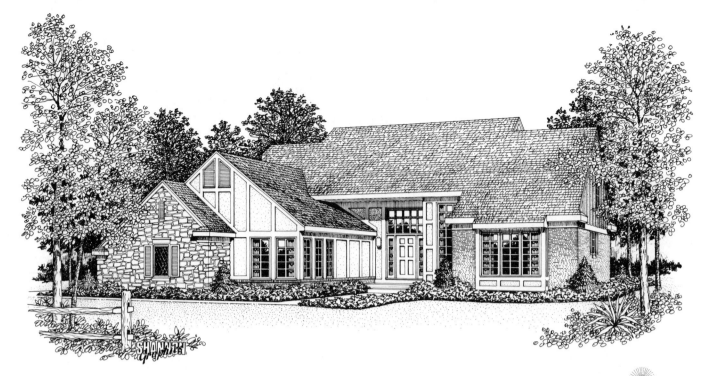

Design V23342 First Floor: 1,467 square feet
Second Floor: 715 square feet; Total: 2,182 square feet

● Just the right amount of living space is contained in this charming traditional house and it's arranged in a great floor plan. The split-bedroom configuration, with two bedrooms (or optional study) on the first floor and the master suite on the second floor with its own studio, assures complete privacy. The living room has a second-floor balcony overlook and a warming fireplace. The full-width terrace in back is counter-balanced nicely by the entry garden court.

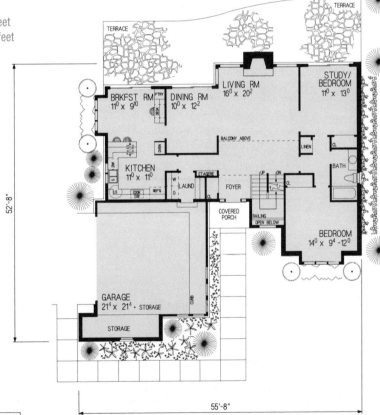

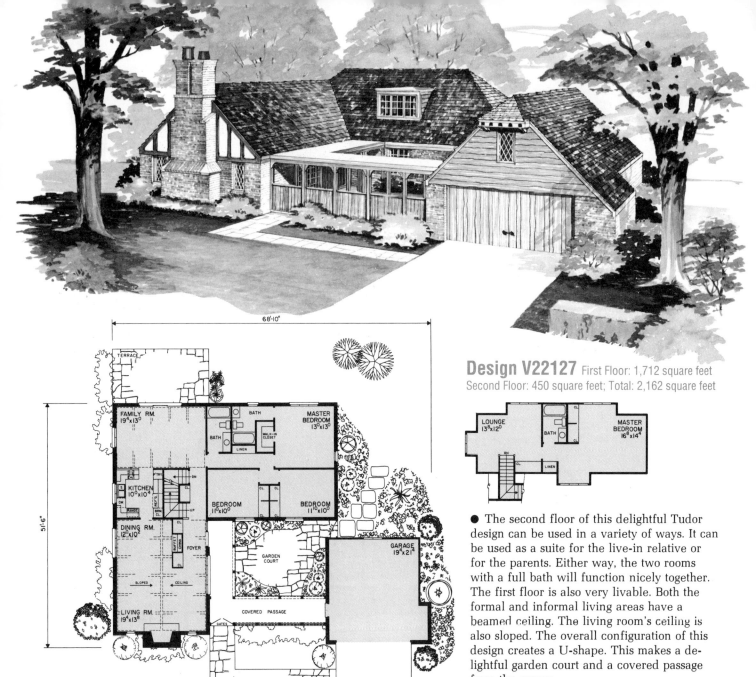

Design V22127 First Floor: 1,712 square feet
Second Floor: 450 square feet; Total: 2,162 square feet

● The second floor of this delightful Tudor design can be used in a variety of ways. It can be used as a suite for the live-in relative or for the parents. Either way, the two rooms with a full bath will function nicely together. The first floor is also very livable. Both the formal and informal living areas have a beamed ceiling. The living room's ceiling is also sloped. The overall configuration of this design creates a U-shape. This makes a delightful garden court and a covered passage from the garage.

Design V22586

First Floor: 991 square feet
Second Floor: 1,003 square feet
Total: 1,994 square feet

● A stately Tudor! With four large bedrooms. And lots of living space . . . formal living and dining rooms, a family room with a traditional fireplace, a spacious kitchen with nook.

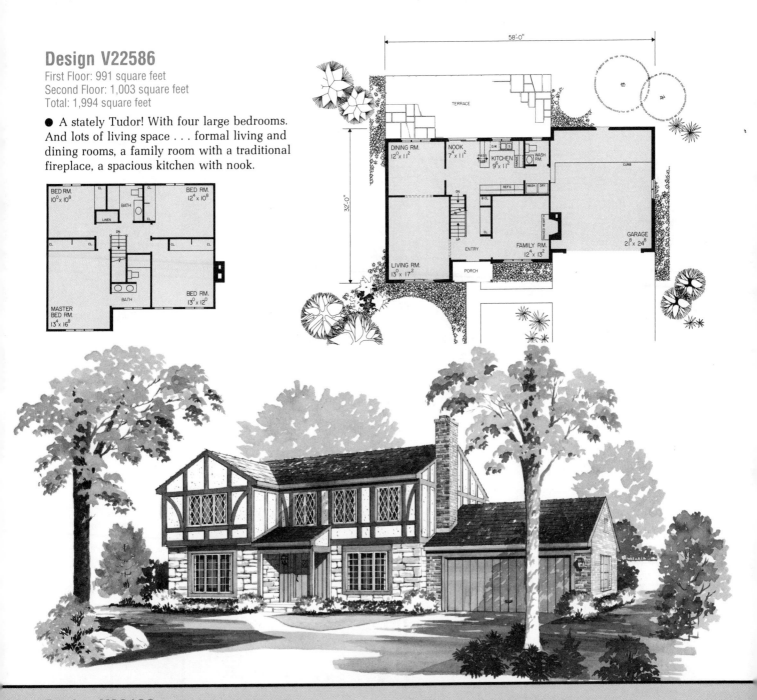

Design V22190
First Floor: 1,221 square feet; Second Floor: 884 square feet; Total: 2,105 square feet

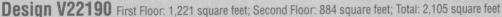

● Here is a Tudor adaptation with a popular floor plan. The open planning of the formal living/dining area results in a spacious atmosphere. Sliding glass doors and a bowed bay window foster an awareness of the rear yard.

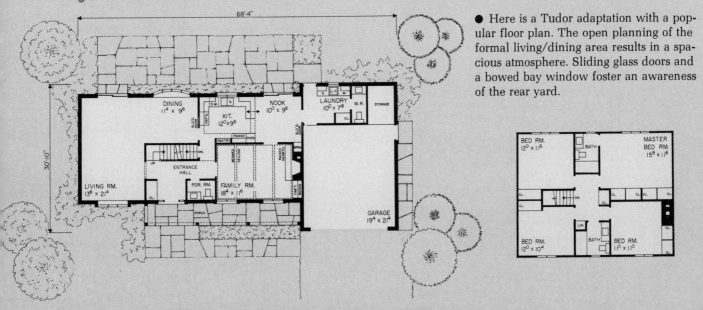

259

Design V23302

First Floor: 1,326 square feet
Second Floor: 542 square feet
Total: 1,868 square feet

● A cottage fit for a king! Appreciate the highlights: a two-story foyer, a rear living zone (gathering room, terrace, and dining room), pass-through snack bar in kitchen, a two-story master bedroom. Two upstairs bedrooms share a full bath.

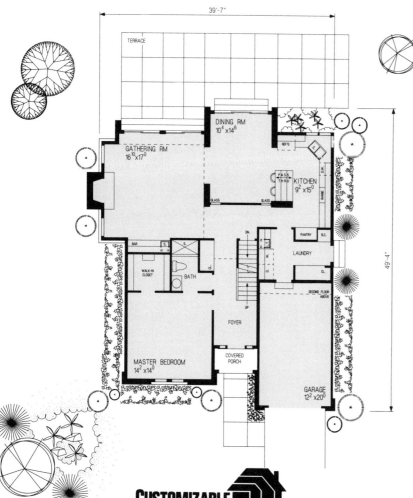

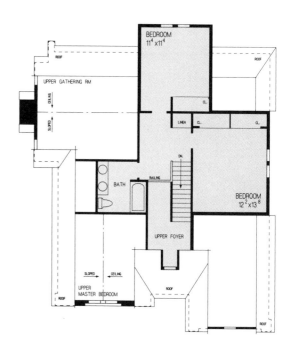

CUSTOMIZABLE

Custom Alterations? See page 413 for customizing this plan to your specifications.

Design V22491

First Floor: 1,060 square feet
Second Floor: 580 square feet
Total: 1,640 square feet

● This modest-looking plan surprises everyone with its wealth of amenities inside. Look for a U-shaped kitchen with snack bar, morning room, sunken gathering room (note fireplace with wood box), and abundant built-ins. The master suite on the second floor is a true eye-catcher.

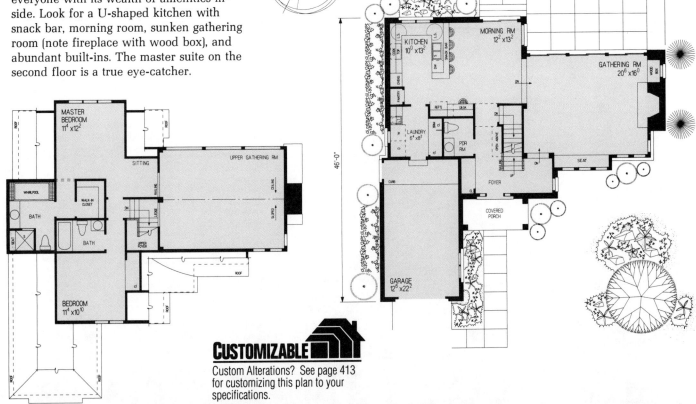

CUSTOMIZABLE
Custom Alterations? See page 413 for customizing this plan to your specifications.

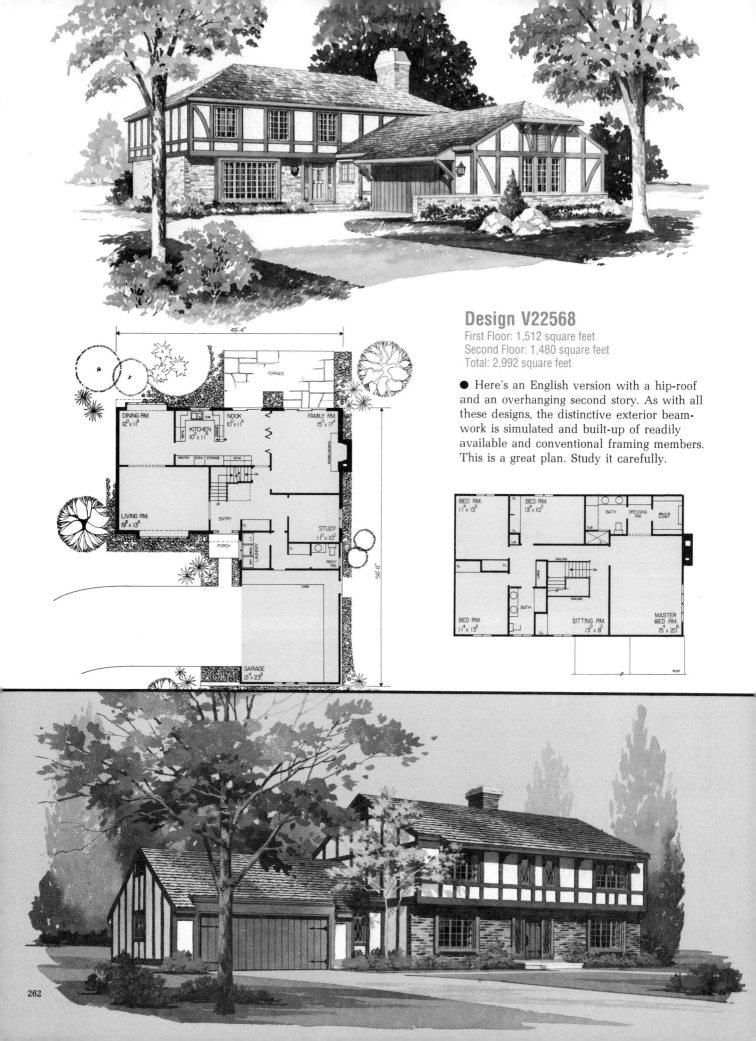

Design V22568

First Floor: 1,512 square feet
Second Floor: 1,480 square feet
Total: 2,992 square feet

● Here's an English version with a hip-roof and an overhanging second story. As with all these designs, the distinctive exterior beamwork is simulated and built-up of readily available and conventional framing members. This is a great plan. Study it carefully.

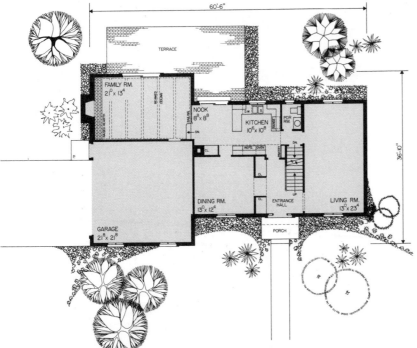

Design V22618

First Floor: 1,269 square feet
Second Floor: 1,064 square feet
Total: 2,333 square feet

● This four bedroom Tudor design is the object of an outstanding investment for a lifetime of proud ownership and fine, family living facilities. Note that the family room is sunken and it, along with the nook, has sliding glass doors.

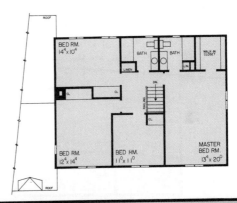

Design V22637

First Floor: 1,308 square feet
Second Floor: 1,063 square feet
Total: 2,371 square feet

● A generous, centered entrance hall routes traffic efficiently to all areas. And what wonderfully spacious areas they are. Note living, dining, sleeping and bath facilities. Don't miss first floor laundry.

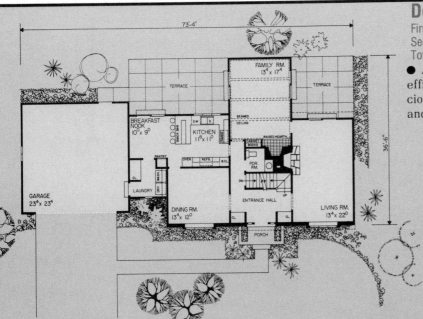

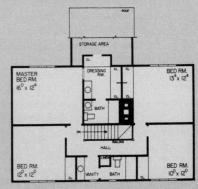

Design V22959
First Floor: 1,003 square feet
Second Floor: 1,056 square feet
Total: 2,059 square feet

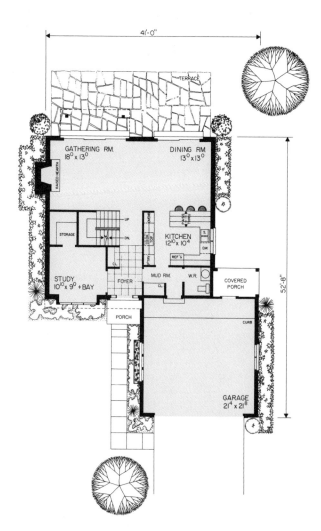

● Here the stateliness of Tudor styling is captured in a design suited for a narrow building site. This relatively low-budget two-story delivers all the livability found in many much larger homes. Imagine, a 31 foot living-dining area that stretches across the entire rear of the house and functions with the big terrace. Then, there is the efficient U-shaped kitchen with built-in cooking facilities and a pass-thru to the snack bar. Just inside the entrance from the garage is the mud room with its adjacent wash room. Enhancing first floor livability is the study with its big walk-in closet. An open staircase leads to the basement recreation area. Upstairs, three bedrooms, two baths and an outdoor balcony.

Design V22964

First Floor: 1,441 square feet
Second Floor: 621 square feet
Total: 2,062 square feet

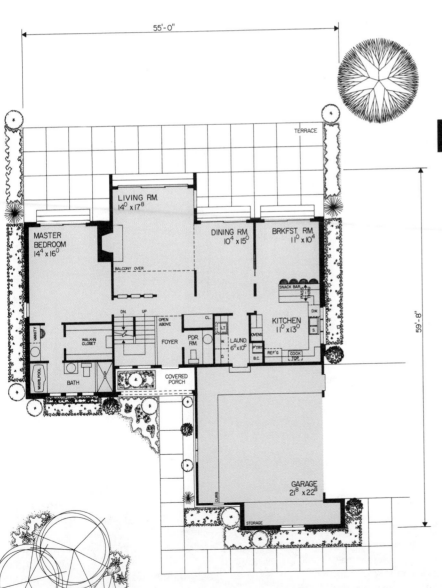

55'-0"

59'-8"

TERRACE

LIVING RM.
14⁰ x 17⁸

DINING RM.
10⁴ x 15⁰

BRKFST. RM.
11⁰ x 10⁴

MASTER BEDROOM
14⁴ x 16⁰

BALCONY OVER

SNACK BAR

KITCHEN
11⁰ x 13⁰

WALK-IN CLOSET

DN UP

OPEN ABOVE

CL.

FOYER

PDR. RM.

LAUND.
6⁰ x 10⁰

OVENS

PTRY.

REF'G

B.C.

COOK TOP

DW

S.

VANITY

BATH

WHIRLPOOL

COVERED PORCH

GARAGE
21⁸ x 22⁸

CURB

STORAGE

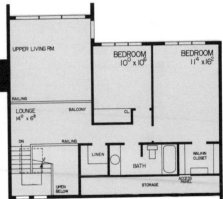

UPPER LIVING RM.

BEDROOM
10⁰ x 10⁶

BEDROOM
11⁴ x 16²

RAILING

LOUNGE
14⁰ x 6⁸

BALCONY

CL.

DN

RAILING

LINEN

BATH

WALK-IN CLOSET

OPEN BELOW

STORAGE

ACCESS PANEL

● Tudor houses have their own unique exterior design features. They include: gable roofs, simulated beam work, stucco and brick surfaces, diamond-lite windows, muntins, panelled doors, varying roof planes and hefty cornices. This outstanding two-story features a first-floor master bedroom, plus two more with lounge upstairs. The living room is dramatically spacious. It has a two-story sloping ceiling which permits it to look upward to the lounge. Large glass areas across the rear further enhance the bright, cheerful atmosphere of this area as well as the bedroom, dining and breakfast rooms. The open staircase to the upstairs has plenty of natural light as does the stairway to the basement recreation area.

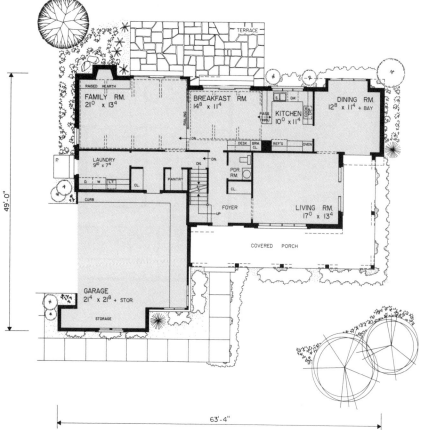

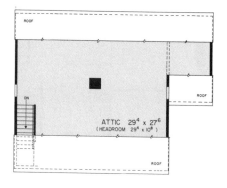

Design V22939 First Floor: 1,409 square feet; Second Floor: 1,020 square feet; Total: 2,429 square feet

● Here's a Tudor adaptation with plenty of warmth and comfort for the entire family! Start with the big wrap-around covered porch in front. Then there's a large attic with headroom, a bonus for bulk storage and even possible expansion. An efficient U-shaped kitchen features many built-ins with

also a pass-thru to a beamed-ceiling breakfast room. Sliding glass doors to a terrace are highlights in both the sunken family room and the breakfast room. A service entrance to the garage has a storage closet on each side, plus a secondary entrance through the laundry area. Recreational activities and

hobbies can be enjoyed in the basement area. There are four bedrooms plus two baths upstairs, isolated from household noise and activity. A quiet corner living room opens to a sizable formal dining room. This room enjoys natural light from a bay window that overlooks the backyard.

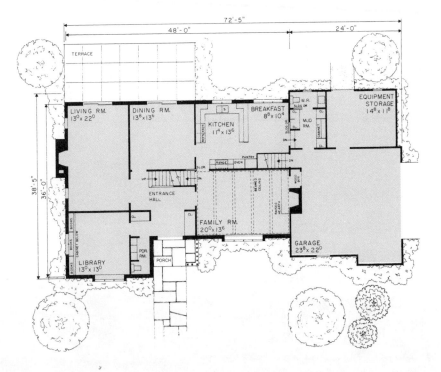

Design V22148

First Floor: 1,656 square feet
Second Floor: 1,565 square feet
Total: 3,221 square feet

● The charm of this Tudor adaptation could hardly be improved upon. Its fine proportion and exquisite use of materials result in a most distinctive home. However, the tremendous exterior appeal tells only half of the story. Inside there is a breathtaking array of highlights which will cater to the whims of the large family. Imagine six large bedrooms, two full baths and plenty of closets on the second floor! The first floor has a formal living zone made up of the big living room, the separate dining room and the sizeable library. A second zone is comprised of the U-shaped kitchen, the breakfast room and the family room — all contributing to fine informal family living patterns. Behind the garage is the mud room, washroom and the practical equipment storage room. Don't miss beamed ceiling, powder room, two fireplaces and two flights of stairs to the basement.

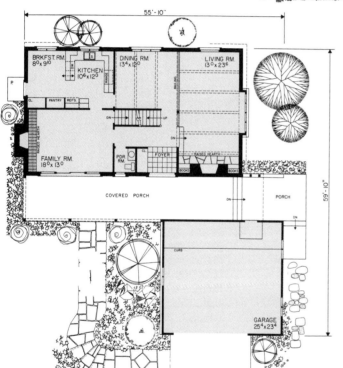

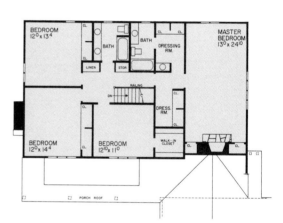

Design V22324
First Floor: 1,256 square feet
Second Floor: 1,351 square feet; Total: 2,607 square feet

● Dramatic, indeed! Both the interior and the exterior of these three Tudor designs deserve mention. Study each of them closely. The design featured here has a simple rectangular plan which will be relatively economical to build. This design is ideal for a corner lot.

Design V22274

First Floor: 1,941 square feet
Second Floor: 1,392 square feet
Total: 3,333 square feet

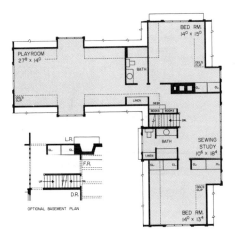

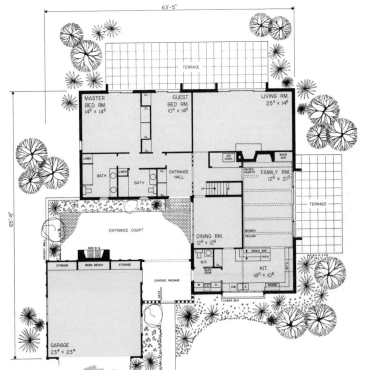

Design V22276

First Floor: 1,273 square feet
Second Floor: 1,323 square feet
Total: 2,596 square feet

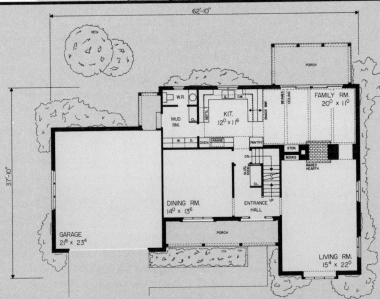

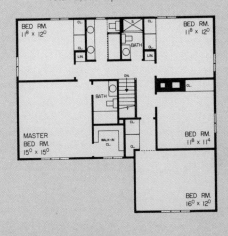

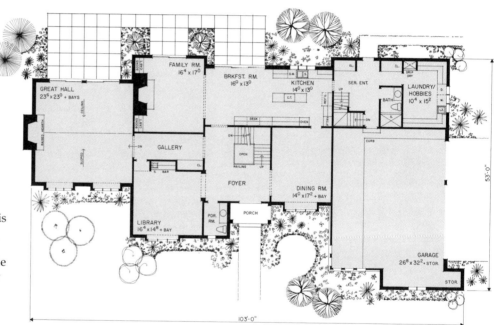

Design V23369

First Floor: 2,740 square feet
Second Floor: 2,257 square feet
Total: 4,997 square feet

● In magnificent Tudor style, this home delivers a stunning facade complemented by a most livable floor plan. The living areas include a library, a great hall and a family room (both with fireplaces) and a formal dining room. The island kitchen has an attached breakfast room. Connecting the main body of the house to the garage is a service area with full bath and laundry/hobby room. Upstairs, there are four bedrooms with walk-in closets and four full baths. The master has a fireplace and His and Hers walk-ins.

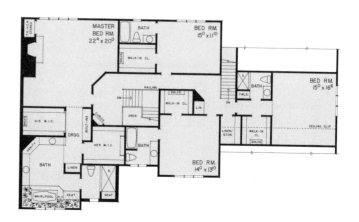

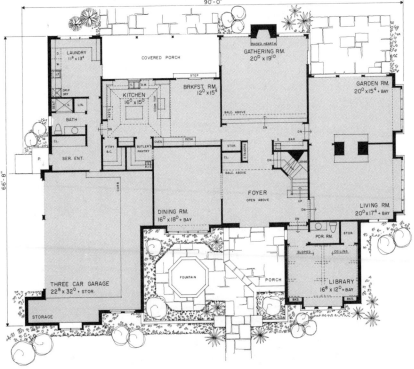

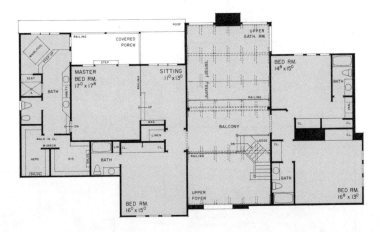

Design V23554

First Floor: 3,275 square feet
Second Floor: 2,363 square feet
Total: 5,638 square feet

● A splendid garden entry greets visitors to this regal Tudor home. Past the double doors is a two-story foyer that leads to the various living areas of the home. A quiet library is secluded directly off the foyer and has a box bay window, private powder room and sloped ceiling. Formal living takes place to the right of the foyer—an attached garden room shares a through fireplace with this area. Formal dining is found to the left of the foyer, accessed from the kitchen via a butler's pantry. The gathering room handles casual occasions and is just across the hall from the wet bar. Upstairs there is a grand master suite with lavish bath and sitting room and three secondary bedroom, each with private bath.

271

Design V22629

First Floor: 1,555 square feet
Second Floor: 1,080 square feet
Total: 2,635 square feet

● This home will really be fun in which to live. In addition to the sizeable living, dining and family rooms, many extras will be found. There are two fireplaces one to serve each of the formal and the informal areas. The back porch is a delightful extra. It will be great to relax in after a long hard day. Note two half baths on the first floor and two full baths on the second floor to serve the three bedrooms. Count the number of closets in the spacious upstairs. The door from the bedroom leads to storage over garage.

Design V22630

First Floor: 1,491 square feet
Second Floor: 788 square feet
Total: 2,279 square feet

● This distinctive version of Tudor styling will foster many years of prideful ownership and unique, yet practical living patterns. The main portion of the facade is delightfully symmetrical. Inside, the family living will focus on the 29 foot great room with its dramatic fireplace and beamed ceiling. The kitchen is outstanding with snack bar and dining nook nearby. Note the three large bedrooms each having its own dressing room. Extra storage space is available above the garage or may be developed into another room. Oversized garage includes a built-in workbench. Study plan carefully. It has much to offer.

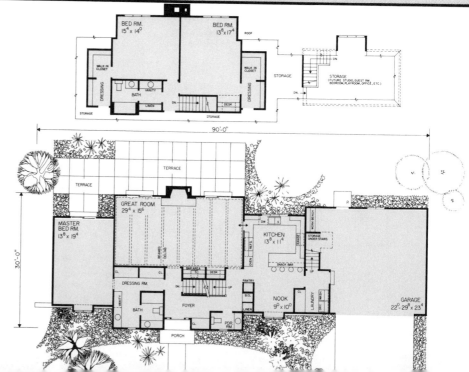

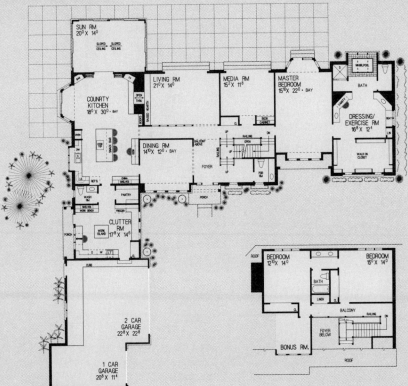

Floor plan labels:

SUN RM 20⁰ X 14⁰ — SLOPED CEILING, SLOPED CEILING

LIVING RM 21⁰ X 14⁰

MEDIA RM 15⁰ X 11⁰

MASTER BEDROOM 15⁰ X 22⁰ + BAY

BATH — WHIRLPOOL

COUNTRY KITCHEN 18⁰ X 30⁰ + BAY

DRESSING/EXERCISE RM 16⁸ X 12⁴

DINING RM 14¹⁰ X 12⁰ + BAY

BALCONY ABOVE — RAILING OPEN

FOYER

WALK-IN CLOSET

PANTRY

CLUTTER RM 17⁸ X 14⁰ — WORK ISLAND

PORCH

2 CAR GARAGE 22⁸ X 22⁸

1 CAR GARAGE 20⁸ X 11⁴

BEDROOM 12¹⁰ X 14⁰

BEDROOM 15⁰ X 14⁰

BATH — LINEN

BALCONY — RAILING

FOYER BELOW

BONUS RM.

ROOF

Design V23354

First Floor: 3,556 square feet
Second Floor: 684 square feet
Total: 4,240 square feet

L D

● Tudor styling forms the basis for this comfortable home. Stone and half-timbering provide the structure, multi-paned windows and window boxes provide the accent. The livability inside is designed for empty-nesters: the main living areas and the master suite are on the first floor; secondary bedrooms are on the second floor. Special features such as a clutter room, an island kitchen and bay or boxed windows provide added attraction. Note the bonus room that can be developed into additional sleeping space or used for storage.

Design V23371

First Floor: 2,486 square feet
Second Floor: 1,553 square feet
Total: 4,039 square feet

● Dramatic and bold, the Tudor reigns supreme among housing styles. This one combines all the favorite elements—stone, brick and half-timbering—on the outside with great livability. This is a perfect family plan. It contains formal and informal living spaces, indoor/outdoor areas, work spaces, spacious bedrooms and plenty of storage. The garage allows space for three cars. Note the extras: four fireplaces, sloped beamed ceilings in the living room and maser bedroom, and an island kitchen.

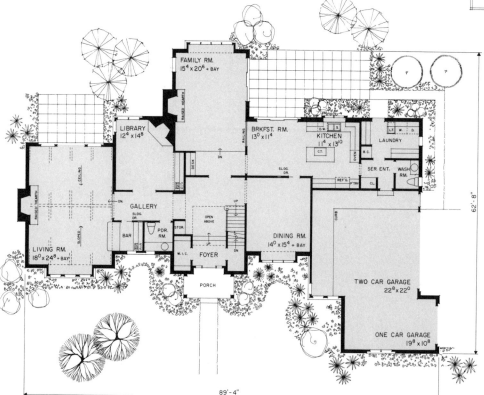

Design V22541

First Floor: 1,985 square feet
Second Floor: 1,659 square feet
Total: 3,644 square feet

● Here is English Tudor styling at its stately best. The massive stone work is complemented by stucco and massive beams. The diamond lite windows, the projecting bays, the carriage lamps and the twin chimneys add to the charm of this exterior. The spacious center entrance routes traffic effectively to all areas. Worthy of particular note is the formal living room with its fireplace, the adjacent family room overlooking the terrace, the quiet study with fireplace, two sizeable dining areas and an excellent master suite. Plus two more sizeable bedrooms.

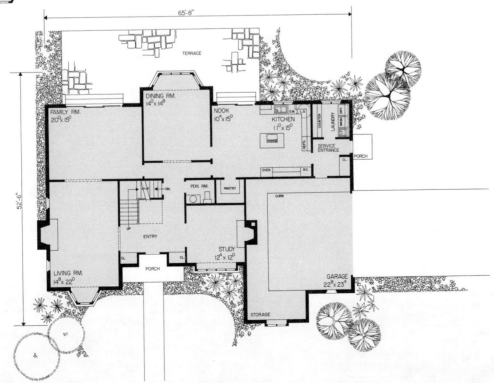

Design V22391

First Floor: 2,496 square feet
Second Floor: 958 square feet
Total: 3,454 square feet

● Here is a stately English adaptation that is impressive, indeed. The two-story octagonal foyer strikes a delightfully authentic design note. The entrance hall with open staircase and two-story ceiling is spacious. Clustered around the efficient kitchen are the formal living areas and those catering to informal activities. The family room with its beamed ceiling and raised-hearth fireplace functions like the formal living/dining zone, with the partially enclosed outdoor terrace. Three bedrooms with two baths comprise the first floor sleeping zone. Each room will enjoy its access to the terrace. Upstairs there are two more bedrooms and a study. Notice the sliding glass doors to the balcony and how the study looks down into the entrance hall. The three-car garage is great. Your own list of favorite features will surely be lengthy.

Design V21991

First Floor: 1,262 square feet
Second Floor: 1,108 square feet
Total: 2,370 square feet

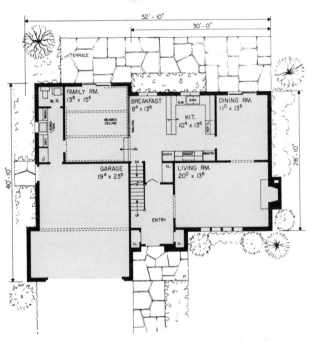

● Put yourself and your family in this English cottage adaptation and you'll all rejoice over your new home for many a year. The pride of owning and living in a home that is distinctive will be a constant source of satisfaction. Count the features that will serve your family well for years.

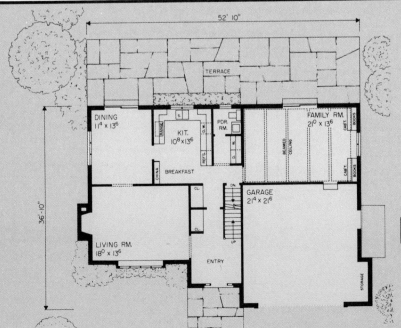

Design V22175
First Floor: 1,206 square feet
Second Floor: 1,185 square feet; Total: 2,391 square feet

● An English adaptation with all the amenities for gracious living. Note built-ins.

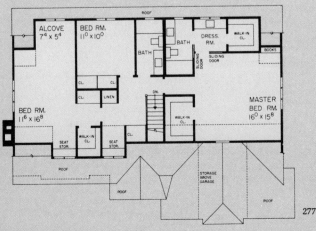

Design V22674
First Floor: 1,922 square feet
Second Floor: 890 square feet; Total: 2,812 square feet

● This delightful Tudor design's configuration permits a flexible orientation on its site with either the garage doors or the front doors facing the street. One-and-a-half-story designs offer great flexibilty in their livability. Complete livability is offered on the first floor then by utilizing the second floor another three bedrooms and bath are available. First floor features include a sunken family room with fireplace and built-in bookshelves, rear living room with sliding glass doors to the terrace, large formal dining room, first floor laundry and two washrooms.

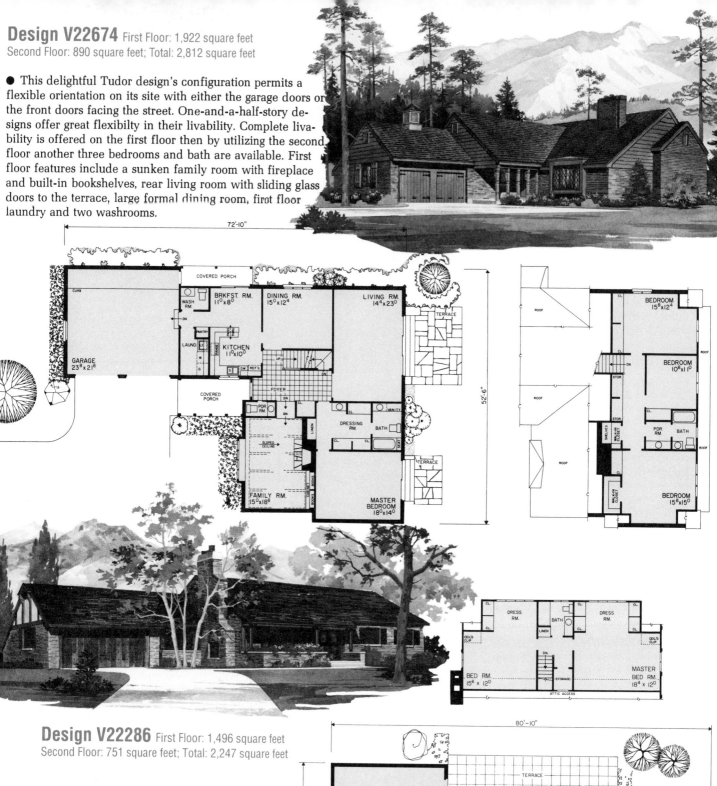

Design V22286
First Floor: 1,496 square feet
Second Floor: 751 square feet; Total: 2,247 square feet

● This charming home has a hint of Tudor styling. It will offer you and your family lots of livability. Take note of the spacious living room with fireplace. Just a few steps away, you can easily entertain family and friends in the sizable family-dining room. It is attractively highlighted with a beamed ceiling. Access to the rear terrace is obtained from both family room and nook area. A nice sized kitchen overlooks the terrace. Two bedrooms and a full bath also are on this floor. The development of the second floor adds two more bedrooms and another bath.

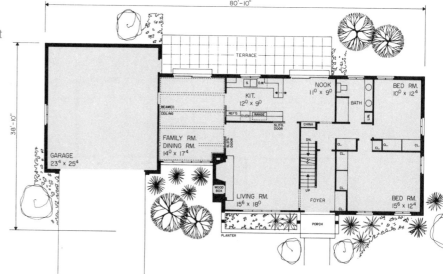

Design V22278 First Floor: 1,804 square feet; Second Floor: 939 square feet; Total: 2,743 square feet

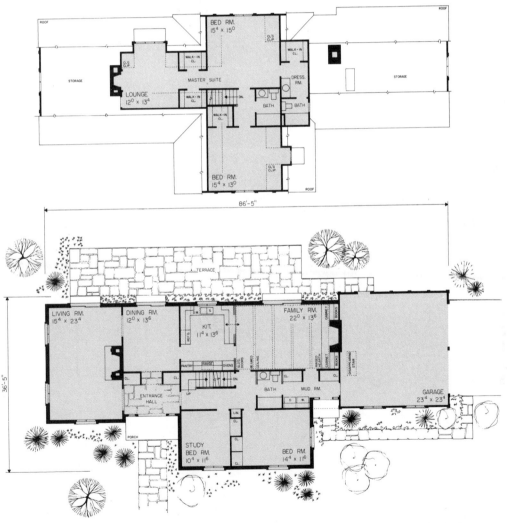

● This cozy Tudor adaptation is surely inviting. Its friendly demeanor seems to say, "welcome". Upon admittance to the formal front entrance hall, even the most casual of visitors will be filled with anticipation at the prospect of touring the house. And little wonder, too. Traffic patterns are efficient. Room relationships are excellent. A great feature is the location of the living, dining, kitchen and family rooms across the back of the house. Each enjoys a view of the rear yard and sliding glass doors provide direct access to the terrace. Another outstanding feature is the flexibility of the sleeping patterns. This may be a five bedroom house, or one with three bedrooms with study and lounge. Don't miss the three fireplaces and three baths.

Design V22373 First Floor: 1,160 square feet; Second Floor: 1,222 square feet; Total: 2,382 square feet

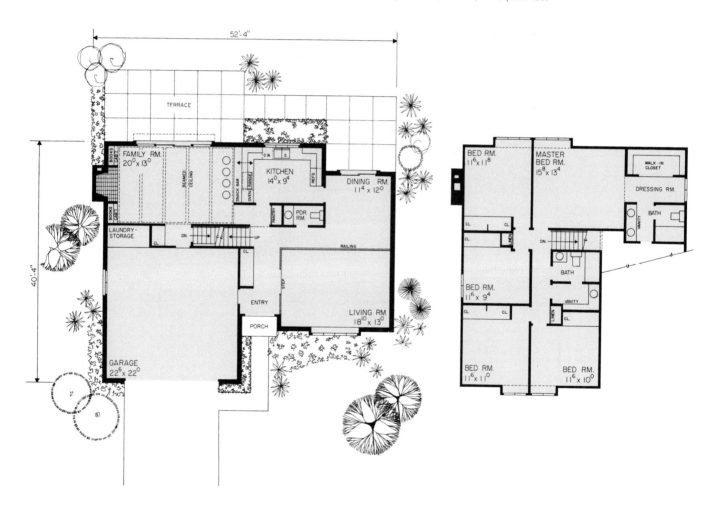

● Finding more livability wrapped in such an attractive facade would be difficult, indeed. This charming Tudor adaptation will return big dividends per construction dollar. It is compact and efficient. And, of course, it will not require a big, expensive piece of property. The location of the two-car garage as an integral part of the structure has its convenience and economic advantages, too. The living room is sunken and is divided from the dining room by a railing which helps maintain the desirable spacious atmosphere. The family room with its beamed ceiling, attractive fireplace wall, built-in storage and snack bar functions well with both the kitchen and the outdoor terrace. Four bedrooms, two baths, plenty of closets and built-in vanities.

Design V23331

First Floor: 1,115 square feet
Second Floor: 690 square feet
Total: 1,805 square feet

● Who could guess that this compact design contains three bedrooms and two full baths? The kitchen has indoor eating space in the dining room and outdoor eating space in an attached deck. A fireplace in the two-story gathering room welcomes company.

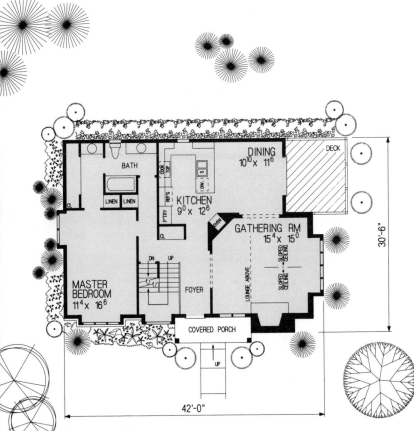

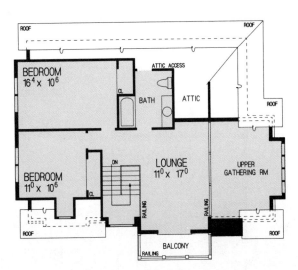

● This Tudor design has many fine features. The exterior is enhanced by front and side bay windows in the family and dining rooms. Along with an outstanding exterior, it also contains a modern and efficient floor plan within its modest proportions. Flanking the entrance foyer is a comfortable living room. The U-shaped kitchen is conveniently located between the dining and breakfast rooms.

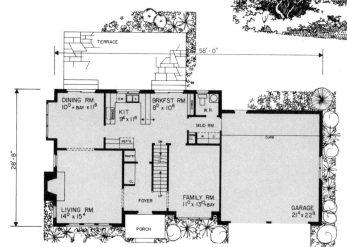

Design V22800 First Floor: 999 square feet
Second Floor: 997 square feet; Total: 1,996 square feet

L D

● The charm of old England has been captured in this outstanding one-and-a-half story design. Interior livability will efficiently serve the various needs of all family members. The first floor offers both formal and informal areas along with the work centers. Features include: a wet-bar in the dining room, the kitchen's snack bar, first floor laundry and rear covered porch.

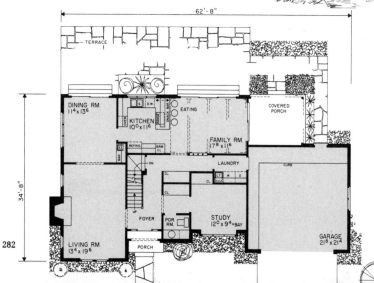

Design V22854 First Floor: 1,261 square feet
Second Floor: 950 square feet; Total: 2,211 square feet

L D

THE SIGNATURE SERIES . . . *is a superior selection of first-quality*

homes. Each plan embodies an admirable assortment of amenities that signal luxury living at its finest. Appreciable features include interior balcony overlooks, unconventional shapes, dramatic styling, and abundant space for living and entertaining. Styles vary from Contemporary to the stately Tudor manor to the charming Victorian estate.

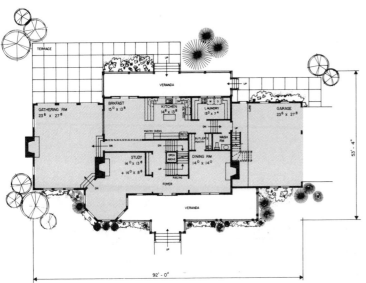

Design V23395

First Floor: 2,248 square feet
Second Floor: 2,020 square feet
Third Floor: 1,117 square feet
Total: 5,385 square feet

L **D**

● This home is a lovely example of classic Queen Anne architecture. Its floor plan offers: a gathering room with fireplace, a study with an octagonal window area, a formal dining room and a kitchen with attached breakfast room. Bedrooms on the second floor include three family bedrooms and a grand master suite. On the third floor are a guest room with private bath and sitting room and a game room with attached library.

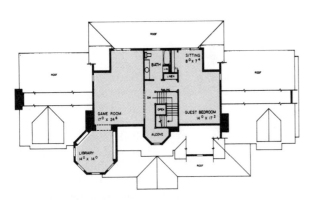

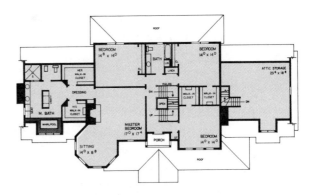

Design V22954

First Floor: 3,079 square feet
Second Floor: 1,461 square feet
Total: 4,540 square feet

● This enchanting manor displays architectural elements typical of the Victorian style: asymmetrical facade, decorative shingles and gables, and a covered porch. The two-story living room with fireplace and wet bar is located at the rear of this home where it opens to the glass-enclosed porch with skylights. A spacious kitchen is filled with amenities including an island cooktop, built-in desk, and butler's pantry connecting to the dining room. The master suite, adjacent to the study, opens to a rear deck, perfect for taking in the night air before retiring. A cozy fireplace keeps the room warm on chilly evenings. Separate His and Hers dressing rooms are outfitted with vanities and walk-in closets, and a luxurious whirlpool tub connects the baths. The second floor opens to a large lounge with built-in cabinets and bookshelves ideal for study or peaceful relaxation. Three bedrooms and two full baths complete the second-floor livability. A three-car garage with disappearing stairs to a huge attic storage area makes this home as practical as it is charming.

● A magnificent, finely wrought covered porch wraps around this impressive Victorian estate home. The gracious two-story foyer provides a direct view past the stylish bannister and into the great room with large central fireplace. To the left of the foyer is a bookshelf-lined library and to the right is a dramatic, octagonal-shaped dining room. The island cooktop completes a convenient work triangle in the kitchen, and a pass-through connects this room with the Victorian-style morning room. A butler's pantry, walk-in closet, and broom closet offer plenty of storage space. A luxurious master suite is located on the first floor and opens to the rear covered porch. A through-fireplace warms the bedroom, sitting room, and dressing room, which includes His and Hers walk-in closets. The step-up whirlpool tub is an elegant focal point to the master bath. Four uniquely designed bedrooms, three full baths, and a restful lounge with fireplace are located on the second floor. Who says you can't combine the absolute best of today's amenities with the quaint styling and comfortable warmth of the Victorian past!

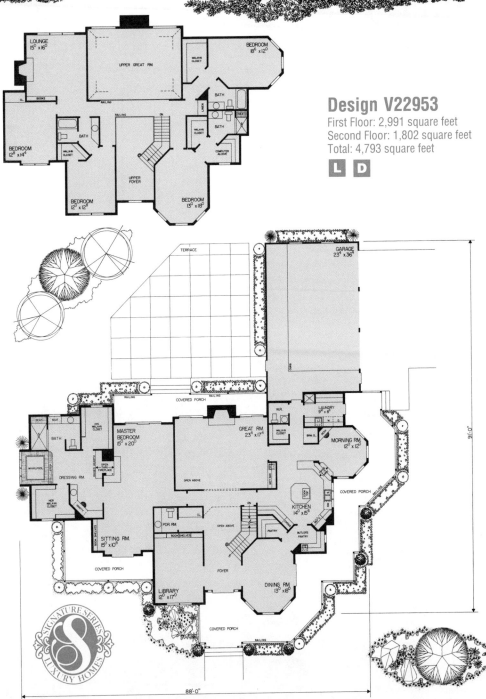

Design V22953

First Floor: 2,991 square feet
Second Floor: 1,802 square feet
Total: 4,793 square feet

L D

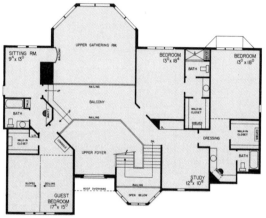

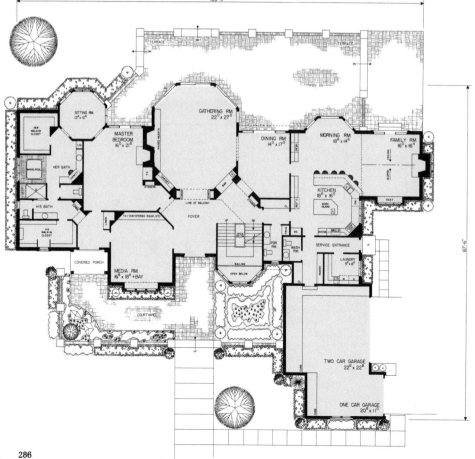

Design V22951

First Floor: 4,195 square feet
Second Floor: 2,094 square feet
Total: 6,289 square feet

● A single prominent turret with two-story divided windows draws attention to this stately Tudor home. The open foyer allows an uninterrupted view into the impressive, two-story great room with wet bar, where a fireplace with raised hearth runs the entire length of one wall. The expansive kitchen, conveniently located near the service entrance, has a U-shaped work area and a snack bar that opens to the morning room. The adjacent sloped-ceiling family room has an additional fireplace and a comfortable window seat. A Victorian-inspired, octagon-shaped sitting room is tucked into the corner of the unique master bedroom. His and Hers baths and walk-in closets complete the impressive first-floor suite. Two bedrooms, a study, and a guest suite with private sitting room are located on the second floor. A magnificent second-floor bridge overlooks foyer and gathering room and provides extraordinary views to guests on the way to their bedroom.

Cross gables, decorative half-timbers, and three massive chimneys mark the exterior of this magnificent baronial Tudor. A circular staircase housed in the turret makes an impressive opening statement in the two-story foyer. A powder room and telephone center are located off the foyer for easy use by guests. Two steps down lead to the elegant living room with music alcove or the sumptuous library with wet bar. The kitchen is a chef's delight with large work island, full cooking counter, snack bar, and a butler's pantry leading to a formal dining room with bow window. The second floor features four bedrooms, two with fireplaces, and each with private bath and abundant closet space. The master suite has an additional fireplace, His and Hers walk-in closets, whirlpool bath and separate shower, and a private sitting room in a windowed alcove. Adjacent to the master suite is a nursery that would also make an ideal exercise room.

Design V22955 First Floor: 4,274 square feet
Second Floor: 3,008 square feet; Total: 7,282 square feet

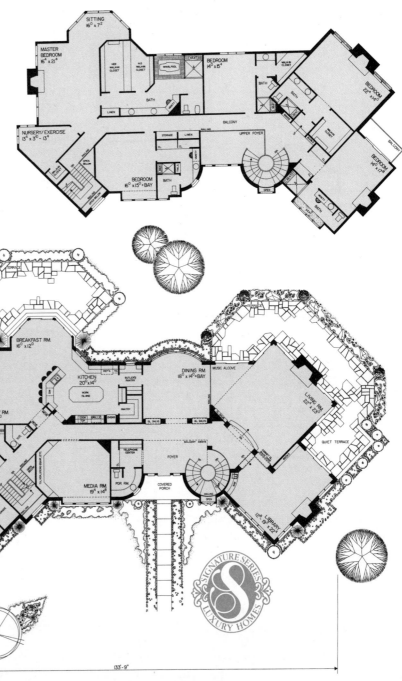

287

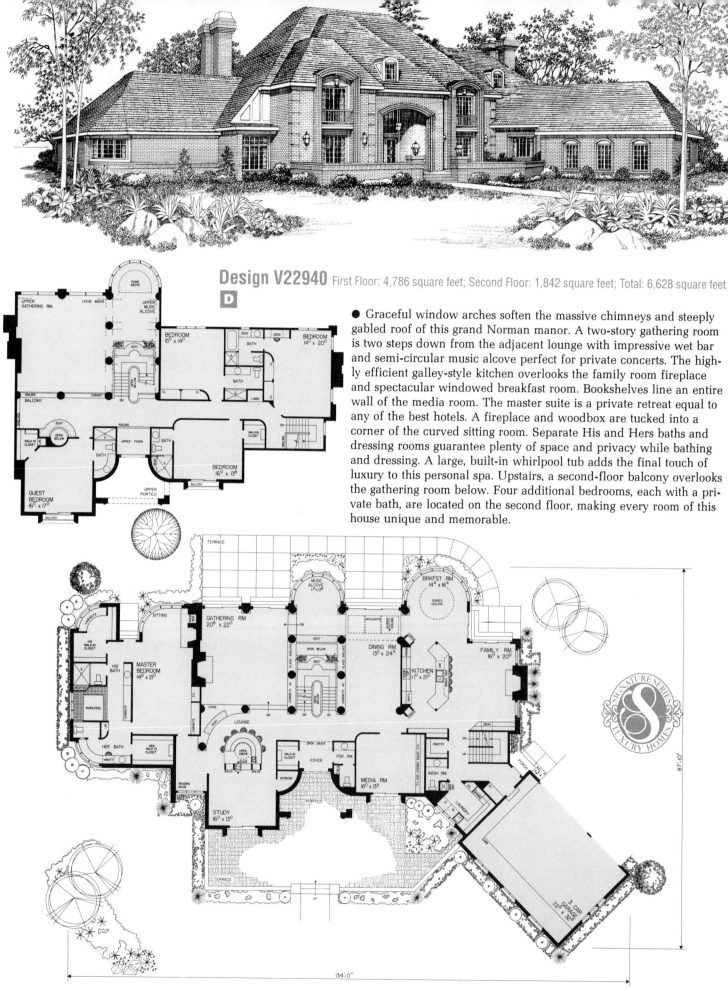

Design V22940 First Floor: 4,786 square feet; Second Floor: 1,842 square feet; Total: 6,628 square feet

D

● Graceful window arches soften the massive chimneys and steeply gabled roof of this grand Norman manor. A two-story gathering room is two steps down from the adjacent lounge with impressive wet bar and semi-circular music alcove perfect for private concerts. The highly efficient galley-style kitchen overlooks the family room fireplace and spectacular windowed breakfast room. Bookshelves line an entire wall of the media room. The master suite is a private retreat equal to any of the best hotels. A fireplace and woodbox are tucked into a corner of the curved sitting room. Separate His and Hers baths and dressing rooms guarantee plenty of space and privacy while bathing and dressing. A large, built-in whirlpool tub adds the final touch of luxury to this personal spa. Upstairs, a second-floor balcony overlooks the gathering room below. Four additional bedrooms, each with a private bath, are located on the second floor, making every room of this house unique and memorable.

Design V22968 First Floor: 3,736 square feet; Second Floor: 2,264 square feet; Total: 6,000 square feet

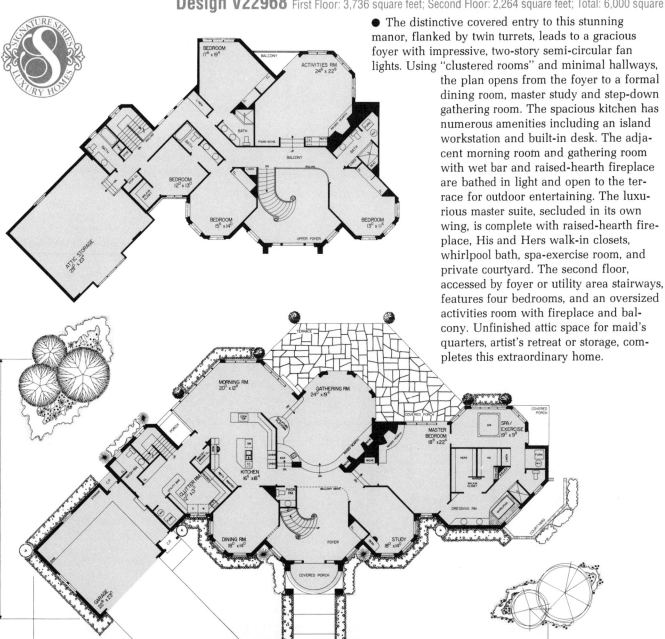

● The distinctive covered entry to this stunning manor, flanked by twin turrets, leads to a gracious foyer with impressive, two-story semi-circular fan lights. Using "clustered rooms" and minimal hallways, the plan opens from the foyer to a formal dining room, master study and step-down gathering room. The spacious kitchen has numerous amenities including an island workstation and built-in desk. The adjacent morning room and gathering room with wet bar and raised-hearth fireplace are bathed in light and open to the terrace for outdoor entertaining. The luxurious master suite, secluded in its own wing, is complete with raised-hearth fireplace, His and Hers walk-in closets, whirlpool bath, spa-exercise room, and private courtyard. The second floor, accessed by foyer or utility area stairways, features four bedrooms, and an oversized activities room with fireplace and balcony. Unfinished attic space for maid's quarters, artist's retreat or storage, completes this extraordinary home.

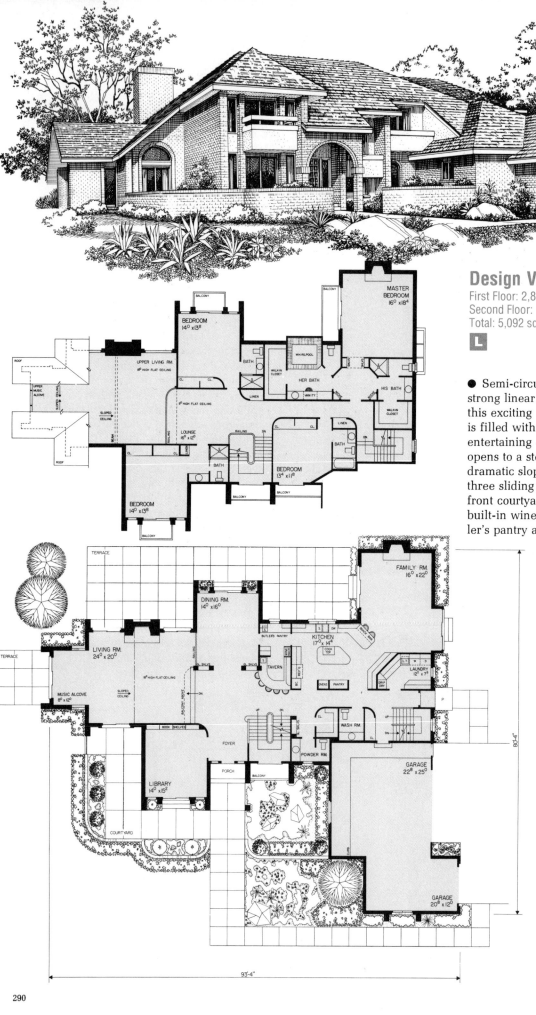

Design V22952

First Floor: 2,870 square feet
Second Floor: 2,222 square feet
Total: 5,092 square feet

L

● Semi-circular arches complement the strong linear roof lines and balconies of this exciting contemporary. The first floor is filled with well-planned amenities for entertaining and relaxing. The foyer opens to a step-down living room with a dramatic sloped ceiling, fireplace, and three sliding glass doors that access the front courtyard and terrace. A tavern with built-in wine rack and an adjacent butler's pantry are ideal for entertaining. The family room features a fireplace, sliding glass door, and a handy snack bar. The kitchen allows meal preparation, cooking and storage within a step of the central work island. Three second-floor bedrooms, each with a private bath and balcony, are reached by either of two staircases. The master suite, with His and Hers baths and walk-in closets, whirlpool, and fireplace, adds the finishing touch to this memorable home.

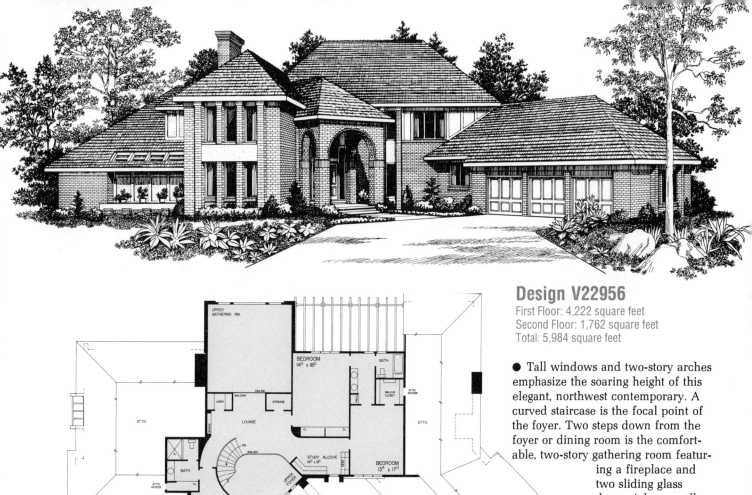

Design V22956

First Floor: 4,222 square feet
Second Floor: 1,762 square feet
Total: 5,984 square feet

● Tall windows and two-story arches emphasize the soaring height of this elegant, northwest contemporary. A curved staircase is the focal point of the foyer. Two steps down from the foyer or dining room is the comfortable, two-story gathering room featuring a fireplace and two sliding glass doors. A large walk-in pantry, work island, snack bar, and view of the family room fireplace make the kitchen functional and comfortable. The master suite is secluded in its own wing. The bedroom, with a curved-hearth fireplace, and exercise room open to the terrace through sliding glass doors. His and Hers walk-in closets and baths (Hers with whirlpool tub) are added luxuries. A media room with wet bar, accessible from master bedroom and foyer, is the perfect place to relax. The second floor stairs open to a lounge which overlooks the gathering room. Three additional bedrooms and a quiet study alcove on the second floor round out the living area of this gracious and functional home.

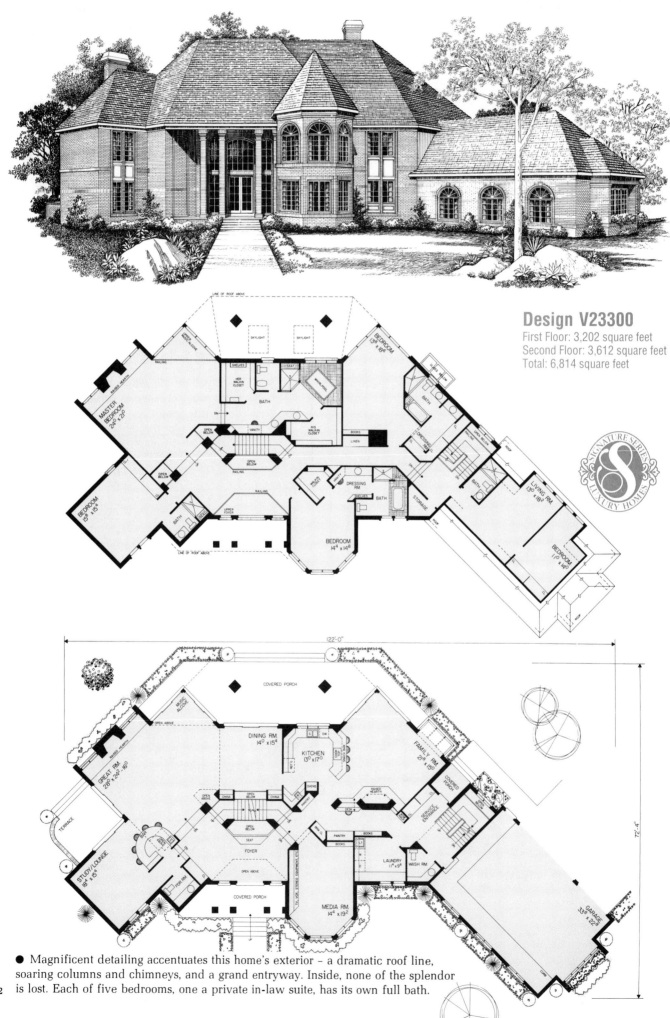

Design V23300

First Floor: 3,202 square feet
Second Floor: 3,612 square feet
Total: 6,814 square feet

Signature Series Luxury Homes

● Magnificent detailing accentuates this home's exterior – a dramatic roof line, soaring columns and chimneys, and a grand entryway. Inside, none of the splendor is lost. Each of five bedrooms, one a private in-law suite, has its own full bath.

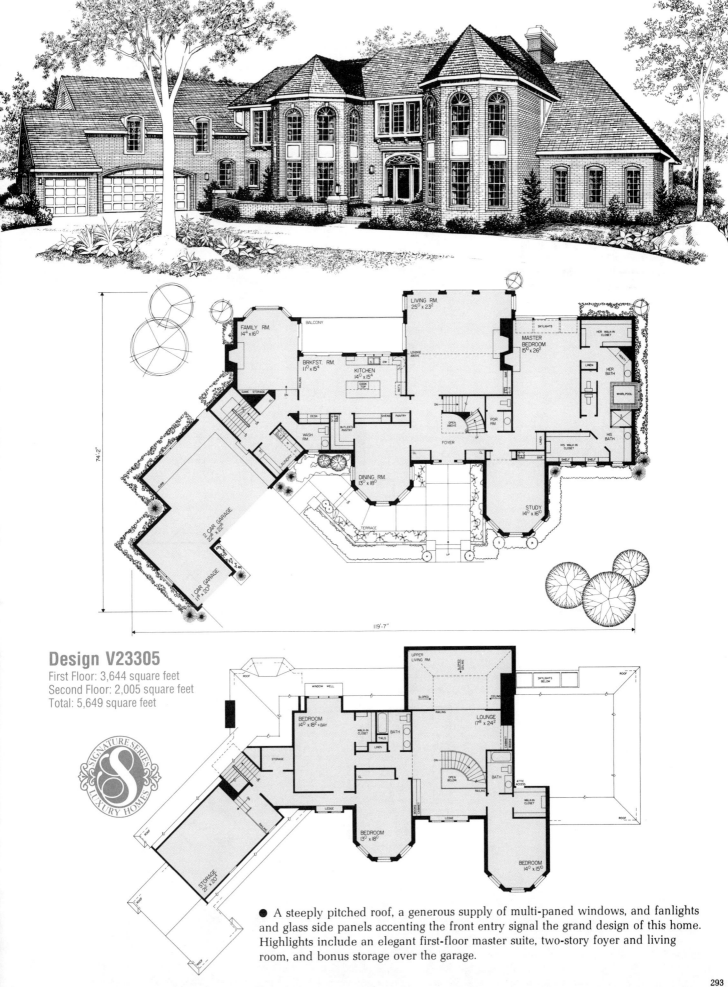

FAMILY RM.
14⁴ x 16⁰

BALCONY

LIVING RM.
25⁰ x 23²

MASTER BEDROOM
15⁰ x 26²

HER WALK-IN CLOSET

SKYLIGHTS

LOUNGE ABOVE

BRKFST. RM.
11⁰ x 15⁴

KITCHEN
14⁰ x 15⁴

COOK TOP

HER BATH

WHIRLPOOL

GAME STORAGE

DESK

OVENS

PANTRY

BUTLER'S PANTRY

WASH RM.

OPEN ABOVE

POR. RM.

HIS WALK-IN CLOSET

HIS BATH

LINEN

DINING RM.
13⁰ x 18⁰

FOYER

BAR

SHELF   SHELF

2 CAR GARAGE
23⁸ x 22⁸

CAR GARAGE
19 x 20⁸

TERRACE

STUDY
14⁰ x 16⁰

UP

74'-2"

119'-7"

Design V23305

First Floor: 3,644 square feet
Second Floor: 2,005 square feet
Total: 5,649 square feet

UPPER LIVING RM.

SLOPED CEILING

SKYLIGHTS BELOW

ROOF

WINDOW WELL

BEDROOM
14⁰ x 18² + BAY

WALK-IN CLOSET

BATH

LINEN

LOUNGE
17⁸ x 24²

CABINET

SHELVES

STORAGE

OPEN BELOW

BATH

ATTIC ACCESS

ROOF

STORAGE
28' x 20'

LEDGE

BEDROOM
13⁰ x 18⁰

LEDGE

WALK-IN CLOSET

BEDROOM
14⁰ x 15⁰

● A steeply pitched roof, a generous supply of multi-paned windows, and fanlights and glass side panels accenting the front entry signal the grand design of this home. Highlights include an elegant first-floor master suite, two-story foyer and living room, and bonus storage over the garage.

Design V23301

First Floor: 3,425 square feet
Second Floor: 2,501 square feet
Total: 5,926 square feet

● Masterful use of space with a profusion of windows and terrace access are all employed in this Tudor treasure. A two-story foyer points the way directly to the living room which features a raised-hearth fireplace, huge bay window, and curved bar. The angular kitchen has a center island and is strategically placed with relationship to the formal dining room, the family room and its gracious fireplace, and a captivating breakfast room. A media room to the left of the foyer provides built-in space for an entertainment system. The sloped-ceiling master bedroom contains a third fireplace and another gigantic bay window. Its adjoining bath is divided into His and Hers dressing areas and closets, and centers around a relaxing whirlpool spa. Guests are easily accommodated in a full suite with its own living room and bath on the second floor. Three other bedrooms and a lounge on this floor share a balcony overlook to the living room below.

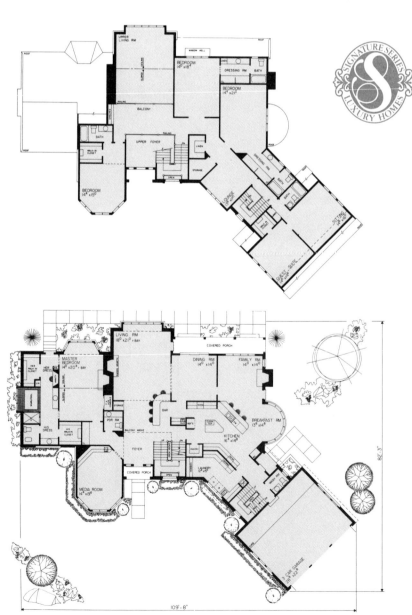

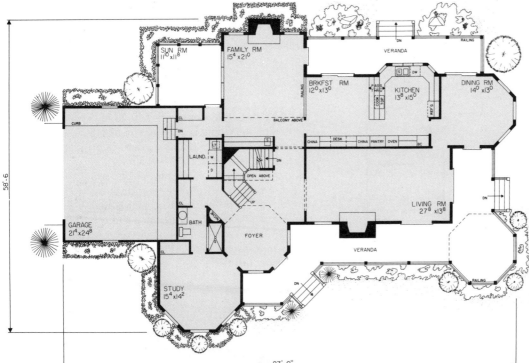

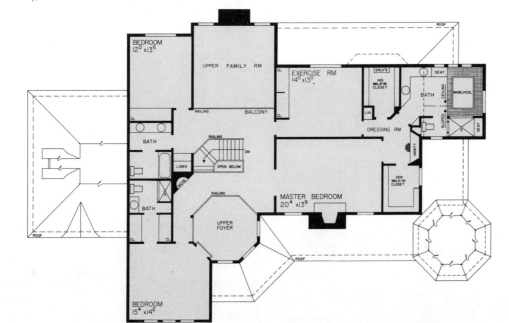

Design V23304

First Floor: 2,102 square feet
Second Floor: 1,971 square feet
Total: 4,073 square feet

L **D**

● Victorian style is displayed in most exquisite proportions in this three-bedroom, four-bath home. From verandas, both front and rear, to the stately turrets and impressive chimney stack, this is a beauty. Inside is a great lay-out with many thoughtful amenities. Besides the large living room, formal dining room, and two-story family room, there is a cozy study for private time. A gourmet kitchen with built-ins has a pass-through counter to the breakfast room. The master suite on the second floor includes many special features: whirlpool spa, His and Hers walk-in closets, exercise room, and fireplace. There are two more bedrooms, each with a full bath, on the second floor.

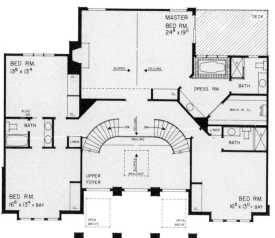

Design V23364
First Floor: 2,883 square feet
Second Floor: 1,919 square feet
Total: 4,802 square feet

● The impressive stonework facade of this
contemporary home is as dramatic as it is
practical — and it contains a grand floor plan.
Notice the varying levels — a family room,
living room, media room, and atrium are
down a few steps from the elegant entry
foyer. The large L-shaped kitchen is highlighted by an island work center and a pass-
through snack bar. A double curved staircase
leads to a second floor where four bedrooms
and three full baths are found.

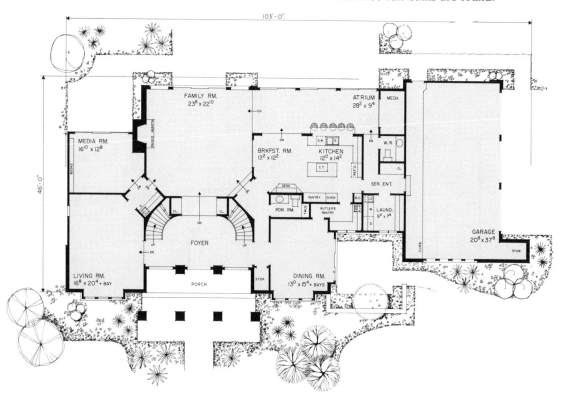

TRADITIONAL VARIATIONS ...

includes the incorporation of traditional design features such as muntined windows, shutters, panelled doors, glass side lights, gabled roofs, horizontal siding, stone chimneys, bay windows, dovecotes, cupolas, carriage lamps, and cornice brackets. All are tastefully blended to result in an appealing and distinctive facade. The examples on the following pages include Spanish, Victorian, Tudor, French, and Georgian adaptations.

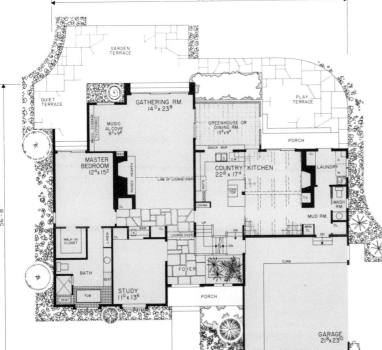

Design V22883 First Floor: 1,919 square feet
Second Floor: 895 square feet; Total: 2,814 square feet

● A country-style home is part of America's fascination with the rural past. This home's emphasis of the traditional home is in its gambrel roof, dormers and fanlight windows. Having a traditional exterior from the street view, this home has window walls and a greenhouse, which opens the house to the outdoors in a thoroughly contemporary manner. The interior meets the requirements of today's active family. Like the country houses of the past, it has a gathering room for family get-togethers or entertaining. The adjacent two-story greenhouse doubles as the dining room. There is a pass-through snack bar to the country kitchen here. This country kitchen just might be the heart of the house with its two areas — work zone and sitting room. There are four bedrooms on the two floors — the master bedroom suite on the first floor; three more on the second floor. A lounge, overlooking the gathering room and front foyer, is also on the second floor.

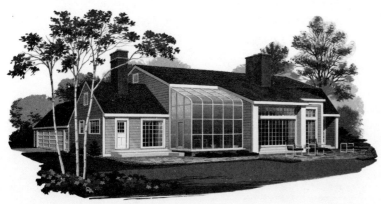

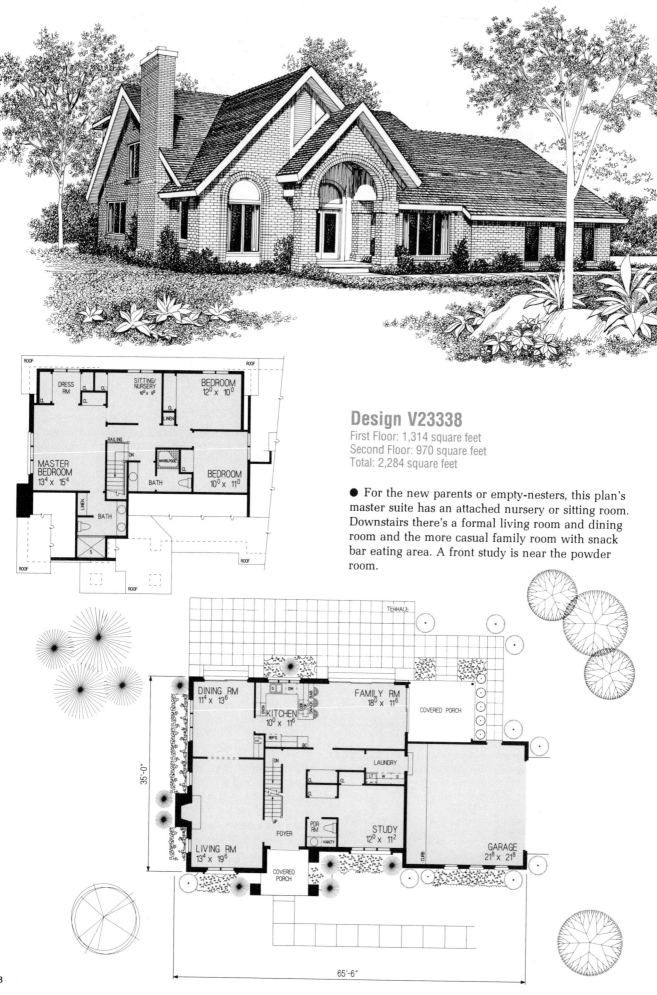

Design V23338

First Floor: 1,314 square feet
Second Floor: 970 square feet
Total: 2,284 square feet

● For the new parents or empty-nesters, this plan's master suite has an attached nursery or sitting room. Downstairs there's a formal living room and dining room and the more casual family room with snack bar eating area. A front study is near the powder room.

ROOF
ROOF

DRESS RM
CL CL CL
SITTING/NURSERY
10⁰ x 9⁰

BEDROOM
12⁰ x 10⁰

CL
LINEN

RAILING
DN

MASTER BEDROOM
13⁴ x 15⁴

WHIRLPOOL
CL
BATH

BEDROOM
10⁰ x 11⁰

LINEN
BATH

S

ROOF
ROOF
ROOF

TERRACE

DINING RM
11⁴ x 13⁶

S DW

KITCHEN
10⁰ x 11⁶

SNACK BAR

FAMILY RM
18⁰ x 11⁶

COVERED PORCH

REF'G

BC

35'-0"

DN

LAUNDRY

UP

LT W D

FOYER

PDR RM

VANITY

STUDY
12⁰ x 11²

GARAGE
21⁸ x 21⁸

LIVING RM
13⁴ x 19⁶

COVERED PORCH

65'-6"

Design V22722

First Floor: 2,330 square feet
Second Floor: 921 square feet
Total: 3,251 square feet

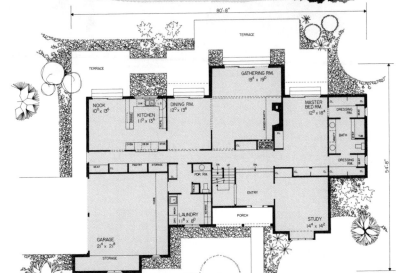

Design V22927

First Floor: 1,425 square feet
Second Floor: 704 square feet
Total: 2,129 square feet

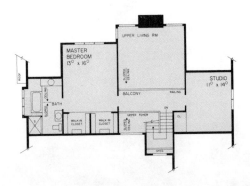

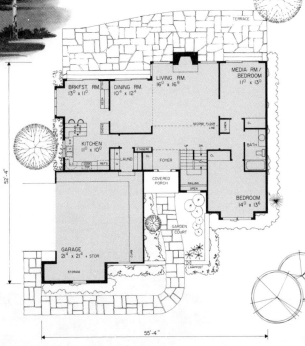

Design V22909 First Floor: 1,221 square feet
Second Floor: 767 square feet; Total: 1,988 square feet

D

● This charming traditional home with striking good looks offers the modern family plenty of contemporary amenities. The first floor features a large gathering room with fireplace, media room for stereos and VCRs, a convenient kitchen with breakfast room, plus a dining room. The second floor includes an upper gathering room, spacious master bedroom suite, and a second bedroom. Notice columns that support a covered porch and window treatments.

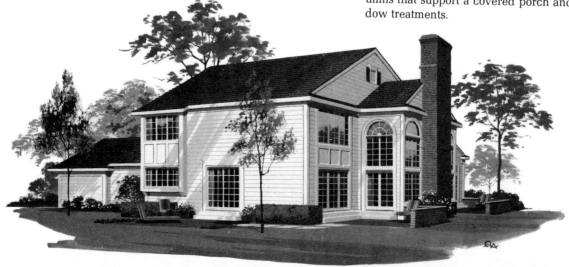

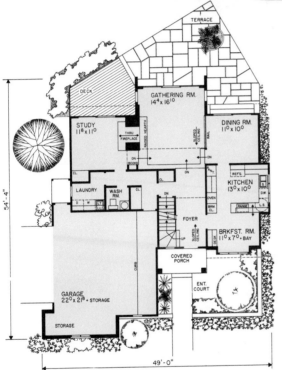

TERRACE

DECK

GATHERING RM.
14⁴ x 16¹⁰

STUDY
11⁸ x 11⁰

DINING RM.
11⁰ x 10⁰

THRU
FIREPLACE

RAISED HEARTH

KITCHEN
13⁰ x 10⁰

REF'D.

OVEN

RANGE

L.S.

D.W.

LAUNDRY

WASH
RM.

BRM.
CL.

FOYER

BRKFST. RM.
11⁰ x 7⁰ + BAY

COVERED
PORCH

GARAGE
22⁰ x 21⁸ + STORAGE

ENT.
COURT

STORAGE

54'-4"

49'-0"

Design V22826 First Floor: 1,112 square feet
Second Floor: 881 square feet; Total: 1,993 square feet

D

UPPER GATHERING ROOM

MASTER
BEDROOM
11⁸ x 13⁸

LOUNGE
10⁰ x 10⁴

BEDROOM
11⁰ x 10⁶

SLOPED CEILING

RAIL

WALK-IN
CLOSET

BATH

CL.

LINEN

BATH

CL.

DN

RAIL

SLOPED CEILING

ATTIC

UPPER
FOYER

BEDROOM
11⁰ x 10⁶

TERRACE

BRKFST. RM.
11⁰ x 7⁰

KITCHEN
13⁰ x 10⁰

RANGE

L.S.

OVEN

D.W.

BRM.
CL.

REF'G.

DINING RM.
11⁰ x 10⁰ + BAY

ALTERNATE KITCHEN / DINING RM /
BREAKFAST RM. FLOOR PLAN

● This is an outstanding example of the type of informal, traditional-style architecture that has captured the modern imagination. The interior plan houses all of the features that people want most - a spacious gathering room, formal and informal dining areas, efficient, U-shaped kitchen, master bedroom, two children's bedrooms, second floor lounge, entrance court and rear terrace and deck. Study all areas of this plan carefully.

Design V22724

First Floor: 2,543 square feet
Second Floor: 884 square feet
Total: 3,427 square feet

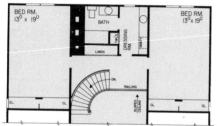

● Impressive at first glance! The interior of this one-and-a-half story home offers an abundance of livability. The master bedroom suite is on the first floor and has a private terrace. The second floor houses two more bedrooms and a bath. A design sure to provide enjoyment.

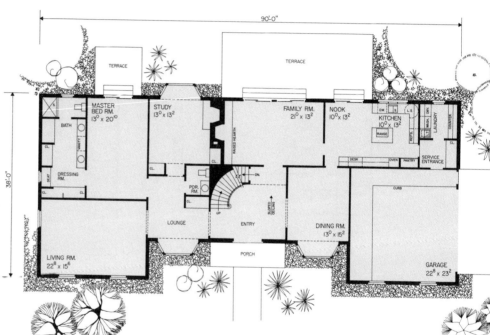

Design V22676
First Floor: 1,889 square feet
Second Floor: 872 square feet; Total: 2,761 square feet

● Here is the perfect home for those who want lots of livability. Note the easy access to each room. A luxurious master bedroom suite will provide all of the comforts you deserve. Take note of the sitting room, his/her dressing and closet areas and the raised tub. Upstairs, two nice sized bedrooms and a full bath.

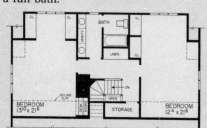

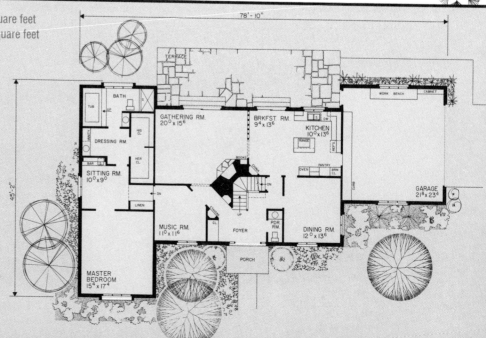

● The inviting warmth of this delightful home catches the eye of even the most casual observer. Imagine, four big bedrooms! Formal and informal living can be enjoyed throughout this charming plan. A private, formal dining room is available for those very special occasions.

Design V21794 First Floor: 2,122 square feet
Second Floor: 802 square feet; Total: 2,924 square feet

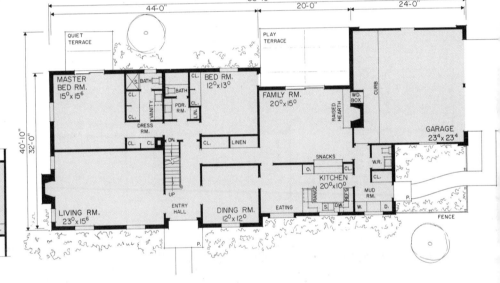

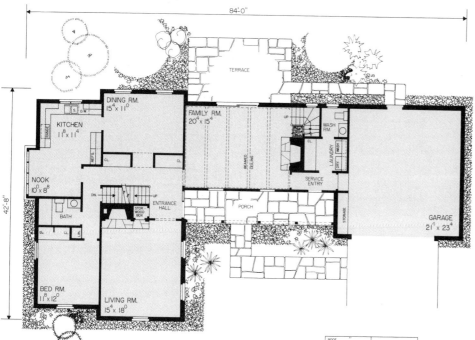

● Pleasing appearance, with an excellent floor plan. Notice how all the rooms are accessible from a hall. That's a plus for easy housekeeping. Some other extras: an exceptionally large family room which is more than 20' x 15', a gracious living room, formal dining room adjacent to the kitchen/nook area, four large bedrooms, a secluded guest suite plus a huge storage area.

Note that the large guest suite, featuring a full bath, is only accessible by the back stairs in the family room. You could use it as a spacious library, playroom, or a hobby area. Two fireplaces (one with a built-in wood box), walk-in closets, covered front porch and rear terrace also highlight this home.

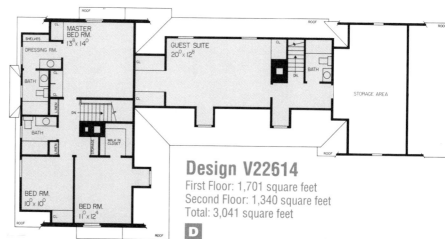

Design V22614

First Floor: 1,701 square feet
Second Floor: 1,340 square feet
Total: 3,041 square feet

D

Design V23363

First Floor: 1,926 square feet
Second Floor: 1,189 square feet
Total: 3,115 square feet

● Timeless traditional style and 1½-story design are highlights in this lovely home. On the first floor, formal living areas are found to the right; more casual living to the left. The spacious family room devotes one full wall to a raised-hearth fireplace with built-in wood box and a built-in barbecue and bookshelves. Just off the dining room is a screened porch, perfect for outdoor eating. Examine the three upstairs bedrooms and you'll find two adjoining baths. His and Hers walk-in closets enhance the master suite.

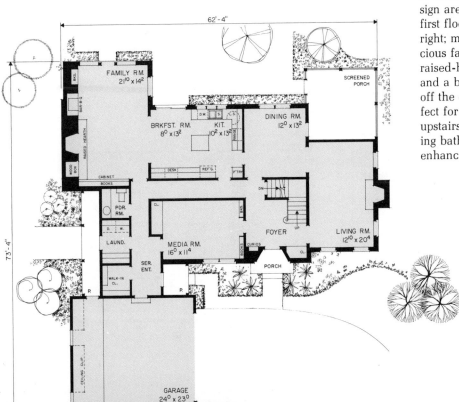

Design V23341 First Floor: 1,055 square feet
Second Floor: 981 square feet; Total: 2,036 square feet

● Designed for the empty-nester, small family, or as a second home, this appealing Tudor adaptation holds a most livable floor plan. Besides the 31' gathering room/dining room area and U-shaped kitchen with nearby washroom, there is a front study with large storage closet on the first floor. Three bedrooms on the second floor meet sleeping needs without a hitch. Notice the walk-in closets and the master-bedroom balcony.

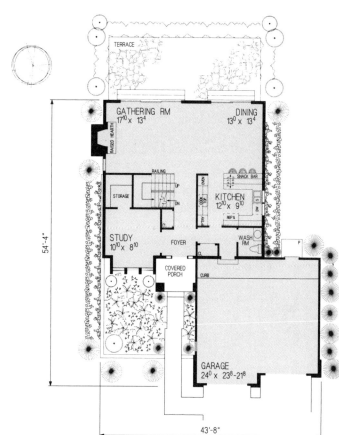

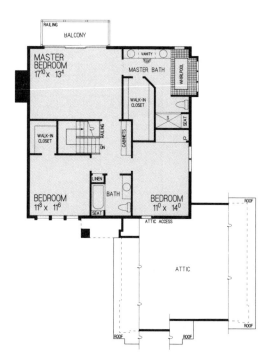

Design V23343

First Floor: 1,953 square feet; Second Floor: 895 square feet
Total: 2,848 square feet

● Beyond the simple traditional styling of this home's exterior are many of the amenities required by today's lifestyles. Among them: a huge country kitchen with fireplace, an attached greenhouse/dining area, a media room off the two-story foyer, split-bedroom planning, and a second-floor lounge. There are three bedrooms upstairs, which share a full bath.

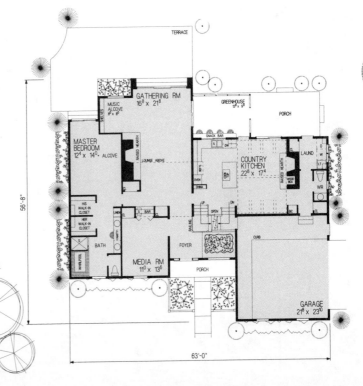

Design V23330

First Floor: 1,394 square feet
Second Floor: 320 square feet
Total: 1,714 square feet

● Outdoor living and open floor planning are highlights of this moderately sized plan. Amenities include a private hot tub on a wooden deck that is accessible via sliding glass doors in both bedrooms, and a two-story gathering room. An optional second-floor plan allows for a full 503 square feet of space with a balcony.

Design V23334

First Floor: 2,193 square feet
Second Floor: 831 square feet
Total: 3,024 square feet

● A traditional favorite, this home combines classic style with progressive floor planning. Four bedrooms are split — master suite and one bedroom on the first floor, two more bedrooms upstairs. The second-floor lounge overlooks a large, sunken gathering room near the formal dining area. A handy butler's pantry connects the dining room and kitchen.

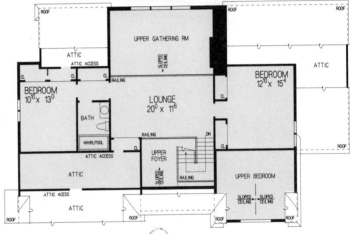

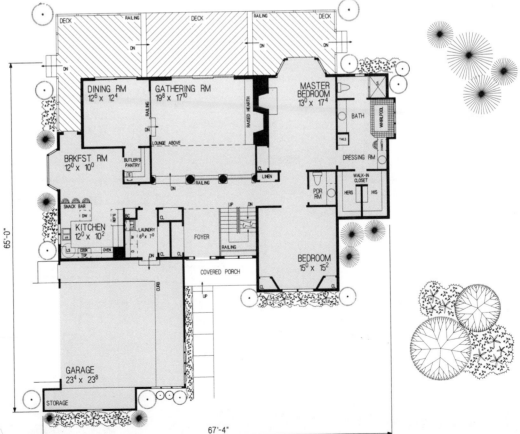

● You and your family will love the new living patterns you'll experience in this story-and-a-half home. The front entry hall features an impressive open staircase to the upstairs and basement. Adjacent is the master bedroom which has a compartmented bath with both tub and stall shower. The spacious dressing room steps down into a unique, sunken conversation pit. This cozy area has a planter, built-in seat and a view of the thru-fireplace, opening to the gathering room as well. Here, the ceiling slopes to the top of the second floor lounge which looks down into the gathering room.

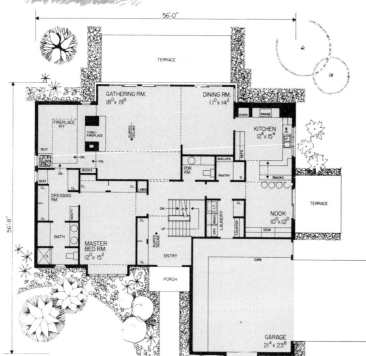

Design V22718 First Floor: 1,941 square feet
Second Floor: 791 square feet; Total: 2,732 square feet

D

Design V22513
First Floor: 1,799 square feet
Second Floor: 1,160 square feet
Total: 3,101 square feet

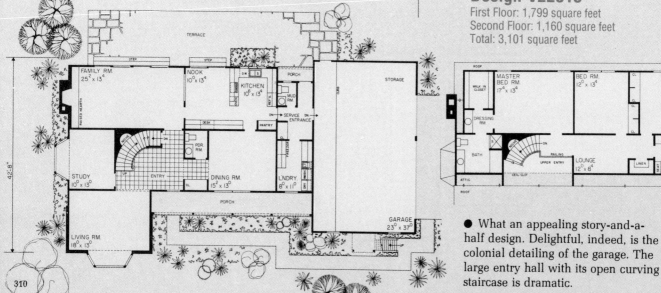

● What an appealing story-and-a-half design. Delightful, indeed, is the colonial detailing of the garage. The large entry hall with its open curving staircase is dramatic.

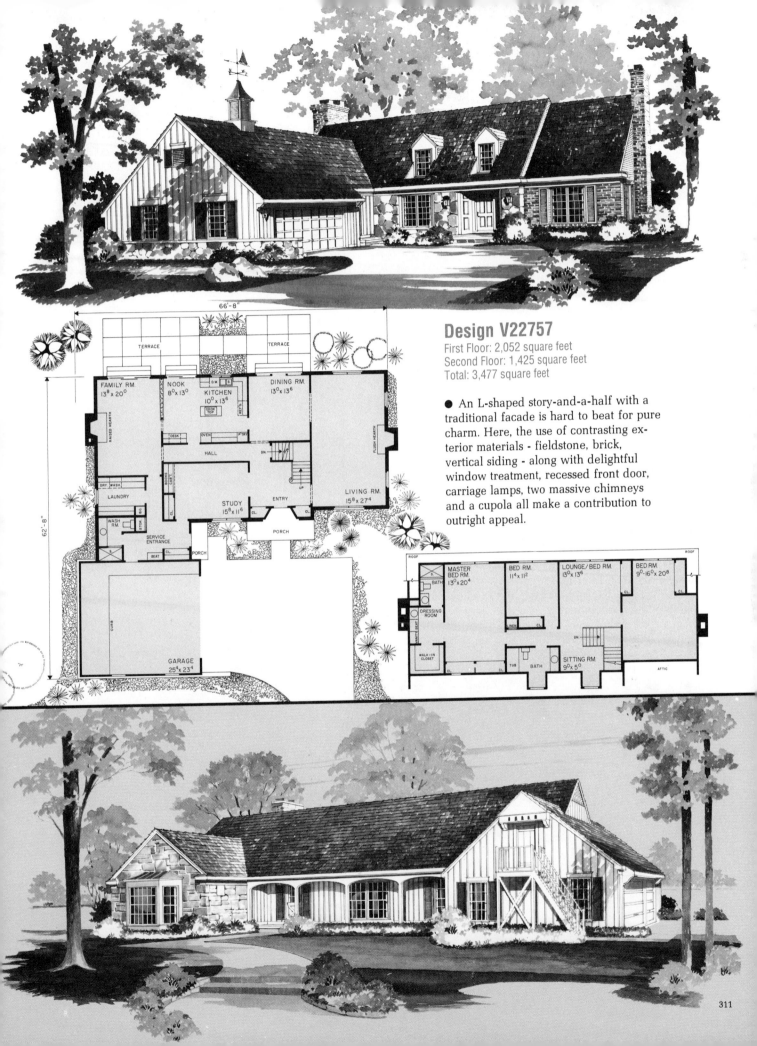

Design V22757

First Floor: 2,052 square feet
Second Floor: 1,425 square feet
Total: 3,477 square feet

● An L-shaped story-and-a-half with a traditional facade is hard to beat for pure charm. Here, the use of contrasting exterior materials - fieldstone, brick, vertical siding - along with delightful window treatment, recessed front door, carriage lamps, two massive chimneys and a cupola all make a contribution to outright appeal.

66'-8"

62'-8"

TERRACE   TERRACE

FAMILY RM.
13⁸ x 20⁰

NOOK
8⁰ x 13⁰

KITCHEN
10⁰ x 13⁶

DINING RM.
13⁰ x 13⁶

DESK   OVEN   PTR'S   REF'S   D.W.   S   COOK TOP   RAISED HEARTH   FLUSH HEARTH

HALL

DRY. WASH.

LAUNDRY

WASH. RM.   STOR.   CL.   STUDY
15⁸ x 11⁶   ENTRY   LIVING RM.
15⁸ x 27⁴

BOOKS   CAB'T   CL.   DN   UP   CL.   CL.

SERVICE ENTRANCE

SEAT   CL.   PORCH

PORCH

GARAGE
25⁸ x 23⁴

CURB

ROOF   ROOF

MASTER BED RM.
13⁰ x 20⁴

BATH

DRESSING ROOM

VANITY SEAT

WALK-IN CLOSET   CL.   CL.   TUB   BATH

BED RM.
11⁴ x 11²

LINEN   CL.

LOUNGE/BED RM.
13⁰ x 13⁶

DN

SITTING RM.
9⁰ x 5⁰

BED RM.
9⁰-16⁰ x 20⁸

CL.   CL.

ATTIC

311

Design V22923

First Floor: 1,100 square feet
Second Floor: 970 square feet
Total: 2,070 square feet

● This Trend Home is as charming on the outside as it is comfortable on the inside. Note the Early American window treatments, second-story over-hang, central fireplace, and textured look of stone and board siding. Inside one finds a large rear gathering room with fireplace, efficient U-shaped kitchen, formal dining room, study, and foyer on the first floor. Upstairs are three bedrooms plus an upper gathering room. The two-car garage includes storage space. Note the view windows and covered porch in the rear.

Design V23550

First Floor: 2,328 square feet
Second Floor: 712 square feet
Total: 3,040 square feet

● A transitional 1½-story home combines the best of contemporary and traditional elements. This one uses vertical wood siding, stone and multi-paned windows to beautiful advantage. The floor plan makes great use of space with first-floor living and dining areas and a first-floor master suite. Two secondary bedrooms, a full bath and an open lounge area are found on the second floor. The garage is accessed from the island kitchen through the laundry.

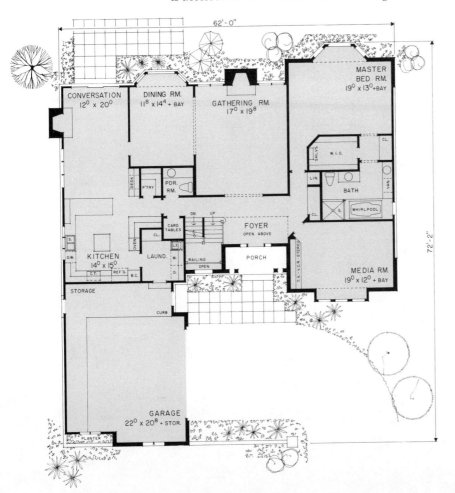

Design V23555

First Floor: 1,948 square feet
Second Floor: 1,669 square feet
Total: 3,617 square feet

● Round-top windows add
elegance to the interior and
exterior of this traditional home.
Large gathering areas on the
first floor flow together for ease
in entertaining. The sunken
gathering room stretches from
the front of the house to the
back, with a terrace at each end
and a fireplace in the middle.
Another fireplace is found in the
conversation area adjoining the
kitchen. The formal dining
room features a bay window.
Sleeping areas upstairs include
a master bedroom with spacious
bath and walk-in closet, three
family bedrooms and two full
baths.

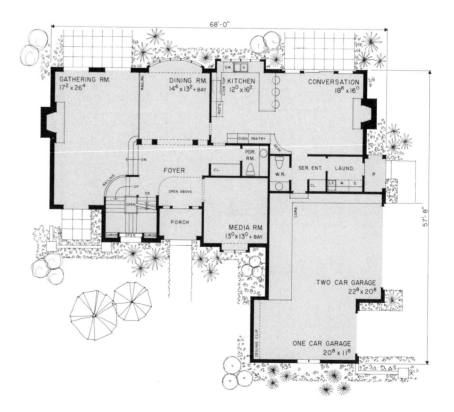

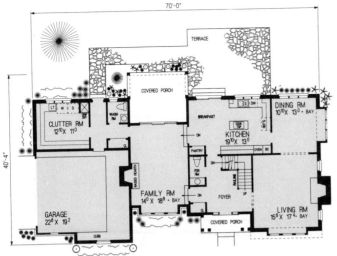

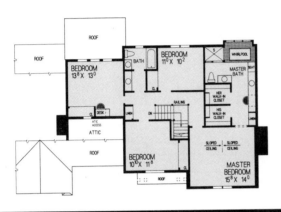

Design V23356

First Floor: 1,610 square feet
Second Floor: 1,200 square feet
Total: 2,810 square feet

L **D**

● Traditionally speaking, this home takes blue ribbons. Its family room has a raised-hearth fireplace and there's a covered porch reached through sliding glass doors for informal eating. The living room also has a fireplace and is near the boxed-windowed dining room. A clutter room off the garage could be turned into a hobby or sewing room. Three bedrooms on the second floor include a master suite with His and Hers walk-in closets and three family bedrooms.

Design V23370

First Floor: 2,055 square feet
Second Floor: 1,288 square feet
Total: 3,343 square feet

L **D**

● The combination of stone and brick allow an impressive facade on this traditional two-story. The symmetrically designed interior will provide efficient traffic patterns. Note the formal living and dining areas to the right and huge family room to the rear. The U-shaped kitchen has an attached breakfast room and built-ins. There are four bedrooms on the second floor. The master features a walk-in closet, double vanity and whirlpool tub.

Design V23381

First Floor: 2,485 square feet
Second Floor: 1,864 square feet
Total: 4,349 square feet

● A place for everything and everything in its place. If that's your motto, this is your house. A central foyer allows access to every part of the home. To the left sits the spacious gathering room with fireplace and music alcove. Straight ahead, the open living and dining rooms offer sweeping views of the back yard. The modern kitchen and conversation area are situated to the right of the home. Near the entrance, a library with bay window and built-in bookcase is found. Look for extra amenities throughout the home: curio cabinets in the foyer, stairwell, conversation area and hall; built-in desk; walk-in closet and a second fireplace. Upstairs, the master suite features an enormous walk-in closet and a pampering bath. Another bedroom has a private bath, while the remaining two bedrooms share a bath with dual lavs.

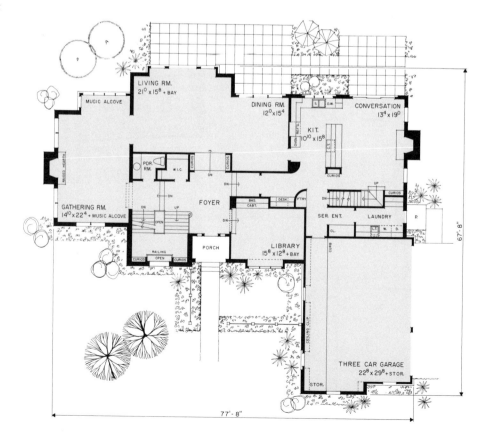

Design V23551

First Floor: 1,575 square feet
Second Floor: 1,501 square feet
Total: 3,076 square feet

● Efficient floor planning provides a spacious, yet economical home. The large kitchen adjoins a breakfast/family room combination with fireplace. A butler's pantry connects the kitchen to the formal dining room with terrace access. A second fireplace is found in the living room. Also on the first floor: a library and convenient powder room. The master bedroom features His and Hers walk-in closets and a grand bath with whirlpool tub. The bedroom next door would make a fine nursury or office. A large bonus room over the garage offers many optional uses.

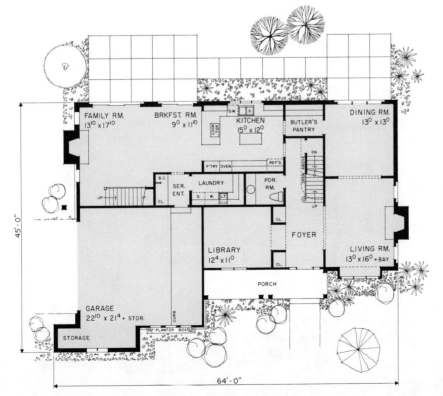

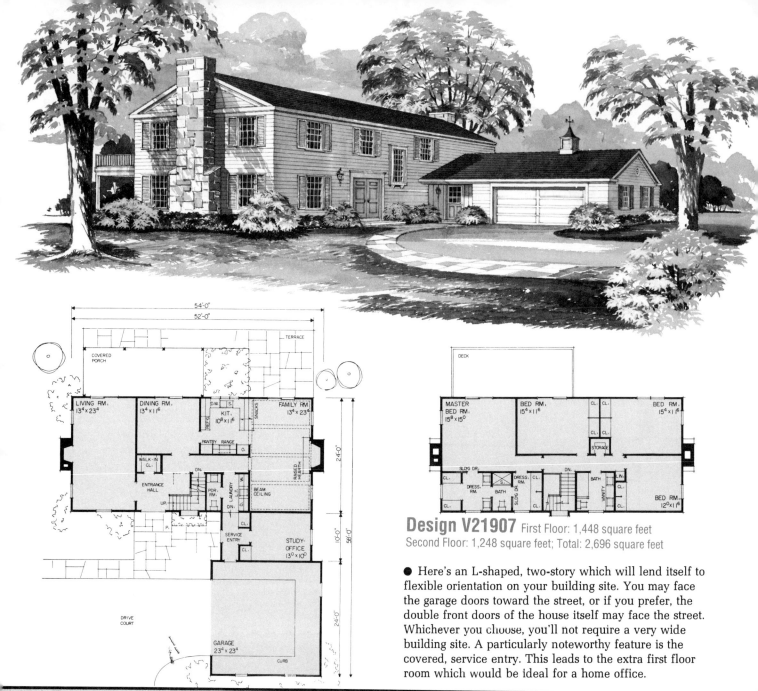

Floor Plan Labels (First Floor)

- 54'-0"
- 52'-0"
- COVERED PORCH
- TERRACE
- LIVING RM. 13⁴ x 23⁴
- DINING RM. 13⁴ x 11⁶
- KIT. 10⁸ x 11⁶
- D.W. S.
- REF.
- SNACKS
- FAMILY RM. 13⁴ x 23⁴
- PANTRY RANGE
- WALK-IN CL.
- ENTRANCE HALL
- PDR. RM.
- LAUNDRY
- BEAM CEILING
- RAISED HEARTH
- UP.
- DN.
- P.
- SERVICE ENTRY
- CL.
- STUDY-OFFICE 13⁰ x 10⁰
- 24'-0"
- 10'-0"
- 58'-0"
- DRIVE COURT
- GARAGE 23⁴ x 23⁴
- CURB
- 24'-0"

Floor Plan Labels (Second Floor)

- DECK
- MASTER BED RM. 15⁸ x 15⁰
- BED RM. 15⁴ x 11⁶
- BED RM. 15⁴ x 11⁶
- CL. CL.
- CL. CL.
- STORAGE
- SLDG. DR.
- DRESS. RM.
- BATH
- DRESS. RM.
- BATH
- SLDG. DR.
- DN.
- VANITY
- LIN.
- BED RM. 12⁰ x 11⁶

Design V21907 First Floor: 1,448 square feet
Second Floor: 1,248 square feet; Total: 2,696 square feet

● Here's an L-shaped, two-story which will lend itself to flexible orientation on your building site. You may face the garage doors toward the street, or if you prefer, the double front doors of the house itself may face the street. Whichever you choose, you'll not require a very wide building site. A particularly noteworthy feature is the covered, service entry. This leads to the extra first floor room which would be ideal for a home office.

Design V22540
First Floor: 1,306 square feet
Second Floor: 1,360 square feet; Total: 2,666 square feet

● This efficient Colonial abounds in features. A spacious entry flanked by living areas. A kitchen flanked by eating areas. Upstairs, four bedrooms including a sitting room in the master suite.

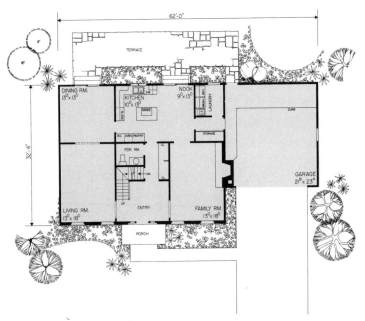

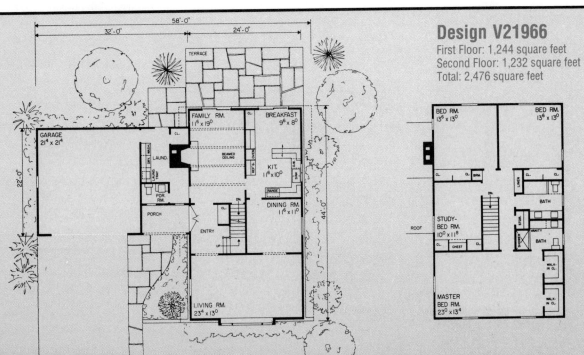

Design V21966
First Floor: 1,244 square feet
Second Floor: 1,232 square feet
Total: 2,476 square feet

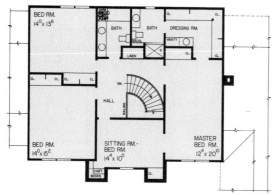

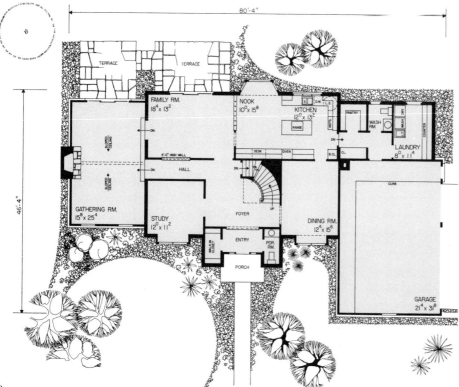

Design V22599

First Floor: 2,075 square feet
Second Floor: 1,398 square feet
Total: 3,473 square feet

 D

● This traditional two-story with its projecting one-story wings is delightfully proportioned. The symmetrical window treatment is most appealing. The massive field-stone arch projects from the front line of the house providing a sheltered front entrance. Inside, there is the large foyer with the curving, open staircase to the second floor. Flexibility will be the byword to describe the living patterns. Not only are there the formal living and informal family rooms, but there is the quiet study and the upstairs sitting room. As for eating, there is a sizeable breakfast nook and a separate dining room. The second floor offers the option to function as either a three, or four, bedroom sleeping zone. That's a fine master bedroom suite when the sitting room is included.

Design V22325

First Floor: 1,154 square feet
Second Floor: 1,188 square feet
Total: 2,342 square feet

● Here is a modest package which
will build economically on a relatively small site. All the elements
are present to guarantee tremendous
livability. Your family is not likely to
outgrow this house. Imagine, four
bedrooms, 2½ baths!

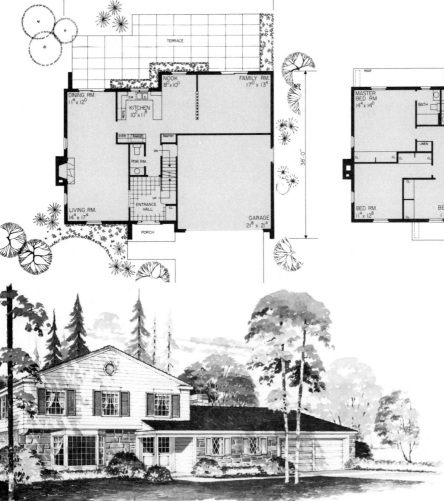

Design V21972

First Floor: 1,286 square feet
Second Floor: 960 square feet
Total: 2,246 square feet

● What an appealingly different
type of two-story home! It is one
whose grace and charm project an
aura of welcome. The large entry
hall routes traffic efficiently to all
areas. Don't miss the covered porch.

Design V21715 First Floor: 1,276 square feet; Second Floor: 1,064 square feet; Total: 2,340 square feet

L D

● The blueprints you order for this design show details for building each of these three appealing exteriors. Which do you like best? Whatever your choice, the interior will provide the growing family with all the facilities for fine living.

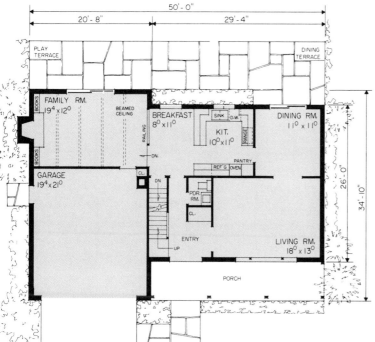

PLAY TERRACE

DINING TERRACE

50'-0"

20'-8"   29'-4"

FAMILY RM.
19⁴×12⁰

BREAKFAST
8⁰×11⁰

SINK   D.W.

DINING RM.
11⁰×11⁰

BEAMED CEILING

KIT.
10⁰×11⁰

RANGE

BOOKS

REF'G   OVEN   PANTRY

GARAGE
19⁴×21⁰

CL.

DN.

PDR.
RM.

CL.

ENTRY

UP

LIVING RM.
18⁰×13⁰

PORCH

26'-0"   34'-10"

BED RM.
10⁴×9⁴

SHOWER   BATH

CL.

MASTER
BED RM.
11⁰×15⁰

CL.

DN

CL.

BATH

CL.

LIN.

CL.

BED RM.
9⁴×10⁰

BED RM.
14⁴×10⁰

Design V21957 First Floor: 1,042 square feet; Second Floor: 780 square feet; Total: 1,822 square feet

L D

● When you order your blueprints for this design you will receive details for the construction of each of the three charming exteriors pictured above. Whichever the exterior you finally decide to build, the floor plan will be essentially the same except the location of the windows. This will be a fine home for the growing family. It will serve well for many years. There are four bedrooms and two full baths (one with a stall shower) upstairs.

Design V23318

First Floor: 1,557 square feet
Second Floor: 540 square feet
Total: 2,097 square feet

● Details make the difference in this darling two-bedroom (or three-bedroom if you choose) bungalow. From covered front porch to covered rear porch, there's a fine floor plan. Living areas are to the rear: a gathering room with through-fireplace and pass-through counter to the kitchen and a formal dining room with porch access. To the front of the plan are a family bedroom and bath and a study. The study can also be planned as a guest bedroom with bath. Upstairs is the master bedroom with through-fireplace to the bath and a gigantic walk-in closet.

CUSTOMIZABLE

Custom Alterations? See page 413 for customizing this plan to your specifications.

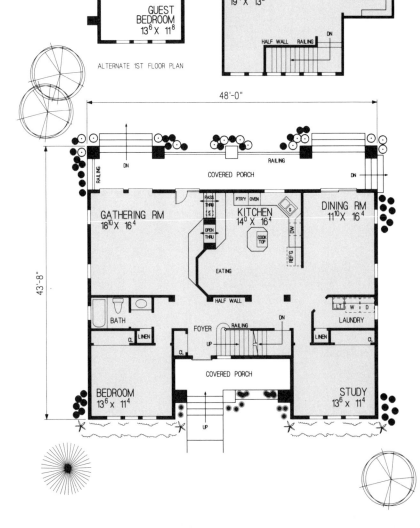

Design V22488

First Floor: 1,113 square feet
Second Floor: 543 square feet
Total: 1,656 square feet

● A cozy cottage for the young at heart! Whether called upon to serve the young, active family as a leisure-time retreat at the lake, or the retired couple as a quiet haven in later years, this charming design will perform well. As a year round second home, the upstairs with its two sizable bedrooms, full bath and lounge area, looking down into the gathering room below, will ideally accommodate the younger generation.

CUSTOMIZABLE

Custom Alterations? See page 413 for customizing this plan to your specifications.

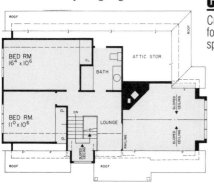

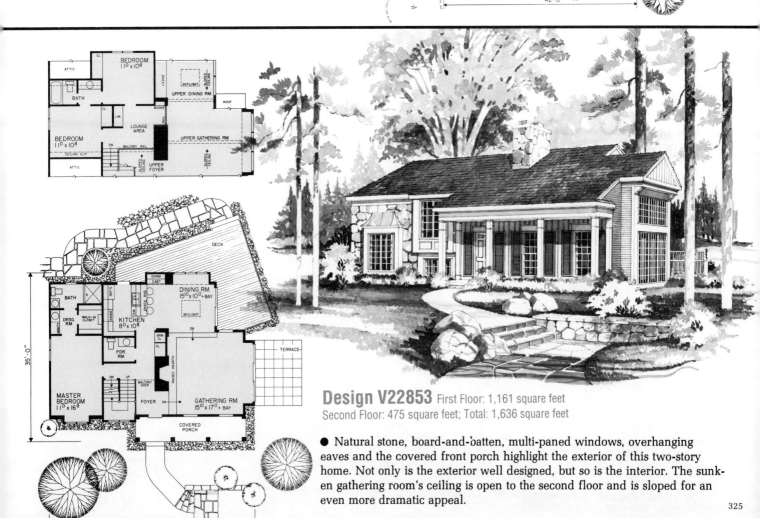

Design V22853
First Floor: 1,161 square feet
Second Floor: 475 square feet; Total: 1,636 square feet

● Natural stone, board-and-batten, multi-paned windows, overhanging eaves and the covered front porch highlight the exterior of this two-story home. Not only is the exterior well designed, but so is the interior. The sunken gathering room's ceiling is open to the second floor and is sloped for an even more dramatic appeal.

325

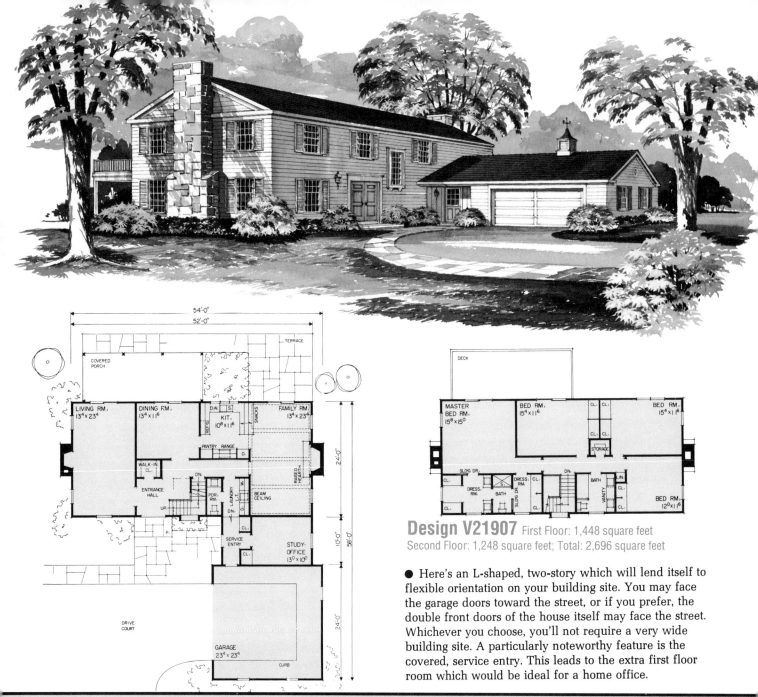

Design V21907 First Floor: 1,448 square feet
Second Floor: 1,248 square feet; Total: 2,696 square feet

● Here's an L-shaped, two-story which will lend itself to flexible orientation on your building site. You may face the garage doors toward the street, or if you prefer, the double front doors of the house itself may face the street. Whichever you choose, you'll not require a very wide building site. A particularly noteworthy feature is the covered, service entry. This leads to the extra first floor room which would be ideal for a home office.

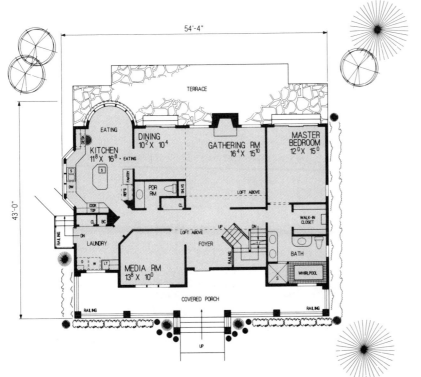

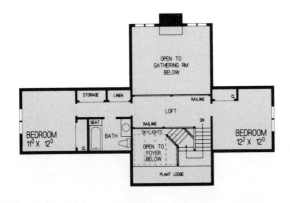

Design V23321

First Floor: 1,705 square feet
Second Floor: 572 square feet
Total: 2,277 square feet

● Cozy and completely functional, this 1½-story bungalow has many amenities not often found in homes its size. The covered porch at the front opens at the entry to a foyer with angled staircase. To the left is a media room, to the rear the gathering room with fireplace. Attached to the gathering room is a formal dining room with rear terrace access. The kitchen features a curved casual eating area and island work station. The right side of the first floor is dominated by the master suite. It has access to the rear terrace and a luxurious bath. Upstairs are two family bedrooms connected by a loft area overlooking the gathering room and foyer.

CUSTOMIZABLE
Custom Alterations? See page 413 for customizing this plan to your specifications.

327

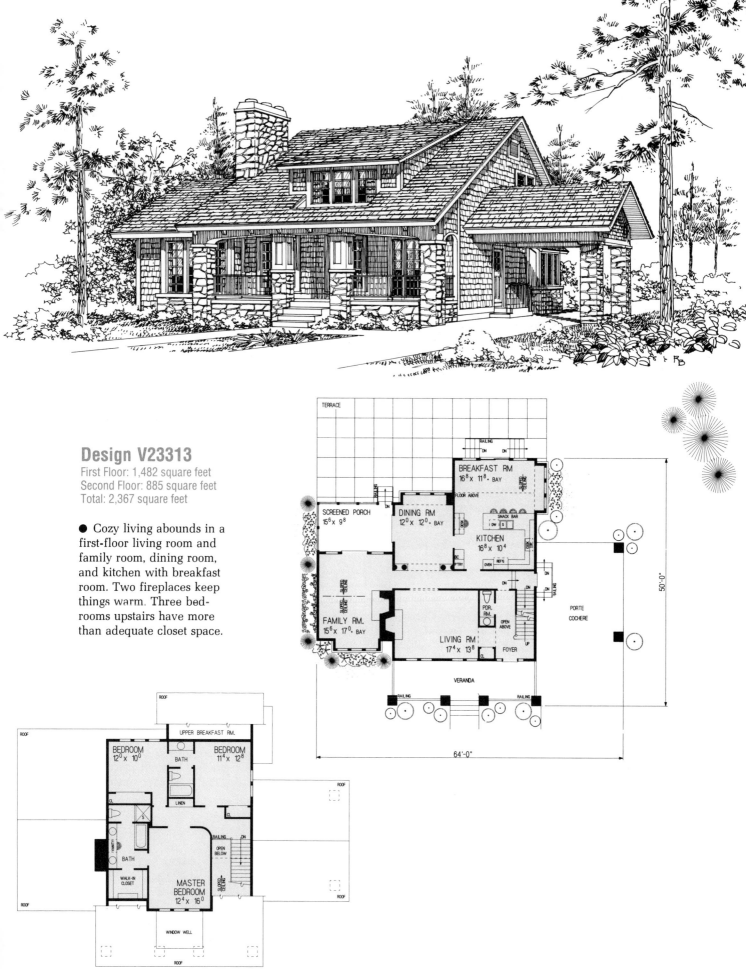

Design V23313

First Floor: 1,482 square feet
Second Floor: 885 square feet
Total: 2,367 square feet

● Cozy living abounds in a first-floor living room and family room, dining room, and kitchen with breakfast room. Two fireplaces keep things warm. Three bedrooms upstairs have more than adequate closet space.

TERRACE

RAILING

BREAKFAST RM
16⁸ x 11⁸ BAY

SCREENED PORCH
15⁶ x 9⁸

DINING RM
12⁰ x 12⁰ BAY

SNACK BAR

KITCHEN
16⁸ x 10⁴

DW

OVEN   REF'G

PTRY

FAMILY RM.
15⁶ x 17⁰ BAY

SUPER CEILING

PDR. RM.

OPEN ABOVE

LIVING RM
17⁴ x 13⁸

FOYER

UP

PORTE COCHERE

50'-0"

VERANDA

RAILING   RAILING

64'-0"

ROOF

UPPER BREAKFAST RM.

ROOF

BEDROOM
12⁰ x 10⁰

BATH

BEDROOM
11⁴ x 12⁸

LINEN

CL

ROOF

RAILING   DN

VANITY

BATH

OPEN BELOW

WALK-IN CLOSET

MASTER BEDROOM
12⁴ x 16⁰

WINDOW WELL

ROOF

ROOF

Design V23316

First Floor: 1,111 square feet
Second Floor: 886 square feet
Total: 1,997 square feet

● Don't be fooled by a small-looking exterior. This plan offers three bedrooms and plenty of living space. Notice that the screened porch leads to a rear terrace with access to the breakfast room. A living room/dining room combination adds spaciousness to the first floor.

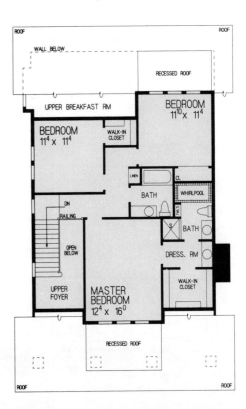

329

● This house combines the best of both worlds: a traditional look and a contemporary feel. Inside, the master bedroom provides many modern amenities, including a study, walk-in closet and deluxe bath with whirlpool tub and dual vanities. The traditional country kitchen with fireplace and built-in desk is spacious and yet cozy. A second fireplace is found in the expansive living room. Each of two bedrooms on the second floor has its own full bath.

Design V23353

First Floor: 2,191 square feet
Second Floor: 874 square feet
Total: 3,065 square feet

WIDTH 106'-8"
DEPTH 32'

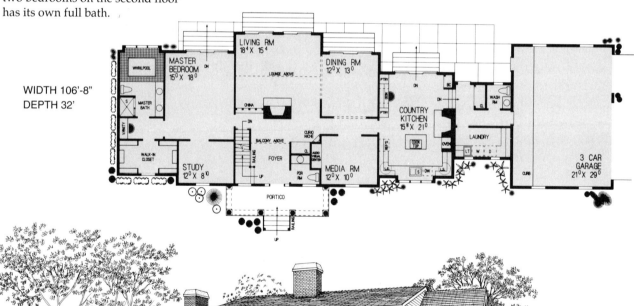

CONTEMPORARY HOMES . . . are known for, and

often identified by, their lack of exterior adornment. Simple, uncluttered lines generally highlight their exteriors. Often, irregular shapes and soaring roof lines achieve a visual impact that is, indeed, dramatic. And as appealing as many of these contemporary forms are, so too are their accompanying, refreshing living patterns. Open planning, dual and multi-use space, sunken living areas, indoor balconies and lounges, cathedral ceilings, effective uses of glass, and functional indoor-outdoor living relationships can all complement one another to assure outstanding family living patterns. The contemporary home can offer an exciting break from the conventions of the past.

Design V22379 First Floor: 1,525 square feet; Second Floor: 748 square feet; Total: 2,273 square feet

L D

● A house that has "everything" may very well look just like this design. Its exterior is well-proportioned and impressive. Inside the inviting double front doors there are features galore. The living room and family room level are sunken. Separating these two rooms is a dramatic thru fireplace. A built-in bar, planter and beamed ceiling highlight the family room. Nearby is a full bath and a study which could be utilized as a fourth bedroom. The fine functioning kitchen has a pass-thru to the snack bar in the breakfast nook. The adjacent dining room overlooks the living room and has sliding doors to the covered porch. Upstairs three bedrooms, two baths and an outdoor balcony. Blueprints for this design include optional basement details.

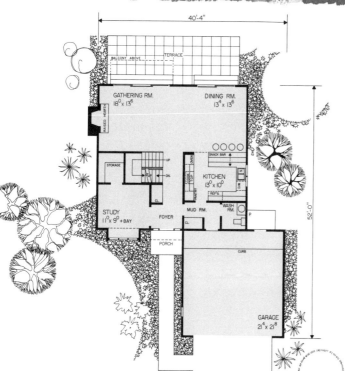

Design V22711
First Floor: 975 square feet
Second Floor: 1,024 square feet; Total: 1,999 square feet

L D

● Special features! A complete master suite with a private balcony plus two more bedrooms and a bath upstairs. The first floor has a study with a storage closet. A convenient snack bar between kitchen and dining room. The kitchen offers many built-in appliances. Plus a gathering room and dining room that measures 31 feet wide. Note the curb area in the garage and fireplace in gathering room.

Design V22748
First Floor: 1,232 square feet
Second Floor: 720 square feet
Total: 1,952 square feet

● This four bedroom contemporary will definitely have appeal for the entire family. The U-shaped kitchen-nook area with its built-in desk, adjacent laundry/wash room and service entrance will be very efficient for the busy kitchen activities. The living and family rooms are both sunken one step.

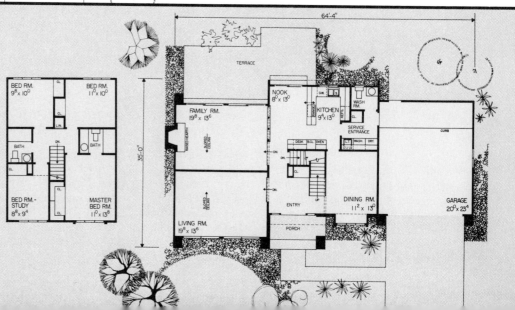

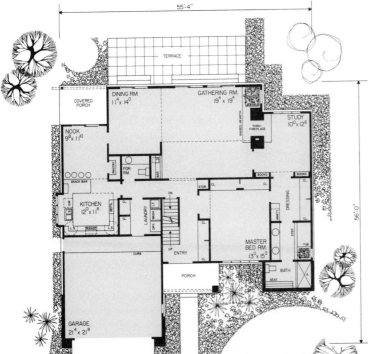

Design V22701 First Floor: 1,909 square feet
Second Floor: 891 square feet; Total: 2,800 square feet

● A snack bar in the kitchen! Plus a breakfast nook and formal dining room. Whether it's an elegant dinner party or a quick lunch, this home provides the right spot. There's a wet bar in the gathering room. Built-in bookcases in the study. And between these two rooms, a gracious fireplace. Three large bedrooms. Including a luxury master suite. Plus a balcony lounge overlooking gathering room below.

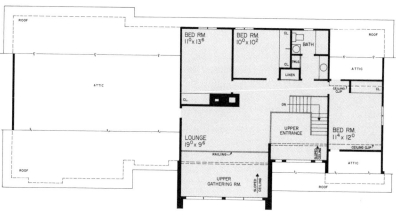

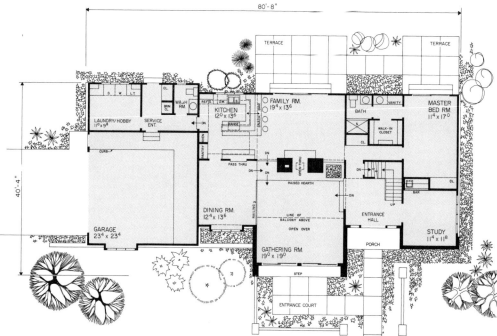

Design V22782

First Floor: 2,060 square feet
Second Floor: 897 square feet
Total: 2,957 square feet

● What makes this such a distinctive four bedroom design? Let's list some of the features. This plan includes great formal and informal living for the family at home or when entertaining guests. The formal gathering room and informal family room share a dramatic raised-hearth fireplace. Other features of the sunken gathering room include: high, sloped ceilings, built-in planter and sliding glass doors to the front entrance court. The kitchen has a snack bar, many built-ins, a pass-thru to dining room and easy access to the large laundry/wash room. The master bedroom suite is located on the main level for added privacy and convenience. There's even a study with a built-in bar. The upper level has three more bedrooms, a bath and a lounge looking down into the gathering room.

Design V22906 First Floor: 2,121 square feet
Second Floor: 913 square feet; Total: 3,034 square feet

D

● This striking Contemporary with Spanish good looks offers outstanding living for lifestyles of today. A three-car garage opens to a mudroom, laundry, and washroom to keep the rest of the house clean. An efficient, spacious kitchen opens to a spacious dining room, with pass-thru also leading to a family room. The family room and adjoining master bedroom suite overlook a backyard terrace. Just off the master bedroom is a sizable study that opens to a foyer. Steps just off the foyer make upstairs access quick and easy. The center point of this modern Contemporary is a living room that faces a front courtyard and a lounge above the living room. Three second-story bedrooms and an upper foyer join the upstairs lounge.

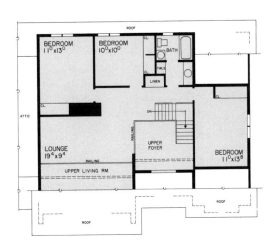

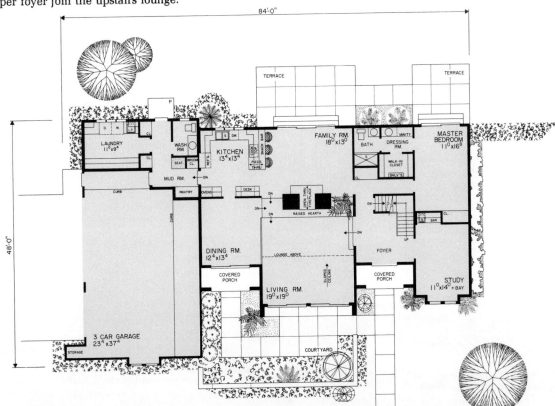

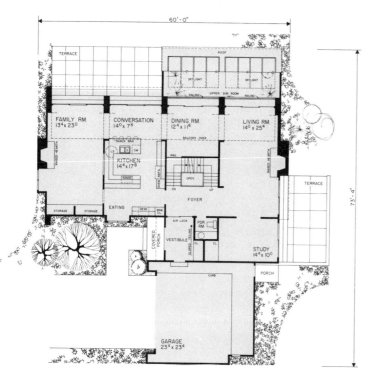

60'-0"

73'-4"

TERRACE

ROOF

SKYLIGHT SKYLIGHT

UPPER SUN ROOM

RAILING RAILING

FAMILY RM.
13⁴ x 23⁰

CONVERSATION
14⁰ x 7⁸

DINING RM.
12⁴ x 11⁶

LIVING RM.
14⁰ x 25⁴

SNACK BAR

BALCONY OVER

KITCHEN
14⁴ x 17⁸

RAL

OPEN

RANGE

DW

OVEN REFS.

DN   UP

RAISED HEARTH

RAISED HEARTH

TERRACE

STORAGE STORAGE

EATING

DESK DRM
RM

FOYER

AIR LOCK

PDR
RM

COVERED PORCH

VESTIBULE

SLOPED CEILING

CL CL

STUDY
14⁴ x 10⁰

PORCH

CURB

GARAGE
23⁴ x 23⁴

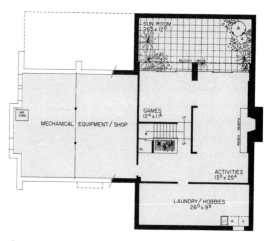

ROOF

SKYLIGHT SKYLIGHT

ROOF

LEDGE

LEDGE

UPPER FAMILY ROOM

UPPER CONVERSATION

SKYLIGHT

UPPER DINING ROOM

UPPER LIVING ROOM

BEDROOM
11⁸ x 12⁰

BALCONY

BEDROOM
11⁴ x 13⁶

CL

LIN
CL

OPEN

MASTER
BEDROOM
14⁴ x 17⁴

BALCONY

BATH

SKYLIGHT

BATH

DRESSING
ROOM

VANITY

CL CL

UPPER
VESTIBULE

SLOPED CEILING

ATTIC

SUN ROOM
26⁶ x 12⁰

BALCONY ABOVE

AIR
COND

MECHANICAL EQUIPMENT / SHOP

GAMES
12⁴ x 11⁶

UP

RAISED HEARTH

ACTIVITIES
13⁰ x 25⁴

LAUNDRY / HOBBIES
26⁶ x 9⁸

Design V22834 First Floor: 1,775 square feet
Second Floor: 1,041 square feet; Lower Level: 1,128 square feet
Total: 3,944 square feet

● This passive solar design offers 3,900 square feet of livability situated on three levels. The primary passive element will be the lower level sun room which admits sunlight for direct-gain heating. The solar warmth collected in the sun room will radiate into the rest of the house after it passes the sliding glass doors. During the warm summer months, shades are put over the skylight to protect it from direct sunlight. This design has the option of incorporating active solar heating panels to the roof. The collectors would be installed on the south-facing portion of the roof. They would absorb the sun's warmth for both domestic water and supplementary space heating. An attic fan exhausts any hot air out of the house in the summer and circulates air in the winter. With or without the active solar panels, this is a marvelous two-story contemporary.

Design V22831 First Floor: 1,758 square feet
Second Floor: 1,247 square feet; Total: 3,005 square feet

D

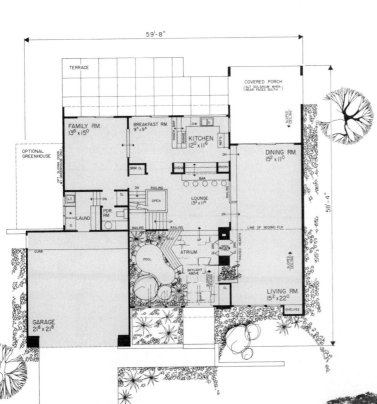

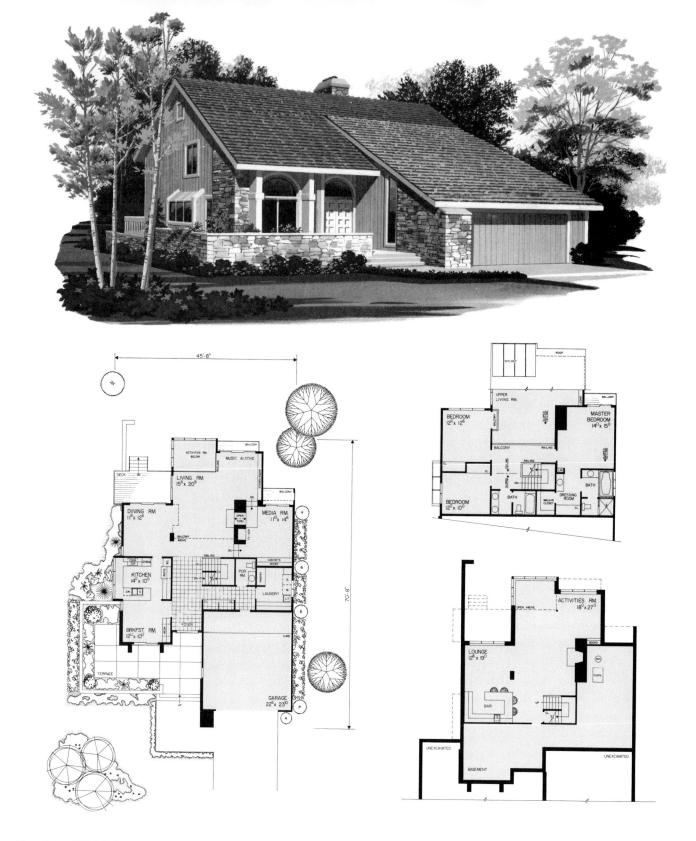

Design V22944 Main Level: 1,545 square feet; Upper Level: 977 square feet; Lower Level: 933 square feet; Total: 3,455 square feet

● This eye-catching contemporary features three stacked levels of livability. And what livability it will truly be! The main level has a fine U-shaped kitchen which is flanked by the informal breakfast room and formal dining room. The living room will be dramatic, indeed. Its sloping ceiling extends through the upper level. It overlooks the lower level activities room and has wonderfully expansive window areas for full enjoyment of surrounding vistas. A two-way fireplace can be viewed from dining, living and media rooms. A sizable deck and two cozy balconies provide for flexible outdoor living. Don't miss the music alcove with its wall for stereo equipment. Upstairs, the balcony overlooks the living room. It serves as the connecting link for the three bedrooms. The lower level offers more cheerful livability with the huge activities room plus lounge area. Note bar, fireplace.

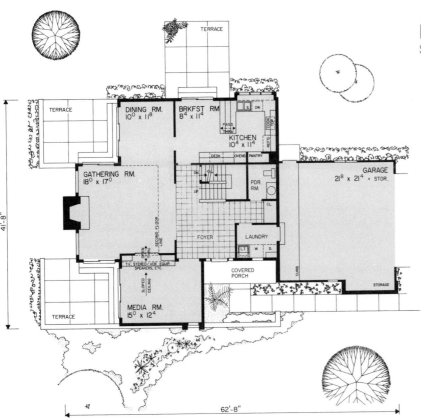

Design V22910 First Floor: 1,221 square feet
Second Floor: 767 square feet; Total: 1,988 square feet

● This two-story home offers excellent zoning by room functions and modern amenities for comfort. A two-story gathering room, with attached dining room, serves the needs of any get-together, both formal and informal.

Sliding glass doors on either side of this room lead to two separate terrace areas. A third terrace can be reached via sliding glass doors in the breakfast room. Be sure to note the special features of this home: dramatic ceiling

heights, built-in storage areas, and pass-throughs. Notice also the media room for stereos/VCRs, plush master bedroom with a whirlpool, modern kitchen, and balcony.

Design V22511

Main Level: 1,043 square feet
Upper Level: 703 square feet
Lower Level: 794 square feet
Total: 2,540 square feet

L D

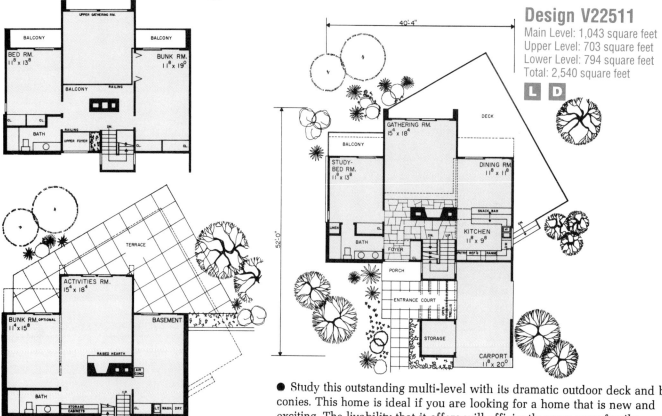

● Study this outstanding multi-level with its dramatic outdoor deck and balconies. This home is ideal if you are looking for a home that is new and exciting. The livability that it offers will efficiently serve your family.

Design V22823

First Floor: 1,370 square feet
Second Floor: 927 square feet
Total: 2,297 square feet

L D

● The street view of this contemporary design features a small courtyard entrance as well as a private terrace off the study. Inside the livability will be outstanding. This design features spacious first floor activity areas that flow smoothly into each other. In the gathering room a raised hearth fireplace creates a dramatic focal point. An adjacent covered terrace, featuring a skylight, is ideal for outdoor dining and could be screened in later for an additional room.

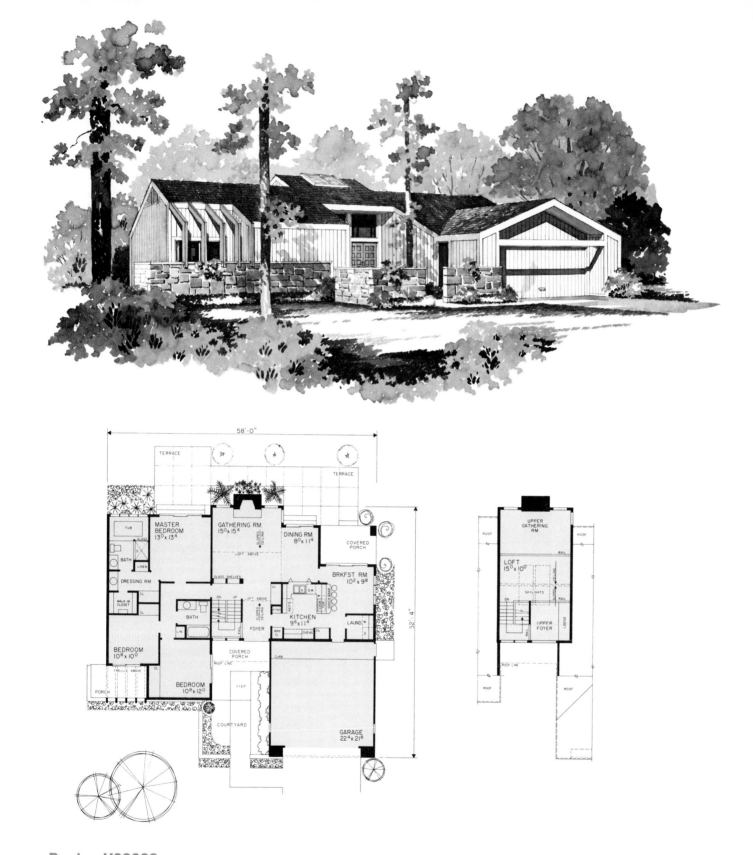

Design V22892 First Floor: 1,623 square feet; Second Floor: 160 square feet; Total: 1,783 square feet

● What a striking contemporary! It houses an efficient floor plan with many outstanding features. The foyer has a sloped ceiling and an open staircase to the basement. To the right of the foyer is the work center. Note the snack bar, laundry and covered dining porch, along with the step-saving kitchen. Both the gathering and dining rooms overlook the back yard. Each of the three bedrooms has access to an outdoor area. Now, just think of the potential use of the second floor loft. It could be used as a den, sewing room, lounge, TV room or anything else you may need. It overlooks the gathering room and front foyer. Two large skylights will brighten the interior.

Design V22887 First Floor: 1,338 square feet; Second Floor: 661 square feet; Total: 1,999 square feet

● This attractive, contemporary one-and-a-half story will be the envy of many. First, examine the efficient kitchen. Not only does it offer a snack bar for those quick meals but also a large dining room. Notice the adjacent dining porch. The laundry and garage access are also adjacent to the kitchen.

An exciting feature is the gathering room with fireplace. The first floor also offers a study with a wet bar and sliding glass doors that open to a private porch. This will make those quiet times cherishable. Adjacent to the study is a full bath followed by a bedroom. Upstairs a large master bedroom suite oc-

cupies the entire floor. It features a bath with an oversized tub and shower, a large walk-in closet with built-ins and an open lounge with fireplace. Both the lounge and master bedroom, along with the gathering room, have sloped ceilings. Develop the lower level for additional space.

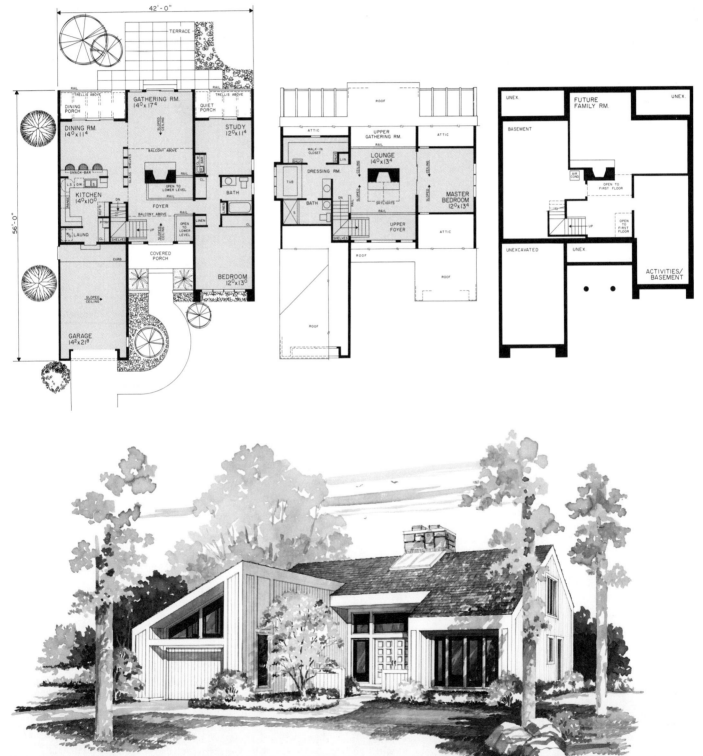

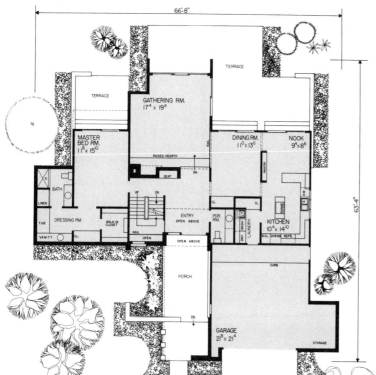

66'-8"

TERRACE

GATHERING RM.
17⁴ x 19⁴

TERRACE

MASTER BED RM.
11⁸ x 15¹⁰

DINING RM.
11⁰ x 13⁶

NOOK
9⁴ x 8⁶

RAISED HEARTH

SEAT

BATH

LINEN

DRESSING RM.

TUB

VANITY

WALK IN CLOSET

UP

DN

RAIL

OPEN

ENTRY
OPEN ABOVE

PDR.
RM.

CL.

LAUNDRY

KITCHEN
10⁴ x 14¹⁰

DRY. WASH.

BCL. OVENS REFS.

RANGE

OPEN ABOVE

DN

PORCH

CURB

GARAGE
21⁸ x 21⁴

STORAGE

63'-4"

BALCONY

BED RM.
11⁸ x 13⁶

OPEN TO
GATHERING RM.
BELOW

SLOPED
CEILING

BED RM.
11⁰ x 13⁶

OPEN

RAIL

CL.

DRESS.
RM.

BATH

VANITY

CL.

DN

RAIL

OPEN

OPEN TO
ENTRY BELOW

RAIL

DRESS.
RM.

BATH

CL.

OPEN

Design V22729 First Floor: 1,590 square feet
Second Floor: 756 square feet; Total: 2,346 square feet

L

● Entering this home will be a pleasure
through the sheltered walk-way to the double
front doors. And the pleasure and beauty does
not stop there. The entry hall and sunken gathering room are open to the upstairs for added
dimension. There are fine indoor-outdoor living
relationships in this design. Note the private
terrace, a living terrace plus the balcony.

Design V21783
First Floor: 2,412 square feet
Second Floor: 640 square feet
Total: 3,052 square feet

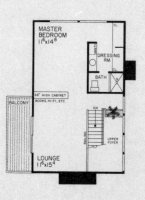

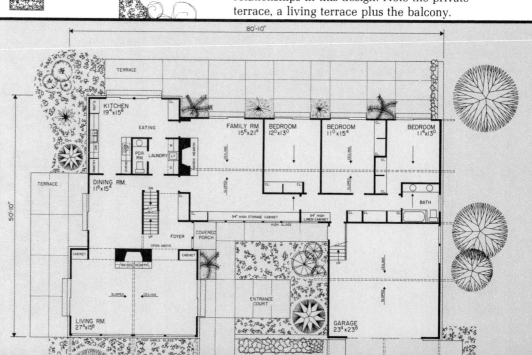

80'-10"

TERRACE

KITCHEN
19⁴ x 15⁸

EATING

FAMILY RM.
15⁶ x 21⁴

BEDROOM
12⁰ x 13⁰

BEDROOM
11⁰ x 15⁴

BEDROOM
11⁴ x 13⁰

MASTER
BEDROOM
11⁶ x 14⁸

DRESSING
RM.

BATH

CL.

PANTRY

COOK

PDR.
RM.

LAUNDRY

RAISED HEARTH

CEILING

SLOPED

SLOPED

CL.

CL.

CL.

60" HIGH CABINET
BOOKS, HI-FI, ETC.

TERRACE

DINING RM.
11⁶ x 15⁴

DN

54" HIGH STORAGE CABINET

54" HIGH
LINEN CABINET

HIGH GLASS

BATH

LINEN

BALCONY

LOUNGE
11⁶ x 15⁴

DN

UPPER
FOYER

UP

OPEN ABOVE

FOYER

COVERED
PORCH

50'-10"

CABINET

RAISED HEARTH

CABINET

SLOPED CEILING

LIVING RM.
27⁴ x 15⁸

HIGH GABLE GLASS

ENTRANCE
COURT

SLOPED

GARAGE
23⁴ x 23⁸

CEILING

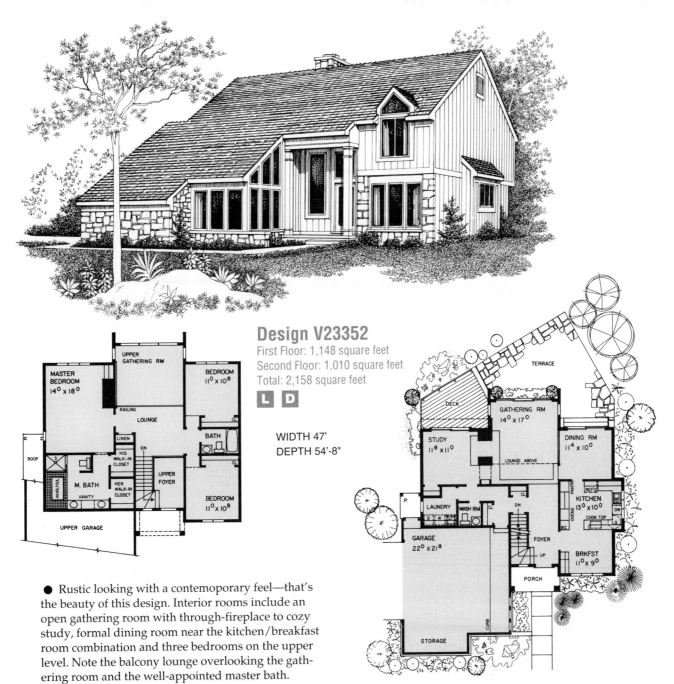

Design V23352

First Floor: 1,148 square feet
Second Floor: 1,010 square feet
Total: 2,158 square feet

L **D**

WIDTH 47'
DEPTH 54'-8"

● Rustic looking with a contemporary feel—that's the beauty of this design. Interior rooms include an open gathering room with through-fireplace to cozy study, formal dining room near the kitchen/breakfast room combination and three bedrooms on the upper level. Note the balcony lounge overlooking the gathering room and the well-appointed master bath.

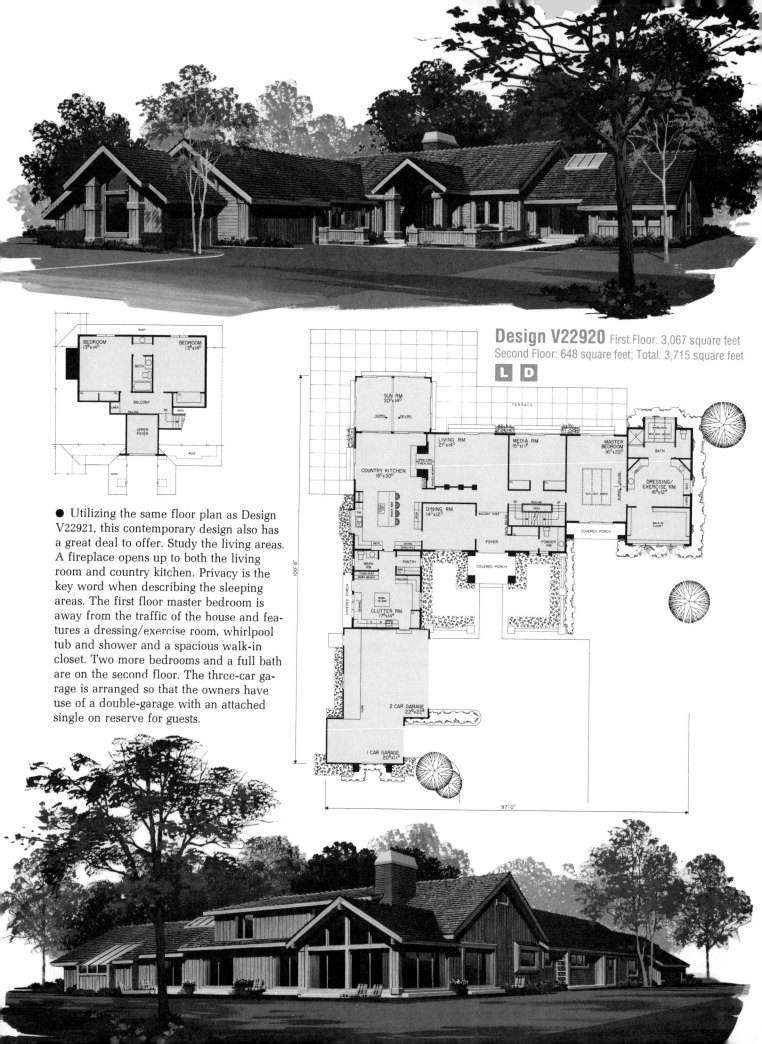

Design V22920 First Floor: 3,067 square feet
Second Floor: 648 square feet; Total: 3,715 square feet

L D

● Utilizing the same floor plan as Design V22921, this contemporary design also has a great deal to offer. Study the living areas. A fireplace opens up to both the living room and country kitchen. Privacy is the key word when describing the sleeping areas. The first floor master bedroom is away from the traffic of the house and features a dressing/exercise room, whirlpool tub and shower and a spacious walk-in closet. Two more bedrooms and a full bath are on the second floor. The three-car garage is arranged so that the owners have use of a double-garage with an attached single on reserve for guests.

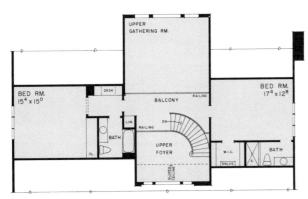

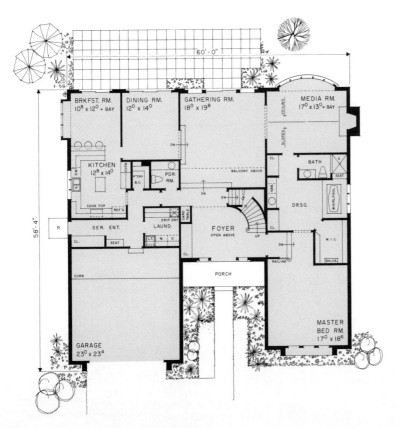

Design V23557

First Floor: 2,897 square feet
Second Floor: 835 square feet
Total: 3,732 square feet

● The owners of this home will be giving themselves a real treat. A large master bedroom is accompanied by a pampering master bath and dressing area with walk-in closet. The master suite also provides access to the media room with bay window and fireplace. A sunken gathering room suits formal or informal occasions. The kitchen contains a snack bar and is convenient to the breakfast and dining rooms. Two large bedrooms upstairs are accompanied by two full baths.

Design V22780
First Floor: 2,006 square feet
Second Floor: 718 square feet
Total: 2,724 square feet

● This 1½-story contemporary has more fine features than one can imagine. The livability is outstanding and can be appreciated by the whole family. Note the fine indoor-outdoor living relationships.

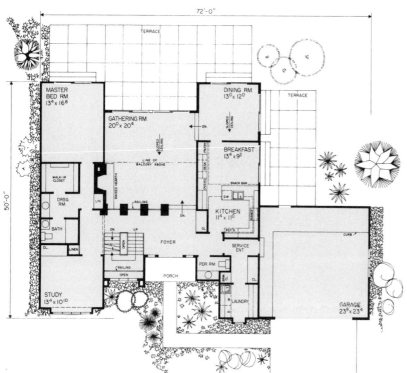

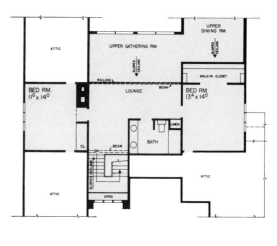

Design V22772
First Floor: 1,579 square feet
Second Floor: 1,240 square feet; Total: 2,819 square feet

● This four-bedroom two-story contemporary design is sure to suit your growing family needs. The rear U-shaped kitchen, flanked by the family and dining rooms, will be very efficient to the busy homemaker. Parents will enjoy all the convenience of the master bedroom suite.

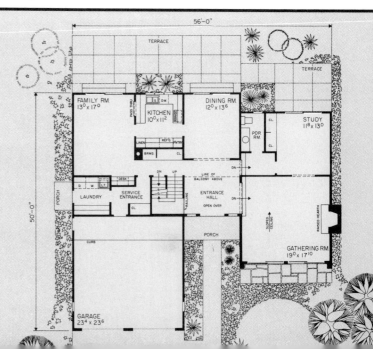

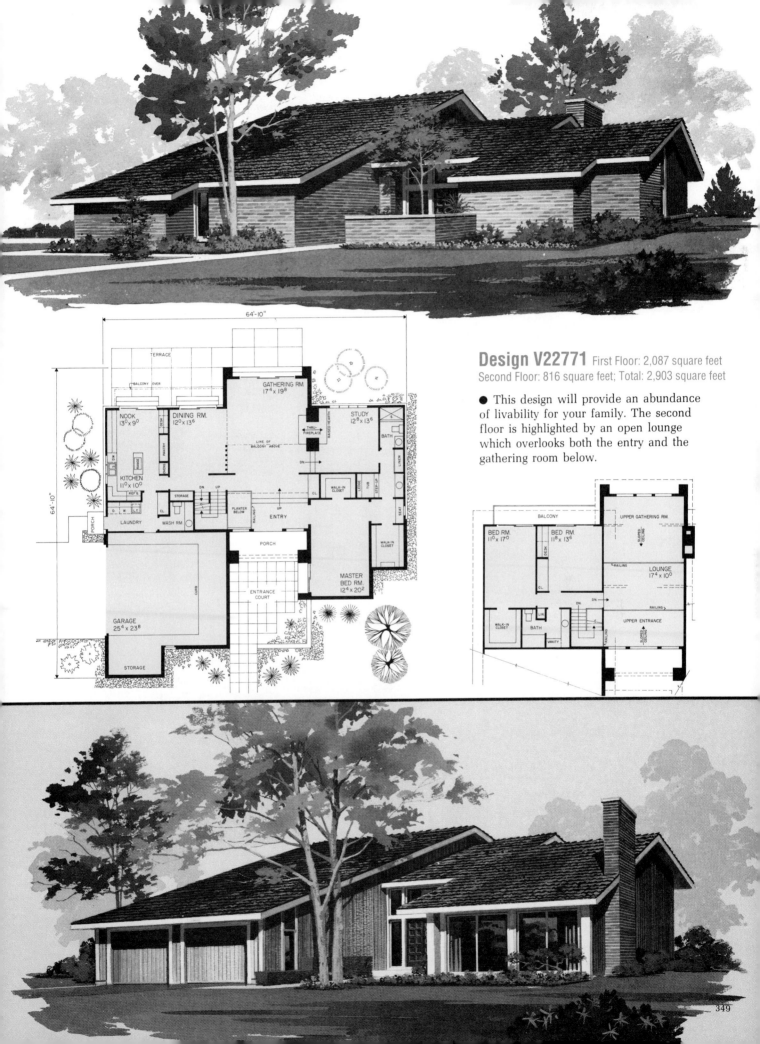

Design V22771 First Floor: 2,087 square feet
Second Floor: 816 square feet; Total: 2,903 square feet

● This design will provide an abundance of livability for your family. The second floor is highlighted by an open lounge which overlooks both the entry and the gathering room below.

Floor plan labels (first floor):

TERRACE
BALCONY OVER
GATHERING RM. 17⁴ x 19⁸
NOOK 13⁰ x 9⁰
DINING RM. 12⁰ x 13⁶
STUDY 12⁸ x 13⁶
BATH
THRU-FIREPLACE
RAISED HEARTH
LINE OF BALCONY ABOVE
KITCHEN 11⁰ x 10⁰
REF'G.
RANGE
OVENS
PANTRY
DRESS
DN
LINEN
WALK-IN CLOSET
CL
LEDGE
TUB
STEP-UP
DW
LT
STORAGE
DN UP
RAILING
PLANTER BELOW
ENTRY
SEAT
UP
CL
LAUNDRY
WASH RM.
WALK-IN CLOSET
PORCH
GARAGE 25⁴ x 23⁸
CURB
PORCH
ENTRANCE COURT
MASTER BED RM. 12⁴ x 20²
STORAGE

64'-10"
64'-10"

Floor plan labels (second floor):

BALCONY
UPPER GATHERING RM.
BED RM. 11⁰ x 17⁰
BED RM. 11⁸ x 13⁶
SLOPED CEILING
DECK
CL
RAILING
LOUNGE 17⁴ x 10⁰
WALK-IN CLOSET
LIN.
BATH
VANITY
DN DN
RAILING
UPPER ENTRANCE
SLOPED CEILING

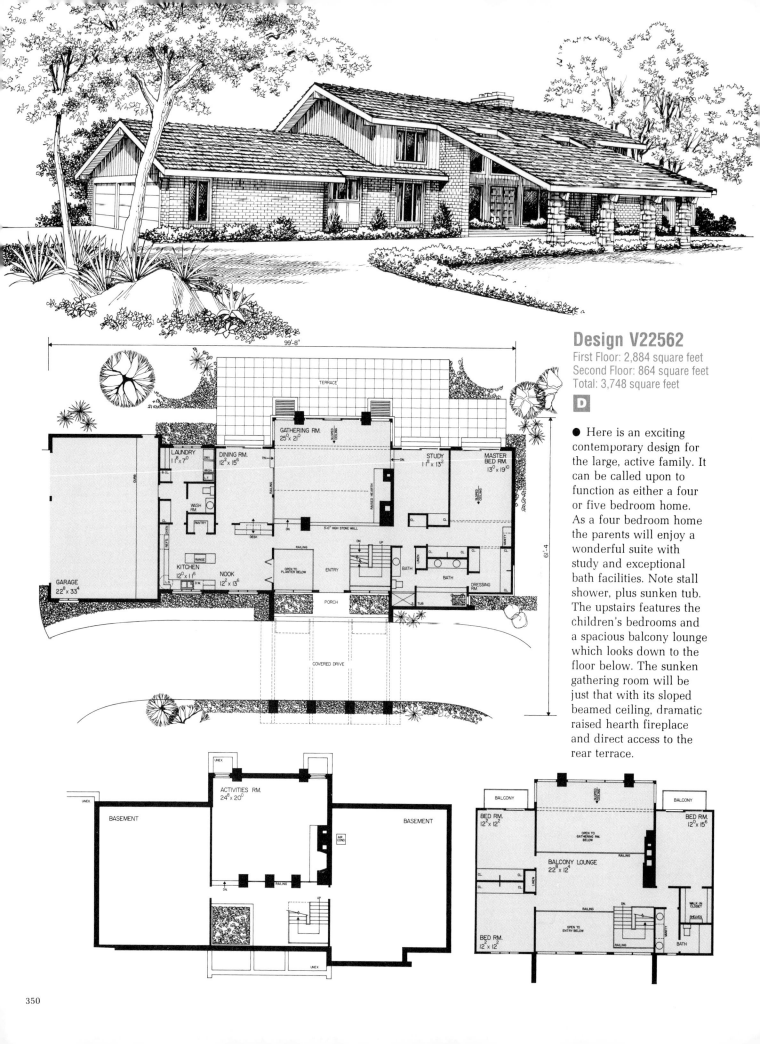

Design V22562

First Floor: 2,884 square feet
Second Floor: 864 square feet
Total: 3,748 square feet

D

● Here is an exciting contemporary design for the large, active family. It can be called upon to function as either a four or five bedroom home. As a four bedroom home the parents will enjoy a wonderful suite with study and exceptional bath facilities. Note stall shower, plus sunken tub. The upstairs features the children's bedrooms and a spacious balcony lounge which looks down to the floor below. The sunken gathering room will be just that with its sloped beamed ceiling, dramatic raised hearth fireplace and direct access to the rear terrace.

Design V23556

First Floor: 1,828 square feet
Second Floor: 1,344 square feet
Total: 3,172 square feet

● Contemporary styling on the exterior, an amenity-filled floor plan—what more could you ask for in a luxury home? First-floor livability includes a huge gathering room/dining room combination with fireplace and terrace access. Another area with fireplace is found just off the kitchen. A sunken media room with greenhouse area is located to the right of the entry foyer. The second floor holds four bedrooms and three full baths. The master bedroom contains a sloped ceiling, a convenient dressing area with double-bowl vanity, and His and Hers walk-in closets. A compartmented toilet and whirlpool tub grace the bath.

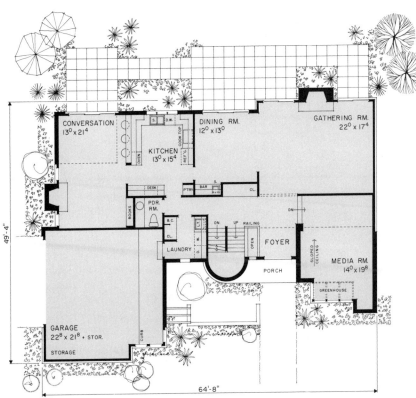

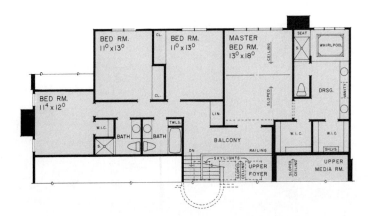

● Varying roof planes, wide overhangs, interestingly shaped blank wall areas and patterned, double front doors provide the distinguishing characteristics of this contemporary design. The extension of the front wall results in a private, outdoor patio area accessible from the living room. There is a fine feeling of spaciousness inside this plan. The living area features open planning. Upstairs, four good-sized bedrooms and two baths.

Design V22602 First Floor: 1,154 square feet
Second Floor: 1,120 square feet; Total: 2,274 square feet

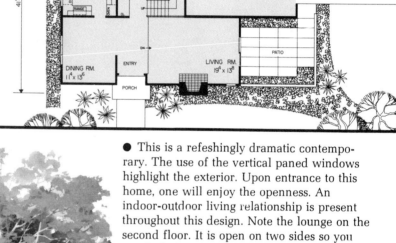

● This is a refeshingly dramatic contemporary. The use of the vertical paned windows highlight the exterior. Upon entrance to this home, one will enjoy the openness. An indoor-outdoor living relationship is present throughout this design. Note the lounge on the second floor. It is open on two sides so you can look down into the gathering room and entry hall below.

Design V22749 First Floor: 1,716 square feet
Second Floor: 1,377 square feet; Total: 3,093 square feet

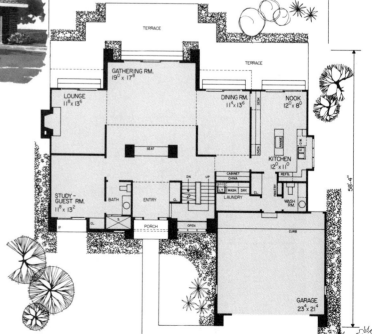

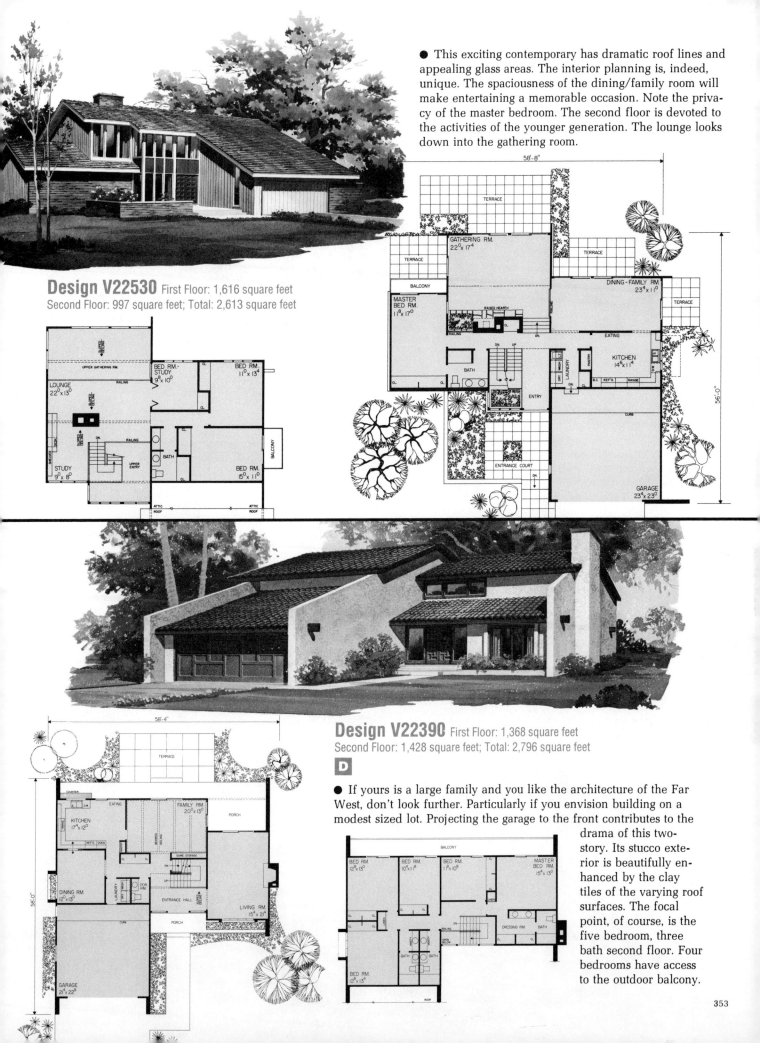

● This exciting contemporary has dramatic roof lines and appealing glass areas. The interior planning is, indeed, unique. The spaciousness of the dining/family room will make entertaining a memorable occasion. Note the privacy of the master bedroom. The second floor is devoted to the activities of the younger generation. The lounge looks down into the gathering room.

Design V22530 First Floor: 1,616 square feet
Second Floor: 997 square feet; Total: 2,613 square feet

Design V22390 First Floor: 1,368 square feet
Second Floor: 1,428 square feet; Total: 2,796 square feet

D

● If yours is a large family and you like the architecture of the Far West, don't look further. Particularly if you envision building on a modest sized lot. Projecting the garage to the front contributes to the drama of this two-story. Its stucco exterior is beautifully enhanced by the clay tiles of the varying roof surfaces. The focal point, of course, is the five bedroom, three bath second floor. Four bedrooms have access to the outdoor balcony.

Design V22377 First Floor: 1,170 square feet
Second Floor: 815 square feet; Total: 1,985 square feet

● What an impressive, up-to-date home. Its refreshing configuration will command a full measure of attention. Note that all of the back rooms on the first floor are a couple steps lower than the entry and living room area. Separating the living room and the slightly lower level is a thru-fireplace, which has a raised hearth in the family room. Four bedrooms, serviced by two full baths, comprise the second floor which looks down into the living room.

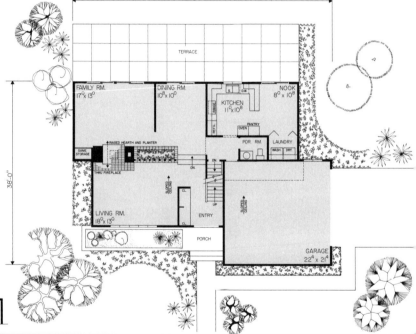

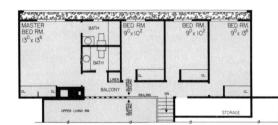

Design V21877 First Floor: 1,162 square feet
Second Floor: 883 square feet; Total: 2,045 square feet

D

● This simple, straightforward plan has much to offer in the way of livability and economical construction costs. Worthy of particular note are the excellent traffic patterns and the outstanding use of space. There is no wasted space here. Notice the cozy family room with its raised-hearth fireplace, wood box and sliding glass doors to the sweeping outdoor deck. The efficient kitchen is flanked by the informal snack bar and the formal dining area. Open planning between the living and dining areas promotes a fine feeling of spaciousness.

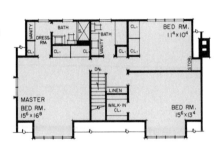

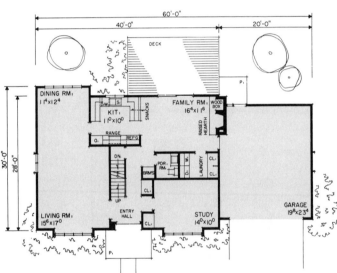

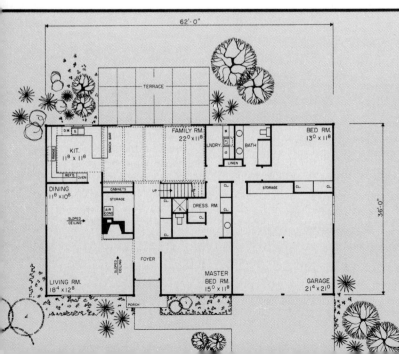

Design V22309 First Floor: 1,719 square feet
Second Floor: 456 square feet; Total: 2,175 square feet

● Study this floor plan carefully. The efficiency of the kitchen could hardly be improved upon. It is strategically located to serve the formal dining room, the family room and even the rear terrace. The sleeping facilities are arranged in a most interesting manner. The master bedroom with its attached bath and dressing room will enjoy a full measure of privacy on the first floor. A second bedroom is also on this floor and has a full bath nearby. Upstairs, there are two more bedrooms and a bath.

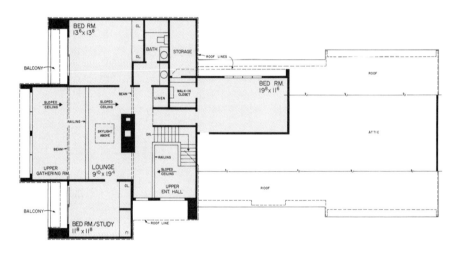

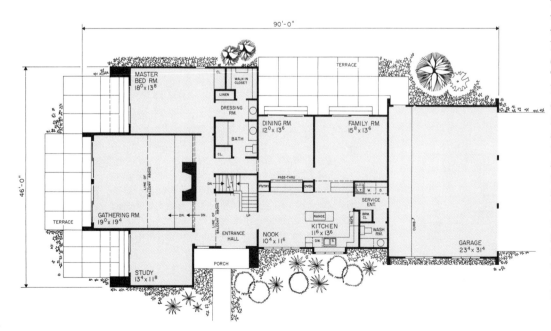

Design V22781

First Floor: 2,132 square feet
Second Floor: 1,156 square feet
Total: 3,288 square feet

● This beautifully designed two-story could be considered a dream house of a
lifetime. The exterior is
sure to catch the eye of
anyone who takes sight of
its unique construction.
The front kitchen features
an island range, adjacent
breakfast nook and pass-
thru to formal dining room.
The master bedroom suite
with its privacy and con-
venience on the first floor
has a spacious walk-in
closet and dressing room.
The side terrace is accessible through sliding glass
doors from the master bedroom, gathering room and
study. The second floor has
three bedrooms and storage
space galore. Also notice
the lounge which has a
sloped ceiling and a sky-
light above. This delightful
area looks down into the
gathering room. The out-
door balconies overlook the
wrap-around terrace. Surely an outstanding trend
house for decades to come.

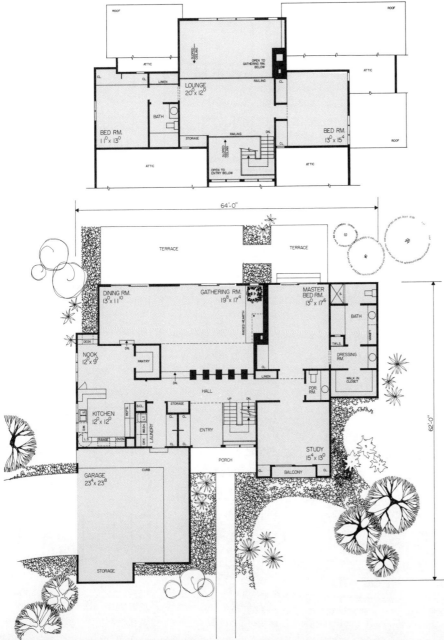

Design V22708

First Floor: 2,108 square feet
Second Floor: 824 square feet
Total: 2,932 square feet

D

● Here is a one-and-a-half story home whose exterior is distinctive. It has a contemporary feeling, yet it retains some of the fine design features and proportions of traditional exteriors. Inside the appealing double front doors there is livability galore. The sunken rear living-dining area is delightfully spacious and is looked down into from the second floor lounge. The open end fireplace, with its raised hearth and planter, is another focal point. The master bedroom features a fine compartmented bath with both shower and tub. The study is just a couple steps away. The U-shaped kitchen is outstanding. Notice the pantry and laundry. Upstairs provides children with their own sleeping, studying and TV quarters. Absolutely a great design! Study all the fine details closely with your family.

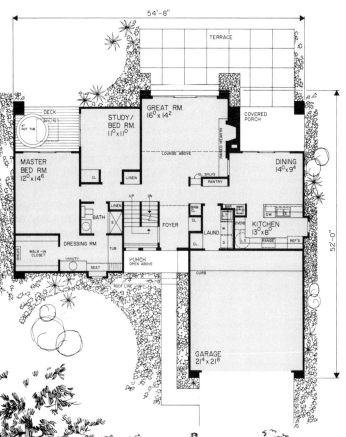

54'-8"

TERRACE

DECK
SKYLITE
3' HOT TUB

STUDY / BED RM.
11⁰ x 11⁰

GREAT RM.
16⁰ x 14²

COVERED PORCH

LOUNGE ABOVE

MASTER BED RM.
12⁰ x 14⁶

CL

LINEN

GL. SHLVS.
PANTRY

DINING
14⁰ x 9⁴

BATH

LINEN

UP

DN

S

DRESSING RM.

TUB

VANITY

SEAT

WALK-IN CLOSET

FOYER

BRM. CL.

OVENS

BAR

CL

LAUND.

DW

KITCHEN
13⁰ x 8⁰

W

L.S.

RANGE

REF'G.

RAISED HEARTH

52'-0"

PORCH OPEN ABOVE

ROOF LINE

CURB

GARAGE
21⁴ x 21⁸

Design V22822

First Floor: 1,363 square feet
Second Floor: 351 square feet
Total: 1,714 square feet

L

UPPER GREAT RM.

RAILING

LOUNGE / HOBBIES
16⁰ x 9²

CL

SKYLITE

CL

DN

RAILING

UPPER FOYER

STOR./ BATH

RAILING

● Here is a truly unique house whose interior was designed with the current decade's economies, life-styles and demographics in mind. While function-ing as a one-story home, the second floor provides an extra measure of livability when required. In addition, this two-story section adds to the dramatic appeal of both the exterior and the interior. Within only 1,363 square feet, this contemporary delivers refreshing and outstanding living patterns for those who are buying their first home, those who have raised their family and are looking for a smaller home and those in search of a retirement home.

BALCONY

LOUNGE / GUEST RM. / GRANDCHILDREN'S RM.
16⁰ x 19²

CL

CL

DN

RAILING

UPPER FOYER

BATH

RAILING

ALTERNATE SECOND FLOOR

Design V23439

First Floor: 1,443 square feet
Second Floor: 937 square feet
Total: 2,380 square feet

● Featuring a facade of wood and window glass, this home presents a striking first impression. It's floor plan is equally as splendid. Formal living and dining areas flank the entry foyer—both are sunken a step down. Also sunken from the foyer is the family room with attached breakfast nook. A fireplace in this area sits adjacent to a built-in audiovisual center. A nearby study with adjacent full bath doubles as a guest room. Upstairs are three bedrooms including a master suite with whirlpool spa and walk-in closet. Plant shelves adorn the entire floor plan.

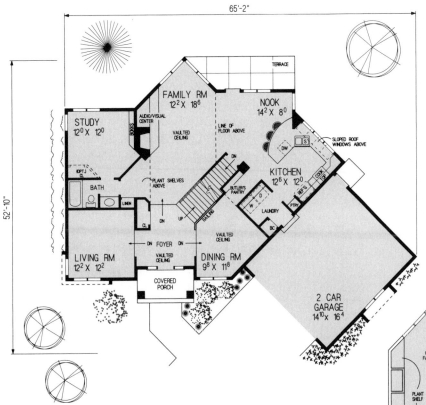

CUSTOMIZABLE

Custom Alterations? See page 413 for customizing this plan to your specifications.

Design V22905

First Floor: 1,342 square feet
Second Floor: 619 square feet
Total: 1,961 square feet

L

● All of the livability in this plan is in the back! Each first floor room, except the kitchen, has access to the rear terrace via sliding glass doors. A great way to capture an excellent view. This plan is also ideal for a narrow lot seeing that its width is less than 50 feet. Two bedrooms and a lounge, overlooking the gathering room, are on the second floor.

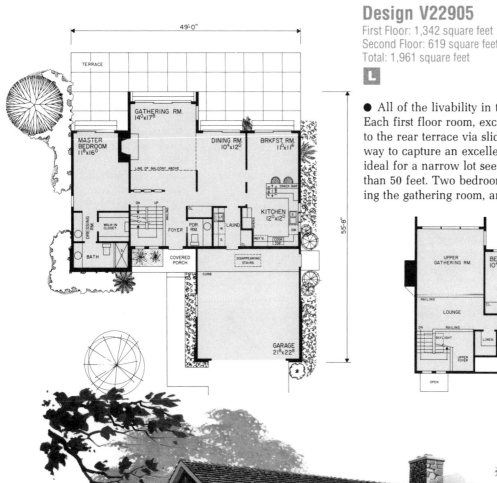

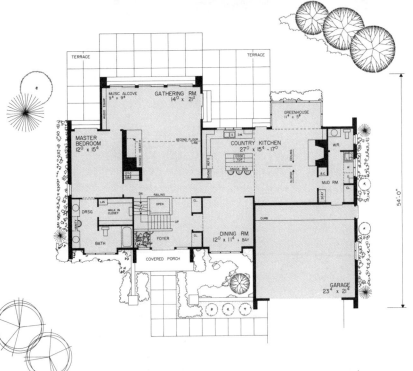

Design V22928

First Floor: 1,917 square feet
Second Floor: 918 square feet
Total: 2,835 square feet

First Floor labels:
TERRACE
TERRACE
MUSIC ALCOVE 9⁴ x 9⁸
GATHERING RM. 14⁰ x 21²
GREENHOUSE 11⁴ x 5⁸
MASTER BEDROOM 12⁰ x 15⁴
SECOND FLOOR LINE
RAISED HEARTH
COUNTRY KITCHEN 27⁰ x 15⁴ - 17⁰
COOK TOP
SNACK BAR
SLOPED CEILING
W.R.
MUD RM.
DRSG
WALK IN CLOSET
OPEN
RAILING
DN
UP
FOYER
BATH
DINING RM. 12⁰ x 11⁴ + BAY
CURB
COVERED PORCH
GARAGE 23⁴ x 21⁴

54'-0"
68'-4"

Second Floor labels:
UPPER GATHERING ROOM
SLOPED CEILING
ROOF
ROOF
BEDROOM 12⁰ x 9⁰
LOUNGE 15⁸ x 12⁴
RAILING
BATH
DL
DL
BEDROOM 12⁰ x 11⁸ + BAY
UPPER FOYER
DN
RAILING
LIN
CL
CL
BEDROOM 12⁰ x 13⁰ + BAY
ROOF
ROOF

Design V22582

First Floor: 1,195 square feet
Second Floor: 731 square feet
Total: 1,926 square feet

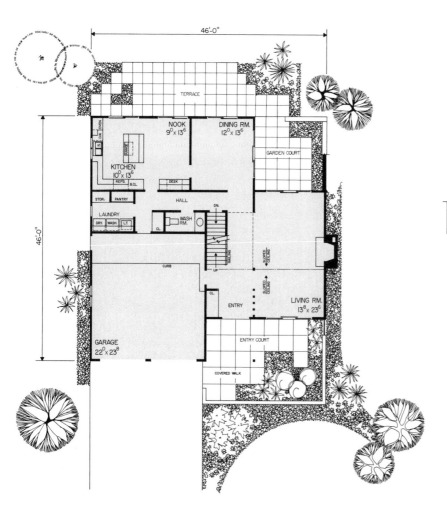

● This distinctive two-story will command attention wherever built. One of its significant features is that it doesn't require a huge piece of property. In slightly less than 2,000 square feet it offers tremendous livability. As a bonus, the basement can function as the family recreation and hobby areas. Of particular interest is the first floor laundry room. Don't miss the fine kitchen layout, the formal and informal dining facilities and the sloping ceiling of the living room. Notice the outstanding outdoor living facilities. Upstairs, three bedrooms and two baths will be found.

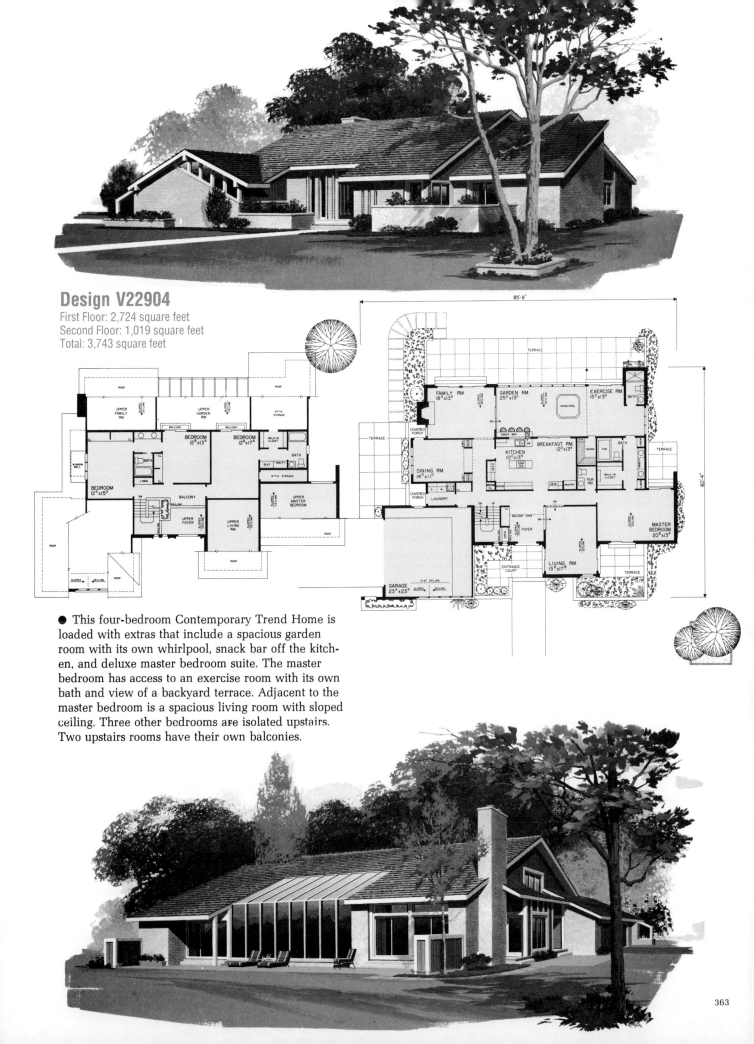

Design V22904

First Floor: 2,724 square feet
Second Floor: 1,019 square feet
Total: 3,743 square feet

● This four-bedroom Contemporary Trend Home is loaded with extras that include a spacious garden room with its own whirlpool, snack bar off the kitchen, and deluxe master bedroom suite. The master bedroom has access to an exercise room with its own bath and view of a backyard terrace. Adjacent to the master bedroom is a spacious living room with sloped ceiling. Three other bedrooms are isolated upstairs. Two upstairs rooms have their own balconies.

TWO COUPLES/SINGLES RESIDENCE

BALCONY | DINING RM. 10⁸ x 10⁴ | BALCONY

LIVING RM. 13⁰ x 21⁸ | OPTIONAL SKYLIGHT | BEDROOM 13⁰ x 11⁴

SNACK BAR | KITCHEN 7⁴ x 8⁴

SLOPED CEILING | LINEN CL. CL.

SKYLIGHT | BATH

ENTRY | CL.

CABINETS SHELVES | SKYLIGHTS | DN UP

UPPER FOYER | STORAGE (OPTIONAL LAUNDRY)

CONVERTIBLE ONE-FAMILY RESIDENCE

BALCONY | BEDROOM/ LOUNGE 10⁸ x 10⁴ | BALCONY

MASTER BEDROOM 13⁰ x 21⁸ | BEDROOM 13⁰ x 11⁴

BATH | CL.

SKYLIGHT | LINEN | BATH

CL. CL. | LINEN

SKYLIGHTS | DN

UPPER FOYER | SEWING/ HOBBIES

Design V22828 First Floor (Living Area): 817 square feet; Foyer & Laundry: 261 square feet
Second Floor (Living Area): 852 square feet; Foyer & Storage: 214 square feet; Total: 2,144 square feet

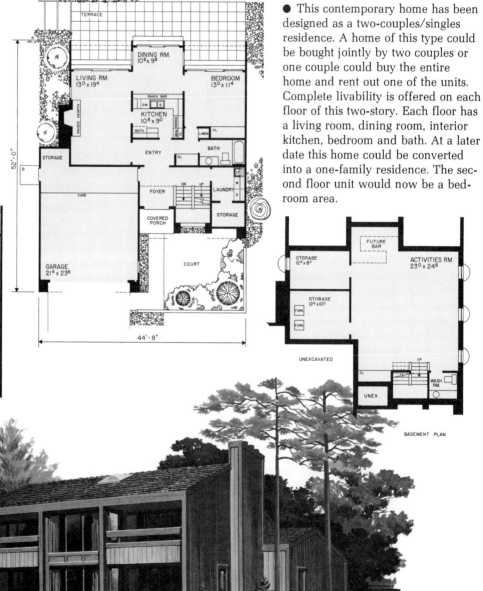

TERRACE

DINING RM. 10⁸ x 9⁸

LIVING RM. 13⁰ x 19⁴ | BEDROOM 13⁰ x 11⁴

SNACK BAR | KITCHEN 10⁸ x 9⁰

RAISED HEARTH | REF'S | RANGE

STORAGE | ENTRY | LINEN CL.

BATH | CL.

52'-0"

CURB | FOYER | DN UP | LAUNDRY | LT.

COVERED PORCH | STORAGE

GARAGE 21⁴ x 23⁶ | COURT

44'-8"

● This contemporary home has been designed as a two-couples/singles residence. A home of this type could be bought jointly by two couples or one couple could buy the entire home and rent out one of the units. Complete livability is offered on each floor of this two-story. Each floor has a living room, dining room, interior kitchen, bedroom and bath. At a later date this home could be converted into a one-family residence. The second floor unit would now be a bedroom area.

FUTURE BAR

STORAGE 12⁸ x 8⁰ | ACTIVITIES RM. 23⁰ x 24⁸

STORAGE 12⁸ x 10⁰ | FURN. | FURN.

UNEXCAVATED | CL. | UP

UNEX. | WASH RM.

BASEMENT PLAN

Design V22884 First Floor: 1,855 square feet
Second Floor: 837 square feet; Total: 2,692 square feet

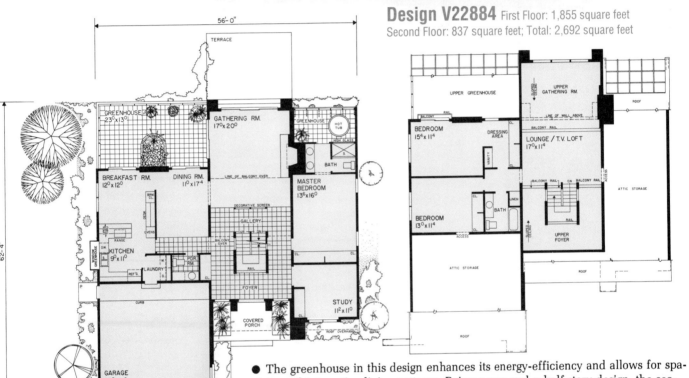

GREENHOUSE
23⁰ x 13⁰

GATHERING RM.
17⁰ x 20⁰

GREENHOUSE

HOT TUB

HIGH GLASS

BATH

BREAKFAST RM.
12⁰ x 12⁰

DINING RM.
11⁰ x 17⁴

LINE OF BALCONY OVER

MASTER BEDROOM
13⁶ x 16⁰

RANGE

OVENS

DECORATIVE SCREEN

GALLERY

KITCHEN
9⁰ x 11⁰

BALCONY OVER

PDR. RM.

LAUNDRY

RAIL

FOYER

CL.

CL.

TERRACE

56'-0"

62'-4"

GARAGE
23⁶ x 21⁶

CURB

COVERED PORCH

STUDY
11² x 11⁰

ROOF OVERHANG

ROOF OVERHANG

UPPER GREENHOUSE

UPPER GATHERING RM.

ROOF

BALCONY

BALCONY RAIL

LINE OF WALL ABOVE

BEDROOM
15⁴ x 11⁴

DRESSING AREA

LOUNGE / T.V. LOFT
17⁰ x 11⁴

VANITY

CL.

BALCONY RAIL

ON BALCONY RAIL

ATTIC STORAGE

BEDROOM
13⁰ x 11⁴

CL.

BATH

LINEN

CL.

ACCESS

UPPER FOYER

RAIL

ATTIC STORAGE

ROOF

ROOF

● The greenhouse in this design enhances its energy-efficiency and allows for spacious and interesting living patterns. Being a one-and-a-half story design, the second floor could be developed at a later date when the space is needed. The greenhouses add an additional 418 sq. ft. to the above quoted figures.

Design V22925 First Floor: 1,128 square feet; Second Floor: 844 square feet; Total: 1,972 square feet

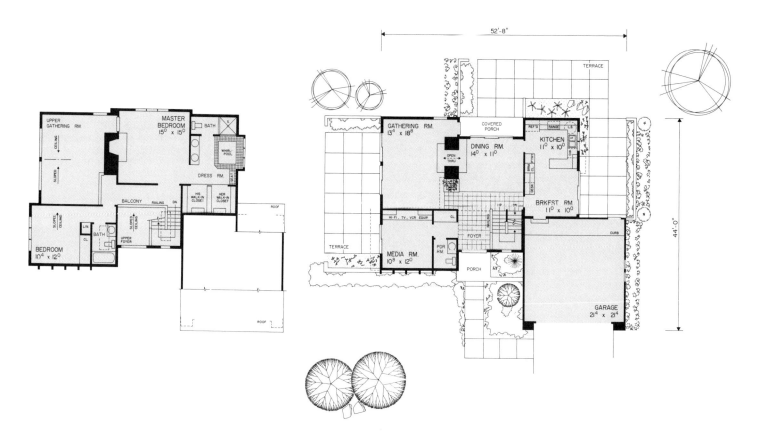

● What a refreshing and exciting two-story contemporary. The expansive wide-overhanging roofs make a distinctive design statement. This is also true of the effective uses of varying exterior materials and surface textures. The front entry area is noteworthy for its panelled double doors below the large radial head window. This window and the two vertical strips of glass to its right permit an abundance of natural light to flood the foyer and open staircases. While enjoying privacy from the street, the various rooms enjoy wonderful views of the rear and side yards. The cathedral ceiling of the gathering room and its windowed wall will make this the family's favorite area. A thru-fireplace serves both the gathering and dining rooms at the same time. The corner kitchen serves both dining areas well. The media room will house all that hi-tech equipment. Upstairs, two bedrooms and baths.

Design V23347 First Floor: 1,915 square feet
Second Floor: 759 square feet; Total: 2,674 square feet

● Open living is the key to the abundant livability of this design. The gigantic gathering room/dining room area shares a through-fireplace with a unique sunken conversation area. An L-shaped kitchen has a pass-through snack bar to the breakfast room. On the second floor, two bedrooms are separated by a lounge with a balcony overlook.

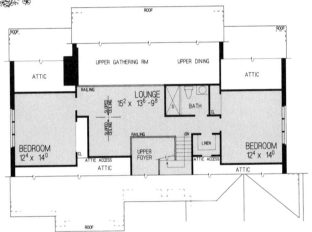

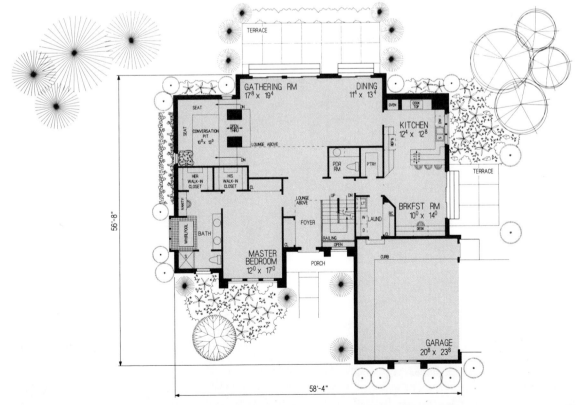

Design V23404

First Floor: 3,358 square feet
Second Floor: 868 square feet
Total: 4,226 square feet

L **D**

● Farmhouse design does a double take in this unusual and elegant rendition. Notice that most of the living takes place on the first floor: formal living room and dining room, gigantic family room with enormous firepit and porch access, guest bedroom or den and master bedroom suite. Upstairs there are two smaller bedrooms and a dramatic balcony overlook to the family room below.

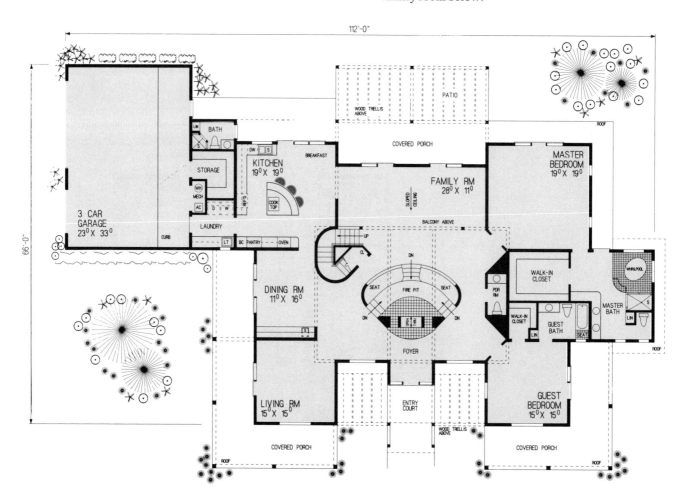

Design V23438

First Floor: 1,489 square feet
Second Floor: 741 square feet
Total: 2,230 square feet

● A unique farmhouse plan which provides a
grand floor plan, this home is comfortable in
country or suburban settings. Formal entertaining areas share first-floor space with family
gathering rooms and work and service areas.
The master suite is also on this floor for convenience and privacy. Upstairs is a guest bedroom, private bath and loft area that makes a
perfect studio. Special features make this a
great place to come home to.

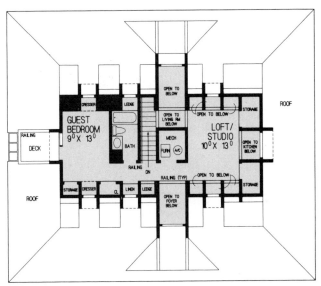

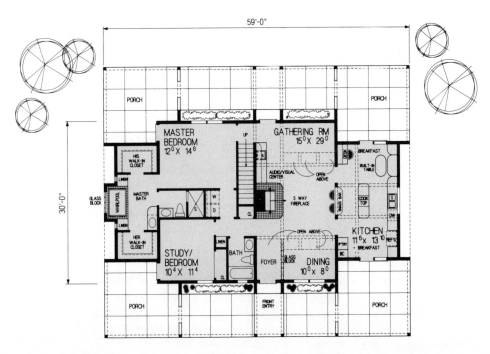

Design V23409

First Floor: 1,481 square feet
Second Floor: 1,287 square feet
Total: 2,768 square feet

● Glass block walls and a foyer with barrel vaulted ceiling create an interesting exterior. Covered porches to the front and rear provide for excellent indoor/outdoor living relationships. Inside, a large planter and through-fireplace enhance the living room and family room. The dining room has a stepped ceiling. A desk, eating area and snack bar are special features in the kitchen. The master suite features a large walk-in closet, bath with double bowl vanity and separate tub and shower, and a private deck. Three additional bedrooms share a full bath.

Design V23403

First Floor: 2,240 square feet
Second Floor: 660 square feet
Total: 2,900 square feet

L **D**

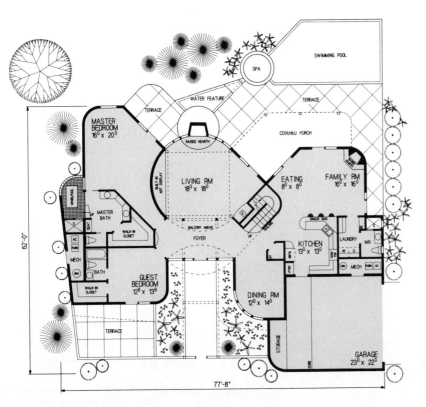

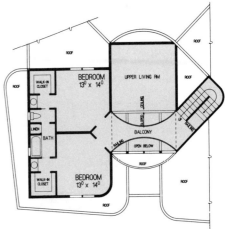

● There is no end to the distinctive features in this Southwestern contemporary. Formal living areas are concentrated in the center of the plan, perfect for entertaining. To the right of the plan, the kitchen and family room function well together as a working and living area. Also note the separate laundry room. The optional guest bedroom or den and the master bedroom are located to the left of the plan. Upstairs, the remaining two bedrooms are reached by a balcony overlooking the living room and share a bath with twin vanities.

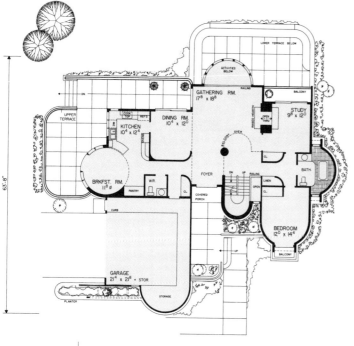

Design V22926 First Floor: 1,570 square feet
Second Floor: 598 square feet; Lower Level: 1,080 square feet
Total: 2,650 square feet

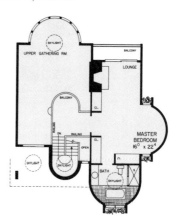

● This striking contemporary design offers plenty of leisure living on three levels including an activities room with bar, exercise room with sauna, a gathering room, circular glass windows, and skylights. Note the outstanding master bedroom suite with skylight over the bath, adjoining lounge, and adjacent upper gathering room.

SUN COUNTRY HOMES . . .

display the spirit and diversity of a relaxed lifestyle. From California Craftsman, Spanish Mission and Monterey to Santa Fe-style, these homes spread across the Southwest in the beginning of the 20th Century. Currently, these styles can be seen in scattered areas throughout the country. Unique features include red tile roofs, towers, exterior porches and balconies. Indoor/outdoor relationships are given special attention.

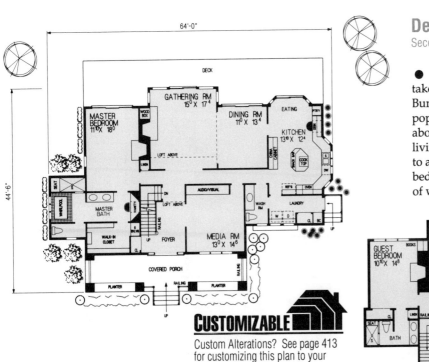

CUSTOMIZABLE

Custom Alterations? See page 413 for customizing this plan to your specifications.

Design V23322 First Floor: 1,860 square feet
Second Floor: 935 square feet; Total: 2,795 square feet

● This cleverly designed Southwestern-style home takes its cue from the California Craftsman and Bungalow styles that have seen such an increase in popularity lately. Nonetheless, it is suited to just about any climate. Its convenient floor plan includes living and working areas on the first floor in addition to a master suite. The second floor holds two family bedrooms and a guest bedroom. Note the abundance of window area to the rear of the plan.

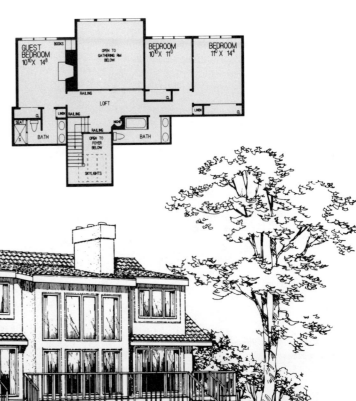

Design V23449

First Floor: 1,336 square feet
Second Floor: 1,186 square feet
Total: 2,522 square feet

● A covered porch leads inside to a wide, tiled foyer. A curving staircase makes an elegant expression in the open space including the living and dining rooms with two-story ceilings. A through-fireplace warms the nook and family room with wet bar and glass shelves. The nook also includes planters on two sides. Just above, light spills into the whirlpool in the master bath with dual vanities and walk-in closet. The master bedroom includes a sitting area, two more closets, and access to a private covered deck. Two family bedrooms share a full bath with dual vanities.

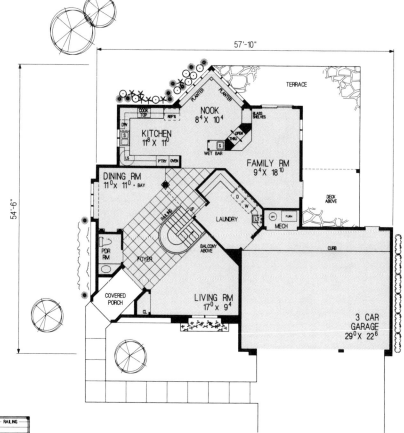

CUSTOMIZABLE

Custom Alterations? See page 413 for customizing this plan to your specifications.

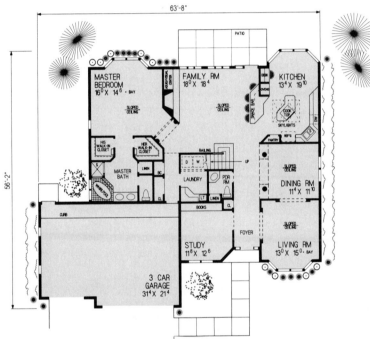

Design V23441

First Floor: 2,022 square feet
Second Floor: 845 square feet
Total: 2,867 square feet

● Special details make the difference
between a house and a home. A snack
bar, audio/visual center and a fireplace make the family room livable. A
desk, island cook top, bay, and skylights enhance the kitchen area. The
dining room features two columns
and a plant ledge. The first-floor master suite includes His and Hers walk-
in closets, a spacious bath, and a bay
window. On the second floor, one
bedroom features a walk-in closet and
private bath, while two additional
bedrooms share a full bath.

CUSTOMIZABLE

Custom Alterations? See page 413
for customizing this plan to your
specifications.

Design V23417
First Floor: 875 square feet
Second Floor: 731 square feet; Total: 1,606 square feet

CUSTOMIZABLE
Custom Alterations? See page 413 for customizing this plan to your specifications.

● Perfect for a starter home, this design is compact yet features great livability. The plan provides both formal and informal living areas. There's a living room with bay window and adjacent dining area. Open to the kitchen, the spacious family room is large enough to accommodate an informal eating area. The second floor boasts a balcony lounge overlooking the family room, master bedroom with bay window and two smaller family bedrooms.

CUSTOMIZABLE
Custom Alterations? See page 413 for customizing this plan to your specifications.

Design V23418

First Floor: 1,283 square feet
Second Floor: 552 square feet
Total: 1,835 square feet

● This home is ideal for the economically minded who don't want to sacrifice livability. The entry foyer opens directly into the two-story living room with fireplace. To the right, the kitchen with peninsula cooktop and snack bar conveniently serves both the breakfast room and the formal dining room. Also on this level, the master bedroom boasts an enormous bath with a whirlpool and His and Hers walk-in closets. Three other bedrooms are located upstairs to ensure peace and quiet. Also notice the abundant storage space in the attic.

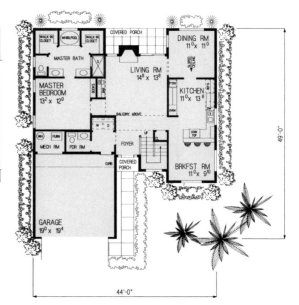

Design V23420
First Floor: 1,617 square feet
Second Floor: 658 square feet; Total: 2,275 square feet

● Here is a moderate-sized house with a wealth of amenities typical of much larger homes. Interesting window treatments include two bay windows, one in the living room and one in the breakfast room. In the kitchen there's a snack bar pass-through to the family room which boasts a corner raised-hearth fireplace. Also on this level, the master suite features a large bath with whirlpool and access to the rear covered porch. Upstairs are three more bedrooms and a shared bath. Notice the attic storage space.

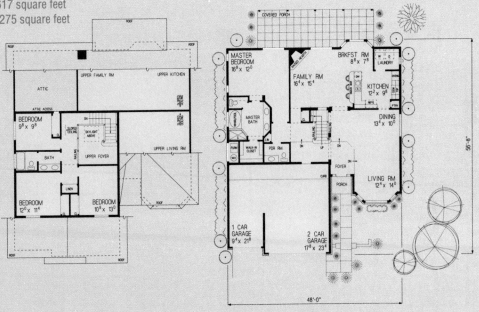

CUSTOMIZABLE

Custom Alterations? See page 413 for customizing this plan to your specifications.

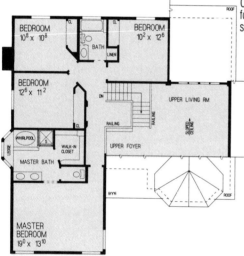

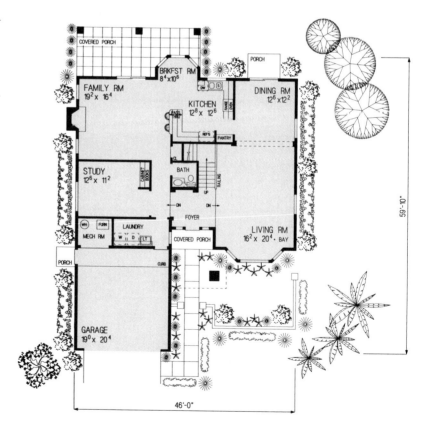

CUSTOMIZABLE
Custom Alterations? See page 413
for customizing this plan to your
specifications.

Design V23427 First Floor: 1,574 square feet
Second Floor: 1,177 square feet; Total: 2,751 square feet

● Varying rooflines and unusual window treatments will make this home a
standout anywhere. The transom-lit
foyer opens onto a cozy study and a spacious living room with dramatic bay
window. To the rear, the kitchen easily
serves the dining room and the bay-
windowed breakfast room. The family
room features a large fireplace. Upstairs
are four bedrooms including a master
with whirlpool bath.

Design V23428 First Floor: 2,623 square feet
Second Floor: 551 square feet; Total: 3,174 square feet

● High sloping ceilings and plenty of windows lend a light, airy feel to this Southwestern design. Flanking the two-story foyer are the sleeping areas, the regal master suite to the left and three more bedrooms (or two plus study) to the right. Overlooking the back yard are the dining room and living room with raised-hearth fireplace. The U-shaped kitchen has a pass-through to the family room which also has a fireplace. Doors here and in the dining room open onto the covered porch. Notice the pot shelves scattered throughout the plan.

CUSTOMIZABLE
Custom Alterations? See page 413 for customizing this plan to your specifications.

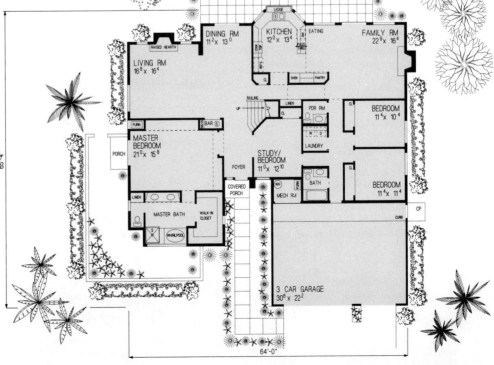

Design V23425

First Floor: 1,776 square feet
Second Floor: 1,035 square feet
Total: 2,811 square feet

[L] [D]

CUSTOMIZABLE

Custom Alterations? See page 413 for customizing this plan to your specifications.

● Here's a two-story Spanish design with an appealing, angled exterior. Inside is an interesting floor plan containing rooms with a variety of shapes. Formal areas are to the right of the entry tower: a living room with fireplace and large dining room. The kitchen has loads of counter space and is complemented by a bumped-out breakfast room. Note the second fireplace in the family room and the first-floor bedroom. Three second-floor bedrooms include a master suite with balcony.

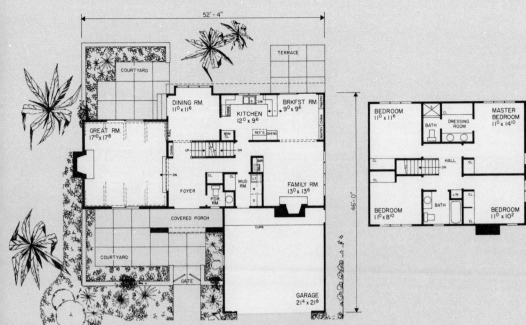

Design V22801

First Floor: 1,172 square feet
Second Floor: 884 square feet
Total: 2,056 square feet

L D

● The great room in this design will be just that. It is sunken two steps, has a beamed ceiling, the beauty of a fireplace and two sets of sliding glass doors to a front and rear courtyard. A built-in wet bar and fireplace are the features of the family room. The foyer of this Spanish design is very spacious and houses a powder room. Four bedrooms and two baths are on the second floor. Don't miss the two enclosed courtyards.

Design V23414
First Floor: 2,024 square feet
Second Floor: 1,144 square feet; Total: 3,168 square feet

● Though seemingly compact from the exterior, this home allows for "wide-open-spaces" living. The two-story entry connects directly to a formal living/dining area, a fitting complement to the more casual family room and cozy breakfast room. Split-bedroom planning puts the master suite on the first floor for utmost privacy. Up the curved staircase are three family bedrooms, a guest room with deck, and two full baths.

CUSTOMIZABLE

Custom Alterations? See page 413 for customizing this plan to your specifications.

CUSTOMIZABLE
Custom Alterations? See page 413
for customizing this plan to your
specifications.

Design V23429

First Floor: 1,739 square feet
Second Floor: 1,376 square feet
Total: 3,115 square feet

● From the dramatic open
entry to the full-width back
porch, this home delivers a
full measure of livability in
Spanish design. Formal living areas (living room and
dining room) have a counter-
point in the family room and
glassed-in breakfast room.
The kitchen is a hub for
both areas. Notice that the
first-floor study has an adjacent bath, making it a fine
guest room when needed.
On the second floor, the
central loft serves two family
bedrooms and a grand mas-
ter suite.

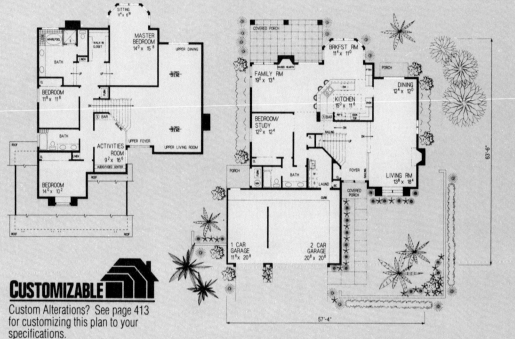

CUSTOMIZABLE
Custom Alterations? See page 413
for customizing this plan to your
specifications.

● You'll find plenty about this Spanish design that will convince you that this is *the*
home for your family. Enjoy indoor/
outdoor living in the gigantic family room
with covered porch access and a sunken
conversation area sharing a through fireplace with the study. An
L-shaped kitchen has an attached,
glass-surrounded breakfast room
and is conveniently located next
to the formal dining room/
living room combina-
tion. Besides the opu-
lent master suite on
the second floor, there
are two family bed-
rooms and a full bath.

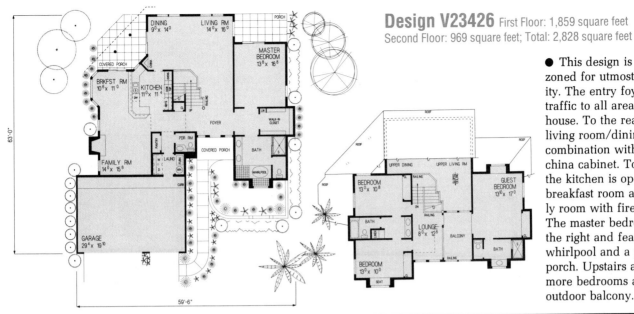

Design V23426 First Floor: 1,859 square feet
Second Floor: 969 square feet; Total: 2,828 square feet

● This design is carefully zoned for utmost livability. The entry foyer routes traffic to all areas of the house. To the rear is the living room/dining room combination with built-in china cabinet. To the left, the kitchen is open to the breakfast room and family room with fireplace. The master bedroom is on the right and features a whirlpool and a private porch. Upstairs are three more bedrooms and an outdoor balcony.

Design V23424 First Floor: 1,625 square feet
Second Flooor: 982 square feet; Total: 2,607 square feet

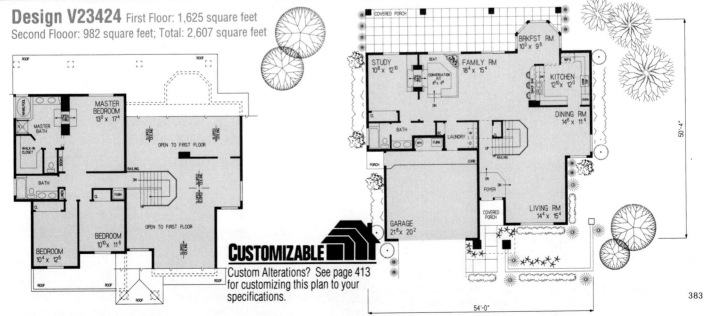

CUSTOMIZABLE
Custom Alterations? See page 413 for customizing this plan to your specifications.

Design V23447

First Floor: 2,296 square feet
Second Floor: 1,027 square feet
Total: 3,323 square feet

CUSTOMIZABLE

Custom Alterations? See page 413 for customizing this plan to your specifications.

● Family activities of all types have a distinct place in this home. The first floor contains a game room, along with a living room/dining room combination with sloped ceiling and a family room with fireplace. The spacious, angled kitchen includes a snack-bar, walk-in pantry, and adjacent breakfast area with a bay. A covered patio in the back makes for pleasant outside dining in any weather. An elegant staircase is accented by a niche and art gallery. The master bedroom features a private deck, two closets and a lavish bath. Two additional bedrooms share a full bath.

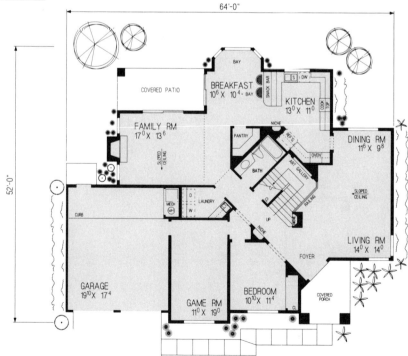

Design V23448

First Floor: 2,504 square feet
Second Floor: 1,673 square feet
Total: 4,168 square feet

● Spacious rooms are the rule in this home. A sunken living room stretches for a full 25 feet. The family room with fireplace is impressive in size, and even the kitchen abounds in space with a separate eating area (with coffered ceiling), a snack bar, island cook top, and a walk-in pantry. The first-floor master suite contains His and Hers walk-in closets, a three-way fireplace, whirlpool, and double bowl vanity. Three bedrooms upstairs share a compartmented bath. Back on the first floor, a fifth bedroom with private bath is perfect for guest quarters.

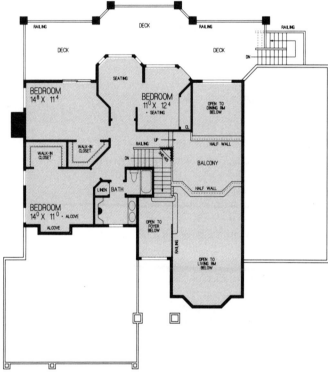

CUSTOMIZABLE

Custom Alterations? See page 413 for customizing this plan to your specifications.

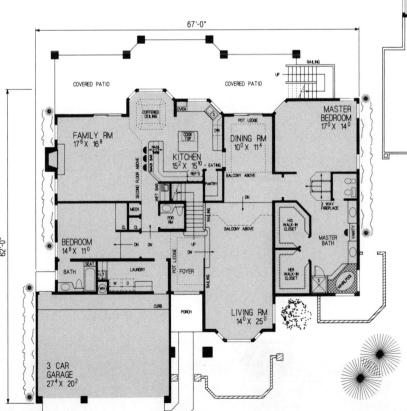

Design V23323

First Floor: 1,923 square feet
Second Floor: 838 square feet
Total: 2.751 square feet

● This two-story southwestern home was designed to make living patterns as pleasant as they can be. Take a step down from the foyer and go where your mood takes you: a gathering room with fireplace and an alcove for reading or quiet conversations, a media room for enjoying the latest technology, or to the dining room with sliding glass doors to the terrace. The kitchen has an island range and eating space. Also on the first floor is a large master suite including a sitting area with terrace access, walk-in closet and whirlpool. An elegant spiral staircase leads to two family bedrooms sharing a full bath and a guest bedroom with private bath.

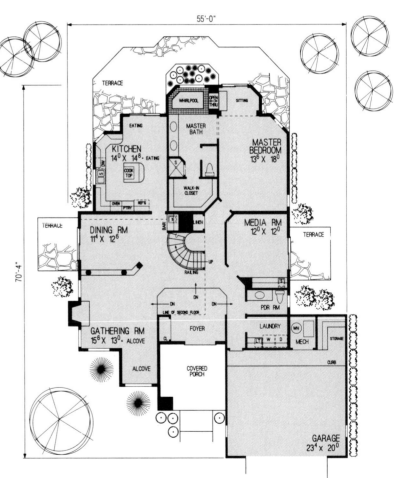

CUSTOMIZABLE

Custom Alterations? See page 413 for customizing this plan to your specifications.

386

Design V23450

First Floor: 1,801 square feet
Second Floor: 1,086 square feet
Total: 2,887 square feet

● A striking facade includes a covered front porch with four columns.
To the left of the foyer is a large
gathering room with a fireplace and bay
window. The adjoining dining room leads
to a covered side porch. The kitchen
includes a snack bar, pantry, desk, and eating area. The first-floor master suite provides a spacious bath with walk-in closet,
whirlpool and shower. Also on the first
floor: a study and a garage workshop. Two
bedrooms and a lavish guest suite share
the second floor.

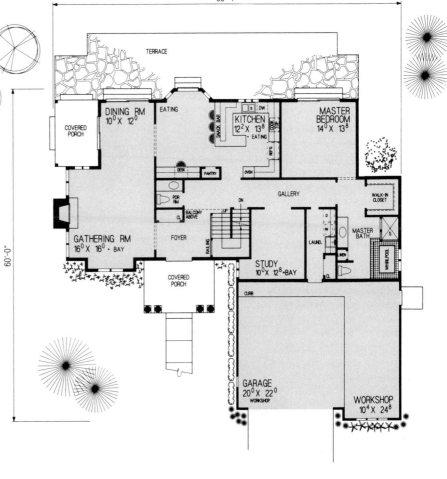

CUSTOMIZABLE
Custom Alterations? See page 413
for customizing this plan to your
specifications.

Design V23435

First Floor: 1,946 square feet
Second Floor: 986 square feet
Total: 2,932 square feet

● Here's a grand Spanish Mission home designed for family living. Enter at the angled foyer which contains a curved staircase to the second floor. Family bedrooms are here along with a spacious guest suite. The master bedroom is found on the first floor and has a private patio and whirlpool overlooking an enclosed garden area. Besides a living room and dining room connected by a through-fireplace, there is a family room with casual eating space. There is also a library with large closet. You'll appreciate the abundant built-ins and interesting shapes throughout this home.

Custom Alterations? See page 413 for customizing this plan to your specifications.

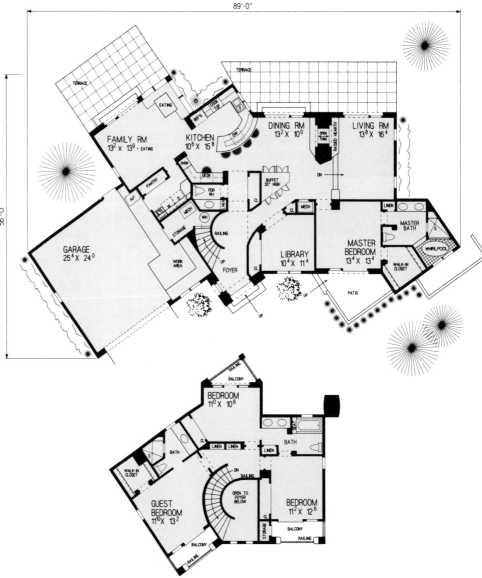

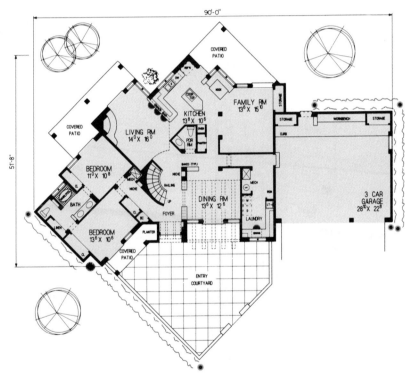

Design V23432

First Floor: 1,966 square feet
Second Floor: 831 square feet
Total: 2,797 square feet

● Unique in nature, this two-story Santa Fe-style home is as practical as it is lovely. The facade is elegantly enhanced by a large entry court, overlooked by windows in the dining room and a covered patio from one of two family bedrooms. The entry foyer leads to living areas at the back of the plan: a living room with corner fireplace and a family room connected to the kitchen via a built-in eating nook. Upstairs, the master suite features a grand bath and large walk-in closet. The guest bedroom has a private bath. Every room in this home has its own outdoor area.

CUSTOMIZABLE

Custom Alterations? See page 413 for customizing this plan to your specifications.

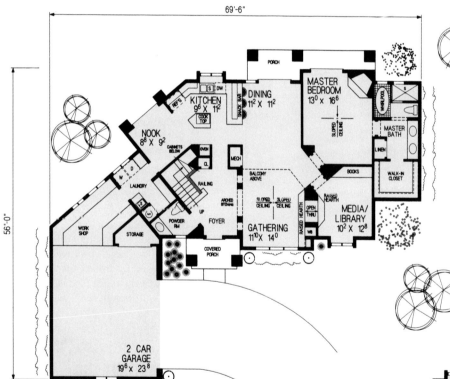

69'-6"

56'-0"

PORCH

KITCHEN
9⁶ X 11²

DINING
11² X 11²

MASTER
BEDROOM
13⁰ X 16⁶

SNACK BAR

COOK TOP

NOOK
8⁸ X 9²

CABINETS BELOW

OVEN

CL

MECH

SLOPED CEILING

MASTER BATH

WHIRLPOOL

LINEN

BOOKS

WALK-IN CLOSET

LAUNDRY

BALCONY ABOVE

RAILING

ARCHED OPENING

SLOPED CEILING

SLOPED CEILING

RAISED HEARTH

RAISED HEARTH

MEDIA/
LIBRARY
10² X 12⁸

WORK SHOP

POWDER RM

UP

STORAGE

FOYER

GATHERING
11¹⁰ X 14⁰

OPEN THRU

COVERED PORCH

2 CAR
GARAGE
19⁶ X 23⁸

CUSTOMIZABLE

Custom Alterations? See page 413 for customizing this plan to your specifications.

Design V23437

First Floor: 1,522 square feet
Second Floor: 730 square feet
Total: 2,252 square feet

● This two-story Spanish Mission-style home has character inside and out. The first-floor master suite features a fire-place and gracious bath with walk-in closet, whirlpool, shower, dual vanities, and linen storage. A second fireplace serves both the gathering room and media room or library. The kitchen with island cook top includes a snack bar and an adjoining breakfast nook. Three bedrooms and two full baths occupy the second floor.

GUEST BEDROOM
10⁰ X 11⁰

BEDROOM
10⁶ X 11⁰

BATH

LINEN

BATH

DN

BALCONY

RAILING

MECH

CL

OPEN TO BELOW

OPEN TO GATHERING RM BELOW

BEDROOM
11² X 10⁴

390

MOST POPULAR ONE-STORY HOUSES . . .

a bonus feature we present for your inspection. From the one-story designs most requested by our customers, this grouping offers a diversity of floor plans and exteriors. Encompassing many of the most popular styles, from Contemporary to Western, they host a wealth of highlights: gathering rooms, luxury master suites, private studies, and great indoor-outdoor relationships.

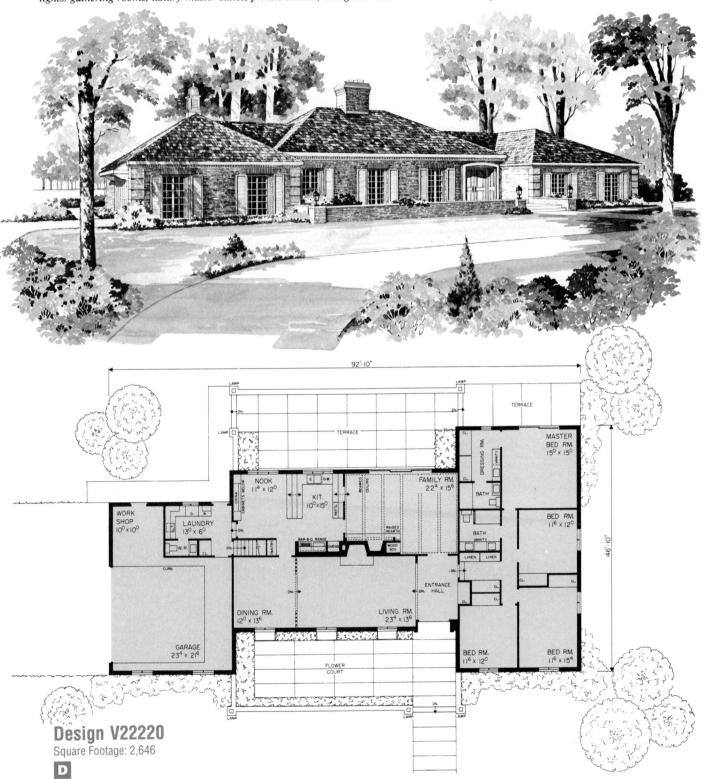

Design V22220
Square Footage: 2,646

D

● The gracious formality of this home is reminiscent of a popularly accepted French styling. The hip-roof, the brick quoins, the cornice details, the arched window heads, the distinctive shutters, the recessed double front doors, the massive center chimney, and the delightful flower court are all features which set the dramatic appeal of this home. This floor plan is a favorite of many. The four bedroom, two bath sleeping wing is a zone by itself. Further, the formal living and dining rooms are ideally located. For entertaining they function well together and look out upon the pleasant flower court. Overlooking the raised living terrace at the rear are the family and breakfast rooms and work center. Don't miss the laundry, extra wash room and work shop in garage.

Clutter Room, Media Room To The Fore

● Something new? Something new, indeed!! Here is the introduction of two rooms which will make a wonderful contribution to family living. The clutter room is strategically placed between the kitchen and garage. It is the nerve center of the work area. It houses the laundry, provides space for sewing, has a large sorting table, and even plenty of space for the family's tool bench. A handy potting area is next to the laundry tray. Adjacent to

the clutter room, and a significant part of the planning of this whole zone, are the pantry and freezer with their nearby counter space. These facilities surely will expedite the unloading of groceries from the car and their convenient storing. Wardrobe and broom closets, plus washroom complete the outstanding utility of this area. The location of the clutter room with all its fine cabinet and counter space means that the often numerous family projects

can be on-going. This room is ideally isolated from the family's daily living patterns. The media room may be thought of as the family's entertainment center. While this is the room for the large or small TV, the home movies, the stereo and VCR equipment, it will serve as the library or study. It would be ideal as the family's home office with its computer equipment. Your family will decide just how it will utilize this outstanding area.

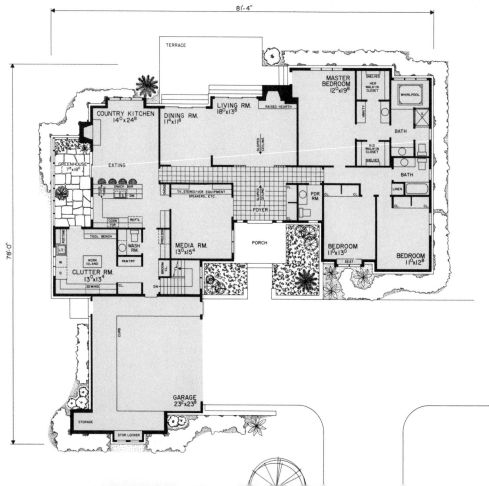

Design V22915 Square Footage: 2,758

L **D**

● The features of this appealing contemporary design go far beyond the clutter and media rooms. The country kitchen is spacious and caters to the family's informal living and dining activities. While it overlooks the rear yard it is just a step from the delightful greenhouse. Many happy hours will be spent here enjoying to the fullest the outdoors from within. The size of the greenhouse is 8'x18' and contains 149 sq. ft. not included in the square footage quoted above. The formal living and dining areas feature spacious open planning. Sloping ceiling in the living room, plus the sliding glass doors to the outdoor terrace enhance the cheerfulness of this area. The foyer is large and routes traffic efficiently to all areas. Guest coat closets and a powder room are handy. The sleeping zone is well-planned. Two children's bedrooms have fine wall space, good wardrobe facilities and a full bath.

The master bedroom is exceptional. It is large enough to accommodate a sitting area and has access to the terrace. Two walk-in closets, a vanity area with lavatory and a compartmented bath are noteworthy features. Observe the stall shower in addition to the dramatic whirlpool installation. The floor plan below is identical with that on the opposite page and shows one of many possible ways to arrange furniture.

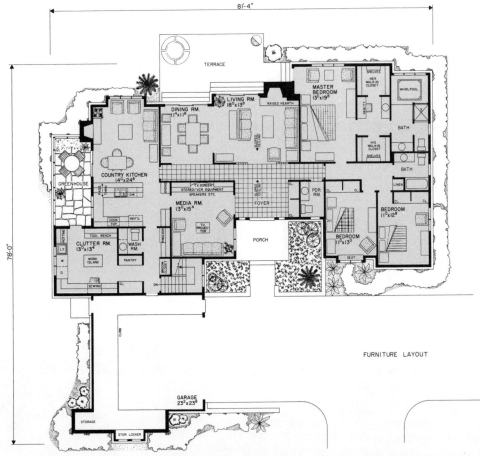

FURNITURE LAYOUT

Design V22534 Square Footage: 3,262

L

● The angular wings of this ranch home surely contribute to the unique character of the exterior. These wings effectively balance what is truly a dramatic and inviting front entrance. Massive masonry walls support the wide overhanging roof with its exposed wood beams. The patterned double front doors are surrounded by delightful expanses of glass. The raised planters and the masses of quarried stone (make it brick if you prefer) enhance the exterior appeal. Inside, a distinctive and practical floor plan stands ready to shape and serve the living patterns of the active family. The spacious entrance hall highlights sloped ceiling and an attractive open stairway to the lower level recreation area. An impressive fireplace and an abundance of glass are features of the big gathering room. Interestingly shaped dining room and study flank this main living area. The large kitchen offers many of the charming aspects of the family-kitchen of yesteryear. The bedroom wing has a sunken master suite.

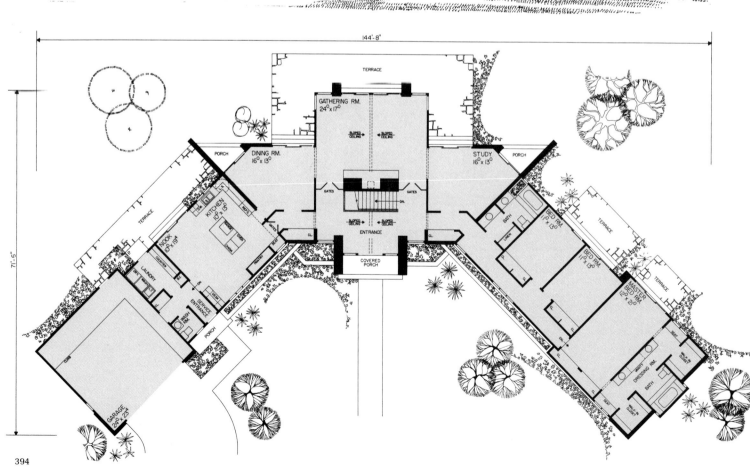

Design V21829

Square Footage: 1,800

L **D**

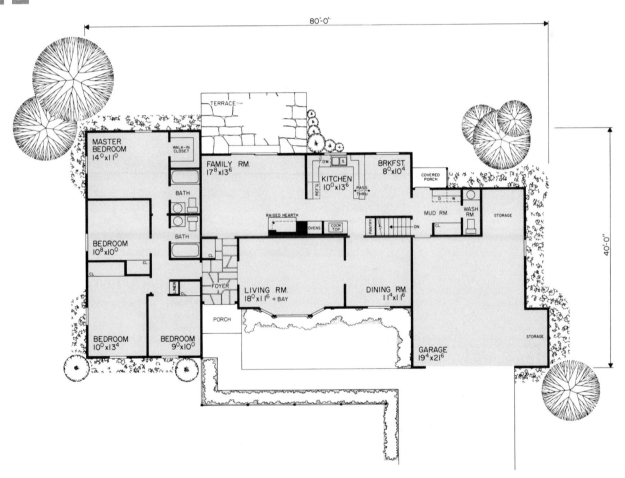

80'-0"

40'-0"

TERRACE

MASTER
BEDROOM
14⁰x11⁰

WALK-IN
CLOSET

FAMILY RM.
17⁸x13⁶

DW.   S

KITCHEN
10⁰x13⁶

REFG.

PASS
THRU

BRKFST.
8⁰x10⁴

COVERED
PORCH

BATH

D   W

MUD RM.

WASH
RM

STORAGE

BEDROOM
10⁸x10⁰

BATH

RAISED HEARTH

OVENS   COOK
TOP

PANTRY

DN

CL

CL

CL

CL

PORCH

FOYER

LIVING RM.
18⁰x11⁶ + BAY

DINING RM.
11⁴x11⁶

STORAGE

BEDROOM
10⁰x13⁴

BEDROOM
9⁰x10⁰

GARAGE
19⁴x21⁶

● All the charm of a traditional heritage is wrapped up in this U-shaped home with its narrow, horizontal siding, delightful window treatment and high-pitched roof. The massive center chimney, the bay window and the double front doors are plus features. In-side, the living potential is outstanding. The sleeping wing is self-contained and has four bedrooms and two baths. The large family and living rooms cater to the divergent age groups. Pay attention to the carefully thought-out room arrangement with living room and dining room to the fore, family room and kitchen to the rear. A service area with laundry and half bath is conveniently located. A rear terrace will surely be a favorite outdoor space.

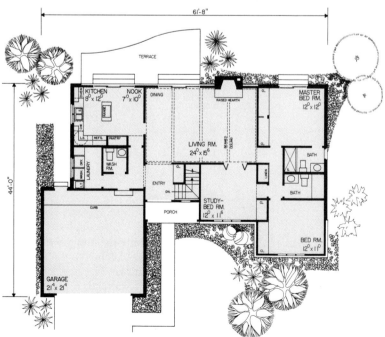

Design V22565
Square Footage: 1,540

L **D**

● This modest sized floor plan has much to offer in the way of livability. It may function as either a two or three bedroom home. The living room is huge and features a fine, raised hearth fireplace. The open stairway to the basement is handy and will lead to what may be developed as the recreation area. In addition to the two full baths, there is an extra wash room. Adjacent is the laundry room and the service entrance from the garage. The blueprints you order for this design will show details for each of the three delightful elevations above. Which is your favorite? The Tudor, the Colonial or the Contemporary?

Design V22505

Square Footage: 1,366

L **D**

● This design offers you a choice of
three distinctively different exteriors.
Which is your favorite? Blueprints
show details for all three optional
elevations. A study of the floor plan
reveals a fine measure of livability. In
less than 1,400 square feet there are
features galore. An excellent return on
your construction dollar. In addition to
the two eating areas and the open
planning of the gathering room, the
indoor-outdoor relationships are of
great interest. The basement may be
developed for recreational activities.
Be sure to note the storage potential,
particularly the linen closet, the pantry,
the china cabinet and the broom closet.

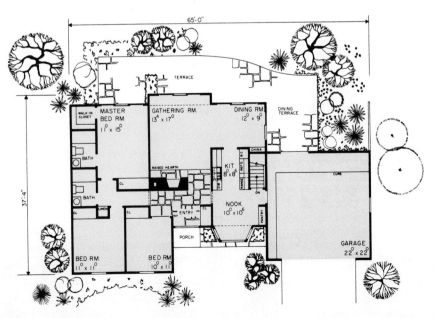

When You're Ready To Order . . .

Let Us Show You Our Home Blueprint Package.

Building a home? Planning a home? Our Blueprint Package contains nearly everything you need to get the job done right, whether you're working on your own or with help from an architect, designer, builder or subcontractors. Each Blueprint Package is the result of many hours of work by licensed architects or professional designers.

QUALITY

Hundreds of hours of painstaking effort have gone into the development of your blueprint set. Each home has been quality-checked by professionals to insure accuracy and buildability.

VALUE

Because we sell in volume, you can buy professional-quality blueprints at a fraction of their development cost. With our plans, your dream home design costs only a few hundred dollars, not the thousands of dollars that custom architects charge.

SERVICE

Once you've chosen your favorite home plan, you'll receive fast efficient service whether you choose to mail your order to us or call us toll free at 1-800-848-2550.

SATISFACTION

Our years of service to satisfied home plan buyers provide us the experience and knowledge that guarantee your satisfaction with our product and performance.

ORDER TOLL FREE 1-800-848-2550

After you've studied our Blueprint Package and Important Extras on the following pages, simply mail the accompanying order form on page 413 or call toll free on our Blueprint Hotline: 1-800-848-2550. We're ready and eager to serve you.

Each set of blueprints is an interrelated collection of floor plans, interior and exterior elevations, dimensions, cross-sections, diagrams and notations showing precisely how your house is to be constructed.

Here's what you get:

Frontal Sheet
This artist's sketch of the exterior of the house, done in realistic perspective, gives you an idea of how the house will look when built and landscaped. Large ink-line floor plans show all levels of the house and provide a quick overview of your new home's livability, as well as a handy reference for studying furniture placement.

Foundation Plan
Drawn to 1/4-inch scale, this sheet shows the complete foundation layout including support

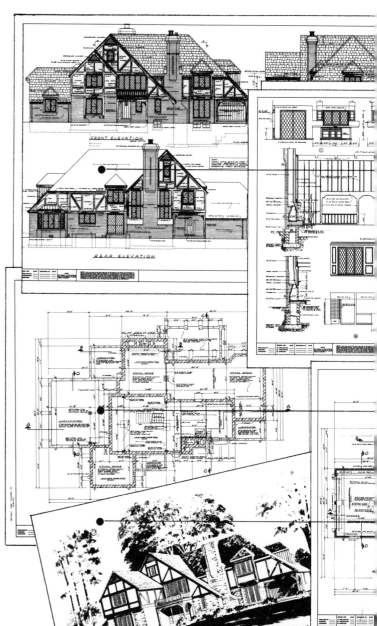

walls, excavated and unexcavated areas, if any, and foundation notes. If slab construction rather than basement, the plan shows footings and details for a monolithic slab. This page, or another in the set, also includes a sample plot plan for locating your house on a building site.

Detailed Floor Plans
Complete in 1/4-inch scale, these plans show the layout of each floor of the house. All rooms and interior spaces are carefully dimensioned and keys are provided for cross-section details given later in the plans. The positions of all electrical outlets and switches are clearly shown.

House Cross-Sections
Large-scale views, normally drawn at 3/8-inch equals 1 foot, show sections or cut-aways of the foundation, interior walls, exterior walls, floors, stairways and roof details. Additional cross-sections are given to show important changes in floor, ceiling or roof heights or the relationship of one level to another. Extremely valuable for construction, these sections show exactly how the various parts of the house fit together.

Interior Elevations
These large-scale drawings show the design and placement of kitchen and bathroom cabinets, laundry areas, fireplaces, bookcases and other built-ins. Little "extras," such as mantelpiece and wainscoting drawings, plus moulding sections, provide details that give your home that custom touch.

Exterior Elevations
Drawings in 1/4-inch scale show the front, rear and sides of your house and give necessary notes on exterior materials and finishes. Particular attention is given to cornice detail, brick and stone accents or other finish items that make your home distinctive.

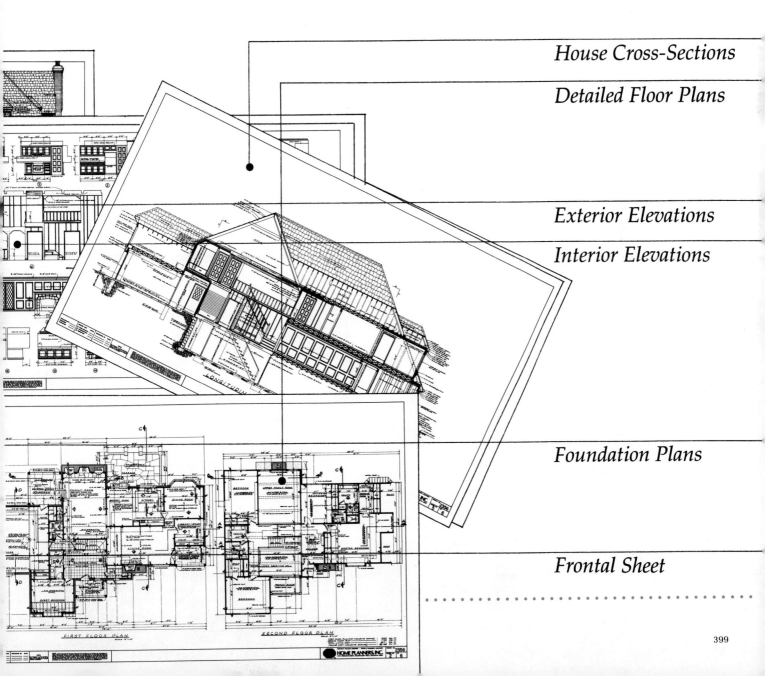

House Cross-Sections

Detailed Floor Plans

Exterior Elevations

Interior Elevations

Foundation Plans

Frontal Sheet

Important Extras To Do The Job Right!

Introducing seven important planning and construction aids developed by our professionals to help you succeed in your home-building project.

To Order, Call Toll Free 1-800-848-2250

To add these important extras to your Blueprint Package, simply indicate your choices on the order form on page 413 or call us Toll Free 1-800-848-2550 and we'll tell you more about these exciting products.

MATERIALS LIST

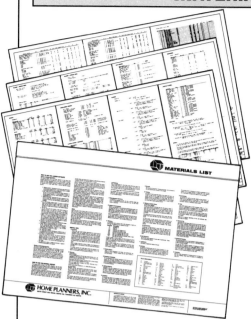

For many of the designs in our portfolio, we offer a customized materials take-off that is invaluable in planning and estimating the cost of your new home. This comprehensive list outlines the quantity, type and size of material needed to build your house (with the exception of mechanical system items). Included are:

- framing lumber
- roofing and sheet metal
- windows and doors
- exterior sheathing material and trim
- masonry, veneer and fireplace materials
- tile and flooring materials
- kitchen and bath cabinetry
- interior drywall and trim
- rough and finish hardware
- many more items

(Note: Because of differing local codes, building methods, and availability of materials, our Materials Lists do not include mechanical materials. To obtain necessary take-offs and recommendations, consult heating, plumbing and electrical contractors. Materials Lists are not sold separately from the Blueprint Package.)

This handy list helps you or your builder cost out materials and serves as a ready reference sheet when you're compiling bids. It also provides a cross-check against the materials specified by your builder and helps coordinate the substitution of items you may need to meet local codes.

SPECIFICATION OUTLINE

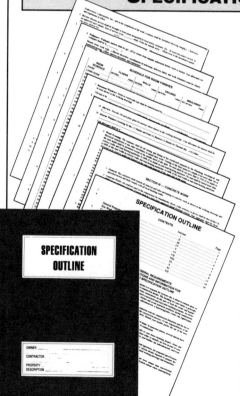

This valuable 16-page document is critical to building your house correctly. Designed to be filled in by you or your builder, this booklet lists 166 stages or items crucial to the building process.

For the layman, it provides a comprehensive review of the construction process and helps in making the specific choices of materials, models and processes. For the builder, it serves as a guide to preparing a building quotation and forms the basis for the construction program.

Designed primarily as a reference for the homeowner, this Specification Outline can become a legally binding document. Once it is filled out and agreed upon by owner and builder, it becomes a complete Project Specification.

When combined with the blueprints, a signed contract and schedule, the Specification Outline becomes a legal document and record for the building of your home. Many home builders find it useful to order two of these outlines—one as a worksheet in formulating the specifications and another to be carefully completed as a legal document.

DETAIL SHEETS

If you want to know more about techniques—and deal more confidently with subcontractors—we offer these remarkably useful detail sheets. Each is an excellent tool that will enhance your understanding of these technical subjects.

Plan-A-Home®

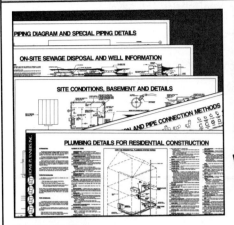

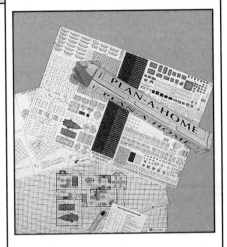

PLUMBING

The Blueprint Package includes locations for all the plumbing fixtures in your new house, including sinks, lavatories, tubs, showers, toilets, laundry trays and water heaters. However, if you want to know more about the complete plumbing system, these 24x36-inch detail sheets will prove very useful. Prepared to meet requirements of the National Plumbing Code, these six fact-filled sheets give general information on pipe schedules, fittings, sump-pump details, water-softener hookups, septic system details and much more. Color-coded sheets include a glossary of terms.

ELECTRICAL

The locations for every electrical switch, plug and outlet are shown in your Blueprint Package. However, these Electrical Details go further to take the mystery out of household electrical systems. Prepared to meet requirements of the National Electrical Code, these comprehensive 24x36-inch drawings come packed with helpful information, including wire sizing, switch-installation schematics, cable-routing details, appliance wattage, door-bell hookups, typical service panel circuitry and much more. Six sheets are bound together and color-coded for easy reference. A glossary of terms is also included.

Plan-A-Home® is an easy-to-use tool that helps you design a new home, arrange furniture in a new or existing home, or plan a remodeling project. Each package contains:

- More than *700 peel-off planning symbols* on a self-stick vinyl sheet, including walls, windows, doors, all types of furniture, kitchen components, bath fixtures and many more. All are made of durable, peel-and-stick vinyl you can use over and over.

- A reusable, transparent, *1/4-inch scale planning grid* made of tough mylar that matches the scale of actual working drawings (1/4 -inch equals 1 foot). This grid provides the basis for house layouts of up to 140x92 feet.

- *Tracing paper* and a protective sheet for copying or transferring your completed plan.

- A *felt-tip pen*, with water-soluble ink that wipes away quickly.

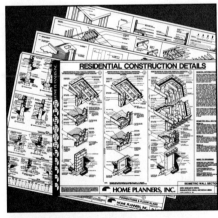

CONSTRUCTION

The Blueprint Package contains everything an experienced builder needs to construct a particular house. However, it doesn't show all the ways that houses can be built, nor does it explain alternate construction methods. To help you understand how your house will be built—and offer additional techniques—this set of drawings depicts the materials and methods used to build foundations, fireplaces, walls, floors and roofs. Where appropriate, the drawings show acceptable alternatives. These six sheets will answer questions for the advanced do-it-yourselfer or home planner.

MECHANICAL

This package contains fundamental principles and useful data that will help you make informed decisions and communicate with subcontractors about heating and cooling systems. The 24 x 36-inch drawings contain instructions and samples that allow you to make simple load calculations and preliminary sizing and costing analysis. Covered are today's most commonly used systems from heat pumps to solar fuel systems. The package is packed full of illustrations and diagrams to help you visualize components and how they relate to one another.

With Plan-A-Home®, you can make basic planning decisions for a new house or make modifications to an existing house. Use with your Blueprint Package to test modifications to rooms or to plan furniture arrangements before you build. Plan-A-Home® lets you lay out areas as large as a 7,500 square foot, six-bedroom, seven-bath house.

◨ *The Deck Blueprint Package*

Many of the homes in this book can be enhanced with a professionally designed Deck Plan. Those home plans highlighted with a ◨ have a matching or corresponding deck plan available which includes a Deck Plan Frontal Sheet, Deck Framing and Floor Plans, Deck Elevations and a Deck Materials List. A Standard Deck Details Package, also available, provides all the how-to information necessary for building *any* deck. Our Complete Deck Building Package contains 1 set of Custom Deck Plans of your choice, plus 1 set of Standard Deck Building Details all for one low price. Our plans and details are carefully prepared in an easy-to-understand format that will guide you through every stage of your deck-building project. See these pages for 25 different Deck layouts to match your favorite house.

SPLIT–LEVEL SUN DECK
Deck Plan D100

BI–LEVEL DECK WITH COVERED DINING
Deck Plan D101

FRESH–AIR CORNER DECK
Deck Plan D102

BACK–YARD EXTENDER DECK
Deck Plan D103

WRAP–AROUND FAMILY DECK
Deck Plan D104

DRAMATIC DECK WITH BARBECUE
Deck Plan D105

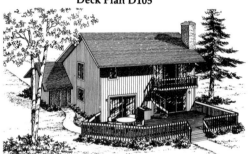

SPLIT–PLAN COUNTRY DECK
Deck Plan D106

DECK FOR DINING AND VIEWS
Deck Plan D107

BOLD, ANGLED CORNER DECK
Deck Plan D108

SPECTACULAR "RESORT–STYLE" DECK
Deck Plan D109

TREND–SETTER DECK
Deck Plan D110

TURN–OF–THE–CENTURY DECK
Deck Plan D111

WEEKEND ENTERTAINER DECK
Deck Plan D112

STRIKING "DELTA" DECK
Deck Plan D113

CENTER–VIEW DECK
Deck Plan D114

KITCHEN–EXTENDER DECK
Deck Plan D115

BI–LEVEL RETREAT DECK
Deck Plan D116

SPLIT–LEVEL ACTIVITY DECK
Deck Plan D117

OUTDOOR LIFESTYLE DECK
Deck Plan D118

TRI–LEVEL DECK WITH GRILL
Deck Plan D119

CONTEMPORARY LEISURE DECK
Deck Plan D120

ANGULAR WINGED DECK
Deck Plan D121

DECK FOR A SPLIT–LEVEL HOME
Deck Plan D122

GRACIOUS GARDEN DECK
Deck Plan D123

TERRACED DECK FOR ENTERTAINING
Deck Plan D124

For Deck Plan prices and ordering information, see page 408.

 Or call **Toll Free,** **1-800-848-2550.**

⌶ *The Landscape Blueprint Package*

For the homes marked with an ⌶ in this book, we have created a front-yard landscape plan that matches or is complementary in design to the house plan. These comprehensive blueprint packages include a Frontal Sheet, Plan View, Regionalized Plant & Materials List, a sheet on Planting and Maintaining Your Landscape, Zone Maps and Plant Size and Description Guide. These plans will help you achieve professional results, adding value and enjoyment to your property for years to come. Each set of blueprints is a full 18" x 24" in size with clear, complete instructions and easy-to-read type. See the following pages for 40-different front-yard Landscape Plans to match your favorite house.

Regional Order Map

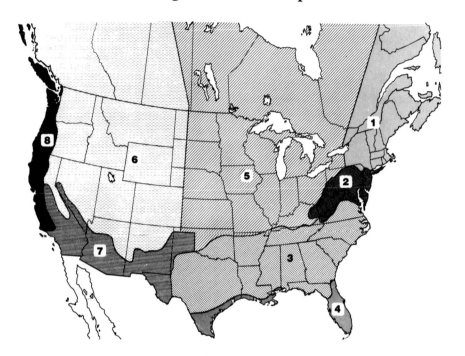

Most of the Landscape Plans shown on these pages are available with a Plant & Materials List adapted by horticultural experts to 8 different regions of the country. Please specify Geographic Region when ordering your plan. See page 408-411 for prices, ordering information and regional availability.

Region	1	Northeast
Region	2	Mid-Atlantic
Region	3	Deep South
Region	4	Florida & Gulf Coast
Region	5	Midwest
Region	6	Rocky Mountains
Region	7	Southern California & Desert Southwest
Region	8	Northern California & Pacific Northwest

CAPE COD TRADITIONAL
Landscape Plan L200

WILLIAMSBURG CAPE
Landscape Plan L201

CAPE COD COTTAGE
Landscape Plan L202

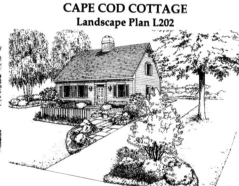

GAMBREL–ROOF COLONIAL
Landscape Plan L203

CENTER–HALL COLONIAL
Landscape Plan L204

CLASSIC NEW ENGLAND COLONIAL
Landscape Plan L205

SOUTHERN COLONIAL
Landscape Plan L206

COUNTRY–STYLE FARMHOUSE
Landscape Plan L207

PENNSYLVANIA STONE FARMHOUSE
Landscape Plan L208

RAISED–PORCH FARMHOUSE
Landscape Plan L209

NEW ENGLAND BARN–STYLE HOUSE
Landscape Plan L210

NEW ENGLAND COUNTRY HOUSE
Landscape Plan L211

TRADITIONAL COUNTRY ESTATE
Landscape Plan L212

FRENCH PROVINCIAL ESTATE
Landscape Plan L213

GEORGIAN MANOR
Landscape Plan L214

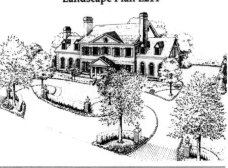

GRAND–PORTICO GEORGIAN
Landscape Plan L215

BRICK FEDERAL
Landscape Plan L216

COUNTRY FRENCH RAMBLER
Landscape Plan L217

FRENCH MANOR HOUSE
Landscape Plan L218

ELIZABETHAN TUDOR
Landscape Plan L219

TUDOR ONE–STORY
Landscape Plan L220

ENGLISH–STYLE COTTAGE
Landscape Plan L221

MEDIEVAL GARRISON
Landscape Plan L222

QUEEN ANNE VICTORIAN
Landscape Plan L223

GOTHIC VICTORIAN
Landscape Plan L224

BASIC RANCH
Landscape Plan L225

L–SHAPED RANCH
Landscape Plan L226

SPRAWLING RANCH
Landscape Plan L227

TRADITIONAL SPLIT–LEVEL
Landscape Plan L228

SHED–ROOF CONTEMPORARY
Landscape Plan L229

WOOD–SIDED CONTEMPORARY
Landscape Plan L230

HILLSIDE CONTEMPORARY
Landscape Plan L231

FLORIDA RAMBLER
Landscape Plan L232

CALIFORNIA STUCCO
Landscape Plan L233

LOW–GABLE CONTEMPORARY
Landscape Plan L234

NORTHERN BRICK CHATEAU
Landscape Plan L235

MISSION–TILE RANCH
Landscape Plan L236

ADOBE–BLOCK HACIENDA
Landscape Plan L237

COURTYARD PATIO HOME
Landscape Plan L238

CENTER–COURT CONTEMPORARY
Landscape Plan L239

For Landscape Plan prices and ordering information, see page 408.

 Or call **Toll Free,** **1-800-848-2550**.

Price Schedule & Plans Index

House Blueprint Price Schedule
(Prices guaranteed through December 31, 1994)

	1-set Study Package	4-set Building Package	8-set Building Package	1-set Reproducible Sepias
Schedule A	$210	$270	$330	$420
Schedule B	$240	$300	$360	$480
Schedule C	$270	$330	$390	$540
Schedule D	$300	$360	$420	$600
Schedule E	$390	$450	$510	$660

Additional Identical Blueprints in same order...............$50 per set
Reverse Blueprints (mirror image).........................$50 per set
Specification Outlines...$7 each
Materials Lists:
      Schedule A-D $40
      Schedule E $50

Deck Plans Price Schedule

CUSTOM DECK PLANS

Price Group	Q	R	S
1 Set Custom Plans	$25	$30	$35

Additional identical sets:.......................................$10 each
Reverse sets (mirror image): ....$10 each

STANDARD DECK DETAILS
1 Set Generic Construction Details .... $14.95 each

COMPLETE DECK BUILDING PACKAGE

Price Group	Q	R	S
1 Set Custom Plans 1 Set Standard Deck Details	$35	$40	$45

Landscape Plans Price Schedule

Price Group	X	Y	Z
1 set	$35	$45	$55
3 sets	$50	$60	$70
6 sets	$65	$75	$85

Additional Identical Sets ....$10 each
Reverse Sets (mirror image)............................$10 each

These pages contain all the information you need to price your blueprints. In general the larger and more complicated the house, the more it costs to design and thus the higher the price we must charge for the blueprints. Remember, however, that these prices are far less than you would normally pay for the services of a licensed architect or professional designer.

Custom home designs and related architectural services often cost thousands of dollars, ranging from 5% to 15% of the cost of construction. By ordering our blueprints you are potentially saving enough money to afford a larger house, or to add those "extra" amenities such as a patio, deck, swimming pool or even an upgraded kitchen or luxurious master suite.

Index

To use the Index below, refer to the design number listed in numerical order (a helpful page reference is also given). Note the price index letter and refer to the House Blueprint Price Schedule above for the cost of one, four or eight sets of blueprints or the cost of a reproducible sepia. Additional prices are shown for identical and reverse blueprint sets, as well as a very useful Materials List. Also note in the Index below those plans that have matching or complementary Deck

Plans or Landscape Plans. Refer to the schedules above for prices of these plans. Some of our plans can be customized through our Home Customizer® Service. These plans are indicated below with this symbol: ⌂ . See page 413 for more information.

To Order: Fill in and send the order form on page 413—or call toll free 1-800-848-2550.

DESIGN	PRICE	PAGE	CUSTOMIZABLE	DECK	DECK PRICE	LANDSCAPE	LANDSCAPE PRICE	REGIONS
V21082	B	137						
V21104	A	88						
V21141	B	54						
V21142	B	41						
V21179	B	22						
V21196	A	92						
V21202	B	40						
V21208	A	195						
V21228	D	218		D124	S	L217	Y	1-8
V21239	C	122						
V21241	A	93		D117	S	L225	X	1-3,5,6,8
V21260	B	220						
V21266	B	40						
V21269	B	136						
V21278	B	50						
V21285	B	135		D117	S	L205	Y	1-3,5,6,8
V21304	B	127				L225	X	1-3,5,6,8
V21318	A	132						
V21339	B	127						
V21354	A	128		D105	R	L200	X	1-3,5,6,8
V21361	A	128		D117	S	L225	X	1-3,5,6,8

DESIGN	PRICE	PAGE	CUSTOMIZABLE	DECK	DECK PRICE	LANDSCAPE	LANDSCAPE PRICE	REGIONS
V21365	A	103		D113	R			
V21368	A	129						
V21372	A	82						
V21394	A	83		D105	R	L202	X	1-3,5,6,8
V21700	C	22						
V21701	B	101		D117	S			
V21711	D	209						
V21715	B	322		D100	Q	L204	Y	1-3,5,6,8
V21718	B	76		D114	R	L210	Y	1-3,5,6,8
V21719	A	29		D105	R	L203	Y	1-3,5,6,8
V21723	A	129						
V21728	C	122						
V21736	B	99						
V21745	B	67						
V21763	C	32						
V21766	B	100		D100	Q			
V21767	C	156						
V21773	B	195						
V21777	B	58						
V21783	C	344						
V21787	C	138		D117	S			

DESIGN	PRICE	PAGE	CUSTOMIZABLE	DECK	DECK PRICE	LANDSCAPE	LANDSCAPE PRICE	REGIONS
V21791	B	80		D114	R	L205	Y	1-3,5,6,8
V21793	C	101		D100	Q			
V21794	C	303						
V21814	B	33						
V21816	C	212						
V21827	B	60						
V21829	B	395		D113	R	L226	X	1-8
V21849	B	37						
V21852	C	158						
V21856	A	36		D117	S			
V21858	C	147		D101	R			
V21868	B	134						
V21870	B	80						
V21877	B	355		D114	R			
V21887	B	68						
V21900	C	24						
V21901	A	88						
V21902	B	77						
V21903	B	89						
V21905	C	130						
V21907	B	318						
V21914	B	66						
V21933	B	136		D117	S	L205	Y	1-3,5,6,8
V21955	B	122						
V21956	A	132	🏠	D117	S			
V21957	A	323		D100	Q	L228	Y	1-8
V21966	B	319						
V21967	B	97						
V21970	C	105		D100	Q			
V21972	B	321						
V21986	B	58				L203	Y	1-3,5,6,8
V21987	B	77		D101	R	L203	Y	1-3,5,6,8
V21991	B	277						
V21993	D	221				L213	Z	1-8
V21996	B	126		D114	R	L205	Y	1-3,5,6,8
V22102	C	35						
V22103	B	46		D124	S			
V22107	A	194						
V22124	B	100		D114	R	L203	Y	1-3,5,6,8
V22127	B	258						
V22128	B	250		D100	Q	L205	Y	1-3,5,6,8
V22131	B	61		D117	S	L203	Y	1-3,5,6,8
V22132	C	151				L201	Y	1-3,5,6,8
V22133	D	208		D106	S	L214	Z	1-3,5,6,8
V22138	B	51						
V22139	B	157						
V22140	C	201				L206	Z	1-6,8
V22141	C	251						
V22145	A	78				L209	Y	1-6,8
V22146	A	79		D114	R	L203	Y	1-3,5,6,8
V22148	C	267						
V22162	A	82		D103	R	L202	X	1-3,5,6,8
V22172	C	133						
V22175	B	277						
V22176	B	156		D112	R	L206	Z	1-6,8
V22184	C	186						
V22185	C	187						
V22188	C	49						
V22190	B	259						
V22192	D	154		D117	S	L218	Z	1-6,8
V22211	B	36		D117	S	L201	Y	1-3,5,6,8
V22220	C	391		D114	R	L217	Y	1-8
V22221	C	158						
V22222	B	216						
V22223	C	131		D112	R	L205	Y	1-3,5,6,8
V22224	B	67				L210	Y	1-3,5,6,8
V22225	D	139						
V22230	D	177						
V22239	C	255						
V22242	B	254		D112	R			
V22250	C	159						
V22253	C	22						
V22274	C	269						
V22276	B	269						
V22278	C	279						
V22281	C	216		D106	S			
V22283	C	175		D114	R	L206	Z	1-6,8
V22286	B	278						
V22295	C	52						
V22308	C	46						
V22309	C	355						
V22320	C	69						
V22322	B	52		D100	Q			
V22324	B	268						
V22325	C	321						
V22326	C	217						
V22336	C	211						
V22342	D	219						
V22346	B	53						
V22356	D	245		D119	S	L219	Z	1-3,5,6,8
V22364	B	60						
V22373	B	280						
V22377	A	354						
V22379	B	331		D120	R	L212	Z	1-8
V22390	C	353		D101	R			
V22391	C	276						
V22395	B	74						
V22396	B	80		D100	Q			
V22399	B	19						
V22488	A	325	🏠	D102	Q			
V22490	A	326	🏠					
V22491	A	261	🏠					
V22500	B	97		D100	Q	L204	Y	1-3,5,6,8
V22503	C	220						
V22505	A	397	🏠	D113	R	L226	X	1-8
V22507	C	220						
V22508	C	250						
V22510	A	83		D105	R	L200	X	1-3,5,6,8
V22511	B	340		D108	R	L229	Y	1-8
V22513	C	310						
V22520	B	169		D105	R	L201	Y	1-3,5,6,8
V22521	B	110						
V22524	A	212		D105	R			
V22530	B	353						
V22531	B	58						
V22534	D	394				L227	Z	1-8
V22538	B	55		D113	R	L201	Y	1-3,5,6,8
V22539	B	54						
V22540	B	319		D113	R	L205	Y	1-3,5,6,8
V22541	C	275						
V22543	D	215		D107	S	L218	Z	1-6,8
V22553	C	197						
V22556	C	164		D103	R			
V22559	B	102		D112	R			
V22562	D	350		D122	S			
V22563	B	74	🏠	D114	R	L201	Y	1-3,5,6,8
V22565	B	396		D101	R	L225	X	1-3,5,6,8
V22568	C	262						
V22569	A	102		D112	R	L200	X	1-3,5,6,8
V22571	A	86		D114	R	L202	X	1-3,5,6,8
V22582	A	362						
V22585	B	141		D113	R	L205	Y	1-3,5,6,8
V22586	A	259						
V22596	B	99		D114	R	L201	Y	1-3,5,6,8
V22598	A	45						
V22599	C	320		D100	Q			
V22600	C	165						
V22602	B	352						
V22610	C	48		D114	R	L204	Y	1-3,5,6,8
V22614	C	304		D114	R			
V22615	D	107		D106	S	L211	Y	1-8
V22618	B	263						
V22622	A	45	🏠	D103	R	L200	X	1-3,5,6,8
V22623	B	33		D100	Q	L205	Y	1-3,5,6,8
V22625	C	32						
V22627	A	213						
V22629	B	272						
V22630	B	272						
V22631	B	104		D112	R	L201	Y	1-3,5,6,8
V22633	C	146						

DESIGN	PRICE	PAGE	CUSTOMIZABLE	DECK	DECK PRICE	LANDSCAPE	LANDSCAPE PRICE	REGIONS
V22636	A	109						
V22637	B	263						
V22638	C	150						
V22639	C	162		D114	R	L215	Z	1-6,8
V22640	B	38		D114	R			
V22641	C	34						
V22644	B	94						
V22645	C	232				L224	Y	1-3,5,6,8
V22646	B	232		D114	R	L224	Y	1-3,5,6,8
V22647	D	233				L224	Y	1-3,5,6,8
V22649	C	39						
V22650	B	121		D117	S	L201	Y	1-3,5,6,8
V22653	C	30						
V22654	A	25						
V22655	A	84				L200	X	1-3,5,6,8
V22656	B	85		D105	R	L203	Y	1-3,5,6,8
V22657	B	98				L200	X	1-3,5,6,8
V22658	A	71						
V22659	B	27		D113	R	L205	Y	1-3,5,6,8
V22660	D	193						
V22661	A	95	🏠	D113	R	L202	X	1-3,5,6,8
V22662	C	153				L216	Y	1-3,5,6,8
V22663	B	214						
V22664	B	192		D113	R			
V22665	D	183						
V22666	B	13						
V22667	B	189				L216	Y	1-3,5,6,8
V22668	B	188				L214	Z	1-3,5,6,8
V22673	C	198						
V22674	C	278						
V22676	C	302						
V22680	C	70		D114	R			
V22681	B	31						
V22682	A	72	🏠	D115	Q	L200	X	1-3,5,6,8
V22683	D	148		D101	R	L214	Z	1-3,5,6,8
V22684	C	207		D114	R	L204	Y	1-3,5,6,8
V22686	C	204		D112	R	L209	Y	1-6,8
V22687	C	18		D117	S	L204	Y	1-3,5,6,8
V22688	B	206						
V22690	C	161						
V22691	B	20						
V22693	D	202						
V22694	C	112				L209	Y	1-6,8
V22695	C	168						
V22696	D	176						
V22697	C	205						
V22699	C	106				L211	Y	1-8
V22700	C	199						
V22701	C	333						
V22708	C	357		D112	R			
V22711	B	332	🏠	D105	R	L229	Y	1-8
V22718	C	310		D105	R			
V22722	C	299						
V22724	C	302						
V22729	B	344				L234	Y	1-8
V22731	B	51		D114	R	L205	Y	1-3,5,6,8
V22732	B	254						
V22733	B	44		D100	Q	L205	Y	1-3,5,6,8
V22748	A	332						
V22749	C	352						
V22752	B	140						
V22757	C	311						
V22762	C	196						
V22771	C	349						
V22772	C	348						
V22774	B	115	🏠	D100	Q	L207	Z	1-6,8
V22775	B	114				L207	Z	1-6,8
V22776	B	117	🏠	D113	R	L207	Z	1-6,8
V22780	C	348						
V22781	C	356		D121	S	L230	Z	1-8
V22782	C	334		D101	R			
V22794	C	246						
V22798	A	224		D100	Q	L200	X	1-3,5,6,8
V22799	A	28						
V22800	B	282		D113	R	L220	Y	1-3,5,6,8
V22801	B	381		D105	R	L232	Y	4,7
V22822	A	358				L229	Y	1-8
V22823	B	341		D112	R	L229	Y	1-8
V22826	B	301	🏠	D116	R			
V22828	B	364						
V22829	D	231		D113	R	L219	Z	1-3,5,6,8
V22831	C	337		D113	R			
V22834	D	336						
V22839	C	200						
V22852	A	86		D105	R	L202	X	1-3,5,6,8
V22853	A	325						
V22854	B	282	🏠	D112	R	L220	Y	1-3,5,6,8
V22855	B	249	🏠	D103	R	L219	Z	1-3,5,6,8
V22865	C	119		D114	R			
V22870	A	29						
V22883	C	297						
V22884	B	365						
V22887	A	343						
V22889	D	171		D107	S	L215	Z	1-6,8
V22890	C	116		D114	R			
V22891	B	64						
V22892	B	342						
V22897	C	65						
V22898	C	185		D118	R			
V22899	C	184						
V22904	C	363						
V22905	B	360		D121	S	L229	Y	1-8
V22906	C	335		D114	R			
V22907	B	124						
V22908	B	125	🏠	D117	S	L205	Y	1-3,5,6,8
V22909	B	300		D103	R			
V22910	B	339						
V22915	C	392		D114	R	L212	Z	1-8
V22920	D	346		D104	S	L212	Z	1-8
V22921	D	90		D104	S	L212	Z	1-8
V22923	B	312						
V22924	B	190	🏠					
V22925	B	366						
V22926	D	372						
V22927	B	299	🏠	D100	Q			
V22928	C	361						
V22939	B	266		D108	R			
V22940	E	288		D114	R			
V22944	C	338						
V22945	B	120	🏠					
V22946	C	118	🏠	D114	R	L207	Z	1-6,8
V22951	E	286						
V22952	E	290				L235	Z	1-3,5,6,8
V22953	E	285		D111	S	L223	Z	1-3,5,6,8
V22954	E	284				L223	Z	1-3,5,6,8
V22955	E	287						
V22956	E	291						
V22957	D	247		D107	S	L218	Z	1-6,8
V22959	B	264						
V22960	B	248						
V22963	D	111						
V22964	B	265						
V22965	D	253						
V22967	B	252						
V22968	E	289						
V22969	C	227		D110	R	L223	Z	1-3,5,6,8
V22970	D	235				L223	Z	1-3,5,6,8
V22971	C	225				L223	Z	1-3,5,6,8
V22972	B	226				L223	Z	1-3,5,6,8
V22973	B	226	🏠			L223	Z	1-3,5,6,8
V22974	A	239				L223	Z	1-3,5,6,8
V22975	D	152						
V22977	D	203				L214	Z	1-3,5,6,8
V22978	C	26						
V22979	C	170						
V22980	C	160						
V22981	D	113						
V22982	C	155						
V22983	A	56						
V22984	E	174						

DESIGN	PRICE	PAGE	CUSTOMIZABLE	DECK	DECK PRICE	LANDSCAPE	LANDSCAPE PRICE	REGIONS
V22987	D	172						
V22988	B	62		D120	R	L201	Y	1-3,5,6,8
V22989	D	17						
V22990	D	15						
V22991	D	210		D111	S	L215	Z	1-6,8
V22992	E	43		D103	R	L203	Y	1-3,5,6,8
V22993	B	173						
V22994	E	16						
V22995	E	63		D106	S	L217	Y	1-8
V22996	E	196						
V22998	D	14						
V22999	E	42						
V23126	A	75		D114	R	L203	Y	1-3,5,6,8
V23189	A	86		D113	R			
V23300	E	292						
V23301	E	294						
V23302	A	260	🏠					
V23303	D	181						
V23304	E	295						
V23305	E	293						
V23307	C	241		D111	S	L207	Z	1-6,8
V23308	E	228						
V23309	B	244						
V23310	C	5		D111	S	L227	Z	1-8
V23313	B	328						
V23316	A	329						
V23318	B	324	🏠			L202	X	1-3,5,6,8
V23320	D	178						
V23321	C	327	🏠	D116	R	L209	Y	1-6,8
V23322	C	373	🏠	D118	R	L234	Y	1-8
V23323	C	386	🏠	D120	R	L223	Z	1-3,5,6,8
V23325	C	3	🏠	D100	Q	L238	Y	3,4,7,8
V23330	A	308						
V23331	A	281						
V23333	C	191						
V23334	C	309						
V23335	C	256						
V23337	D	180						
V23338	B	298						
V23339	B	179						
V23341	B	306						
V23342	B	257						
V23343	C	307						
V23347	D	367						
V23349	E	163		D107	S	L216	Y	1-3,5,6,8
V23351	C	108		D115	Q	L209	Y	1-6,8
V23352	B	345		D108	R	L229	Y	1-8
V23353	C	330		D113	R	L206	Z	1-6,8
V23354	E	273		D104	S	L212	Z	1-8
V23356	C	315		D103	R	L217	Y	1-8
V23363	C	305						
V23364	D	296						
V23365	C	167						
V23367	D	166						
V23369	E	270						
V23370	D	315		D119	S	L235	Z	1-3,5,6,8

DESIGN	PRICE	PAGE	CUSTOMIZABLE	DECK	DECK PRICE	LANDSCAPE	LANDSCAPE PRICE	REGIONS
V23371	E	274		D115	Q	L214	Z	1-3,5,6,8
V23372	C	92		D102	Q	L200	X	1-3,5,6,8
V23379	B	21						
V23380	E	223						
V23381	E	316						
V23382	C	238		D110	R	L202	X	1-3,5,6,8
V23383	C	236		D111	S	L205	Y	1-3,5,6,8
V23384	C	236		D115	Q	L207	Z	1-6,8
V23385	C	240		D100	Q	L207	Z	1-6,8
V23386	C	229		D111	S	L216	Y	1-3,5,6,8
V23387	E	243		D110	R	L224	Y	1-3,5,6,8
V23388	D	230		D111	S	L207	Z	1-6,8
V23389	C	234		D115	Q	L205	Y	1-3,5,6,8
V23390	C	240		D106	S	L207	Z	1-6,8
V23391	C	237		D116	R	L207	Z	1-6,8
V23392	D	242		D110	R	L223	Z	1-3,5,6,8
V23393	C	234		D115	Q	L207	Z	1-6,8
V23394	D	230		D111	S	L207	Z	1-6,8
V23395	E	283		D111	S	L223	Z	1-3,5,6,8
V23396	C	144		D111	S	L207	Z	1-6,8
V23397	D	142		D110	R	L209	Y	1-6,8
V23398	C	145		D111	S	L224	Y	1-3,5,6,8
V23399	C	143		D110	R	L224	Y	1-3,5,6,8
V23403	C	371		D115	Q	L237	Y	7
V23404	D	368		D106	S	L230	Z	1-8
V23409	C	370						
V23414	C	381	🏠					
V23417	A	376	🏠					
V23418	A	376	🏠					
V23420	B	377	🏠					
V23424	B	383	🏠					
V23425	C	380	🏠					
V23426	C	383	🏠					
V23427	C	378	🏠					
V23428	C	379	🏠					
V23429	C	382	🏠					
V23432	C	389	🏠			L233	Y	3,4,7
V23435	D	388	🏠	D104	S	L227	Z	1-8
V23437	C	390	🏠					
V23438	C	369				L209	Y	1-6,8
V23439	C	359	🏠					
V23441	C	375	🏠					
V23447	D	384	🏠	D120	R	L237	Y	7
V23448	E	385	🏠			L233	Y	3,4,7
V23449	C	374	🏠					
V23450	C	387	🏠	D106	S	L229	Y	1-8
V23550	D	313						
V23551	D	317						
V23552	C	47						
V23553	D	96						
V23554	E	271						
V23555	D	314						
V23556	D	351						
V23557	D	347						
V23558	C	5		D105	R	L203	Y	1-3,5,6,8

Before You Order . . .

Before completing the coupon at right or calling us on our Toll-Free Blueprint Hotline, you may be interested to learn more about our service and products. Here's some information you will find helpful.

Quick Turnaround
We process and ship every blueprint order from our office within 48 hours. On most orders, we do even better. Normally, if we receive your order by 5 p.m. Eastern Time, we'll process it the same day and ship it the following day. Because of this quick turnaround, we won't send a formal notice acknowledging receipt of your order.

Our Exchange Policy
Since blueprints are printed in response to your order, we cannot honor requests for refunds. However, we will exchange your entire first order for an equal number of blueprints at a price of $40 for the first set and $10 for each additional set; $60 total exchange fee for 4 sets; $90 total exchange fee for 8 sets... *plus* the difference in cost if exchanging for a design in a higher price bracket or *less* the difference in cost if exchanging for a design in a lower price bracket. (Sepias are not exchangeable.) All sets from the first order must be returned before the exchange can take place. Please add $8 for postage and handling via ground service; $20 via 2nd Day Air.

About Reverse Blueprints
If you want to build in reverse of the plan as shown, we will include an extra set of reversed blueprints (mirror image) for an additional fee of $50. Although lettering and dimensions appear backward, reverses will be a useful visual aid if you decide to flop the plan. Right-reading reverses of Customizable Plans are available through our Customization Service. Call for more details.

Modifying or Customizing Our Plans
With such a great selection of homes, you are bound to find the one that suits you. However, if you need to make alterations to a design that is customizable, you need only order our Customizer® kit or call our Customization representative at 1-800-322-6797, ext. 800, to get you started (see additional information on next page). It is possible to customize many of our plans that are not part of our Home Customizer® Service.

If you decide to revise plans significantly that are not customizable through our service, we strongly suggest that you order reproducible sepias and consult a licensed architect or professional designer to help you redraw the plans.

Architectural and Engineering Seals
Some cities and states are now requiring that a licensed architect or engineer review and "seal" your blueprints prior to construction. This is often due to local or regional concerns over energy consumption, safety codes, seismic ratings, etc. For this reason, you may find it necessary to consult with a local professional to have your plans reviewed. This can normally be accomplished with minimum delays, for a nominal fee. In some cases, we can seal your plans through our Customization Service. Call for more details.

Compliance with Local Codes and Regulations
At the time of creation, our plans are drawn to specifications published by Building Officials Code Administrators (BOCA), the Southern Standard Building Code, or the Uniform Building Code and are designed to meet or exceed national building standards. Some states, counties and municipalities have their own codes, zoning requirements and building regulations. Before starting construction, consult with local building authorities and make sure you comply with local

ordinances and codes, including obtaining any necessary permits or inspections as building progresses. In some cases, minor modifications to your plans by your builder, local architect or designer may be required to meet local conditions and requirements. We may be able to make these changes to Customizable Plans providing you supply all pertinent information from your local building authorities.

Foundation and Exterior Wall Changes
Most of our plans are drawn with either a full or partial basement foundation. Depending upon your specific climate or regional building practices, you may wish to convert this basement to a slab or crawlspace. Most professional contractors and builders can easily adapt your plans to alternate foundation types. Likewise, most can easily convert 2x4 wall construction to 2x6, or vice versa. If you need more guidance on these conversions, our handy Construction Detail Sheets, shown on page 401, describe how such conversions can be made. For Customizable Plans, we can easily provide the necessary changes for you.

How Many Blueprints Do You Need?
A single set of blueprints is sufficient to study a home in greater detail. However, if you are planning to obtain cost estimates from a contractor or subcontractors—or if you are planning to build immediately—you will need more sets. Because additional sets are cheaper when ordered in quantity with the original order, make sure you order enough blueprints to satisfy all requirements. The following checklist will help you determine how many you need:

_____Owner

_____Builder (generally requires at least three sets; one as a legal document, one to use during inspections, and at least one to give to subcontractors)

_____Local Building Department (often requires two sets)

_____Mortgage Lender (usually one set for a conventional loan; three sets for FHA or VA loans)

_____TOTAL NUMBER OF SETS

 Toll Free 1-800-848-2550

Normal Office Hours:
8:00 a.m. to 8:00 p.m. Eastern Time
Monday through Friday
Our staff will gladly answer any questions during normal office hours. Our answering service can place orders after hours or on weekends.

If we receive your order by 5:00 p.m. Eastern Time, Monday through Friday, we'll process it the same day and ship it the following business day. When ordering by phone, please have your charge card ready. We'll also ask you for the Order Form Key Number at the bottom of the coupon. Please use our Toll-Free number for blueprint and book orders only.
For Customization orders call 1-800-322-6797, ext. 800.

By FAX: Copy the Order Form on the next page and send it on our International FAX line: 1-800-224-6699.

Canadian Customers
Order Toll-Free 1-800-848-2550
For faster, more economical service, Canadian customers may now call in orders on our Toll-Free line. Or, complete the order form at right adding 30% to all prices, and mail in Canadian funds to:

Home Plans
3275 W. Ina Road, Suite 110
Tucson, AZ 85741

By FAX: Copy the Order Form on the next page and send it on our International FAX line: 1-800-224-6699.

The Home Customizer® 🏠

Many of the plans in this book are customizable through our Home Customizer® service. Look for this symbol 🏠 on the pages of home designs. It indicates that the plan on that page is part of The Home Customizer® service.

Some changes to customizable plans that can be made include:

- exterior elevation changes
- kitchen and bath modifications
- roof, wall and foundation changes
- room additions
- and much more!

If the plan you have chosen to build is one of our customizable homes, you can easily order the Home Customizer® kit to start on the path to making your alterations. The kit, priced at only $19.95, may be ordered at the same time you order your blueprint package by calling on our toll-free number or using the order blank at right. Or you can wait until you receive your blueprints, spend some time studying them and then order the kit by phone, FAX or mail. If you then decide to proceed with the customizing service, the $19.95 price of the kit will be refunded to you after your customization order is received. The Home Customizer® kit includes:

- instruction book with examples
- architectural scale
- clear acetate work film
- erasable red marker
- removable correction tape
- ¼" scale furniture cutouts
- 1 set of Customizable Drawings with floor plans and elevations

The service is easy, fast and *affordable*. Because we know and work with our plans and have them available on state-of-the-art computer systems, we can make the changes efficiently at prices much lower than those charged by normal architectural or drafting services. In addition, you'll be getting custom changes directly from a company whose dedication to excellence and long-standing professional experience are well recognized in the industry.

Call now to learn more about how simple it can be to have the *custom home* you've always wanted.

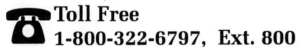

☎ Toll Free
1-800-322-6797, Ext. 800

ORDER FORM

HOME PLANS, 3275 WEST INA ROAD
SUITE 110, TUCSON, ARIZONA 85741

THE BASIC BLUEPRINT PACKAGE
Rush me the following (please refer to the Plans Index and Price Schedule in this section):

_____ Set(s) of blueprints for plan number(s) _____.	$_____
_____ Set(s) of sepias for plan number(s) _____.	$_____
_____ Additional identical blueprints in same order @ $50 per set.	$_____
_____ Reverse blueprints @ $50 per set.	$_____
_____ Home Customizer™ Kit(s) for Plan(s)_____ @ $19.95 per kit.	$_____

IMPORTANT EXTRAS
Rush me the following:

_____ Materials List @ $40 Schedule A-D; $50 Schedule E	$_____
_____ Specification Outlines @ $7 each.	$_____
_____ Detail Sets @ $14.95 each; any two for $22.95; any three for $29.95; all four for $39.95 (save $19.85).	$_____

❏ Plumbing ❏ Electrical ❏ Construction ❏ Mechanical
(These helpful details provide general construction advice and are not specific to any single plan.)

DECK BLUEPRINTS

_____ Set(s) of Deck Plan _____.	$_____
_____ Additional identical blueprints in same order @ $10 per set.	$_____
_____ Reverse blueprints @ $10 per set.	$_____
_____ Set of Standard Deck Details @ $14.95 per set.	$_____
_____ Set of Complete Building Package (Best Buy!) Includes Custom Deck Plan _____ (See Index and Price Schedule) Plus Standard Deck Details	$_____

LANDSCAPE BLUEPRINTS

_____ Set(s) of Landscape Plan _____.	$_____
_____ Additional identical blueprints in same order @ $10 per set.	$_____
_____ Reverse blueprints @ $10 per set.	$_____

Please indicate the appropriate region of the country for Plant & Material List. (See Map on page 404): Region _____

SUB-TOTAL $_____

SALES TAX (Arizona residents add 5% sales tax; Michigan residents add 6% sales tax.) $_____

POSTAGE AND HANDLING	1-3 sets	4 or more sets	
COMMERCIAL SERVICE (Requires street address - No P.O. Boxes)			
•Ground Service Allow 4-6 days delivery	❏ $6.00	❏ $8.00	$_____
•2nd Day Air Service Allow 2-3 days delivery	❏ $12.00	❏ $20.00	$_____
•Next Day Air Service Allow 1 day delivery	❏ $22.00	❏ $30.00	$_____
POST OFFICE DELIVERY If no street address available. Allow 4-6 days delivery	❏ $8.00	❏ $12.00	$_____
OVERSEAS AIR MAIL DELIVERY	❏ $30.00	❏ $50.00	$_____
Note: All delivery times are from date Blueprint Package is shipped.	❏ Send COD		

TOTAL (Sub-total, tax, and postage) $_____

YOUR ADDRESS (please print)

Name _____

Street _____

City _____ State _____ Zip _____

Daytime telephone number (_____) _____

FOR CREDIT CARD ORDERS ONLY
Please fill in the information below:

Credit card number _____

Exp. Date: Month/Year _____

Check one ❏ Visa ❏ MasterCard ❏ Discover Card

Signature _____

Please check appropriate box:
❏ Licensed Builder-Contractor
❏ Home Owner

Order Form Key

CHP2BP

☎ **ORDER TOLL FREE**
1-800-848-2550

 **CREATIVE HOMEOWNER PRESS®**

How-To Books for...

Quick Guide:
Ceramic Tile

Includes projects on tiling walls, floors, countertops and backsplashes; showers and tub surrounds, fireplaces and wood stoves, steps and stairs.

80 pages   **$7.95**

Quick Guide:
Floors

Focuses on ways of restoring old floors and preparing floors for new surfaces. Includes how to install hardwood floors, carpeting, tiling and more.

80 pages   **$7.95**

Quick Guide:
Decks

Covers every stage from developing a site plan to the final construction. Includes plans for freestanding, attached, or raised decks.

80 pages   **$7.95**

Quick Guide:
Ponds & Fountains

Topics incude: selecting a site, basic materials, formal and natural pools, waterfalls, filtration options, plumbing and electrical requirements, installing a pump, pool maintenance and more.

80 pages   **$7.95**

Quick Guide:
Fences & Gates

Covers site construction and installation for different styles of wood fences, plus chain link and sectional aluminum fences.

80 pages   **$7.95**

Quick Guide:
Interior & Exterior Painting

Topics include both interior and exterior painting projects, preparing surfaces for paint, color selection and design, choosing a finish, surface treatments, painting tools and more.

80 pages   **$7.95**

Quick Guide:
Trim & Molding

Topics include: types of molding and trim, tools needed and how to use them. Projects include decorating with molding and trim, door and window applications, maintenance, repair and more.

80 pages   **$7.95**

Quick Guide:
Storage Sheds

Every facet of planning and construction is covered from design selection to the installation of windows, doors and finishing trim.

80 pages   **$7.95**

Quick Guide:
Patios & Walks

Covers designing the area, selecting materials, creating patterns and using surface textures. Includes techniques for working with stone, concrete and brick.

80 pages   **$7.95**

Quick Guide:
Walls & Ceilings

Covers simple cracks to replacing entire surfaces. Includes surface repair and preparation, painting, wallpapering and tiling.

80 pages   **$7.95**

the Home Planner, Builder & Owner

Quick Guide:
Plumbing
Covers all areas of home plumbing including all the techniques necessary for working on sinks, toilets, baths, showers and water heaters.
80 pages   **$7.95**

Quick Guide:
Windows & Doors
Provides complete up-to-date, step-by-step instructions for the installation of original or replacement windows and doors.
80 pages   **$7.95**

Quick Guide:
Small Gasoline Engines
Small gasoline engine powered equipment for the homeowner includes lawnmowers, grass trimmers, hedge trimmers, leaf blowers, chain saws, edgers, snow blowers and more.
80 pages   **$7.95**

Quick Guide:
Wiring
Demonstrates the basics of wiring so the do-it-yourselfer can repair a lamp, replace an outlet, or extend electrical circuits in the home.
80 pages   **$7.95**

Basic Wiring
Learn how to repair a lamp, replace an outlet, extend electrical circuits, install ceiling and attic fans and programmable thermostats. Includes pertinent sections from the National Electrical Code. Over 350 illustrations.
160 pages   **$12.95**

Modern Home Plumbing
Take the guesswork out of plumbing repair and installation for old and new systems. Projects include replacing faucets, unclogging drains, installing a tub, replacing a water heater and much more. 500 illustrations and diagrams.
160 pages   **$12.95**

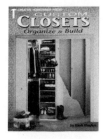

Custom Closets:
Organize & Build
Learn how to build wooden, laminate and coated-wire organizer systems tailor-made to the specific needs of men, women and children. Over 350 illustrations and color photographs.
160 pages   **$9.95**

Walls, Floors & Ceilings
Fifty projects to beautify a home's interior. Features many remodeling ideas including installing skylights, recessed lighting, ceiling fans, hardwood floors, and laying wall-to-wall carpet. Over 500 illustrations and color photographs.
160 pages   **$12.95**

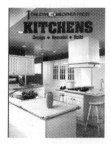

Kitchens
Design, Remodel, Build
Whether tackling a small kitchen project or a major overhaul, this title offers both creative and practical ideas in over 100 step-by-step projects. Over 300 color photographs and line drawings.
176 pages   **$12.95**

Dream Kitchens
The kitchen designs, plans and projects offered in this book can transform an average or dull kitchen into a more functional and beautiful one. 40 step-by-step projects range from replacing cabinets to installing skylights. Over 70 full-color photographs and 300 illustrations.
160 pages   **$9.95**

Place Your Order ...

Decks & Patios

Create additional living space and learn how to beautify an outdoor setting. Includes deck and patio building basics plus projects for overhead covers, benches, outdoor furniture, screens, lighting, barbecues and firepits. Over 350 illustrations and color photographs.
160 pages   **$9.95**

Spas & Hot Tubs
Saunas & Home Gyms

How to create the environments in which to exercise, relax, unwind or entertain. Step-by-step instructions will guide you in installing and maintaining a spa, hot tub, sauna or exercise room. Over 300 line drawings and color photographs.
160 pages   **$9.95**

Design, Remodel and Build
Your Bathroom

Floor plans are provided for all bathroom shapes and sizes. Instructions for building cabinets, platform and sunken tubs, plumbing repairs, tiling, wiring and more. Over 350 illustrations and color photographs.
160 pages   **$9.95**

Swimming Pools

A pool will enhance your health and relaxation, as well as add to the beauty and value of your home. Features both inground/above ground and indoor pools. Also included are ponds, cabanas, gazebos, fountains, fences, spas and hot tubs. 400 illustrations and color photos.
160 pages   **$9.95**

Fireplaces

How to build, install, renovate and maintain fireplaces of many types. Discusses the elements of fireplace efficiency and decor. Includes wood stoves, recycling systems, energy conservation, safety and wood use. Over 300 illustrations and color photographs.
128 pages   **$9.95**

Decks

Design and build your dream deck. Parts of a deck and materials used in construction are explained. Features step-by-step instructions on railing and step construction, overhead deck covers and deck maintenance. Outdoor lighting and how to install it is included. Over 400 illustrations and color photographs.
160 pages   **$12.95**

✂

BOOK ORDER FORM   *Please Print*
SHIP TO:

Name:

Address:

City: State: Zip: Phone Number:

(should there be a problem with your order)

Quantity	Title	CHP #	Price	Cost
	Quick Guide: Ceramic Tile	287730	$ 7.95 ea.	
	Quick Guide: Decks	287720	7.95 ea.	
	Quick Guide: Fences & Gates	287880	7.95 ea.	
	Quick Guide: Floors	287734	7.95 ea.	
	Quick Guide: Ponds & Fountains	287804	7.95 ea.	
	Quick Guide: Interior & Exterior Painting	287784	7.95 ea.	
	Quick Guide: Trim & Molding	287745	7.95 ea.	
	Quick Guide: Patios & Walks	287778	7.95 ea.	
	Quick Guide: Plumbing	287863	7.95 ea.	
	Quick Guide: Small Gasoline Engines	287849	7.95 ea.	
	Quick Guide: Storage Sheds	287815	7.95 ea.	
	Quick Guide: Walls & Ceilings	287792	7.95 ea.	
	Quick Guide: Windows & Doors	287812	7.95 ea.	
	Quick Guide: Wiring	287884	7.95 ea.	
	Basic Wiring	277825	12.95 ea.	
	Custom Closets	277132	9.95 ea.	
	Decks: Design & Build	277174	12.95 ea.	
	Decks & Patios	277100	9.95 ea.	
	Dream Kitchens	277067	9.95 ea.	

Quantity	Title	CHP #	Price	Cost
	Fireplaces	277174	9.95 ea.	
	Kitchens, Design, Remodel, Build	277060	12.95 ea.	
	Modern Home Plumbing	277612	12.95 ea.	
	Spas, Hot Tubs, Saunas, Home Gyms	277845	9.95 ea.	
	Swimming Pools	277850	9.95 ea.	
	Walls, Floors & Ceilings	277694	12.95 ea.	
	Your Bathroom: Design, Remodel, Build	277040	9.95 ea.	

Number of Books Ordered _____   Total for Books _____

Prices subject to change without notice.   NJ residents add 6% tax _____

Sub-total _____

Postage/Handling Charges _____
$2.50 for first book / $1.00 for each additional book

TOTAL _____

Make checks (in U.S. currency only) payable to:
CREATIVE HOMEOWNER PRESS®
P.O. Box 38, 24 Park Way
Upper Saddle River, New Jersey 07458-9960.